Our Onward
March

To my parents, Marilyn and David
—
and for Margaret

A portion of Chapter 1 first appeared, in somewhat different form, as "A Building Very Useful: The Grand Army Memorial Hall in US Civic Life, 1880–1920," in *The War Went On: Reconsidering the Lives of Civil War Veterans,* edited by Brian Matthew Jordan and Evan C. Rothera, copyright © 2020 by Louisiana State University Press.

A portion of Chapter 2 first appeared, in somewhat different form, as "'Produce Patriots As Well As Scholars': GAR Educational Reform and the Establishment of Mason City's Memorial University," *The Annals of Iowa* 79, no. 3 (Summer 2020), copyright © 2020 by the State Historical Society of Iowa.

Copyright © 2025 Fordham University Press

All rights reserved. No part of this publication may be reproduced, stored in a retrieval system, or transmitted in any form or by any means—electronic, mechanical, photocopy, recording, or any other—except for brief quotations in printed reviews, without the prior permission of the publisher.

Fordham University Press has no responsibility for the persistence or accuracy of URLs for external or third-party Internet websites referred to in this publication and does not guarantee that any content on such websites is, or will remain, accurate or appropriate.

Fordham University Press also publishes its books in a variety of electronic formats. Some content that appears in print may not be available in electronic books.

Visit us online at www.fordhampress.com.

Library of Congress Cataloging-in-Publication Data available online at https://catalog.loc.gov.

Printed in the United States of America

27 26 25   5 4 3 2 1

First edition

Our Onward March

The Grand Army of the Republic in the Progressive Era

Jonathan D. Neu

Fordham University Press
New York 2025

RECONSTRUCTING AMERICA
Andrew L. Slap, series editor

Contents

	Introduction: Our Onward March | 1
1	Practical Monuments | 13
2	A Grand Army of Scholars | 43
3	West of Appomattox, South of Richmond | 73
4	Clasping Hands Across the Sea | 105
5	Rally Once Again | 137
	Conclusion: From Their Battlements in Heaven | 172

Acknowledgments	*181*
Notes	*185*
Bibliography	*245*
Index	*275*

OUR ONWARD MARCH

Introduction

Our Onward March

> *The more intimately I have been associated with my Comrades in the work of our Order, the more assured have I become that the Grand Army of the Republic is the grandest civic organization the world has knowledge of.*
>
> —Iowa GAR Department Commander John J. Steadman, 1893

During the waning days of May 1916, every school and college in and around Emporia, Kansas, hosted a Union veteran to say a few appropriate remarks to commemorate Memorial Day and the Civil War, now half a century past. The College of Emporia welcomed sixty-nine-year-old James Whitehead, a prominent town elder. Born in Wisconsin to a devout Methodist family, Whitehead enlisted in the Union army at fifteen on the Fourth of July 1862. Nearly succumbing to disease that winter, he recovered in time to take part in the siege of Petersburg and the capture of Richmond. By all accounts a dutiful soldier, he earned the praise of a regimental officer who declared later that Whitehead "went to the war to fight, and he did it like a hero." After mustering out of the service, he married and farmed in his native state until 1884. Whitehead then applied for a homestead in Custer County, Nebraska, where he established a productive tract and served the public through the years as tax collector, land office bureaucrat, and member of the state legislature. Ordered by his physician to "seek a lower altitude" for his health, he and his family arrived in Emporia in 1907.[1]

Whitehead fully embraced the role of community patriarch, exercised through his membership in the era's largest and most influential organization of Union veterans, the Grand Army of the Republic (GAR). He first joined the GAR soon after his arrival in Nebraska, where he remarked in 1902 that the fraternity's fundamental role was to assist "our onward march to that higher & more perfect civilization that embraces in its creed all races, colors, & conditions of men." Upon settling in Emporia, he transferred his membership to the town's well-respected GAR chapter, the Preston B. Plumb Post (see Figure 1). Over the next several years, Whitehead and scores of his post comrades kept active by hosting musical and literary soirees at their headquarters, organizing educational public programs, commemorating patriotic holidays, denouncing government plans to disband African American units in the US military, and spearheading the town's recruitment efforts during the First World War. At the College of Emporia in 1916, as guns blazed anew in a deadly, modern war across the Atlantic, Whitehead boosted the sacrifices of his GAR fellows, then in the twilight of their lives, and eulogized the legacy of their fading organization. "The object and aim of the Grand Army is not to indulge merely in personal recollections and dwell in [a] reminiscent mood—as some seem to think—on the past," contended Whitehead, "but, to inculcate rather lessons of patriotism and love of country among the young and impress while yet we may upon the generation that has followed the cost and sacrifice by which the privileges we enjoy as a nation were purchased and thus stimulate to greater love, and if possible, greater devotion to this our common country."[2]

Figure 1 Members of the Preston B. Plumb Post of Emporia, Kansas, pose with wives, family members, and other civic leaders circa 1911. James Whitehead may be among them. Courtesy of Lyon County Historical Society.

INTRODUCTION: OUR ONWARD MARCH 3

This work examines the local GAR post as an active and assertive community fixture during the Progressive Era, a period in the organization's history that has remained routinely understudied and largely mischaracterized. Contrary to expectations, the order during this time was still potent, functioning largely as a decentralized civic association whose aging members worked locally and regionally to instill a commitment to community reform, participation in public life, engagement with pressing social issues, and a pride in the democracy that they had defended as young men. This reconsideration counters stubborn notions that the GAR was merely a pension advocacy group, a heedless voting bloc for the Republican Party, or—as Whitehead himself disclaimed—an insular bastion of nostalgia, particularly as the Civil War generation aged into its golden years. Scholars have often identified 1890 (the year of the GAR's peak membership and the passage of a transformational veterans' pension bill that it promoted) as the fraternity's culminating moment, after which, it is said, the GAR declined steeply and quickly into senescence, sentimentality, and, ultimately, extinction. This work instead sees 1890 as an important juncture, after which veterans for the next thirty years refocused their activism away from self-interested aims spearheaded by prominent, nationally recognized GAR officials and toward cooperative, community-building objectives guided by rank-and-file members. By shifting the investigation to the period between 1890 and 1920, what we uncover is the persistent visibility and civic engagement of the GAR in shaping the activities, values, and relationships within and between Progressive Era American communities.[3]

GAR members stood prominently among the diverse constellation of turn-of-the-century social reformers, utilizing their memory of the Civil War to direct a range of robust, veteran-led advocacies. By situating Union veterans in this context, we see a more accurate portrait of the Grand Army post room or memorial hall in American culture—as a local hub of progressive activism, interconnected with thousands of other nodes in the nationwide GAR network of like-minded community centers. Here, crusading veterans and their auxiliaries inspired neighborhood projects and advocated broad-based civic participation, while reaffirming and even redefining the meaning of the wartime sacrifices that they made a generation earlier. At the same time, Americans underwent wrenching domestic challenges such as industrialization, urbanization, and immigration, while also coming to terms with the nation's growing influence in the world. Instead of shying away from these developments and seeking refuge within the ritualized boundaries of their fraternity, GAR veterans boldly faced them and deployed their venerated status to remake US society from the community level outward. In short, turn-of-the-century GAR activism, influenced by the veterans' own collective memory of their Civil War experience, was itself a strain of Progressive Era reform.

Of course, adding Union veterans and their advocacies to the already overwrought amalgam of what constitutes "progressivism" comes with challenges. For decades, historians have debated—often with little consensus—the identities of the progressives, the principles and creed of progressivism, and the achievements and failures of the Progressive Era. Some have rightly pointed to the movement's ambiguities and the "unprogressive" values that the era's reformers at times advanced. Still, this study sees value in a more recent notion of plural "progressivisms" that helps unite a diverse and ideologically imprecise movement and allows for a modest advancement of a few characteristics of the progressives and their broad agenda. In the decades around 1900, many middle-class Americans (or, at least, those finding themselves pinned between an insatiable, capitalist elite and a recalcitrant, impoverished working class) organized into numerous coalitions with interests in ameliorating various social ills and reforming the nation in a way that would ensure the continuation of their preferred lifestyles and ideals. Bearing a faith in collectivist activism, engaged citizenship, and interventionist government, these progressives felt empowered to tackle the most challenging problems of their day—big business and monopolism, poverty and economic unrest, political corruption, evolving gender norms, and more—by perfecting individuals and, in turn, remaking the communities and cultures from which they came. It is only logical that aging GAR members are part of this story. Organized in one of the largest voluntary associations in the country and with a vested interest in maintaining harmony in the nation that they had saved in their youth, many veterans belonged to this bold, visionary middle class and used their fraternal activism to devise ways to improve civic health alongside other progressives. Yet they addressed it with unique moral suasions and patriotic prescriptions informed by their Civil War service from decades past.[4]

Situating GAR veterans under the umbrella of the progressives means confronting another key criticism of the Progressive Era. Despite many legitimate accomplishments made by reformers around the turn of the twentieth century, the intensification of racial segregation during this period is an area in which they are justifiably criticized. Even as an optimistic, crusading middle class used the power of association and faith in an activist government to devise creative remedies for various political, economic, and social dilemmas, it expressed few concerns for the onset of Jim Crow, the reemergence of the Ku Klux Klan, rapacious empire building in nonwhite lands, and what one commentator famously dubbed the "nadir" of US race relations. The GAR, however, deserves partial credit for bucking this tendency as it was one of the few associations of the period that was explicitly, even proudly, interracial. White and Black members intermingled, often in integrated posts, while sharing the bonds of comradeship and collective memory of their common wartime sacrifices. At GAR meetings, white veterans warmly recalled their involvement in hastening emancipation while African American veterans enjoyed a type of social equality rarely experienced in other aspects of US culture. However, as historian Barbara A. Gannon correctly notes, "[e]ven white veterans who passionately embraced the Memory of black freedom made no connection between freeing slaves in 1865 and protecting their civil rights in 1895." For most white GAR members, extending the hand of fraternal friendship to their Black comrades was enough and few felt a need to go further outside the post room. Still, the GAR merits some commendation as a Progressive Era bastion of interracial camaraderie that, just as importantly, provided the space for African American veterans to become paragons of Black civic engagement who led vital community uplift activities.[5]

To uncover the Grand Army's local-level reformist spirit, a new methodology is needed that deemphasizes the conventional scholarly characterization of the order as a powerful lobbying group with clout at the highest levels of national politics. To be sure, the fraternity's broad influence at the end of the nineteenth century brought it incredible success in mobilizing on behalf of favored politicians, campaigning for military service pensions, and securing other important veterans' benefits. By instead placing the local GAR post at the center of the story, however, a new interpretation emerges of the civic activities and grassroots significance of the Union veteran later in his life, at a time when reformers of all stripes were reshaping their communities. The Civil War soldier of 1861—typically provincial, community-oriented, and surrounded by comrades who were his friends and neighbors—in many ways remained localistic in his outlook a generation later as a veteran in his Grand Army post. By keeping the story of the GAR local and centered on the thousands of individual posts that dotted the postwar United States, we discover that the fraternity's members maintained a dynamic, pragmatic, and active presence well into the twentieth century. Although drawing on larger lessons from the past about patriotism, service, and loyalty to the Union, GAR activism nonetheless fit comfortably within the members' modern, fast-changing, and reform-swept communities.

This work alludes throughout to a Grand Army memory of the Civil War, which veterans invoked to inspire and direct the reform of their towns and cities. In other words, GAR members employed the lessons learned in their war-wrought and, often, trauma-filled youth to influence, organize, and perfect the nation that they knew they had saved decades before. This GAR memory was grounded in part by the constitutional and democratic principles for which many veterans enlisted in the 1860s—republican government, representative institutions, majority rule, social order, and equality under the law. It also encouraged the exaltation of the Union—through personal and public avowals of loyalty, the visual display and emotional expression of patriotism and love of country, and the embrace of service and sacrifice (not just militarily, but also civically). Emphatically acknowledging emancipation as a sacred outcome of the Civil War, white and Black GAR veterans also encouraged younger generations who had no direct memory of the war to carry on this legacy and, to at least some degree, endorsed the notion that freedom, opportunity, and (manhood) suffrage belonged to all Americans, irrespective of race. Together, these principles informed the GAR's memory of the Civil War that subsequently guided Union veterans' contributions to the era's progressive and activist intent to structure, order, and improve an increasingly fractious and heterogeneous society.

It hardly should be surprising that the GAR's Progressive Era influence was so conspicuous given the sheer number of soldiers who returned home after Appomattox with, for many, decades of life left to live. Estimates suggest that roughly 1.5 million Union soldiers and sailors emerged from the war in 1865 to readjust to civilian life (including nearly 200,000 African Americans). Many of these returning veterans immediately organized to cultivate companionship out of the hardships and trauma of their war experience. A host of societies sprang up in the months after the Union army's disbandment, many organized around the units in which the ex-soldiers had served. The largest and most influential, however, was the GAR, established in 1866 in Decatur, Illinois. During its first few years, the GAR prospered as veterans in the Midwest, and soon in the East, supported the order's open-ended promise of fellowship around members' war service and commitment to its foundational principles—Fraternity, Charity, and Loyalty. Membership declined steeply in the 1870s, however, as many balked at the GAR's overt partisanship on behalf of Republican office seekers and the imposition of unpopular fraternal rituals. From this low point, the GAR rebranded by the 1880s with a renewed emphasis on comradeship, nonpartisanship, and charity, while becoming an efficient lobbying machine for veterans' pensions. Moreover, GAR auxiliaries—chiefly the Woman's Relief Corps (WRC) and Sons of Veterans (SV)—were founded in the 1880s and brought hundreds of thousands of veterans' wives, daughters, and sons into the organization's orbit, further revitalizing it.[6]

GAR membership peaked at over 400,000 in 1890, the year that a federal census tabulated around one million surviving Union veterans (among roughly sixty-three million Americans). Thus, nearly half of the Union veteran population belonged to some 7,000 local posts nationwide, which sprang up wherever these men could be found, even out West, in the states of the former Confederacy, and abroad. Virtually every northern community of any size had a post, often led by its most prominent citizens. Despite periodic debates on the boundaries of membership through the years, regulations barred all but honorably discharged Union veterans, placing the GAR on the path to eventual demise. By the end of World War I, only 15 percent of the Civil War's original survivors remained (of whom around 100,000 belonged to the GAR). The Grand Army limped along for another generation, with its formal end marked by the death of the last Union veteran in 1956.[7]

During its existence, the organization was meticulously structured and inflected with militaristic trappings. Members typically called each other "comrade" and dubbed their community-level units "posts," led by an annually elected "commander." Posts also included several other lower-level officers—senior and junior vice commanders, quartermaster, adjutant, chaplain, surgeon, and more. Occasionally, local posts coalesced into loose, regional affiliations (some examples include the Southeastern Michigan GAR Association, the Southern Oregon Veterans Association of the GAR, and Pittsburgh's Allegheny County Grand Army Association). At the state level, the network of local posts formed "departments," such as the Department of Massachusetts or the Department of California and Nevada. Departments held yearly state encampments (the host cities rotating from year to year) where delegates from the local posts elected a department commander for a one-year term. Together, all the departments fell under the dominion of the GAR's national headquarters, led by an influential and often politically prominent veteran elected each year to serve as "commander in chief." National encampments were held annually in a different host city, large enough to accommodate sometimes tens of thousands of veterans who arrived to fraternize with other comrades, elect officers, and set the organization's agenda for the coming year. Previous scholarship often analyzes the GAR as a national association, overlooking the fact that, for the average American, its most persistent and visible activities occurred as a familiar local organization through the first decades of the twentieth century.

Our Onward March therefore extends the boundaries of what constituted America's post–Civil War era, asserting that Union veterans' activism—particularly at the local level—was both longer lasting and more outwardly engaged than previous historians have acknowledged. We can reach this conclusion by shifting the analytical timeframe of the Grand Army's ninety-year lifespan (1866–1956) from its well-understood first quarter century to its overlooked middle thirty years (1890–1920). Much GAR scholarship has viewed 1890 as an end point for the organization—a rational inference given Congress's passage that year of the GAR-endorsed Dependent Pension Act, after which membership steadily declined. These studies emphasized the GAR's politically partisan roots (largely on behalf of office seekers from the Party of Lincoln) and its lobbying for veterans' interests. In an early treatment of the GAR, Mary Dearing underscored that members "became efficient cogs in the Republican machine" and evolved into a successful political pressure group best evidenced by their ability to direct one-fifth of the federal government's revenue toward pensions. Decades later, political scientist Theda Skocpol similarly bolstered the GAR's lobbying significance in her top-down, policy-heavy *Protecting Soldiers and Mothers*, which declared Union veterans' pensions as "America's first national system of public old-age and disability benefits." Skocpol's analysis laid the foundation for a range of subsequent studies by economists, social scientists, and historians that complemented her innovative work by examining pensions from a variety of political, legal, and cultural angles that further instilled the idea of the Grand Army as a highly adept pension lobby.[8]

These studies, although vital in understanding the development and complexities of social welfare in the United States, have nonetheless pegged the GAR as a single-issue and self-interested organization. This obscures the fact that the Grand Army of 1890 reached not its *end* point, but rather its *turning* point. In other words, after securing broad-based pension rights for themselves and their dependents, GAR veterans increasingly turned their organizational power outward—by influencing their neighborhoods then undergoing significant social, economic, and cultural change as the United States transformed into a more urban and diverse society. Scholarship has missed this trend by also overlooking the influence that GAR members still wielded at the community level, even though most turn-of-the-century Union veterans were nearing the end of their lives. Stuart McConnell's *Glorious Contentment*, the first modern social history on the GAR, has contributed to this notion by concluding that the order "was clearly in decline (both numerically and politically) by the late 1890s" and ending his study in 1900, after which he declares that the GAR simply became "an organization for the promotion of patriotism and the commemoration of Memorial Day." Although it is undoubtedly true that the GAR would never again rival its 1890 peak of over 409,000 members, there were still 276,000 in 1900 and 214,000 in 1910—many of whom represented their communities' most respected and engaged citizens at a time when progressive reform movements swept the country.[9]

A recent trend in post–Civil War studies has emphasized Union veterans' social marginality and cast them as victims of a nonveteran populace eager to put the memory of the war behind it. Eric T. Dean Jr.'s *Shook Over Hell* and James Marten's *Sing Not War* track those veterans whose transition back to civilian life proved turbulent because of post-traumatic stress disorder, physical disability, poverty, and more. In a similar vein, Brian Matthew Jordan's *Marching Home* highlights the strained relationship between demobilized Union soldiers and northern civilians unwilling to dwell on the war's effects and adverse to provisioning returning veterans with excess care, benefits, or plaudits. All of these studies are novel and important in understanding the devastating effects of war on a generation of veterans who were prohibited from fully expressing the horrors of their combat experience. Further, each treats primary source material—veterans' writings, pension files, and soldiers' home records, for example—more seriously than previous work on Union veteran culture. However, this so-called "dark turn" in the scholarship must not be taken too far. As historian Paul A. Cimbala counters, "being a Civil War veteran was not some sort of pathology that alienated most of the men from their communities." Indeed, the far-reaching influence of GAR members in their local posts shows that many Union veterans were neither helpless in the face of indifferent civilians nor powerless in effecting civic reform that was meaningful to them, even as the war years grew increasingly distant.[10]

Any current study on Union veterans must also reckon with the ever-evolving scholarship on Civil War memory, which influences this work's conceptualization of a GAR-endorsed memory of the war. When David W. Blight published his groundbreaking *Race and Reunion*, historians wrestled as they never had before with the ideological consequences of the Civil War—those conflicting and unresolved questions about the war's legacies, largely dealing with race. As Americans sought to heal the personal and sectional wounds the war wrought, Blight argues that a reconciliationist memory of the war overwhelmed all others by adapting many of the tenets of white supremacism, valorizing the white soldiers of both North and South, and suppressing all remembrance of slavery as the war's root cause.[11]

While indebted to Blight's conceptualization, methodologies, and terminologies of Civil War memory, this work nonetheless contributes to the ongoing revision of his influential reconciliationist paradigm by identifying GAR veterans' own passionate remembrance of their war experience as an overlooked but vital aspect of the nation's messy reunification process. As scholar James E. Young has succinctly declared, "[m]emory is never shaped in a vacuum." This holds especially true for the memory of the Civil War, a wrenching event in American history so consequential to the millions of Americans—North and South, male and female, white and Black—who, after the war, recalled the same events differently, depending upon, as Barbara A. Gannon explains, "the social and cultural contexts of those who remember." For individual GAR veterans who came together with comrades in their local posts, individual memories melded over time into a collective memory of their Civil War experience. These men remembered their war service as a (perhaps *the*) defining moment in their lives and would cede the meaning of their sacrifices to neither the southerners whom they defeated in their youth nor the younger generations of Americans who had no lived experience of the war. Union veterans' collective memory of their military service thus presented a stubborn obstacle to white northerners' and white southerners' reconciliationist tendencies. For many Grand Army veterans that appear in the pages that follow, the costs of war were too immense, the past actions of Confederate veterans were too treasonous, and (especially for Black GAR comrades, but also for many white Union veterans) the outcome of African American freedom was too vital not to vigorously assert their own conception of what postwar US society should be. As the GAR applied its reform and civic activism at the local level, they did so while powerfully influenced by their collective memory of the war with its dual outcomes—the Union's preservation and slavery's abolition.[12]

Our Onward March rests on research conducted in thirty-two repositories across eighteen states. Given the following chapters' emphasis on the GAR's community role, it was necessary for the source base to comprise records scattered across state and local libraries, archives, and historical societies in a wide range of places. Indeed, the fraternity's dispersed paper trail presents one of the great challenges in comprehensively studying the organization. Surprisingly, for a fraternity so preoccupied by its legacy, GAR national headquarters devised no thorough record preservation strategy. A few state departments mandated that disbanding posts send their papers to a centralized location, usually a state archive. More typically, however, when the last members of a GAR post passed away, their records fell to the community Veterans of Foreign Wars or American Legion post, SV camp, or a local library. Often, post records were simply discarded or otherwise lost to history. What remains, then, is a patchwork collection of records in repositories near and far. Thus, the researcher must be extremely discerning in selecting archives that both house a diverse range of materials *and* represent an adequate race, class, and geographic cross sampling.

To achieve this outcome, this author was most dependent upon local post records, wherever they exist. The basic unit of GAR organizational recordkeeping was the post minute book. As is the case with most voluntary membership associations, GAR minutes are usually formulaic and rarely provide much personal expression from the post adjutant. The typical minute book entry lists the names of post officers present at the meeting, names of veterans added or removed from the roster, expense and relief fund reports, and other sundry information. What proves most useful to this study, however, are the occasional incidences when adjutants recorded events at which post members interacted with their auxiliaries or other nonmembers either within or outside the fraternity walls. Also vital are the rarer, but often more detailed, post documents—incoming and outgoing letters, interpost communications, official directives from state or national headquarters, and other types of correspondence. These sources not only provide great detail about the interworking of the local GAR post and its interactions with nearby posts, but also offer insights into how GAR veterans communicated with a wide range of nonveteran community members. Newspapers are the other key element used in this study to glean vital details and provide cultural textures that are often absent in other types of source material. This is especially true in tracking GAR post involvement in the community, for which newspapers provide a vital complement to comparatively reticent minute books. Newspapers—particularly those that were Black-owned—are also often the only source available that uncovers the interests and advocacies of African American posts whose records were even less likely to survive.

In five chapters, this book examines a variety of ways that aging Grand Army veterans promoted civic engagement and reform activism in their Progressive Era communities. Chapter 1 reframes the local GAR post room or memorial hall, dispelling the notion that these fraternal sites were guarded and insular. Instead, post records demonstrate that they were dynamic and community-oriented venues that Union veterans utilized for public outreach and the inculcation of GAR values and lessons about the Civil War. Chapter 2 considers GAR educational reform interest in the nation's burgeoning institutions of learning—particularly libraries and universities—illustrating how veterans viewed these sites as key to disseminating principles of loyalty, public service, and citizenship to younger generations of Americans. Chapter 3 highlights the migration of Union veterans to the South and West, showing how the Grand Army's institutional legacy expanded into new territories while members' outreach techniques adapted to distinct challenges in communities far from the GAR's northern and eastern points of origin. Chapter 4 explores how GAR veterans came to terms with US imperial expansion, believing that the (often forcible) spread of American values abroad cemented democracy, order, and progress at home. Chapter 5 details GAR veteran activity during World War I, revealing that these now-elderly men utilized their revered civic status to direct their communities' mobilization efforts for the nation's latest global crisis. A brief conclusion traces the decline of Union veterans' civic activism at the end of the Progressive Era and the emergence of a new generation of veterans, more conservative and traditionalist than their progenitors of the GAR.

From 1890 to 1920—the heart of the US Progressive Era—Union veterans leveraged their membership in the Grand Army of the Republic to influence and direct the reform and improvement of their communities. Drawing on what they learned and valued from their Civil War service—lessons about broad principles like democracy, loyalty, and freedom—GAR members in their local posts turned to grassroots, community-building activism to address what they viewed as the rampant social ills associated with US modernization. "Every Post of the Grand Army is a school of patriotism, a school of intelligent Americanism, a school of high obedience to law and order," avowed Minnesota GAR member John Ireland in 1897, "and it is a blessing to any town or village in America when a Grand Army Post is organized." Investigating that public-spirited commitment, *Our Onward March* argues that the sacrifices and services of Union soldiers did not end in 1865. Rather, their legacy marched on through their GAR veteran activism, well into the twentieth century, as they mobilized again to perfect the nation that they had once saved.[13]

1   Practical Monuments

I am always glad, when opportunity offers, to testify to my high appreciation of your body as a civic organization of the greatest usefulness.

—President William H. Taft, address before Grand Army veterans in Rochester, New York, 1911

Before dawn on February 27, 1904, fire broke out in the Wisconsin capitol. Flames gutted the building, but its steel-lined, fireproof vaults (and some daring Madison citizens) saved most of the state's important public records. "Considering the magnitude of the capitol fire," reported one newspaper, "the loss on the contents, especially on the valuable and, in many cases, priceless papers, records and books, was . . . remarkably small." Not spared, sadly, were the scrapbooks, photographs, and relics of the Grand Army Memorial Hall, a space that the legislature reserved specifically for veterans' fraternal functions. Lost too was the taxidermized mascot of the 8th Wisconsin Volunteers, a beloved bald eagle named after Abraham Lincoln, which was a favorite among school groups. "Boys and girls have come to the room . . . in troops," recollected heartbroken veteran Hosea W. Rood, "to stand around Old Abe's glass case and talk in hushed tones about him and what he typifies—American liberty." Construction on the new state capitol building took over a decade. When at last the GAR state headquarters moved into the building's north wing in 1917, veterans set to work re-creating a library, archives, and exhibits for civic use. They called on the public to donate "pictures of good soldiers and war-time events and scenes, history books, biographies, war stories of all kinds, patriotic literature . . . [and] all sorts of war relics with stories attached to them." By 1919, the now-aged Rood reported an outpouring of donations that would help make the memorial hall "a source of research for information concerning wars of the United States, especially our Civil War." Reaching out to younger generations, Rood welcomed "children and grandchildren of veterans, as well as all others interested in what we have here," to visit the new venue "and take a look at the old battle flags and books, pictures and relics."[1]

Like Rood and his comrades, Grand Army members at the state and local levels emphasized grassroots, community-building activities that help redefine the organization as part of the emerging Progressive Era reform coalition. Particularly after 1890, many veterans viewed the GAR as uniquely qualified to combine community activism with patriotic culture—a vision that comprised exaltation of the Union that they had preserved, incorporation of nonveterans into a disciplined and harmonious national polity, and coalition-building with other civic groups to engage an increasingly urban and heterogeneous population. To be sure, these objectives largely aligned with those of the era's other voluntary associations that grew increasingly committed to civic life and invested in solving the social ills linked to the country's modernization. Indeed, Robert D. Putnam has suggested that during this period, fraternities and other societies began moving away from the inward-looking, self-interested concerns of their members and instead turned their attentions outward to address the needs of the community through civic engagement and political action. However, Union veterans' efforts to edify and build meaningful relations with the public at large are a crucial part of the GAR's community presence that historians have largely overlooked. A close examination of members' local-level activities restores the GAR to its rightful place in what Theda Skocpol has described as a "civic nation."[2]

Understanding Union veterans' fundamental engagement in community activism requires reinterpreting the local GAR post or memorial hall as a key node in the social network of emphatically civic-minded entities of the late nineteenth and early twentieth centuries. Much existing scholarship suggests little about veterans' progressive activism and outreach undertaken beyond the sanctum of the post, instead painting the fraternal space as an inward-looking, reactionary refuge against social change and the threatening forces of immigration, urbanization, and industrialization. To be fair, some of the members' own writings suggested as much. General William T. Sherman, for instance, believed comrades got together in their posts simply "to be of good cheer; to meet often at campfires; sing their old songs; tell their stories with reasonable exaggerations, and always cultivate the comradeship begotten of war." Pronouncements like these, however, have misconstrued local GAR posts as exclusive retreats for members to idly hark back on a romantic and sanitized version of the war. One historian, for instance, argued that veterans joined the order for "the opportunity for an escape from humdrum existence," and another characterized the "conservative, backward-looking" GAR post room as a place that could not foster a memory of the war "that implied major social or personal change." When discussed at all, GAR activism encompassed only self-involved lobbying campaigns for soldiers' homes, preferential hiring policies for veterans, unemployment assistance, and the ever-widening procurement of state and federal service pensions.[3]

By closely examining the fullness of turn-of-the-century GAR activities, a more accessible and community-oriented image of the fraternity emerges. The first section below enters the local post room to rediscover a range of veteran-led civic and educational programs devised there. Public programming in GAR venues aimed not merely to remember but also to apply the Civil War's lessons in the emerging Progressive Era. Distinct from other fraternal joiners, Union veterans positioned themselves as elders whose unique service and special status qualified them as effective civic organizers and instructors. African American veterans, in particular, harnessed the edifying power of their local GAR posts and deployed it in their struggle to remind their neighbors—white and Black—about the meaning of their war service. The second section reconsiders the GAR post quarters both culturally (connected to broad social networks and the daily rhythms of civic life) and spatially (conspicuous in the layout of the community). With thousands of posts across the country, most communities of any size constructed or designated space in which veterans not only socialized among themselves, but also organized and collaborated to shape local affairs. Particularly emphasized is the GAR memorial hall—a typically freestanding architectural and civic project undertaken in scores of communities nationwide. These commemorative edifices, unlike other monuments, served as practical and multipurpose public facilities, open to veterans and nonveterans. The final section focuses on Pittsburgh's Soldiers and Sailors Memorial Hall, a massive structure that demonstrated how Civil War commemoration could forge functional new spaces for civic engagement.

Throw Your Doors Open to the Public

Before his death in 1915, Albert C. Leonard of Lancaster, Pennsylvania, compiled a long list of achievements in both military and public service. Enlisting with the 54th Pennsylvania Volunteers, Leonard fought in the Shenandoah Valley before his capture and internment in the notorious Andersonville prison. After the war, he worked as a county clerk, served as the "moral instructor" at the local prison, and headed the Harrisburg capitol police. Leonard enjoyed a prominent GAR career as well. A member of Lancaster's Admiral Reynolds Post, he edited the *Grand Army News*, served as his post's commander, and penned a brief war memoir in 1904. Two decades earlier, before the order attained robust membership, Leonard had also published his *Grand Army of the Republic Hand Book*, written in part to help members explain "the aim, object and doings of the organization" to veterans who had not yet joined the fraternity. In it, Leonard tacitly admitted the struggles that the GAR then faced in gaining adherents. In a chapter entitled "How to Keep the Post Alive," Leonard blamed the "thoughtless lack of sociability" exhibited by some comrades and the intrusion of "matters of little or no account" in business meetings. He offered a solution too, although it was one unusual for a fraternity bound by secret rituals. "Occasionally, throw your doors open to the public," Leonard recommended, "invite the members of your family, as well as your friends and neighbors, in to see you, and let them hear your story of the camp, march, skirmish, battle or prison; have them join in the patriotic song, and thus get the community . . . interested in the Post."[4]

Leonard suggested a role for the local GAR post—open, inclusive, civic-minded—at odds with the typical interpretation of the late nineteenth-century fraternal lodge. At that time, many long-established secret fraternities including the Freemasons, the Order of Red Men, and the Odd Fellows enjoyed a resurgence, while a host of new ones cropped up including the Knights of Pythias, Order of Elks, and Knights of Columbus. Indeed, one contemporary remarked that the period "might well be called the Golden Age of fraternity." Historians and social scientists have argued that this fraternal upsurge occurred in part because of the increasing social alienation prompted by the era's capitalist expansion, immigrant influx, urban growth, and intensifying wealth disparities. Fraternal joiners—largely white, native born, Protestant, and middle class—sought in the lodge a safe place apart from this bewildering array of social disorders. These scholars have attributed this refuge-seeking to a variety of factors. On the one hand, fraternity members might use their organization as a protection *from* external threats—economic disruptions, newly assertive women, and an increasingly heterogeneous population. On the other hand, they also used the lodge as a haven *for* the preservation of cherished things—white, middle-class moral standards, professional respectability, and masculine solidarity. In either case, one's maleness and whiteness typically provided the precondition to access the place of escape while fraternal ritual served as the privileged ceremonial to guard it. All told, the secrecy and exclusivity that marked the late nineteenth-century fraternal lodge enhanced its reputation as a place of sanctuary, self-segregation, and male camaraderie.[5]

The base principles of the Grand Army of the Republic's founders seemed to augur a similar role for the fledgling fraternity. Established in 1866, the early GAR adopted many traditions and rituals influenced by Freemasonry. Its triad of tenets—Fraternity, Charity, and Loyalty—echoed the mottoes of other Masonic-inspired groups, such as the Odd Fellows (Friendship, Love, and Truth) and the Knights of Columbus (Charity, Unity, Fraternity, and Patriotism). Like many fraternal orders of the era, the GAR developed its own unique series of secret grips, passwords, and initiation procedures for its recruits. Although adopting a martial bent, the organizational structure nevertheless mirrored other fraternal orders with local (post), state (department), and national levels, each with its own president (commander), treasurer (quartermaster), secretary (adjutant), and more. GAR discipline—although meted out in unique, military-style courts-martial—mostly revolved around questions of temperance and morality, as it did in other fraternities of the time. Particularly reminiscent of its Masonic roots was the spatial arrangement of the GAR post room. An altar stood at the center with a Bible placed on top, surrounded by ample space for initiation rituals and the conduct of regular business meetings. Along the room's perimeter sat the members, with designated seating for officers. Guards (or "sentinels" in the GAR parlance) stood at the post room door to challenge interlopers. Like the arrangement of other fraternal spaces, the overall effect was to preserve the quarters as a retreat from the profane and disjointed world outside.[6]

Despite these parallels with contemporary fraternities, the GAR also embodied intrinsic differences that prepared it to shed some of its secrecy and ritualism in favor of more open, civic-minded, and service-oriented objectives. Crucially, recruits needed proof of honorable Union military service to join, underscoring an important distinction from other fraternities' members. GAR veterans had proven their manhood and loyalty on the battlefield years earlier and needed no such validation from their fraternal affiliations. Compared with nonveterans, GAR joiners already possessed a mark of heroism to wield against perceived threats from the outside world. Further, GAR membership based on Civil War service, although an inherently exclusive demarcation, could also be uniquely democratizing in other ways. Hundreds of thousands of African Americans and immigrants served in the Union army and enjoyed the postwar pride of veteranhood. One member, preaching the inclusivity of the GAR, stated the order was "non-sectarian, non-political and thoroughly international—men of all creeds and colors, all religions and political beliefs and natives of nearly every civilized nation are members of the organization." In theory (although not always in practice), this service on behalf of the nation better ensured that Grand Army members came from a more heterogeneous racial and ethnic makeup than other fraternities of the era. Further, the GAR recognized its women's auxiliaries—the Woman's Relief Corps (WRC) and the Ladies of the Grand Army of the Republic (LGAR)—in the 1880s, earlier than many fraternities. Veterans often cited the domestic sacrifices women made on the wartime home front that, although gender-specific, were deemed akin to the martial sacrifices of men.[7]

During the GAR's early years, some Union veterans balked at the covert political partisanship of the fraternity's founders, stunting membership and deterring potential recruits from joining. Leading officers often directed their comrades to vote for Republican politicians, while clumsily maintaining that the true aim of the order was to provide charity for underprivileged veterans and their families. Subsequently, GAR membership dropped precipitously through the 1870s. Autopsies of this period admitted that "'politics' was killing the order" and that veterans "looked upon it as a huge political machine, used by unscrupulous office-seekers to further their own aims and ends. The people, taking the same view of the case, were also disgusted with it, and refused to countenance or help it along." Many veterans also loathed the order's Masonic-inspired grade system, enacted in 1869, which required aspiring members to pass through three stages—Recruit, Soldier, and Veteran—before attaining full membership. Intended to bring fraternal discipline to the order and attract men who might alternatively join other degree-granting fraternities, the "Veteran" grade instead offended current and prospective members who already *were* veterans.[8]

Charges of political partisanship and criticism of the degree system encouraged remaining members to reconsider the order's objectives. During the 1870s, officials took note of the declining membership, waning interest among regular members, and stagnant attendance. Their comments suggest typical fraternal proceedings and ritualism did not interest veterans as it did other men. At an 1873 department meeting in Ohio, GAR officer J. Warren Keifer warned that "[i]f nothing more is done at the [post] meetings than the usual business routine . . . the interest will very soon die out." The following year in Massachusetts, department inspector Edward B. Blasland noted similar trends. Acknowledging the difficulty of getting members to come to meetings, Blasland deduced that "comrades [were] getting tired of attending meetings where there is nothing to interest them—where nothing is done save reading the Ritual." Boredom in the ranks emboldened officials to differentiate the GAR from competing fraternities by gaining the interest and acceptance of nonveterans in their communities. Keifer suggested that "[a]ddresses, lectures, declamations, recitals, theatricals, [and] musical soireés" should be held by the posts and the public invited to enjoy these events. Blasland similarly recognized that "[o]ur order depends more upon the public than any other secret organization," and suggested that after closing the regular business of the meeting, posts hold "debates, musical or literary entertainments" to attract both veterans and nonveterans.[9]

These suggestions anticipated wider reforms from the 1880s onward that dispelled the unsavory aspects of the order, both in a bid to attract new members and to gain the public's respect. Although veterans typically remained adherents of the Party of Lincoln for the rest of their lives, the Republican bent of the organization became more subdued. In 1884, Grand Army founder and Illinois Senator John A. Logan alleged that his order was "misunderstood by a great many people" but asserted that it was "a non-political organization for charitable purposes." More importantly, the GAR consciously separated itself from other contemporary fraternities by downplaying its secrecy and ritualism. One Pennsylvania recruitment flyer targeted those veterans who might be "averse to joining a secret organization" and promised there were "not as many secrets in the Grand Army, to be hidden from public view, as there are in every family, and if the laws of organization and discipline would permit, there would be no reason why any man, woman or child could not be present at any meeting of any Post or Encampment." Similarly, one veteran warned against the post becoming a "close and secret conclave" and urged members to adopt "the broad open door of good-fellowship." Energized to separate itself from its previous insularity and old partisan proclivities, the GAR sought to foster among both veterans and civilians a warm regard for its existence.[10]

To further diminish charges of GAR secretiveness, advocates increasingly underscored the organization's benefits to the community at large. The order began a rebranding campaign, portraying itself as a service-oriented organization long before many other fraternities of the era did. At the 1875 national encampment, Commander in Chief Charles Devens Jr., conceded that the GAR was a "secret organization" with grips and signs that allowed "members to recognize each other." However, Devens assured veterans that "its secrecy is limited to these; in all its real purposes and objects it has no concealments or reservations, nothing it is not ready to spread before the world fully and frankly." During the organization's silver anniversary, one local newspaper admitted that the GAR's "aims and purposes were misunderstood," but that more recent evidence suggested that the organization was "becoming better understood and appreciated. It is now becoming recognized as a great benevolent order, the principal purposes of which are to preserve the spirit of comradeship . . . to minister to the sick and disabled, bury the dead and assist the widow and orphan." At public events, officials were quick to highlight the charity work of the GAR, presenting itself as a valuable community organization. At the 1893 Potomac Department encampment in Washington, D.C., Commander Solomon E. Faunce admitted that there were "a few signs and passwords" that only members were privileged to know, but that "[w]e want you to get a little nearer to us and know a little more of us." Boasting about the $4,400 in charitable giving done at the department level and the $300,000 disbursed by the organization at large, Faunce proudly noted that "[t]his is one of the secrets of the Order we desire you to know." An emphasis on outreach coincided with an 1880s spike in membership and a broader shift in public opinion that increasingly considered the GAR to be a welcome fixture in community culture.[11]

With membership rebounding alongside the fraternity's renewed commitment to service, more and more GAR officials recognized the value of local posts hosting public events. The shift portended a dissolving of post room barriers and a new responsibility for veterans to serve as their communities' patriotic teachers. Embracing their special status as war heroes, Grand Army members hosted activities for nonveterans that promoted loyalty to the Union, exalted their wartime sacrifices, and inspired participants to adopt a more active citizenship. Among the most common examples of post outreach was the annual installation of officers—an event that often evolved from a guarded and private fraternal ritual to an open and public affair. Local post members annually elected a slate of comrades to fill various officers' positions and then held installation ceremonies to formally elevate the officers-elect to their positions. As portrayed in early GAR manuals, these ceremonies were typically sacred fraternal events, characterized by martial pageantry. Led by a designated "mustering officer" (usually a state-level department officer, past post commander, or commander from a neighboring post), officers-elect would be brought before the post altar, reminded of their duties for the coming year, and directed to recite an oath, verifying the officers' obligation to "[e]xercise a spirit of fraternal confidence and good fellowship, and be ready to extend a helping hand to every comrade when opportunity offers." All told, such ceremonies during the early years were typical of other fraternities' installation events—secretive, sacred, and ritualistic.[12]

By the end of the nineteenth century, however, GAR installation ceremonies deviated from the fraternal norm, shedding some of its pomp and—at the post's discretion—opening up to public viewing. At the 1885 national encampment in Portland, Maine, officials endorsed changes to local posts' installations, recommending that the event "may be conducted publicly at a special meeting held for that purpose" so long as "no part of the opening or closing services or signs of recognition shall be used." Thereafter, state-level departments touted the benefits of public installation ceremonies and urged their local posts to open up their once-secretive rituals to nonveteran observation. In California, for instance, the department commander lauded the "propriety and desirability of open meetings for this purpose." Officials in Michigan similarly commended these public ceremonies as "pleasing and interesting to our Comrades, the [Woman's Relief] Corps, their families and friends." GAR handbooks, once advocating private installation ceremonies, were revised after the 1885 decree and publicized the benefits of public involvement. "[A]n evening spent in witnessing an occasion of this kind," read one manual, "especially by one who never attended an installation of Grand Army officers, will certainly never be regretted, as it is a very entertaining ceremony." Public officer installations could also serve as more than mere entertainment. As one commentator explained, "the custom of inviting friends, wives, sons and daughters of comrades and all who take an interest in the doings of old soldiers to witness the annual ceremonies of installation has grown in favor" and that there was "no better or more attractive way of teaching lasting lessons of patriotism and loyalty to the rising generation and the people at large." Veterans saw the event as a unique exhibition of patriotic pageantry, better employed to elucidate rather than remain under fraternal seclusion.[13]

Across the country, local posts took up the call to make their officer installation ceremonies public, providing entertainment and instruction for nonveteran guests. At its 1891 installation, one New York post invited the public to its headquarters, promising guests a "jolly good time" with "vocal and instrumental music, recitations ... [and] a generous supper." Another post in Pittsburgh similarly prepared an evening of music, lectures, and a meal after its officers' installation, earning plaudits from the local newspaper for "mak[ing] a very brilliant showing of the manner in which earnest workers can make themselves felt in a community." Often, GAR veterans shared their public installations with their women's auxiliaries. In Leavenworth, Kansas, members of the Custer Post and its affiliated Ladies' Circle used their installation event to broadcast their civic contributions and nonpartisan nature. The women reported on their charity work while the post's commander reminded guests that the GAR did not have "politics in it, calling attention to the fact that the officers just installed were of all parties and creeds." All told, GAR public installations were among the first and most effective events that dismantled the protective walls of the post room.[14]

Officer installations were not just features of urban life, but also served as a key form of civic entertainment and Civil War remembrance for small-town residents. In remote Menominee, Michigan, for instance, the adjutant of the Lyon Post recorded in detail the proceedings of an 1898 public installation. After brief addresses by the retiring and newly elected post commanders, visitors listened to arrangements sung by the daughter of a Confederate soldier who was now "a true Blue Yankee," followed by a "Pantomine [sic]" performance of the Lord's Prayer by a local deaf woman. Songs and recitations with antislavery themes rounded out the program and reminded guests of Union veterans' role in hastening emancipation. One guest sang the minstrel song, "The Poor Old Slave Has Gone to Rest," whose lyrics intimated that only death brought freedom and an end to suffering for an antebellum slave. Afterward, a comrade recited the poem "Banty Tim," which told the story of Tilmon Joy, a Union soldier wounded at Vicksburg and rescued by a slave. "Banty Tim" went North after the war as the servant of the soldier, who was subsequently pressured to expel his Black savior from town by racist white "Dimocrats." "He trumped Death's ace for me that day / And I'm not goin' back on him!" responded Joy, revealing the bond between the white veteran and Black freedman. Although steeped in racial stereotypes, the program nonetheless allowed the Lyon Post's guests to enjoy an evening that recalled the Union's emancipatory objectives during the war.[15]

African American GAR posts also opened up their quarters for their officer installation ceremonies, matching the activities of their white comrades. This is probably unsurprising, as historian Barbara A. Gannon has noted parallels between white and Black fraternal interests and that a guest of an all-Black post meeting "would have found them little different from the thousands of other GAR meetings" held in communities across the country. Newspapers announcing that the "public is invited" to officer installations for the Ives Post of Providence, Rhode Island, or the Sumner Post of Lexington, Kentucky, are largely indistinguishable from those that informed readers about these same events for white or integrated GAR posts. Nevertheless, African American veterans' public installations likely provided an annual reminder to their neighborhoods' civilian white and Black communities about their special sacrifices on behalf of emancipation and freedom. For instance, before "a large crowd of visitors and friends," the officers of Indianapolis's Martin R. Delaney Post were sworn in to their positions, after which one WRC member gave a speech on "the struggles of the civil war and evidences of the progress of the colored race" that "aroused much enthusiasm." Because the installing official assigned to swear in an all-Black post's officers was often a white veteran from a neighboring post, installation ceremonies sometimes brought together members of a community's white and Black chapters, along with their respective families and friends. The turn-of-the-century installation service for New York's all-Black William Lloyd Garrison Post was an example of this interracial accord with local newspapers admiring how "[c]omrades, white and black, walked arm in arm" and with a "spirit of equality and brotherhood."[16]

Another form of local post civic outreach was the open meeting, a public event held with great frequency after the GAR reached its peak membership in 1890. For these events, veterans threw open the doors of their post halls and hosted public entertainments designed to instill patriotic sentiment among guests. Members responded to state-level officials' directives to transform their quarters into civic forums and exploit the aging veterans' revered standing in their communities by promoting good citizenship. In New Hampshire, one high-level officer urged veterans in the state "to get the public interested" in their communities' GAR posts by hosting open events that "rehears[ed] the story of the war, calling to their aid neighboring Posts, well-known comrades, and public speakers." Minnesota Department Commander Colin F. Macdonald, recognizing his comrades' respected status, advocated that posts engage in "Field Work" for the benefit of their communities. Citing public events as "the most beneficial method of furthering the great objects of our organization," Macdonald believed "[t]hese gatherings are schools of patriotism, in which the young are taught lessons of loyalty to the government, and their elders are strengthened in devotion to the Republic." Recognizing veterans' unique ability to impart a Union-centered memory of the war in their communities, Grand Army officers promoted freer access to post room events.[17]

Many local posts responded to these calls to loosen the restrictions to their quarters, transforming their fraternal refuge into a civic and educational resource. Routinely, members selected a handful of comrades to serve on an entertainment committee, charged in part with planning and advertising open meetings. Contact and correspondence with influential community leaders and local media helped publicize the event and fill out the program with popular entertainments. Coordination with local teachers, principals, or superintendents was common to secure the participation of schoolchildren—either as singers, presenters, or simply observers. Members of the post's auxiliaries and comrades from neighboring posts were often invited as well, in a show of the post's dynamism, strength, and influence. On the evening of the event, post officers welcomed the assembled comrades and guests and, frequently, the post's chaplain offered an invocation before the start of the proceedings. The bulk of the program was lent to music, recitations, and prepared addresses, typically ending with audience participation in a war-era song or other patriotic numbers. Occasionally, if the post was wealthy or the open meeting also served as a fundraiser, guests then moved to a larger venue for dinner, usually prepared by the post's women's auxiliary or the female relations of the comrades.

Although open meetings typically followed this formula, the thematic focus of the event or the particulars of the speakers' addresses varied widely and reflected the diverse interests of the local posts and their communities. Some veterans, for instance, took a special interest in celebrating the lives of George Washington and Abraham Lincoln with their guests, hosting open meetings around the birthdays of these much-admired presidents. In 1897, the Sedgwick Post of Reading, Pennsylvania, prepared an evening of song, devotionals, and lectures on the first president in their post hall, inviting student Lillie Steiner to present her recitation on "The Boy Washington." Similarly, young Frank Green presented his paper on Abraham Lincoln before those gathered at a local Nebraska post's Lincoln Social, held on the ninety-fifth anniversary of the president's birth. Ahead of Washington's birthday in 1900, comrades in Bay City, Michigan, prepared a litany of lectures, including Washington as "Soldier," as "the President and Statesman," and as "the Man and Patriot."[18]

Frequently, Grand Army veterans used the open meeting to present lectures on Civil War battles in which the post's comrades fought, an alternative form of war storytelling akin to the many veteran-written histories that proliferated in the late nineteenth and early twentieth centuries. An eyewitness account of the 1862 clash between the *Monitor* and *Merrimack* was the hallmark of an 1893 open meeting in Indiana, Pennsylvania, while Chicago's George H. Thomas Post featured a lecture on the campaigns of the Army of the Frontier (in which many area veterans served). During an 1889 open meeting in Lincoln, Nebraska, comrade O. E. Baker presented a history of Confederate cavalryman John Hunt Morgan's raid through Indiana and Ohio. Because Baker himself belonged to a unit sent to track and capture Morgan's raiders, his lecture fused history and memory. Baker's account subsequently gained further circulation when it was published in the local newspaper. Post lectures often coincided with battle anniversaries, adding commemorative weight to the open meetings in which they were featured. On the thirtieth anniversary of the Battle of Corinth, the Blue Post of Topeka, Kansas, invited citizens to hear informative speeches on the event, along with period music. In Duluth, Minnesota, comrades prepared a presentation on Lee's surrender for the event's forty-fifth anniversary. Beyond retelling the events of battles long past, some posts entertained their guests with programs that immersed nonveterans in Civil War army life. Veterans in Scranton, Pennsylvania, regaled audiences at one such event with wartime reveilles and tattoos by their three-man music corps. One comrade in Pasadena, California, prepared an army signaling demonstration for his post's open meeting in 1906.[19]

In keeping with the Grand Army's interracial membership, some open meetings emphasized the emancipationist outcome of the war and reminded participants of the crucial role that African Americans played in Union victory. One Pittsburgh post hosted an integrated entertainment in 1894, at which the city's newspaper reported on good-natured banter about which soldiers—Black or white—did more to win the war. Veterans of the United States Colored Troops (USCT) brought an "able orator" to the event to defend their sacrifices, consigning their white comrades to make only "feeble efforts to rob the colored braves of their brightest laurels." In one integrated Kansas post, members invited the wife of African American poet Albery A. Whitman to recite his poem, "The Veteran," before the assembled guests. Dedicated by Whitman to "Those Who Have Borne the Battle," the verses doubtless centered both veterans' and nonveterans' thoughts on the war's legacy of emancipation:

> To-day, no poor slave drags the chain
> That manacles the limb and brain,
> But all are free;
> And brothers white, with brothers dark,
> Kindle the fires of freedom's spark,
> From sea to sea.

Meanwhile in Portland, Oregon, the Reverend Daniel Drew, a former enslaved person and USCT veteran, made regular rounds to the city's GAR posts and became for white listeners a living testament to the meaning of the Civil War. Through the years, Drew gave well-received lectures on the horrors of antebellum slavery and the condition of African Americans in the postwar South, including a talk about Black self-reliance in the realms of business, education, and religion. Further, he applauded his white comrades, stating that he was "glad to know you are not ashamed to have had a hand in freeing the Negro from slavery." The presence of African Americans in public GAR meetings and post discussions about slavery and emancipation vividly demonstrated that members were unwilling to obscure the root cause of the war and forcefully reminded nonveteran participants to acknowledge Black participation in northern victory.[20]

Of course, public entertainments and ceremonies organized by African American posts were among the most vital GAR activities that reminded attendees about the stain of slavery and the valor embodied by the Black military experience. Details are often scarce and usually warrant only a few lines in local newspapers. Still, it is evident that African American veterans hoped to impart the collective memory of their Civil War experience upon the younger generations in their communities. The commemoration of emancipation centered many all-Black posts' public events. For many years in Topeka, Kansas, the Fort Pillow Post opted to celebrate around September 22nd—the release date of the 1862 preliminary Emancipation Proclamation—with day-long programs that included speeches "emphasiz[ing] the important part which the Negro had taken in the war which led to his freedom" and an integrated parade with old veterans carrying "banners displaying portraits of Lincoln, John Brown, and Charles Sumner." The all-Black posts of New York City saved their biggest celebrations to align with citywide commemorations on January 1st (when Lincoln's proclamation formally took effect in 1863), while those in Washington, D.C., preferred to commemorate April 16th (when slavery was abolished in the district in 1862). Other posts organized public entertainments that underscored the heroism of Black soldiers. The Ives Post of Providence, Rhode Island, invited a member of the famed 54th Massachusetts Regiment to lecture on the unit's service history while Black veterans in Indianapolis invited the public to hear a history of their post and its civic role. Still other posts encouraged their communities to honor figures crucial to the Black freedom struggle. For instance, the all-Black post in Lancaster, Pennsylvania, organized citywide observances of Lincoln's birthday and led children and other members of the public to Shreiner Cemetery to decorate the grave of ardent abolitionist Thaddeus Stevens.[21]

In Black, white, and integrated posts, aging Civil War veterans volunteered for a new type of service by lending both their fraternal quarters and their patriotic expertise in support of a GAR-endorsed memory of the Civil War. In communities across the country, Grand Army members invited nonveterans within the walls of the post room, wielding their revered veteran status to promote programs and activities that reminded citizens of their wartime sacrifices. They hoped that by offering this instruction, younger generations of Americans would not only reflect on the nation's past, but also use the war's lessons about duty, loyalty, and freedom to exemplify, in the present, a higher level of citizenship. As one grateful newspaper reported, the openness of the local GAR post helped the community "be taught lessons of our history, not only of war but of peace."[22]

A Building More Useful Than a Monument

For years after Appomattox, the citizens of Rockville, Connecticut, considered erecting a commemorative marker to honor their town's Civil War heroes.

During Memorial Day ceremonies in 1884, community leaders reminded the audience of its obligations to the Union's defenders and recommended that the town appropriate sufficient funds to erect a soldiers' monument. However, Rockville patriarch and wartime congressman Dwight Loomis demurred. Instead of a mere monument, he advocated "a large and handsome building" that would "not only be a fitting memorial for the soldiers, but at the same time be of use and benefit to the town." Veterans and nonveterans agreed, ultimately directing some $90,000 in public funds toward the construction of a memorial building. Upon its completion in 1890, the three-story Romanesque structure was a spectacular example of multifunctional design, encompassing a 1,000-seat auditorium, municipal offices, courtrooms, a law library, and police headquarters. Occupying much of the second floor was the meeting hall of Rockville's GAR chapter, the Thomas F. Burpee Post, organized in 1884 and named for a local man killed at Cold Harbor. Opening their September 1890 meeting in their new quarters, the post's veterans passed resolutions thanking the town for "erect[ing] a magnificent edifice as a lasting Memorial" and vowing to be "doubly mindful of our duties as citizens and freemen and [to] always strive to merit the confidence reposed in us as loyal citizens." In subsequent years, the comrades built up an impressive library and relic collection in their GAR hall, which they frequently opened for public lectures, recitals, and school programs. Together, Rockville soldiers and civilians created a dynamic community center—a place at once commemorative of the war dead, practical for the town's day-to-day business, and essential for the community's GAR veterans to meet and communicate their memory of the Civil War.[23]

The construction of the Rockville Memorial Building is just one example underscoring an overlooked relationship between Grand Army members and northern nonveterans. In the postwar decades, both sides cooperatively mobilized to create freestanding memorial structures that not only assumed *fraternal* utility as meeting places for GAR veterans, but also provided *civic* utility for citizens at large. In communities of all sizes, the GAR and its civilian allies collaborated in support of these memorial halls that honored the soldier dead and veteran living in a more impressive (and, typically, more expensive) commemorative expression than the more familiar soldiers' monuments that cropped up after the Civil War. At the same time, these expansive structures had ample space to serve the needs of nonveterans as well, becoming many towns' newest civic centers. Meanwhile, aging Union veterans proved remarkably successful in promoting these ventures, not only leveraging GAR post influence to propose the structures, but also negotiating with town and state officials, architects, urban planners, voters, and other key groups whose support was necessary to raise them. Veterans were thus deeply enmeshed in the social and political networks of their communities and adept in combining Civil War commemoration with Progressive Era civic reform impulses.[24]

Like Connecticut's Burpee Post, the roughly 7,000 individual GAR posts across the country required as many designated community spaces for members to conduct their fraternal business. The location of these quarters varied widely and was determined by a number of factors: comrade preferences, resources and revenue of the local post, and the magnanimity of nonveterans, to name a few. For many posts, especially those in small towns and rural areas where members were usually fewer and poorer, comrades were likely to rent humble quarters with just enough space for basic functions. Leasing a spare room at a nearby business was a common option for many posts, arrangements that mingled commerce with GAR fraternity. Members in rural Mason County, Michigan, for instance, outfitted a "very pleasant post room" atop the main floor of the Pere Marquette Lumber Company after establishing their post in 1880. Others made arrangements to share space with their communities' better-established fraternities like the Odd Fellows or Freemasons (often, GAR members belonged to these orders too, helping facilitate the negotiations). For a time, veterans in Olympia, Washington, rented their quarters from the local Odd Fellows temple, while in Nebraska, John A. Dix Post members rented rooms in their community's Masonic hall. Unable to purchase their own quarters, many poorer and low-membership posts were thus reliant on forging friendly ties with their communities' commercial and civic leaders to secure adequate meeting space.[25]

This was especially true for African American GAR posts whose members often faced economic hardship and lacked the resources to allocate excessive funds for fraternal quarters. Still, the very existence of an all-Black post in any given community also usually meant the presence of a vibrant African American social network that veterans could rely on for support. In Lancaster, Pennsylvania, for instance, many members of the Sergeant Benn Post also belonged to the city's historic Bethel A.M.E. Church, which had purchased a nearby building with ample meeting space. Around the turn of the twentieth century, not only did Benn Post use the church's property for its activities, but so did other social organizations including the local Black chapters of the Freemasons and the Hod Carriers' Union. Similarly, the Sumner Post of Kansas City, Kansas, met for many years at the Sons of Protection Hall, which became a political and social center for the city's African American community. Besides the benevolent society for which the hall was named, the veterans shared the space over the years with other Black men's and women's groups such as the Colored Men's Garfield and Arthur Club, the Knights of Tabor, the Royal Circle of Friends, and the Golden Rule Tabernacle. Frequently, the venues that veterans selected for their meetings were places that had a long history in providing opportunity and uplift for the African American community. The members of the all-Black post in Lexington, Kentucky, doubtless realized that their turn-of-the-century meeting place—Ladies' Hall—had housed one of the first formal schools for the community's African American children in the years immediately following the Civil War. Although it may have lacked funds to establish independent quarters, the typical Black GAR post at the turn of the century was a vital extension of the activist, cooperative, and interlaced web of institution-building organizations in African American neighborhoods around the country.[26]

For a few especially resourceful posts with wealthier members, owning fraternal quarters was a particularly worthy achievement that indicated a healthy and cooperative membership. Indeed, top GAR officials deemed hall ownership to not only be a smart investment and the mark of a dynamic post, but also a way to cultivate further interactions with nonveterans and earn their aid and respect. "Every post should have a permanent place of meeting, and if possible own its own hall," urged one Ohio officer. "Get up reunions, picnics, lectures, etc., and have small payments for admission to raise money for future payments. Citizens will help you when they know that you have a nucleus, and that you are in earnest and will help yourselves." Owning a meeting place was a luxury few posts could afford. Still, a small number of particularly enterprising posts—especially larger and more urban ones—pooled resources and garnered public support to purchase their own accommodations. For instance, members of Pittsburgh's John W. Patterson Post bought a four-story building for $11,000—the top two floors reserved for meetings and the post library, and the remainder of the structure and its outbuildings rented out as office and living space to help defray their debts. To enjoy the benefits of hall ownership, aging veterans proved that they could be quite intrepid and commercially shrewd.[27]

Other posts benefited from the generosity of fellow citizens and local officials who granted Grand Army veterans quarters in their communities' public spaces. In Germantown, Pennsylvania, for instance, the Ellis Post first received the support of Philadelphia's mayor and council to occupy the top floor of the community's town hall in 1896. Over the years, the city's Bureau of City Property extended the lease free of rent. When veterans in Yorkville, Illinois, began dying off and survivors found it difficult to pay the rent for their quarters, remaining members and their WRC affiliate petitioned the local board of supervisors in

1899 to authorize rent-free space for the post to continue meeting. As the town had recently constructed a new courthouse, the board permitted the post to use the basement of the obsolete structure, which included the old jail and a sheriff's quarters, granting it "free of all expense, even furnishing heat and light."[28]

The most ostentatious venue for GAR quarters, however, was the memorial hall, an architectural and cultural phenomenon that erupted across the country in the years surrounding the turn of the twentieth century. When a town sought to erect a tribute to its defenders, preference for a memorial hall often centered on the belief that such a gesture was the most permanent and touching testimonial to the war generation. "Monuments erected to the memory of the brave become defaced with the lapse of years," reasoned one commentator. "In a memorial hall their names might be kept green in memory, as long as time itself shall last." For other advocates, these structures better preserved additional facets of Civil War history besides solely the memory of a town's war heroes. One supporter, for instance, suggested that "in a [memorial] hall could be placed relics, documents and portraits bearing upon the rebellion. Here they would be carefully preserved for all time for the use of those that might be interested in the study of the history of a great struggle." Still others touted memorial hall projects because they proved to be more practical for the benefit of all citizens. Indeed, promises of "usefulness" and "utility" pepper the many building proposals advanced by both GAR veterans and other advocates. In this vein, one hall promoter stated that such a structure in his town "would be a monument in every sense of the word and one that while commemorating the heroic deeds of the dead would also prove of benefit to the living."[29]

To be sure, not everyone welcomed the prospect of a memorial hall in their communities. When, for instance, the Iowa General Assembly deliberated in the late 1880s and early 1890s over erecting a commemorative structure on the capitol grounds "for the purpose of perpetuating an expression of the patriotism, courage and distinguished soldiery" of its defenders (financed in part by a refunded federal war tax), a designated commission appraised the merits of a memorial hall. One hall supporter asked the state's Grand Army posts to consider whether they wanted to invest the funds in a traditional monument of "'dead marble' with its proverbial iron fence and notice to 'keep off the grass,'" or a memorial hall that would be "in keeping with a progressive practical people in that which is *useful* and instructive and consequently more pleasing to the eye." Ultimately, however, it was decided that a memorial hall risked devolving into a "patriotic storage room" for war relics where "flags decay and turn to dust, and arms lose interest as years roll on." When put to a vote by the Grand Army posts of the state, veterans ultimately agreed with the monument commission's assessment (though some posts spurned using the funds for *either* a monument *or* a memorial hall, preferring instead that the money go to disabled veterans in the state's soldiers' home at Marshalltown). The result was the raising of the $150,000 Iowa Soldiers' and Sailors' Monument, completed in 1896.[30]

In other instances, citizens felt memorial halls were an unwarranted expense or even an improper commemorative offering. In Kalamazoo, Michigan, the GAR veterans of the Orcutt Post were repeatedly stymied in their attempts to construct a memorial hall with public funds for many years before the realization of a building in 1908. One reason for the delay was the indignation of those citizens residing on the county's periphery who saw no value in building up the county seat. "There are but few old soldiers in the county outside of Kalamazoo who are physically and financially qualified to take advantage of the benefits of such an institution," one community complained, "and the whole matter is looked upon as a 'graft' on the part of Kalamazoo people to beautify their city at the expense of the county." Relying instead on friendly area businessmen, civic-minded citizens, and their own funds, the Orcutt Post secured the $8,000 for the building without reaping public financing. During the fundraising phase for a memorial hall in New York, some disgruntled citizens took to the local newspaper to editorialize their displeasure at the community's transfer of public funds from a monument to a memorial hall. One rankled critic asked whether it was "right for us to give our money to build a monument to perpetuate the memory of the 'gallant dead,' and then have the money diverted to build a hall?" Another, citing the types of public activities that might threaten the sanctity of a memorial structure feared that "the memory of the gallant dead will be perpetuated by holding high carnival in the monumental hall."[31]

Despite these qualms from some quarters, the construction of memorial halls nonetheless received widespread backing and became a cultural sensation across the North. In several states, legislators passed bills empowering county commissioners or other local entities to appropriate money for Civil War markers. Grand Army veterans were active both in petitioning for these taxation measures, and occasionally, for widening the scope of these laws to include memorial halls. In Iowa, for instance, the state's General Assembly approved a law in 1884 authorizing each county to levy a tax to erect a soldiers' monument to that county's Union dead. Two years later, the efforts of state representative and Union veteran Rufus S. Benson amended the law to permit counties to collect the tax for the construction of a monument *or* a memorial hall. Grand Army veterans in rural Franklin County responded immediately, petitioning the county to put the taxation question on the ballot. The board of supervisors conceded and in the 1887 spring election, voters authorized a tax to finance a memorial hall at the county seat of Hampton. Supplemented by donations gathered by the veterans and aided by the town council's donation of land for the building, Franklin County's Grand Army men moved their post meetings to the brick structure after its 1890 dedication.[32]

Indiana veterans were also active in establishing a memorial hall in Porter County, working to extend the intent of the state's law on commemorative building projects. After the war, the state's legislature empowered boards of county commissioners to appropriate funds for soldiers' monuments. As early as 1885, veterans and civilian allies of Valparaiso's Chaplain Brown Post organized to establish a monument to the town's defenders, aided by a $500 contribution collected by the post's WRC auxiliary. By this point, public opinion shifted toward using the funds to create a more impressive memorial hall. Former Post Commander A. Lytle Jones drew up an amendment to the existing state law and comrades journeyed to Indianapolis to press their case in person. During the 1891 legislative session, Jones's amendment passed, and the Brown Post was free to solicit subscriptions for the memorial hall, assign a building committee to plan construction, and hire an architect and contractors to erect the $15,000 structure. Assisted by the Board of County Commissioners who leased the building's site free of charge, the dedication took place in November 1893. Besides housing the post's fraternal hall and quarters for the WRC, Valparaiso's newest civic center included a 1,200-seat auditorium, stage, and ticket office for community events.[33]

Elsewhere, Union veterans proved exceptionally proficient in tailoring their memorial hall advocacy strategies to the specific needs of their communities. In rural areas across the North, for instance, GAR members recognized that commemorative structures could double as their regions' first centers for entertainment or civic functions. The southwest corner of sparsely populated Livingston County, New York, is illustrative. Here, three memorial halls cropped up within a ten-mile radius and in the span of a quarter century. The first was raised in the village of Portage in 1880 to pay tribute to the thirty-five area soldiers who had died during the Civil War. As early as 1865, the community's Soldiers' Monument Association began collecting money for a marble monument. Earning contributions from individual donors and various fundraisers, the association had amassed nearly $2,000 by the late 1870s. By that time, however, many veterans and civilians now surmised that a memorial hall was "the most sensible way to expend the money" as it "would be of some use to the living and as honorable to the dead." Portage ultimately constructed a modest brick structure, which became the new GAR headquarters of the William C. Hall Post. Eight years later in nearby Dalton, members of the local GAR post worked with citizens in erecting their own memorial hall. Comparable in size and expense to the Portage structure, Dalton's hall was similarly lauded as "a building that will be found very useful for general gatherings of the people."³⁴

The memorial hall at Nunda (see Figure 2) was the last in the region to be constructed, largely due to the villagers' comparative apathy to raise a commemorative testament to its defenders. Despite the fundraising efforts of the members of the Craig W. Wadsworth Post to erect a monument in the 1880s, the local news-

Figure 2 Completed in 1906, the GAR Memorial Hall in Nunda, New York, became a center of civic activity for both veterans and villagers at large. The fraternal quarters for the Craig W. Wadsworth Post were located on the second floor. From author's collection.

paper reported that citizens did "not appear . . . very anxious to contribute" even though "they concede that it should be done." Efforts hibernated for the next two decades until native son John J. Carter gifted $20,000 to erect a stately memorial hall in the middle of town. Carter, a Congressional Medal of Honor recipient who had earned his wealth in the Pennsylvania oil fields after the war, intended the building to serve Nunda's GAR and other patriotic organizations for the benefit of "the old soldiers and citizens of Nunda and the rising generation—the hope of the future." Completed in 1906 and transferred to the Nunda Memorial Hall Corporation, the building became the headquarters of the Wadsworth Post and its auxiliaries.[35]

Livingston County's memorial halls quickly assumed broad functionality. To be sure, the structures played important roles in commemorating the soldier dead, providing meeting places for Grand Army veterans, and serving as focal points for Memorial Day observances. However, perusal of the local newspapers reveals that these sites also became vital civic centers. Portage's memorial hall, for example, served as the headquarters of the town's chapter of the Women's Christian Temperance Union, the local Grange, and the Red Cross sewing circle, and even acted as a storage facility for area farmers' produce. During one particularly active span from 1895 to 1896, the structure hosted a temperance lecture sponsored by a local Baptist church, an oyster supper for the benefit of the local cornet band, a maple sugar social for the junior missionary society of an Episcopal church, and voter registration for the fall elections. Nunda's hall became the site of the American Legion's public fairs and a consultation clinic for nearby Mt. Morris's pulmonary treatment facility. In Dalton, the memorial hall became the villagers' venue for square dances and moving picture shows during the 1910s and 1920s. All told, Livingston County's memorial halls served not just as sites of memory or preserves set aside for GAR use. They were also centers for rural entertainment and civic assembly for all citizens.[36]

Meanwhile, in many small towns across the postwar United States, residents came together in improvement associations to promote municipal planning and public works projects. Enterprises were broad—ranging from civil or sanitary engineering undertakings, village beautification schemes, and the establishment of libraries or other public institutions—all which markedly enhanced provincial life. Through their advocacy of memorial halls, small-town GAR posts were part of this movement to bring new amenities to their communities. They advertised the civic and educational benefits of their projects, secured donations from interested backers, appealed to public officials and voters for appropriations and tax support, and cultivated grassroots civic engagement. The post at Paw Paw,

Michigan, demonstrated this spirit of improvement. Initially seeking to erect a soldiers' monument, the veterans "upon mature consideration" opted to build a memorial hall, "which would be of greater benefit to the community at large and would serve equally well as a memorial to the veterans of the Civil War." Upon its completion in 1912, the post advertised its new home as a place for the general public: "[b]right, clean, light and warm—a place to congregate with your brothers and sisters, feast and visit and commune." The front room of the memorial hall was equipped as a public "rest room" with seating and reading material for all comers to enjoy, a mark of the post's "appreciation of the help [they] received from the community in building their new hall." In a short time, the memorial hall not only served as the headquarters of the GAR post, but also became a regular meeting place for the local branches of the Grange, the Knights of Pythias, the Lady Maccabees, and the Royal Neighbors.[37]

Similarly in Windsor Locks, Connecticut, the members of the Joseph H. Converse Post coordinated to bring their small town a useful building. The veterans bought a tract of land from their own funds in 1889 and then united with wealthy local mill owner Charles E. Chaffee, a "warm sympathizer with the veterans" who donated the money to erect a two-story memorial hall that included a library, meeting rooms, and the post quarters. One town elder deemed the new structure, dedicated in 1891, "an education to future generations" that would teach "how much a free people thought of their government and that men found something beyond themselves worth dying for." Jealous of the valuable amenities that the memorial hall offered, some citizens of neighboring Thompsonville feared that Windsor Locks was now the more attractive community. Noting that there was always "some rivalry between the towns as to public improvements," one commentator suggested that Thompsonville compete with its adversary to erect a similar building that would serve "partly for the Grand Army and largely furnish accommodations for public institutions." Although the town never erected such a structure, interest in doing so illustrates how small communities sought to improve livability with these useful GAR-backed structures.[38]

Grand Army members in larger towns also advocated commemorative tributes but had the resources to propose bigger and costlier structures. These veterans proved particularly adept at leveraging their influence to coordinate carefully planned municipal-building endeavors designed to enhance civic life. In Rockford, Illinois, for instance, the local post placed a proposition on the 1900 ballot advocating the construction of a testament to the county's Union veterans. After voters overwhelmingly backed the measure, Post Commander Thomas G. Lawler presented a petition before the Winnebago County Board of Supervisors.

Signed by some two hundred area veterans, the petition proposed that the board "make their appropriation for a Memorial Hall, believing that such a building, where the records and relics of the different wars could be preserved, would be more useful than a monument." The county's investigative committee approved the memorial hall scheme the following year, insisting "that if a hall was built it be made large enough to be used for county purposes as well as for ornament and for keeping of records." Rockford's Soldiers and Sailors Memorial Hall—which included a GAR post room, a large library, and an auditorium—was dedicated in 1903 at a cost of nearly $60,000. Insistent that the memorial hall remain widely accessible, veterans directed the hall's custodian to observe liberal operating hours for the public's benefit.[39]

In large cities, efforts to construct memorial halls often corresponded with broader community efforts to improve, beautify, and reform urban spaces. Participating in this trend, veterans negotiated with powerful state legislatures, city councils, planning boards, estimators, and architects to raise structures that not only consecrated the Union dead and accommodated GAR veterans, but also promoted urban artistry and utility. The establishment of the Soldiers Memorial Building in Toledo, Ohio, fits these criteria. In 1879, fifteen individuals (five GAR veterans, five women's auxiliary members, and five "citizens in civil life") created the Toledo Soldiers Memorial Association to raise money "to erect a memorial building in the City of Toledo, in which the records of our soldiers and relics of the war may be suitably kept, and to make the same building answer a practical purpose." To meet that end, the memorial association envisioned that the building would include ample space for a city armory, national guard drill hall, banquet hall, and quarters for an artillery battery. Through the efforts of the memorial association and funds authorized by the state legislature, the building was completed in 1886. At the dedication services, GAR veteran J. Kent Hamilton proclaimed, "[a]t last we have a Soldiers' Monument worthy of the name. Not of useless marble or bronze, but a structure which commemorates the valor, the sacrifices, the triumphs, and glories, of the soldiers of the Republic, and is also a temple where is to be taught all civic virtues."[40]

In neighboring Michigan, GAR officials appointed a committee in 1891 to research the feasibility of a memorial hall in Detroit that would serve area posts as a meeting place and records repository. Mindful of a time when the GAR would cease to exist, the building would "then be devoted to the preservation of the records, museum and library of the Grand Army of the State of Michigan for ever [sic], and it shall thereafter be an armory and War Museum." The five veterans on the committee were granted great latitude to solicit and handle funds, choose and purchase a site, canvass architectural designs, and select cost-effective construction proposals. The GAR took to the newspapers to gain public support for the project that would "stand for all time, as an educator . . . [so] the young may gather inspiration from the object lesson it would teach." Despite difficult negotiations with tightfisted city officials, the project at last received the approval of the city council and board of estimates in 1898, which issued $38,000 in bonds (complemented by a $6,000 donation from the state GAR department). Completed in 1900, Detroit's Grand Army of the Republic Building was, according to one comrade, "a monument . . . of more practical value to present and to coming generations than any stately shaft or simple pile of stone."[41]

In communities across the country, GAR veterans around the turn of the twentieth century established a wide range of designated spaces to conduct their fraternal activities. Occasionally, members worked with supportive nonveterans—auxiliary members, civic leaders, local and state politicians, and interested citizens at large—to erect enduring memorial halls that became their communities' newest civic venues. Whether in humble post quarters or lavish halls, they would come to use these spaces to reach out to the public—through lectures, programs, museum displays, and community projects—in ways that definitively marked Union veterans as active participants in Progressive Era local service and reform.

Constructed with a View to Practicality

Perhaps no other GAR-established structure combined magnificence and multifunctionality more distinctly than Pittsburgh's Soldiers and Sailors Memorial Hall (see Figure 3). The project began humbly. On June 14, 1902, members of the William G. Lowry Post of Wilkinsburg, Pennsylvania, prepared resolutions "to erect a suitable monument to the memory of the soldiers and sailors of the Civil War." The post forwarded their proposal to representatives of the Allegheny County Grand Army Association (ACGAA), a select committee of socially prominent GAR members representing thirty-three posts in the Pittsburgh area. ACGAA had existed since 1894 and performed a variety of services for local veterans, including advocacy for destitute comrades, preferential hiring practices, and pension rights. In this case, the Lowry Post called on the politically influential ACGAA "to use their best endeavors" to petition county officials to act on their monument proposal. One week later, members of the ACGAA's Monument and Memorial Committee met to consider the proposal and submit a formal report. "We are in favour [sic] of the county authorities erecting some memorial to the memory of the men who so nobly represented Allegheny County upon the many battle-fields of the Rebellion," the committee agreed, "but we do not favour a monument." Instead, the report continued, "[w]e believe that this County should erect a Memorial Hall." The committee thus surpassed the Lowry Post's vision, calling for a true community center whose purpose would not only memorialize the sacrifices of the Civil War generation, but also serve Pittsburgh as a vibrant meeting place, educational institution, and lasting testament to civic pride. Members also imagined a library, spacious meeting rooms, a 5,000-seat auditorium, and a GAR repository. Here, local posts' scattered records, battle flags, and relics could be "gathered together and placed in a building . . . [where] they would be an incentive to patriots and to generations yet unborn."[42]

The Allegheny County veterans' campaign for what would become Soldiers and Sailors Memorial Hall occurred alongside a larger urban renewal movement designed to bring moral uplift, aesthetic grandeur, and public amenities to the teeming industrial city. For years, commentators had pointed to the severe social ills, wealth disparities, and environmental degradation that had accompanied Pittsburgh's unbounded growth and economic productivity. To combat the city's degraded social conditions and the unsavory publicity they generated, civic leaders responded with a range of ameliorative urban renewal projects that coincided with a nationwide spate of planning initiatives, popularly dubbed the City Beautiful Movement. This urban trend, largely directed by middle- and upper-class civic leaders, stressed a re-creation of American cities into orderly and attractive entities by promoting new architectural and public works projects that blended both aesthetic grandeur and physical functionality. In Pittsburgh's case, these efforts centered on Oakland, a district situated just east of the downtown commercial area, where city leaders fashioned a true civic center to showcase Pittsburgh's culture and provide citizens with opportunities for entertainment, education, and self-improvement. Here, a cluster of colleges, museums, galleries, theaters, and places of worship cropped up thanks to a considerable investment in coordinated planning and construction.[43]

It was amid Oakland's cultural profusion that Allegheny County's GAR veterans and their allies determined to flaunt their memorial hall. Starting in 1902, they undertook an eight-year campaign of concerted advocacy and negotiation to bring about their vision. Beginning with a massive petition drive, veterans persuaded the county's commissioners and courts to support the endeavor. By 1905, the state legislature—under steady GAR pressure—authorized the project, permitting Pittsburgh's veterans to select ten of their own to form an oversight committee to work alongside the commissioners. Veterans next mobilized to

Figure 3 Dedicated in 1910 after a yearslong campaign by local Union veterans, the monumental Soldiers and Sailors Memorial Hall in Pittsburgh, Pennsylvania, became perhaps the grandest example of the merging of civic utility and GAR commemorative function. Even today, the multifunctional structure serves as a memorial, a museum, and a vibrant civic space. From author's collection.

garner the support of the county's voters whose approval was needed to fund the endeavor. GAR flyers and other literature circulated throughout the city in the weeks ahead of the fall vote and on election day, post commanders ordered their men to stake out the polling places to encourage a favorable referendum. With the ballots tallied, 47,902 voters supported the project and just 5,487 came out against—a stunning 90 percent approval rate. "It is especially gratifying," GAR members concluded, "that this Memorial has not been accorded grudgingly, but by an overwhelming favorable vote by our fellow Citizens." With taxpayer funding secured, Pittsburgh veterans assisted the county commissioners in the arduous consultations with the city planners, county officials, architects, and construction teams needed to make the memorial hall a reality. After more than two years of construction and a final price tag exceeding $1.7 million, Allegheny County's imposing testament to its Civil War defenders was complete.[44]

From the start, Pittsburgh's veterans intended Soldiers and Sailors Memorial Hall to serve the public at large and were deeply invested in endowing the structure with the power to teach the masses national loyalty and civic patriotism.

For the three-day dedication in October 1910, they cajoled area businesses to close in order to have as many workers join in the proceedings as possible and coaxed school districts to dismiss their students from class, "believing that such a course would be a lesson in patriotism for the children." Attendees witnessed members of the county's GAR posts—joined by Sons of Veterans (SV) members, national guardsmen, Spanish-American War veterans, and others—step off in a parade of 9,000 that wended its way through Oakland's streets. Afterward, veterans and guests crowded the hall's auditorium to hear addresses from prominent politicians and military heroes. Governor Edward S. Stuart commented on the versatility of the memorial hall, noting that it had "been constructed with a view to practicability" all the while standing "as a monument to the valorous deeds of the brave men who went to the front when they heard the call of duty." The *Pittsburgh Gazette* echoed Stuart's praise that this new institution was "not a shaft of marble and an inscription, but a landmark, a structure of usefulness and milestone in new ideas and typical of the times."[45]

Meanwhile, the dedication of the memorial hall was a remarkably integrated affair. Historically, Pittsburgh had an active and well-respected coterie of African American veterans who led their neighborhoods' commemorations of emancipation, held events celebrating Frederick Douglass's and Abraham Lincoln's birthdays, and organized annual Memorial Day programs at the all-Black Lincoln Memorial Cemetery. The city's white and Black veterans shared a particularly friendly bond. Many of the county's posts willingly accepted African American members and the city's all-Black Robert G. Shaw Post was among the most engaged in the region. White veterans frequently visited the Shaw Post meetings, while Shaw Post members were often invited to speak at all-white or white-majority posts.[46]

Reflecting the cordial relations between Pittsburgh's Black and white veterans, the oversight committee intended the memorial hall dedication to be an integrated celebration, with Union veterans' sacrifices to abolish slavery made paramount. When a representative of the county's African American GAR members approached the committee to request "that a time be fixed during the week of dedication in which the colored people might hold such exercises as they desired," the all-white committee balked. They reminded their African American compatriots "that no distinction could be made between Comrades of the Grand Army, and inasmuch as the Memorial building was erected by the people of this county, colored citizens have the same rights as others." The committee accommodated their African American guests by inviting the Reverend Dr. R. French Hurley of Pittsburgh's Bethel A.M.E. Church to speak. Hurley used the opportunity to reawaken the audience's attention to the war's legacy as it related to emancipation and, according to the *Pittsburgh Post*, "delivered a speech . . . on behalf of 186,000 black men who had enlisted in the Federal army and of the 4,000,000 negroes whose yoke of slavery had been lifted." The memorial hall remained a place dedicated to an integrated memory of the Civil War as the Shaw Post began using the hall's post rooms to hold its fraternal meetings one month after the dedication. At a time when African Americans suffered intense discrimination and racial segregation, Soldiers and Sailors Memorial Hall stood as a proud testament to Black-white GAR camaraderie. White comrades insisted on this. Although largely silent about supporting African American civil rights around the turn of the century, most white veterans nonetheless honored the service of their Black brothers in arms and the role they had all played in hastening emancipation in their youth.[47]

For years afterward, Soldiers and Sailors Memorial Hall demonstrated its civic utility as thousands of veterans and nonveterans made use of its facilities. Many of the county's GAR posts shuttered their meeting halls and moved their monthly events to the specially designated post rooms set aside for GAR members, rent free. The SV, WRC, United Spanish War Veterans camps, and posts of the American Veterans of Foreign Service were also welcome to use the memorial hall's facilities without charge. Meanwhile, to benefit the public, the veteran-led board of managers approved ample visitation hours. Fraternal groups, ladies' societies, commercial and civic clubs, and professional organizations all utilized the capacious facilities in the months following the dedication. An examination of the memorial hall's guest register reveals that the building enjoyed seasonal visitation cycles from a wide variety of groups. During the spring, school field trips brought hundreds of students in to see the magnificent structure with its relics to a bygone war. Summer attracted high volumes of out-of-state travelers vacationing in Pittsburgh, as well as troops of the newly established Boy Scouts. Autumn months most frequently attracted the regimental reunions of Pittsburgh-area veterans. And in winter, a brief rush of pre-Christmas holiday field trips in early December gave way to well-attended January and February programs for McKinley's, Lincoln's, and Washington's birthdays complete with lectures, songs, and hymns. One New York veteran doubtless captured the sentiment of many of the hall's visitors as he scrawled his concise praise in the guest book: "This is the best Memorial to the GAR I have seen."[48]

Citing the "social aspects" which made the Grand Army of the Republic "a most attractive organization," Union veteran and former Wisconsin Governor Lucius

Fairchild anticipated the civic promise of the local GAR post. "Proper [post] rooms," he explained in 1881, should be not only "occupied for the ordinary business meeting," but also "for not infrequent social gatherings; [where] camp fires are held, when the wives and children and friends are invited in, and pleasant, healthful amusements enjoyed; an occasional dance and supper, or the reading of a paper by a brother upon some subject interesting to the members . . . [on] the issues growing out of the struggle." Tracking the community-level activities of local veterans suggests that their post rooms and memorial halls, particularly after 1890, became the types of venues that Fairchild envisioned—not ones of insulation and escapism, but rather of dynamic interaction and socialization between veterans and nonveterans. By examining the interests of Progressive Era Grand Army members in a range of locations, a clearer picture develops of a vast network of local posts imparting lessons from the Civil War to citizens a generation or more removed from the conflict itself. Now, faced with the new challenges of a fractious, turn-of-the-century populace, the veterans confidently believed that their experience and instruction could serve as society's panacea. Meanwhile, not all Grand Army civic activity remained within the walls of the post room or memorial hall. Veterans also became active participants in advocating, financing, and even creating institutions of learning whose influence would be grounded with GAR-endorsed lessons and principles instructive in bringing order, progress, and improvement to a quickly modernizing nation.[49]

2

A Grand Army of Scholars

Knowledge goes hand in hand with liberty, justice and equal rights.

—John R. Paxton, Lafayette Post, New York, New York, 1888

As the Civil War's semicentennial approached, GAR members in Kansas grew impatient. Compared with the appropriations that other state governments had allocated to honor Union veterans, these aging Jayhawkers felt that their legislators neglected them. "Nearly every loyal state," chided Department Commander William A. Morgan in 1908, "has erected either a monument or a memorial building to commemorate the services of the Union soldiers of 1861-'65. Kansas stands almost alone in its dereliction in this matter." For decades, GAR-supported monument or memorial hall funding bills died in Topeka. At last, well into the twentieth century, the state GAR partnered with the Kansas State Historical Society, which sought government aid to properly house its growing collections. Together, officials from the allied organizations proposed a bill to erect a building where "memoir and history" could coexist, and ultimately persuaded the legislature to appropriate funds for a memorial hall in 1909. Completed five years later, the three-story building housed office space, storage facilities, book stacks, and a public reading room for the historical society, as well as meeting rooms, an auditorium, and relic displays for the GAR state headquarters. "Memorial Hall commemorates not alone the glorious record of the soldiers in arms," reflected one commentator, "it stands as a monument to their achievements in state building." By uniting the GAR and historical society under one roof, Kansas veterans thought creatively about how to both commemorate and educate. The initiative fused the memory of the Union soldier's sacrifice on behalf of democracy and freedom to a civic institution inherently designed to preserve and inform. Together, the unique combination of "memoir and history" might inspire and teach rising generations about public service and the weighty responsibilities of citizenship.[1]

Around the turn of the twentieth century, Grand Army veterans at the state and local levels promoted civic education by investing considerable time and resources to support institutions of learning—especially universities and libraries. Department and post records reveal imaginative projects initiated by aging Union veterans to prod, assist, and empower nonveterans in their communities to devote themselves to civic engagement, social reform, and educational improvement. This activism was an alternative to traditional GAR commemorative exercises that aimed not merely to unify (or reunify) the body politic but also to inculcate an ethic of public service that would solidify and perpetuate the war's lessons about loyalty, sacrifice, and ardent citizenship. To be sure, Grand Army educational activism among schoolchildren is well studied, with one scholar arguing that Union veteran presence in schools was part of the "hectic campaign to instill patriotism through worship of the Constitution, the flag, and America's heroes." Historians of Civil War memory have also highlighted the raging textbook debates between Union and Confederate veterans and their allies. But it is perhaps anticipated that Union veterans felt comfortable entering the schoolhouse or weighing in on classroom curricula since so many of them had enjoyed the benefits of, at least, a primary school education in their youth. James McPherson has further observed that "Civil War armies were the most literate in history to that time," noting that 90 percent of Union soldiers could read and write. Yet except for some officers, few of the boys in blue were college boys—which *does* make it surprising that the GAR expended untold energies toward civic training in higher education and related institutions.[2]

Other scholars studying this period have identified institutions of learning as key locations in US communities that fostered order, progress, and improvement in a society undergoing wrenching changes. One historian, for instance, has demonstrated that contemporaries viewed university attendance as the best means to mitigate the problems associated with urban life by nurturing "civic responsibility" among students. Similarly, scholars have long indicated that American libraries tended to instill white, middle-class reformers' definitions of order and control over an unruly citizenry. The story of Progressive Era reform in these institutions has overlooked the role of the GAR veteran, quite curiously given the fact that patriotic education was as transmissible here as it was in public schools. In fact, compared with the schoolchild, targeting the university student or the library patron with patriotic lessons may have been even more impactful to the GAR activist since many of the individuals occupying these learned sites already enjoyed the benefits of full citizenship and could contribute to the good of the community and the country straightaway.[3]

The first section below examines the GAR's influence on the postwar nation's growing network of public libraries, a civic and cultural venue crucial to properly understanding the fraternity's educational activism. While many communities across the country established their first libraries in the decades around the turn of the century, local posts immediately sensed their edifying potential. When harnessed to their influence, veterans recognized these neighborhood institutions as powerful disseminators of a proper interpretation of Civil War history. The second section demonstrates how GAR educational advocacy expanded from schoolhouses to the nation's growing system of normal (teachers') schools, colleges, and universities. Post records show a wide range of supportive, veteran-led activities—monetary contributions, flag donations, scholarship endowments, and of course, ubiquitous veteran interactions with students, faculty, and administrators. Together, GAR members' involvement in American higher education reflected their understanding that the first generations of professionalized business, political, and community leaders needed to learn and apply the lessons of the Civil War to responsibly shape a modern nation. Nevertheless, most white GAR members gave little thought to educational advancement for African Americans, a vacuum that Black veterans admirably filled to benefit their descendants even as they so rarely enjoyed the fruits of a college education themselves. The last section presents a case study of Memorial University— a short-lived college, normal school, and preparatory academy in Mason City, Iowa. Although the institution folded before achieving the national reputation that the region's veterans envisioned, it represented the fullest expression of the GAR's embrace of higher education and its potential to uplift Americans to new heights of civic and patriotic devotion.

The Safeguards of Free Institutions

Thirty-six-year-old Charlotte Templeton rose to address the veterans and interested citizens who had gathered in Fremont, Nebraska, to attend the state's annual GAR encampment in May 1913. Lauded for her "executive ability" and "particular knowledge of library work," Templeton served ably as executive secretary of the Nebraska Public Library Commission and worked closely with civic leaders in building up the state's network of free public libraries. Invited to speak at the encampment, Templeton lectured on "what we librarians are doing in the line of promoting patriotism" and what veterans could do to "confer with your own librarians and see what they are already doing and what they can do by cooperating with your Post." Templeton went on to proudly inform the audience that librarians across the state were "putting on our shelves books dealing with the history of our country . . . for it is only by knowing how this country of ours has developed, what it has cost in labor, in thought, and in human life that we can come to have a true sense of its value." Yet Templeton understood that public—especially youth—engagement with these materials was key to promoting civic learning and laid some of the responsibility on the continued activism of the Civil War generation. To the GAR veterans before her, Templeton urged that posts select "a veteran who loves children . . . to come in and tell army experiences to the older boys." Laying out a cooperative vision uniting librarians' professionalism and veterans' lived experience, Templeton promised that the public library would remain "the most patriotic institution that we have, for its whole purpose is to realize in our citizenship the ideals of the most democratic and progressive nation on earth."[4]

Templeton's lecture before the Nebraska veterans reveals an overlooked relationship—close and often symbiotic—between the GAR and public libraries nationwide. Around the turn of the twentieth century, these institutions centered community reform efforts and provided services designed to cultivate middle-class norms and values among an increasingly heterogeneous population. No longer simply the realm of scholarly pursuits, libraries expanded their offerings to address a wider range of societal needs. During this period, networks of library branches extended to reach underprivileged communities, provided space for civic activities, and offered more outreach to children and immigrants. To meet these growing responsibilities was an expert and efficient cadre of library professionals (often women), educated in new, specialist schools, trained in modern classification systems, and legitimized by a professionalized organization. Meanwhile, the era's wealthy entrepreneurs steered some of their postwar prosperity toward the establishment and maintenance of cultural institutions like libraries in a bid to ameliorate the masses and maintain the existing capitalist order. Most notable was Andrew Carnegie, who hoped that his benefaction toward some 1,600 public libraries in the United States would help "make men not violent revolutionists, but cautious evolutionists; not destroyers, but careful improvers." Sharing these commitments to social order and the alleviation of urban ills, many Grand Army members, too, felt a moral responsibility to support public libraries and ensure that the knowledge they disseminated exemplified the GAR's memory of the Civil War and promoted the lessons that Union victory had achieved.[5]

Union veterans' support for public libraries began soon after their demobilization—in some communities, constituting the earliest example of GAR educational and civic reform. With the end of the Civil War and a populace coming to terms with its massive scale of death, a shift occurred in the ways in which mourners manifested their grief, memorialized their dead, and found adequate justification for their loss. In the urban centers of the prewar Northeast, the park-like garden cemetery acted as a cultural and recreational amenity. Here, amid manicured lawns dotted with obelisks and mausoleums, urban dwellers could escape the confines of the city and commune with the dead, all while taking in a peaceful, natural setting. After the Civil War, citizens increasingly looked to the public library as a place that could simultaneously commemorate the war's sacrifices while serving as a useful institution to uplift the moral and intellectual status of its neighborhood. This change occurred alongside the mid-nineteenth-century public library movement in which state legislatures, particularly in New England, passed laws permitting communities to support these buildings through taxation. Characteristic was the law passed by the Massachusetts legislature in 1866, providing that "[a]ny town may, at a legal meeting, grant and vote money for the establishment, maintenance, or increase of a public library therein, and for erecting or providing suitable buildings or rooms therefor." As libraries already purveyed culture, democratic norms, and morality in the communities that had them, it was reasonable to yoke the memory of the men who had died in the war to these institutions.[6]

With supportive laws already on their state's books, it was Massachusetts veterans, civic leaders, and interested allies that launched their towns' first permanent public libraries, simultaneously linking these institutions to the remembrance of their communities' fallen. Lancaster and Foxboro provide early examples of the movement, with both towns dedicating public libraries just three years after the war. At the June 1868 dedication of the Lancaster memorial hall and library, minister Christopher T. Thayer noted the dual nature of the community's newest institution. "[T]hrough the public spirit, generosity, and excellent taste of the citizens," Thayer said, "has been added . . . a noble memorial of the patriotic dead, coupled with an intellectual mine of inexhaustible and immeasurable wealth, which shall improve and bless the present and succeeding generations." Thayer noted that this would not be just a mere static monument, but rather a building of utility where the dead were "linked inseparable with a great and good object and work, in which the *dulce et utile* are admirably mingled." Similarly, Foxboro's civic leaders believed that to appropriately honor the two hundred townsmen who enlisted in the Union army (and the twenty-three who perished), something "more is required at the hands of the town than simply a monument." Considering what would best commemorate the Union's defenders and simultaneously inspire Foxboro's youth, they settled on a memorial building that would double as a library. "That intelligence which would be diffused by such a library and reading room," the town's memorial committee reasoned, "is ever one of the safeguards of free institutions. Intelligence will tend to fit the future young men of the town to emulate the patriotism of those who went before them."7

As the public library movement spread throughout the commonwealth, so did local GAR posts whose members participated in the commemorative creation of town libraries. For instance, veterans in Canton, Massachusetts, petitioned the town for $500 in 1874 to furnish books for a reading room established at their post's meeting hall. The appropriation was granted, and the reading room became the Canton Public Library, where the veterans pledged that the books would remain free for use by the townspeople. In Manchester-by-the-Sea, the local post and its civilian allies dedicated in 1887 the Memorial Library and Grand Army Hall and recognized the educational contributions they would afford the new institution. "Here we will make our home," said Post Commander Henry T. Bingham, "and here around our camp-fires will be told the thrilling personal experiences . . . of the late conflict, wherein we learn the unpublished history of the war." In the western Massachusetts town of Adams, townspeople and GAR comrades collaborated on a similar memorial library building completed in 1899 that brought President William McKinley to the cornerstone-laying ceremony two years earlier. Placing a time capsule into the stone, McKinley told the thousands gathered before him that the building would be "a monument to duty well done and is a lesson in patriotism to the generations that are to follow." After the structure's completion, members of the George E. Sayles Post held their meetings on the second floor while the townspeople enjoyed the library's benefits below.8

Although Massachusetts first and most frequently linked the memory of the fallen citizen-soldier with commemorative libraries, the practice extended to other New England locations with strong GAR influence and taxation laws dedicated to erecting public libraries. In Vermont, two posts coordinated with townspeople in creating the Rutland Memorial Hall. Completed in 1889 at a cost of $100,000, the building stood as a memorial to the soldier dead, a meeting place and relic repository for the veteran living, and the site of the town's public library for citizens at large. "It was wisely thought," remarked one editorialist, "that the free reading feature was the best gift that could be given the people as a memorial of those who had fought for them." In Rockland, Maine, veterans of the Edwin Libby Post generously donated a parcel of land that they acquired in 1891, envisioning its use for a community project. The lot, reported the local newspaper, "will be donated for public library purposes, with the proviso that a Grand Army memorial hall be set aside in the upper story for the use of the veterans during life, to revert to the Public Library Association on their demise." In May 1893, trustees of the nascent Rockland Public Library deliberated with a designated committee of the Libby Post to hash out details of the donation, which would remain "very accessible to the citizens wishing to patronize the library."[9]

By the 1870s, laws authorizing communities to use tax revenue to establish public libraries reached the Midwest, and GAR members there followed the lead of their New England comrades. Veterans and nonveterans of Aurora, Illinois, for instance, formed the Soldiers' Monument Association in 1869, established to raise funds for an appropriate monument to the town's soldier-heroes, living and dead. Over the next several years, the association accumulated a hefty sum and hounded the city council to approve construction of a memorial building, which was completed in 1877 but initially remained underutilized. Four years later, townspeople acted on a recently passed Illinois state statute permitting them to petition their council "to establish and maintain a public library and reading room" using taxpayer funds. With the library initiative flush with tax revenue, the empty memorial building stood ready to house the facility. The Soldiers' Monument Association eagerly presented the building to host the library free of charge, which opened on May 30, 1882—Memorial Day—not coincidentally, the GAR's sacred holiday. By the end of the year, the Aurora Public Library held 5,500 volumes, served 2,700 patrons, and lent an average of 800 books per week. Almost immediately, the new public library became too cramped to house its growing collections. In 1885, Aurora's GAR post donated $2,000 of the roughly $13,000 needed to build an addition for more library stacks and a reading room, but with a catch—that it have use of the second story addition as a GAR meeting hall, "free of rent, during [the] life of [the] Post."[10]

Even for those communities whose veterans did not lead a public library movement, many local GAR chapters created their own post libraries as a resource for members, and often, for the community at large. With the steady growth of the GAR in the early 1880s, the *National Tribune*—the most influential newspaper published for the benefit of GAR veterans—recognized that "[t]he establishment of libraries in connection with Posts of the Grand Army is a thing much to be desired" and an asset that would give "the rising generation ... an opportunity to become acquainted with the true history of the war." Indeed, one mark of a healthy and active GAR post became the existence of a post library. Many posts assigned members to a library committee charged with soliciting books and tending to the collections. One of the oldest and most active chapters in Pennsylvania, the George G. Meade Post of Philadelphia, boasted that its library was established in 1877 and rapidly grew to one hundred volumes by the end of the decade. "This was the beginning," reported the post historian in 1889, "and for some time thereafter at nearly every muster, books of some kind were presented, until now the Post has a large and valuable library." Similarly, the veterans of Bangor, Maine, appointed a library committee in 1887 "to solicit contributions, of books, papers relating to the war, any article of historic value in the nature of war relics, or contributions of money." Over the next several months, their post received donations from comrades, sympathetic civilians, and even representatives of Congress to establish a respectable collection.[11]

Some GAR posts endeavored to make their collections public, thereby circulating Civil War histories to younger generations of readers. In April 1888, Minneapolis veterans set out "to gather up every printed book or pamphlet in any way relating to the war," and after proper cataloguing, deposit the collection "with some public institution of the city, there to be perpetuated for the public use under the name of the 'John A. Rawlins Post Historical Collection.'" Advocates asked post members to contribute additional dues of five dollars and donate titles from their own libraries. With an eye to its legacy, the veterans expected that "[t]he facts of our army experience will be sought for, after we are all gone, with an eagerness which cannot now be realized. . . . *Everything* relating to the military or political history of the war period belongs in such a collection as we are making." Whatever its impressive designs, however, the Rawlins Post endeavor died quietly, likely hampered by the inability to find a suitable site for the collection. More successful were the efforts of the Joshua B. Culver Post to educate the citizens of Duluth, Minnesota. For years, the Culver Post assigned comrades to serve on its library committee—whose members selected, bought, and shelved the books in the post's Civil War library. Eager to bestow the collection for the public good, aging members in 1910 decided on "moveing [sic] our books to some place where they could be used." The most reasonable destination was the newly established Duluth Public Library. The Culver Post's library committee conferred with the public library's board of directors, which "formally accepted the offer of this Post . . . in accordance with instructions of this Post to place our War Library upon its shelves for the use of the General Publick [sic]."[12]

The *National Tribune* also threw its significant influence behind efforts to circulate the best material on the Civil War and build up the network of post libraries. In the early 1880s, when the organ sought to boost its circulation, it offered to send posts select volumes in exchange for subscriptions. For instance, in an effort to help posts "obtain a war library at small cost," the *Tribune* offered to trade volumes of Scribner's *Campaigns of the Civil War* for newspaper subscriptions. Elliot W. Ford, an intrepid Massachusetts comrade, secured forty-nine new subscribers to the *Tribune*, netting him nine complimentary volumes of the series that he pledged to contribute to his post's fledgling library. Commending Ford's "individual effort," the *Tribune* reminded its readers that "a good military library is a thing which no Post should be without." When the US War Department compiled the ninety-six volume *Official Records of the War of the Rebellion* in the 1880s, the *Tribune* lauded the undertaking and advocated the free distribution of the series to every post in the nation. When Representative Lewis D. Apsley of Massachusetts introduced a House resolution in 1894 to have the series freely delivered to each GAR post, the *Tribune* printed an interview with Apsley to advertise the effort. Touting the interest and excitement that such an effort would drum up among veterans, Apsley avowed that "[t]he books will have a wonderful educational power, and the veterans will take pride in bringing their sons to their quarters to show them just what the official record is of their father's prowess."[13]

GAR veterans occasionally even recommended titles penned by women memoirists and historians, particularly widows of military heroes and Union army nurses. The *National Tribune*, for instance, bestowed ample praise to Elizabeth Bacon Custer's histories of her husband's military exploits. In *Boots and Saddles* (1885) and *Tenting on the Plains* (1887), she portrayed the military heroics of George Armstrong Custer as he transitioned from Union army cavalryman to Plains Indian fighter and the hardships that she faced as the dutiful wife of her career military husband. The *Tribune* featured Custer's work in its "recent literature" reviews and praised it as "exceedingly interesting and instructive," whose author possessed "a keenly-observant eye" and "a graphic pen." Similarly, when beloved Civil War nurse and Red Cross founder Clara Barton published her memoir, *The Story of My Childhood* (1907), the newspaper reviewed the work and reported favorably to its subscribers. Lauding the work as "the first real history of her life," it predicted that the volume would "be welcomed by millions of friends everywhere." Soon after, Wisconsin native Janet Jennings, whose reputation as a nurse during the Civil War and Spanish-American War carried the esteem of two generations of citizen-soldiers, penned *The Blue and the Gray* (1910). This chronological history of the war was written, Jennings asserted, to "inspire in younger generations that spirit of steadfast loyalty, perfect justice, and unexampled magnanimity." Frank A. Walsh, commander of the GAR's Wisconsin department recommended Jennings's work to his state's comrades, appraised to be "of great value to the reading public" and that "deserved a place in numerous libraries."[14]

The Woman's Relief Corps (WRC) similarly prescribed particularly worthy volumes deemed to impart good influence on the reading public while shaping a proper memory of the war. WRC members rankled after the May 1909 dedication of a monument to Captain Henry Wirz, the commandant of the notorious Andersonville prison. In response, they campaigned to broadly circulate Norton P. Chipman's *The Tragedy of Andersonville* (1911) as a way to quash Wirz's historical restoration at the hands of Lost Cause apologists, chiefly the United Daughters of the Confederacy. Chipman, best known for his successful prosecution of Wirz (who became the only Civil War participant tried and executed for war crimes), was called upon by Grand Army officials "to place within reach of the public the facts relating to this trial." Chipman agreed and relitigated Wirz in his 500-page assault on the infamous commandant, presenting it as a "vindication of the verdict rendered in this remarkable case, and as the record of sufferings such as no prisoner of war in any country . . . were ever called upon to endure." If it was the work of the GAR to propose the volume, and Chipman to write it, it became the WRC's task to disseminate the volume widely. At the organization's state-level encampments in 1912, officers were "requested to call attention" to Chipman's volume and to urge "each Corps [to] purchase a copy for presentation to its local public library, as it is of great importance that the libraries be furnished with a correct record of Andersonville that will impress future generations with the justice of the cause for which thousands of Union heroes suffered and died."[15]

As Grand Army members faced old age and impending death, they often looked to the local public library as a sympathetic institution that could accommodate the disbandment of their posts and serve as a lasting repository for the memory of the fast-fading Union veteran. In 1906, for instance, the Thomas Espy Post of Carnegie, Pennsylvania, arranged with the trustees of the community's recently erected Andrew Carnegie Free Library to relocate their quarters to the building's second floor. Members sought accommodations that would "stand 1st as HdQrs for our Post so long as a member was left, and 2d that the Room was to remain as we left it to be known as [the] GAR Memorial Room for all time." When the last veteran of the post died in 1937, the group's papers and relics reverted to the ownership of the library for safekeeping. Similarly, the post in Menominee, Michigan, anticipated the need to preserve their records as infirmity crept into the ranks. At their 1923 Memorial Day meeting, the handful of surviving veterans agreed to transmit their records to the local Spies Public Library "for reference by any one interested" when the post ceased to meet. That day came two years later. Post Commander Arminius W. Bill, speaking on behalf of Menominee's seven surviving comrades, turned over the post's minute books, flags, and other possessions to the library's board president at a small community ceremony. "There were wet eyes," reported the local newspaper, "and their wrinkled cheeks were dampened as the veterans clasped hands and separated, leaving behind the written record of [their] glorious past."[16]

As public libraries became the vital founts of knowledge for many turn-of-the-century American communities, Grand Army veterans recognized their instructional value and began shaping these institutions so the diverse range of patrons who accessed them came away with an appropriate history of the Civil War and GAR-endorsed lessons about patriotism and civic duty. Almost immediately after their homecoming, Union soldiers recognized the value in entwining the record of their service with the buildings where citizens came to reflect and learn. For towns without libraries, some GAR posts opened their own Civil War collections to the public, ensuring that nonveterans received access to a veteran-sanctioned assortment of titles. Later, when local posts began to dissolve, the public library often became the logical repository for their records. Here, the veterans hoped, their legacy of service—as both soldiers and citizens—might live on.

Education for the Duties of Life

Ahead of the 1905 Grand Army national convention in Denver, officials charged a three-man committee with documenting the progress that veterans were making in promoting patriotic education in public schools. Augustus G. Weissert of Wisconsin, James D. Bell of New York, and James L. Merrick of Maine were well-suited to the task, drawing on decades of both GAR and civic service. The trio reported that veterans' involvement in the public schools had been of "inestimable value" in teaching the "basis of good citizenship and uplifting manhood and womanhood." Yet the committee claimed that the order was overlooking the nation's burgeoning colleges and universities. Remarking that "the teaching of patriotism had been to this time confined largely to the public schools of the land," the men advised "that every effort should be made to extend the work,— have it taken up by the more advanced institutions of learning." The committee was perceptive in suggesting a more expansive view of where GAR members might influence educational reform. However, these high-level officers failed to recognize that their comrades at the local and regional level were *already* using their GAR networks to transmit patriotic education outside the public schools to the nation's colleges and universities.[17]

GAR veterans were active participants in reforming American higher education as it underwent significant changes as a result of the Civil War. During the prewar period, predominantly white male students were taught a classical curriculum and typically attended college to affirm their social position or enter into a limited selection of professions. Occupational training largely remained the domain of apprenticeship or hands-on instruction. Meanwhile, federal and state governments largely ceded higher-education planning to religious or other private groups. With the disruptions caused by war, however, colleges and universities underwent reforms in institutional organization, curricula, and student enrollment. Under the Morrill Land Grant Act of 1862, the federal government assumed a vested interest in college education by offering the states grants of public lands to sell, the proceeds of which would "promote the liberal and practical education of the industrial classes in the several pursuits and professions in life." Specifically, the Morrill Act stipulated that grant revenues support agricultural, mechanical, and military instruction—indicating the federal government's interest in training useful citizens. Meanwhile, higher education after the Civil War opened up to an increasingly diverse student body, with more women, African Americans, and lower-class individuals taking advantage of less restrictive enrollment criteria. Although the ratio of students to the total number of young adults remained small (about 2 percent in 1900), the number of colleges and universities grew rapidly. As the war commenced, fewer than 400 institutions existed. Forty years later, the number ballooned to nearly a thousand. As a result, more and more communities across the country came to shape—and be shaped by—their institutions of higher education.[18]

As the nation's colleges and universities became more influential after the Civil War, Americans—especially Union veterans—increasingly looked to them as powerful disseminators of cherished values. As they did with public schools, Grand Army members at the local level looked to their communities' institutions to transmit these values—particularly industry, duty, and patriotism—to their scholars. Frequently, GAR gestures were fairly conventional and not unlike those conveyed at public schools. For instance, New York's Lafayette Post—whose members maintained especially cordial relations with area colleges—promoted patriotic higher education through careful oratory and prominent display of the national colors. In June 1888, the post presented the City College of New York with an American flag, an event attended by members of the post, college administrators, and students. With the veterans' donation, Post Commander Floyd Clarkson hoped that the students before him "preparing for the activities of life" would recognize "that love for country, for the flag, has a mighty influence in developing noble citizens." Upon accepting the donation, President Alexander S. Webb—himself a distinguished Union general—thanked his fellow comrades and commanded his students never to allow "American destiny fall . . . into the hands of the uninstructed" and urged them to "become more contemplative of the necessity on your part for a better understanding of your duties to a National Government."[19]

Nearby Columbia College also drew the Lafayette Post's interest in cultivating patriotism through rhetorical and iconographic displays. Members offered the school flags, a staff, and a pedestal—a $5,000 gift paid for by donations from the post and its supporters. The initiative proceeded in two stages, the first comprising the post's presentation of two flags at an 1896 ceremony. Upon accepting the donation, Columbia President Seth Low guaranteed his and his students' commitment "to die for [the flag] in case of need . . . striving always to make the country over which it floats ever worthier to be loved." The dedication of the flagstaff and pedestal came two years later in May 1898—just weeks after the United States declared war on Spain—felicitously testing Columbia's commitment to the flag that was previously promised. President Low, once again accepting the Lafayette Post's gift to the university, did not know the precise number of Columbia men who pledged their services in the latest conflict, but he thought it "enough, certainly, to bring home to those who are left a realizing sense of the paramount claims of the country, and to assure you that your trust in the men of Columbia has not been misplaced." Whether the Lafayette Post's campus presence or flag donation spurred enlistment is unknowable. However, many college-aged men nationwide found outlet in the Spanish-American War to prove their manliness on the battlefield rather than in the suspect halls of the academy. Citing the many enlistees to his "Rough Riders" unit who came from elite colleges like Columbia, Colonel Theodore Roosevelt commended these young men who joined the ranks "eagerly as if it meant something widely different from hard work, rough fare, and the possibility of death."[20]

Elsewhere, GAR veterans were a part of the reciprocal relationship that many colleges and universities cultivated with their surrounding communities in the decades after the Civil War. The best example of this was in Madison, where the progressive-oriented University of Wisconsin linked its growing commitment to applied research and democratic enrollment standards with community outreach and public service. Veterans of the Lucius Fairchild Post responded favorably to this approach, fostering a fruitful interaction between its members (see Figure 4), Wisconsin legislators, and university leadership that resulted in the placement of an Abraham Lincoln statue on campus (1909) and the construction of a memorial arch (1912) on the same site that had once hosted the Camp Randall training grounds during the Civil War. Concurrent with these efforts,

Figure 4 Members of the Lucius Fairchild Post of Madison, Wisconsin, pose in 1916 to mark the fiftieth anniversary of their organization's founding. These Union veterans fostered a close relationship with the nearby University of Wisconsin and developed educational and public programming that occasionally brought students and administrators to their post quarters. Courtesy of Panoramic Photographs of Veterans Organizations Collection, Wisconsin Veterans Museum.

the Fairchild Post and the students and faculty of the university frequently traded invitations to their respective public events, providing an opportunity for academics and young scholars to learn what values the old soldiers hoped to instill in the rising generation. For instance, during an era in which African Americans were barred from many of the basic privileges of citizenship, the post nonetheless indicated their openness to hear demands for civil rights. In 1910, the veterans invited African American university student Will N. Johnson to speak and warmly received his message on the "intensely human" nature of his race and the plight of the Black community. "The negro does not fight for his country with a black energy, a black courage; nor does [he] love with a black love," Johnson reasoned before the veterans. "When, then, should there be doled out to him black rights? Why discriminate against mere color?"[21]

Around the turn of the twentieth century, some Grand Army members assumed an active role in promoting more democratic higher education opportunities by providing funds for poor—and particularly worthy—scholars to attend college. In Pittsburgh, for instance, veterans, nonveteran allies, and administrators at Western University (now the University of Pittsburgh) collaborated on financial aid schemes for needy students. After the city hosted a GAR national encampment in 1894, veterans discovered a surplus of several thousand dollars that they intended to spend usefully. University Chancellor William J. Holland pitched a novel idea designed to benefit both his institution and the memory of the city's veterans. Proposing "Grand Army scholarships," Holland reasoned that the encampment surplus could be "invested as a permanent fund and the revenue . . . annually applied in aiding the descendants of the veterans of the war of the rebellion in securing the education fitting them for the duties of life." Garnering local GAR post endorsements, roughly $6,000 was set aside for scholarships to deserving students the following academic year. Several years later, wealthy GAR comrade Henry M. Curry died and, in his will, directed that $10,000 of his fortune go to Western University "to be invested, and to use and apply the income therefrom as payment of the tuition of students nominated by the Allegheny County Posts of the Grand Army of the Republic, for entrance to the University." Much like the earlier scholarships, Curry directed that "preference shall be given when they are eligible, to descendants of men who served in the civil war [sic]." Into the 1920s, the University of Pittsburgh offered three Grand Army scholarships and four Curry scholarships for financially needy descendants of Union veterans, all of whom were carefully selected upon the recommendations of the Allegheny County GAR posts.[22]

As American universities expanded their commitment to graduate work during the late nineteenth century, many GAR veterans identified advanced degrees as a worthwhile accomplishment in the pursuit of productive, engaged citizens. In Rhode Island, GAR officer Alonzo Williams, a professor at Brown University, rallied the state's comrades to donate funds benefiting the students of the institution's fledgling graduate programs. Over a period of several months in 1891, veterans raised $10,000, the interest on which was awarded annually to a Brown alumnus of good character pursuing graduate studies. The recipient of this "Grand Army of the Republic Fellowship" was not required to have a familial connection to a Union soldier. However, school administrators made it clear that "[d]escendents of Union Veterans of the Civil War are always to be preferred when the other qualifications of candidates are equal." Contributions to the fund were not only recognition for the nearly 300 students and five faculty members that Brown sent to the war, but also an implicit acknowledgment of the growing importance of graduate studies in American higher education. The fellowship, according to the state GAR department, was not only "an enduring memorial of the character of the Union soldier," but also proof that veterans were attentive to "all the high interests of the State." Three decades after the initiation of the fellowship, Brown's graduate students in a wide range of fields—classical and modern languages, music, philosophy, psychology, biology, and chemistry, to name a few—had benefited from GAR educational philanthropy. The funds had thus succeeded in the contributors' goal to prepare recipients "more thoroughly for the duties of life than otherwise they might be able to do."[23]

Grand Army involvement in higher education also extended to normal (teachers') schools—fertile ground for veterans to support the nation's educators in training. Part of an educational reform movement centered in New England before the Civil War, normal schools exploded in number, geographic range, and graduating students by the turn of the twentieth century. Union veterans recognized the contributions of the nation's teachers in shaping young minds and maintained a presence on the proliferating normal school campuses. The post in Plymouth, New Hampshire, for instance, arranged a twelve-lecture course on patriotic instruction, taught by Commander Joseph Parker, with the state normal school in 1895. Two years later, state-level GAR officers visited the 2,400 women students at the Normal College of the City of New York (now Hunter College) to speak on "the methods of teaching history and patriotism to the young." In Minnesota, Eliakim "Ell" Torrance stepped down in 1903 as commander in chief of the GAR only to be appointed by the governor to the state normal board—a position he maintained for the next two decades. Employing martial rhetoric, Torrance acknowledged the influence of the normal school and credited the state's trained teachers as "an army without banners or weapons of war, but an army essential to the preservation of the institutions upon which rest the welfare, intelligence and happiness of the people."[24]

GAR activism in higher education turned southward as well, where states of the former Confederacy invested more heavily in colleges and universities than ever before. Here, institutions proliferated that frequently melded classical curricula with practical programs in agriculture, mechanics, and teacher training. Of particular interest to GAR veterans were a pair of eastern Tennessee institutions—Grant Memorial University and Lincoln Memorial University—where Union veterans joined contemporaneous efforts to uplift Appalachia through educational reform. Here, they saw a region of the South that not only included some of the Union's most hard-fought and consequential battles—Knoxville, Chattanooga, and Chickamauga, for example—but also a populace where wartime Unionism was comparatively strong, and many residents had been friendly to occupying northern soldiers. Moreover, GAR veterans and other supporters of these schools believed the denizens of the area to be "the people from whom Lincoln sprang, the mountaineer folk of the Cumberland Gap region."[25]

The two institutions gained the organizational and financial support of Union veterans, thanks in part to the schools' famous namesakes and the indomitable energy of their chief backers who happened to be beloved idols of the GAR. Grant Memorial University in Athens, Tennessee, was originally incorporated in 1867 as East Tennessee Wesleyan University. After the death of Ulysses S. Grant in 1886, university president and respected GAR officer John F. Spence spearheaded the school's renaming and actively fundraised among wealthy northern posts, citing "a general desire that a living monument be erected and dedicated to the memory of that greatest soldier and statesman of our age." The cash-strapped GAR posts in the South contributed what they could as well. Beginning in 1889, the university permitted each Tennessee post to recommend one student— "poor, of good character, and otherwise acceptable to the authorities of the Institution"—to earn a "beneficiary scholarship" awarding the recipient reduced tuition. Thanks to the assistance from the GAR and its auxiliaries, the university at the turn of the century boasted that among its graduates, "three hundred have practiced law, five hundred medicine, eight hundred have preached the gospel, and fifteen hundred have taught school."[26]

A hundred miles northeast of Grant Memorial University, Oliver Otis Howard, the former Union general who had headed the Freedmen's Bureau, secured a charter for a university at Cumberland Gap in 1897. Using Abraham Lincoln's name for the school's appellation, Howard asserted that "no monument in stone or in bronze or in marble or on the canvas can ever do more than indicate a little of the superb man whom now all nations praise. . . . [T]he word University is a deserved honor to Lincoln." Giving support to their comrade's vision, posts nationwide rallied to the educational testament to the martyred president. The GAR's Department of Tennessee, for example, deemed the school "worthy of patronage and advantageous to the proper upbuilding of the country's youth." With donations rolling in from veterans around the country, the national organization passed resolutions in favor of the school as well, stating that it "commend[ed] its methods of teaching, its moral tone, its tolerant spirit and steadfast patriotic instruction, and commend[ed] said institution to whoever has children to educate or money to give for education." After Howard's death in 1909, university administrators not only had Lincoln's memory to encourage donations, but also Howard's. In a fundraising letter circulated widely through the GAR network, school officials suggested contributions between ten and twenty-five dollars per post to recognize "General Howard's services to the country during the time of war, and his faithful and untiring efforts to carry out the wish of President Lincoln, by assisting to educate a class of children, located without any advantage for education except through these schools."[27]

Although the GAR clearly valued and invested in the opportunities offered to young scholars at predominantly or exclusively white colleges and universities, providing tangible aid for the higher education of African Americans was mostly not part of its reformist vision. That is not to say that expressions of support for Black improvement and learning are impossible to uncover. On the contrary, many white veterans in the GAR—probably more than most nonveterans—recognized that literacy was vital to African Americans' ability to enjoy the rights and privileges of citizenship in the reconstructing nation. Before an integrated state encampment in 1904, Delaware Commander William G. Baugh acknowledged that education yielded a "higher perfection" among all men and encouraged his white peers that "we must not only educate ourselves but see to it that our colored comrades have the same opportunity." Indeed, white veterans commended their peers who devoted time and energy to bringing educational opportunity to African Americans. When William MacMullin fell on hard times in 1895, his Pittsburgh comrades asked GAR posts across the country to donate to his relief, citing his earlier efforts in establishing schools for Maryland and Virginia freedmen that helped "raise the colored race out of its second bondage—*ignorance*." Similarly, when George C. Round sought election to become commander of the GAR's Department of Virginia and North Carolina in 1910, members of his Richmond post emphasized his work in writing the charter for the Manassas Industrial School for Colored Youth and for serving as the institute's legal counsel "without fee." On the whole, however, fraternal records are largely silent on issues concerning Black education and suggest that white GAR veterans and their local posts paid scant attention to the matter. As historian Barbara A. Gannon has observed, these white veterans' memory of a civil war "fought to free black Americans only rarely prompted these men to action" when it came to preserving or nurturing Black rights and opportunities after the war.[28]

This relative GAR disinterest in African American higher education extended to the growing postwar network of what are now known as historically Black colleges and universities (HBCUs). Rooted in a handful of institutions founded on free soil before the Civil War, HBCUs proliferated in the final decades of the nineteenth century throughout the former Confederacy, most prominently at places like Fisk, Howard, Hampton, and Atlanta universities. Often, these institutions became strongholds for clergy and teacher training, as well as the industrial education of freedmen and their descendants—what famed Black educator and Tuskegee Institute founder Booker T. Washington believed "lift[ed] labor up out of toil and drudgery into the plane of the dignified and the beautiful." Initiated with sparse resources and hampered by intensifying segregationist policies at both the state and national levels, HBCUs nevertheless became proud citadels of racial uplift and self-improvement for the Black community. Many white northern observers looked favorably upon the institutions' capacity to instill values of thrift, enterprise, and economic self-help among African Americans, particularly as Washington's accommodationist approach to southern race relations by the end of the century discouraged the cultivation of political consciousness among college-educated Blacks. The average white GAR veteran probably agreed with a column in the *National Tribune* that encouraged Black students "of good character and marked talent" to learn "the industrial arts" at these institutions "and thus awaken the desire for distinction in some profession that is free from the debasing influence of politics."[29]

Of course, in the immediate aftermath of the Civil War, it was often white, progressive-minded Union army officers who stood at the intersection of a federal government obligated to provision the formerly enslaved, philanthropic societies eager to spread their charity to the reconstructing South, and freedmen with an insatiable thirst for educational opportunity. Generals Oliver O. Howard and Clinton B. Fisk—both revered in GAR circles for their wartime and postwar accomplishments—leveraged their lofty positions in the Freedmen's Bureau to support educational advancement for southern Blacks, earning sufficient esteem to lend their names to two of the oldest and most prominent HBCUs. Samuel C. Armstrong, who ably commanded United States Colored Troop (USCT) units during the war, also joined the Bureau after Appomattox and coordinated with the American Missionary Association (AMA) to establish the Hampton Normal and Agricultural Institute (now Hampton University). Although undoubtedly interested in the uplift of freedmen after the war, Armstrong's pedagogical philosophy also espoused a crude belief in the limitations of Hampton students. They were, according to Armstrong, "docile, impressible, imitative, and earnest, and come to us as *tabula rasa* so far as real culture is concerned." Convinced that "over-education" was a "danger with the weak races," Armstrong led the institution for a quarter century with the intent to primarily nourish the industrial rather than intellectual development of its Black pupils. As scholar Eric Foner has explained, these Freedmen's Bureau administrators with Union army backgrounds "brought to their posts a combination of paternalist assumptions about race and sensitivity to the plight of blacks."[30]

This characterization accurately describes a smattering of white GAR veterans who maintained an interest in African American higher education through the end of the nineteenth century and beyond. Erastus M. Cravath, a graduate of the integrated and abolitionist-minded Oberlin College, settled in Nashville, Tennessee, after the war with the intent, as one admirer remembered, to "establish a school for the benefit of the colored race, to give them the same opportunities as their brothers in white." Leveraging his membership in the AMA, Cravath cofounded Fisk University and served as its president for more than two decades. A beloved officer in the GAR's Department of Tennessee, he died in 1900 and was buried in Nashville National Cemetery "among his comrades who had given up their lives to emancipate the race to the uplifting of which he gave a lifetime of devotion." New Hampshire-born Charles H. Shute was another Union veteran who remained in the South after the war, establishing himself as a prominent New Orleans banker who commanded the city's GAR post. Known for his "interest in the colored schools" of Louisiana, Shute served on the board of trustees at Straight University (now Dillard University) for many years and upon his death in 1907, bequeathed $1,000 to the HBCU. James A. Beaver, a one-term governor of Pennsylvania, was also a trustee at Lincoln University for some thirty years. Speaking to graduates at the southeastern Pennsylvania HBCU in 1882, Beaver not only applauded the "streams of useful and happy influences" that the institution provided, but also expressed a surprising degree of regret for the entire country's participation in the blot of slavery. "[N]ot by the South alone," Beaver averred, "but by us also these people were enslaved, and they now call upon us to make them amends for the wrongs they have sustained, or that the race has sustained, at our hands." Still, whatever the praiseworthy words and efforts of men like Cravath, Shute, Beaver, and others, it is important to note that they were acting not so much as representatives of a race-conscious GAR, but rather as reasonably enlightened white citizens for their time who also happened to wear the Grand Army badge.[31]

Regrettably, it is difficult to interpret the meaning that higher education may have had for members of all-Black GAR posts or for African American veterans who belonged to integrated posts. As other historians have shown, educational opportunities for Black veterans were deficient in the postwar period and illiteracy was fairly common. Extant records from African American posts or columns from Black-owned newspapers rarely comment on veterans' views about the burgeoning HBCUs or the modest number of predominantly white institutions that also accepted Black students. Certainly, African American veterans would have been even less likely than their white peers to take advantage of a college education after their military service ended. Still, a few Black veterans *did* attend colleges and universities in the North and South and, as evidence suggests, the experience likely enhanced opportunities to secure leadership positions in the GAR. For instance, James H. Wolff was elected department commander of the Massachusetts GAR in 1905, doubtless due in part to the professional success he achieved after attending the New Hampshire College of Agriculture and the Mechanic Arts and Harvard Law School. George Washington Williams, who achieved distinction for penning a history of Black soldiers in the Civil War, became judge advocate of the GAR's Ohio Department after stints at Howard University and various theological institutions. In the integrated Blundon Post of Charleston, West Virginia, William H. Davis surprisingly rose to post commander, likely due in part to his work in establishing the West Virginia Colored Institute (now West Virginia State University) and for the distinction of serving as the first teacher of the much-admired Booker T. Washington. In a postwar world in which the GAR provided one of the few opportunities for African Americans to enjoy a degree of social equality, higher education helped at least a few Black veterans exercise leadership with the support of their white comrades.[32]

Even for the many Black veterans who did not attend college, records indicate that they still found higher education opportunities to be valuable for their descendants. For instance, at a time when many African American veterans named their posts after military or political figures prominent in their freedom struggle, those in York, Pennsylvania, opted to name their chapter after David E. Small—unusual given that Small was a local white businessman with no military experience. In fact, the veterans likely chose to honor Small—recognized upon his death in 1883 as "a devoted friend of the colored people"—in part because he bequeathed $10,000 to the historically Black Lincoln University. Elsewhere, evidence suggests that the Robert Gould Shaw Post put forth the names of worthy Black students in hopes of securing Grand Army scholarships for them to attend the University of Pittsburgh. For instance, Martha Basella Hill, the granddaughter of a deceased USCT veteran, won a scholarship that allowed her to graduate with a bachelor's degree in 1926 thanks to the post's recommendation. Other African American veterans spoke out in support of HBCUs in front of their white peers who might not otherwise have known the work that these institutions were doing in uplifting young Blacks. Daniel Drew of the integrated General Compson Post of Portland, Oregon, visited a nearby white post and informed them of the "500 colleges and normal schools [in the South]" where "youths acquire knowledge of some useful trade in addition to a knowledge of books, and develop habits of industry." Even women members of the Black GAR circle spoke on behalf of these institutions. Alice M. Scott, a former enslaved person and administrator of Missouri's Western College and Industrial Institute, served as her state's WRC delegate to the 1897 GAR national encampment in Buffalo. Remarkably, Scott was provided a speaking slot and lectured before a white-majority audience about the advances in African American education, after which she was "vigorously cheered" with "the greatest enthusiasm among the veterans." All told, African Americans recognized the GAR as a prospective advocacy vehicle that, if harnessed carefully, might bring resources to their communities' young scholars and interracial recognition for the good work being done at institutions for Black education.[33]

Grand Army members readily acknowledged their communities' turn-of-the-century colleges and universities as key venues that, if properly mobilized to reinforce GAR objectives, might disseminate their chosen interpretation of the Civil War and produce graduates ready to uphold the legacy and values that the veterans would soon leave behind. In their youth, many northern soldiers forewent the opportunity to receive a complete education when the crisis of the Union intervened and demanded their military service. As old men, GAR veterans sought to restore and expand the privileges of higher education to the next generations, particularly their own progeny. But GAR support for this outcome came with a stipulation—that scholars bear in mind the significance of the Union soldier's sacrifice, the greater worthiness of the Union Cause, and the importance of loyalty and freedom to the reunited nation. If young men and women incorporated those lessons during the course of their studies, they would emerge as a rising cohort who could be depended upon to defend the nation against resurgent threats that had imperiled the Union once before.

A Sore Need of This Very Kind of School

From the republic's earliest days, Americans debated the value of planting an elite institution of higher education in the nation's capital, established and supported by the federal government. Luminaries across the political spectrum articulated the merits of a so-called "national university" and its potential to instill in its students a devotion to the state and to civic service. Notably, George Washington bequeathed $25,000 toward the endowment of such an institution to train young citizens "in acquiring knowledge in the principles of politics and good government" and to help "spread systematic ideas through all the parts of this rising empire, thereby to do away [with] local attachments and State prejudices." Other early advocates for a national university included Benjamin Franklin, John Adams, Thomas Jefferson, James Madison, and John Quincy Adams. Nevertheless, antebellum critics consistently thwarted the efforts. They doubted a national university's constitutionality and feared the consolidation of US higher education under federal control.[34]

The idea again gained traction after the Civil War, when advocates argued that a national university's unifying influence might have averted the sectional crisis in which so many Americans, specifically college-aged men, had died. The string of postwar Republican veteran-presidents—Ulysses S. Grant, Rutherford B. Hayes, and James A. Garfield—supported the university concept, corresponding with their party's intention to consolidate the reunited country and strengthen the federal government. In 1877, for instance, Hayes delivered a message to Congress arguing that it would be "to the great and lasting benefit of the entire country, that this [educational] system should be crowned with a university in all respects in keeping with the national capital and thereby realize the cherished hope of Washington." Further, postwar proponents of a national university tied its establishment to the era's powerful nationalistic impulses, deeming an education from the proposed institution to be a foundation for its graduates' loyal public service. One advocate asserted that the university's prospective scholars "would in time return to their thousands of homes more ardent patriots, the better qualified to serve their country, the more resolute in purpose to protect it from perils of every nature."[35]

Union veterans subscribed to this rhetoric too, linking a national university education with civic-minded patriotism. Like their former army commanders who they had helped to send to the White House, GAR members imagined the establishment of the institution as the educational culmination of their efforts to restore a unified nation. The *National Tribune* steadfastly supported the venture for many years, seeing in its creation the fount for a powerful state and a devoted citizenry. Indicating a national university's ability to "place the United States at the very head, in comparison with similar institutions in other lands," the education it offered would combine "the highest learning with the purest patriotism." At their 1898 state encampment, Massachusetts GAR officials—acting on local post resolutions in support of a national university—urged comrades to pressure Congress to authorize the institution. Citing the project as one that "appeals directly to our patriotism," the veterans advised that a national university "would be a most fitting thing for a great nation, ambitious to lead the world in civilization." Reminiscent of antebellum opposition to the university scheme, stiff resistance to the plan reappeared after the war. Critics (including many wary white southerners) still distrusted the centralization of US higher education and several influential university presidents proved hostile to competition from a federally sponsored institution. The national university never amounted to the vision that George Washington had proposed a century earlier.[36]

Grand Army veterans and their auxiliary allies, however, remained strongly supportive of an elite national institution of higher education—one that might groom devoted patriots from every region of the country and prepare them for service on behalf of a reunited nation. The vision of such service evoked memories of the Union soldier, torn away from the educational and professional pursuits he might have enjoyed as a young man, had the requirements of war not intervened. Proponents of a GAR-endorsed national university believed that knowledge and education provided safeguards against the ignorant and debasing social currents that had once corrupted white southerners, namely, secessionism and slavery, and subsequently led to the death, debility, and stunted opportunities for millions of northern men (not to mention suffering and sacrifice on the part of northern women). A world-class institution under veteran guidance would help prevent a similar recurrence for future generations, as young scholars would learn more intently about the tragedy of the 1860s, the rightness of the Union Cause, the abhorrence of the Lost Cause, and how to prevent a similar catastrophe. By emphasizing disciplines such as history, politics, civics, and ethics, instructors would teach their students the importance of service, liberty, and love of country, all of which would be guided by the memory of the Union soldiers' sacrifice. Graduates would then leave the institution, steeled to the dangers of anarchy, tyranny, and bigotry, and prepared to exercise their citizenship on behalf of order, community, and justice. As one advocate of the proposal simply stated in the *National Tribune*, "build a college and you hold a fortress."[37]

It was in the heart of the country, where so many veterans and their families migrated after the war, that supporters envisioned establishing this national testament to patriotic education and Unionist principles. Leading the effort was Alexander Louis "Al" Sortor Jr. Born in Iowa City, Iowa, in 1867, Sortor (whose father had served in an Ohio battery during the war) reportedly "never wearied of stories of heroism; of the camp-fire; of death in the trenches; of fierce fights where thousands fell" and became an enthusiastic member of the GAR's Sons of Veterans (SV) auxiliary. As a young man, Sortor settled in Mason City and as early as 1896, envisioned "a college here . . . that will be a memorial to the union [sic] soldiers of the Civil war [sic] . . . devoted to the education of their children." At the annual SV convention the following year, delegates favored Sortor's proposal and began drumming up interest and pledges of financial support for the institution among GAR veterans and other patriotic societies. Mason City was selected as the site, not only for its "intelligent, hospitable, and progressive" citizens, but also for the town's pledge to supply forty acres for the campus, as well as a gift of $75,000 for the construction of the embryonic university's first academic building. As initiative on a federally sponsored national university stalled, veterans and their allies assumed the burden of creating a national *memorial* university that would graft the sacrifices of the war generation to the goals of an institution centered around patriotic education and public service.[38]

Progress on what became Memorial University proceeded quickly, aided by the support of enthusiastic Grand Army veterans and members of the organization's auxiliaries. Mason City's own Charles H. Huntley Post contributed twenty dollars from its modest treasury while the veterans from nearby Clear Lake's Tom Howard Post chipped in another ten. The women of Iowa's WRC pulled in especially impressive fundraising numbers. Department President Georgia B. Worker declared December 3, 1901, "Memorial University Day," and urged members across the state "to prepare on that day an entertainment of a patriotic nature, the proceeds to go as Iowa's contribution to help carry out this work . . . to commemorate the lives and deeds of the loyal men and women of the Civil War." The individual corps responded generously. By early the following year, state WRC officials reported that members had contributed over $800 to the project. Meanwhile, Sortor, his SV allies, and the institution's other civic backers drew up incorporation papers, secured the awarded land in the southeast quadrant of town, sold lots to raise funds (garnering some $200,000), and authorized construction on the campus's first academic building. At the cornerstone-laying ceremony in June 1901, Minnesota GAR officer Eliakim "Ell" Torrance dubbed the celebratory crowd of 10,000 a "great army of freedom," and declared that "[t]his is certainly an hour and this the place for a new baptism of patriotism."[39]

With the physical construction of Memorial University begun, the founders next turned to developing unique reasons for prospective students to choose this institution over the host of others cropping up across the country. To do this, they needed to address many commentators' concerns that college education was not molding the type of graduates needed for the modern era. Supposed threats to the republic, such as socialists and anarchists, throngs of unschooled immigrants, urban and industrial unrest, and resistance to law and order, required a new generation of trained leaders instilled with values of public-spiritedness, service, and devotion to country. In 1892, before students at the University of Michigan, President Grover Cleveland argued that "[t]here is a great need of educated men in our public life, but it is the need of educated men with patriotism. The college graduate may be, and frequently is, more unpatriotic and less useful in public affairs than the man who, with limited education, has spent the years when opinions are formed in improving contact with the world instead of being within college walls and confined to the study of books." New York Republican (and later senator) Chauncey M. DePew more simply put it that US educators must "[t]each, first and last, Americanism."[40]

For a university honoring the men and women who had saved the republic, these concerns were particularly germane, and the school's founders prided themselves on three distinct offerings for anticipated enrollees. First was an emphasis on teaching American history and the Union soldier's place within it. Ell Torrance (now the GAR's commander in chief) selected a committee of prominent Union veterans for the task, who subsequently recommended a four-year course of instruction that emphasized the history of the Civil War, the role of slavery in the antebellum republic, and the creation of the US Constitution. Second, administrators proposed an unprecedented curricular focus on what they dubbed "Applied Patriotism"—a hazily defined subject designed "to assist in raising the standard of citizenship by bringing about a greater appreciation of the blessings of a free government." Elevated to department-level status, applied patriotism was not taught in specific courses; rather, it was something university founders intended to "be woven into the warp and woof" of the students' character during their entire academic experience. Finally, the school predictably made military drill a key part of the curriculum and used imagery of the past to inspire the next generation of America's defenders. In a pointed display of the institution's adherence to the memory of Union victory, administrators decided that all male preparatory and college students take part in drill and tactics twice a week while wearing cadet uniforms not "grey as at other schools," but rather "of union blue." All told, the school's extraordinary curricular triad—American history, applied patriotism, and military instruction—shaped Memorial University students into an image reminiscent of the Union soldier of the past, girded to defend the nation of the present. With this training, the university vowed that "every graduate shall become a missionary to the country in altruistic patriotism," sending out scholars to do battle to uphold the GAR's cherished principles.[41]

With its curriculum solidifying and construction of its first academic building complete, Memorial University formally opened its doors to roughly sixty students on September 10, 1902 (see Figure 5). The school's speedy inauguration, however, belied the fact that it was not initially a university at all. Rather, the institution "[f]or the present . . . will be run as a Military academy and until the larger design has been successfully reached. The academic course will be a three year course and will fit students for the collegiate course when it is established." Still, the first academic year passed largely successfully. The school was proudly coeducational (young men boarded in nearby Lincoln Hall, young women in Barton Hall—nods to the war generation's male and female paragons). Mirror-

Figure 5 Completed in 1902, this structure served as the sole academic building for the Memorial University in Mason City, Iowa. Although the institution was short-lived, it represented one of the most inventive educational reform initiatives undertaken by GAR veterans and their auxiliary allies. From author's collection.

ing trends in other contemporary colleges, the students assertively organized a wide range of extracurricular activities. Enrollees had the opportunity to join the newly established Lincoln-Fritchie Literary Society or the board of the student-run *Varsity Review*. Besides the requirement to take part in military drill, young men also joined the school's football, basketball, and baseball teams, taking part in a nationwide turn toward collegiate athletics. By the end of the second term, total enrollments more than doubled to some 150 students.[42]

A particular point of pride was the school's first graduation ceremony in June 1903 and the identity of its lone graduate that year. James Leggett was an African American student, born in Alabama in 1869 to parents who had been enslaved. Leggett transferred to Memorial University after studying for three years at the Illinois State University in Normal, Illinois. He and his wife, Menarvia, boarded at Mason City's Wilson Hotel while he completed one year of study in the College of Liberal Arts. Granted his diploma from trustee W. A. Morris, who "expressed the pleasure" of "being able to give the diploma to one so worthy," Leggett was then feted afterward by "the ladies of the W.R.C." who "presented the young man with handsome bouquets of American beauty roses." Leggett continued his education at the State Normal and Industrial College for Colored Students in Tallahassee, Florida (now Florida A&M University—a prominent HBCU). Newspapers commented that it was appropriate for the first graduate of Memorial University to be Black since "the men in whose memory" the university was dedicated "fought thru to many bloody years for the liberation of the slave." Leggett, then, was perhaps to Memorial University what an African American member was to an integrated GAR post—to use historian Barbara A. Gannon's terminology, a "living reminder" of white veterans' "wartime triumph."[43]

Notwithstanding measurable achievements made in its first years in operation, Memorial University consistently faced numerous obstacles. Enrollment lagged behind the number needed to keep the institution functionally and financially afloat, compelling the school's leadership to lean heavily on the GAR and its auxiliaries for help. Although many veterans and their families were enthusiastic, they often lacked deep pockets. In 1905, for instance, Iowa's WRC department raised $850 for Memorial University—admirable, but insufficient. Worse, the institution failed to shed its image as a preparatory academy merely plucking young Iowans from a public school education in or around Mason City. Indeed, it became known as an educational option for a certain type of student—"largely boys and girls from the more remote agricultural districts, sons and daughters of poor soldiers who would not otherwise be sent to school." Total enrollments stagnated, usually fluctuating from year to year between 100 and 150 students (mostly enrolled in the preparatory academy). Many of Memorial University's college-aged students apparently transferred out of Mason City to further their education at more prestigious institutions. Fatally, the patriotic societies that had once sustained Memorial University cooled in their support. Isabel Worrell Ball, an officer in the WRC Potomac Department, complained that her organization was losing sight of its true mission. "The Woman's Relief Corps must go straight ahead in its work of caring for the veterans," Ball rebuked. "As long as there is a survivor of the Civil War left, all the energies of my life shall be devoted to his welfare and comfort, and when he is laid to rest I may then turn my attention to Chairs of Applied Patriotism, but not before." By 1911, the SV withdrew its affiliation with the university and ceased further appropriations. Choked of funds, the administration formally closed Memorial University's doors during the 1911–1912 academic year.[44]

With the shuttering of Memorial University came the end of one of the most daring educational experiments in GAR memorialization—the establishment of an institution of learning that guaranteed a space for young scholars to honor and learn from the sacrifices of the Union soldier and the principles of his cause, even as much of the rest of the country capitulated to sectional reconciliation. Here, under the watchful supervision of veterans, their wives, and their children, educators and administrators instructed students by means of a unique curricular triad designed to inculcate a GAR-endorsed memory of the war and prepare graduates to lead lives of service with it in mind. Through the educational development of scholars' character, courage, and (perhaps most importantly) loyalty to the nation, Memorial University's young men and women could construct a bulwark against those "imbibing ideas of contempt for law and government"—a defense not unlike that which Union soldiers provided against an earlier generation of disruptive secessionists.[45]

Despite Memorial University's unfulfilled legacy, the failed endeavor nonetheless revealed the powerful influences that turn-of-the-century Grand Army veterans and their auxiliaries maintained in shaping higher education. Through its reform-minded curricula, Memorial University promised a progressive education that both looked backward on Union veterans' past sacrifices while promoting a forward-thinking mastery in modern patriotism, citizenship, and service to the nation. In 1912, WRC members gave their final word about the then-defunct institution. "[There was] a sore need of this very kind of school," that taught the "nameless miseries that followed the men and that remained with the women [of the Civil War generation] . . . and a college that [would] instill into the minds of our youth—whether they are native born or children coming to us from foreign shores—this patriotic love and devotion."[46]

GAR members closely observed the scholarly pursuits occurring in turn-of-the-century institutions of learning and worked to harness them to their own clear educational objectives. This included propagation of a lasting and veteran-endorsed memory of the Civil War and, by extension, the forging of an educated, engaged citizenry who would shield and glorify the nation that they had saved. Despite rarely benefiting from the edifying influence of such institutions as young men, aging veterans nonetheless identified them as important disseminators of knowledge and culture. Like other reformers, they viewed these sites as crucial to the development of a more disciplined, productive, and enlightened society. Further, drawing on their memories of the Civil War, members believed these wellsprings of democracy to be the training ground on which a Grand Army of scholars would learn the proper meaning of the war and ensure that new generations remembered the veterans' sacrifices on behalf of Union and liberty for all time. Meanwhile, GAR veterans' activism was by no means confined to the states of the 1861 Union. In the decades after the war, GAR veterans migrated widely—out West and to the states of the former Confederacy—guaranteeing that their legacy became enmeshed across an expanding and modernizing transcontinental nation.

3   West of Appomattox, South of Richmond

Grand Army men have pushed themselves out into the far West and have built up towns and cities . . . until to-day the saying, Go west and grow with the country, is resented by the stalwart Westerner because the country is full grown.

—Illinois GAR Department Commander Joel M. Longenecker, 1900

Few sites provided a more unusual setting for a Grand Army national encampment than Salt Lake City in 1909. For years, GAR officials accused Utah's Mormons of being "steeped in disloyalty" and akin to Confederate rebels because of their own insurrection against the federal government in 1857–1858. The sect's practice of plural marriage also offended many veterans, provoking Commander in Chief Paul Vandervoort in 1883 to condemn it as "a crime as hideous as treason, and as damnable as slavery." By the turn of the century, however, veterans gradually tempered their disdain. Particularly after the Mormon church renounced polygamy in 1890, the GAR noted improvements in the group's allegiance to the nation. In 1907, one officer optimistically announced that "the Mormon forgot who was Brigham Young and . . . with one accord all the people in their hearts sang hosannahs to 'the flag that makes us free.'" Two years later, the roughly 300 members of the small but vocal Department of Utah succeeded in coaxing the national encampment to the state, inviting thousands of veterans from across the country to teach the Mormons their lessons "of patriotism and loyalty and devotion to country and flag." One full day was reserved for the GAR's grand parade, whose "bent and gray" participants were buoyed by some 100,000 spectators who heard how this land, once "so desolate," was now "dotted over with prosperous communities" planted in part by itinerant Union veterans. Many GAR attendees commented on the friendliness and hospitality of the local Mormons—a remarkable contrast to the sentiments uttered decades before. "The Mormons are great folks for fun," reported back one comrade to his Wisconsin post, "and we all had lots of it."[1]

Grand Army veterans left their footprints far beyond the expected northern and eastern power bases, establishing posts that served as hubs of civic engagement and community upbuilding in all regions of the expanding postwar nation. Union veterans in the South and West confronted unique challenges in new territories—obstacles to GAR-led edification and influence unknown to their comrades who remained in the states of the 1861 Union. Demobilized Yankees became postwar migrants who marched southward and westward, taking with them a predilection to connect with their veteran and nonveteran neighbors and establish close-knit communities reflecting all the principles that the GAR stood for: civic activism and education, loyalty and patriotism, social order and progress. Foregoing rugged individualism, these veteran-migrants remained avid joiners as they took part in US expansion. GAR posts often became one of the first pillars of "community" as Union veterans trekked far from their old homes and battlefields. Utilizing many of the outreach techniques perfected back East—open and inclusive fraternal halls, public programming, and education advocacy—GAR-affiliated migrants set out to instruct a diverse and mobile citizenry in their version of the war's major lessons surrounding ideals like freedom, union, and opportunity. To be sure, turn-of-the-century GAR reform activity in these regions sometimes foundered. Union veterans in the former Confederacy often surrendered to native whites' antagonism, prompting dissociation from their African American comrades and redirection of post activity toward reconciliationist ends. In the West, young and fractious settlers were not always receptive to aging veterans' civic leadership and modern social ills sometimes proved unresponsive to GAR prescriptions. Still, Union veterans formed persistent and, often, thriving departments in the South and West that were vital components of the GAR's nationwide community building and rebuilding efforts.

Understanding Union veterans' civic activism in these areas requires assessing the Grand Army post within regionally specific analyses of Progressive Era community culture and reform—a challenge when scholars more commonly mine fraternal records in the East, which tend to be richer and better preserved. However, preoccupation with GAR posts in the more populous urban and industrial areas of the country has led historians to treat southern and western comrades as curiosities in a story otherwise firmly rooted in the Northeast, mid-Atlantic, and Midwest. Perhaps this is understandable given that the organization was founded in Illinois; drew the most members from the large veteran populations of New York, Pennsylvania, and Ohio; and often elected its national-level leadership core from the states in the North and East. Scholarly focus on the earlier years of the organization also prevents full assessment of southern and western GAR departments, as they were still relatively weak and unorganized before 1890. Extending the geographic and temporal focus of the GAR allows integrating southern and western veterans into a larger picture of how they coalesced into influential posts and fused themselves to local and regional fraternal networks with palpable social and cultural clout. Further, this approach aligns with recent scholarship that encourages bringing the assumed "peripheries" to the interpretive center and, in this chapter, allows investigation of the GAR veteran as a key player in the transnational consolidation of the postwar US nation-state. Indeed, it would be a mistake to assume that veterans in the South and West were merely peripheral figures. Between 1890 and 1920, 20 percent of all GAR posts were located in these regions. Over that same period, Union veterans in the South and West comprised a steadily *growing* proportion of overall GAR membership—from one in seven comrades in 1890 to more than one in five comrades by 1920. Emphasizing the geographically widespread nature of the GAR's presence illuminates Union veterans' civic and moral leadership in regions whose communities were maturing (or, in the South, reconstructing) around the turn of the century.[2]

The first section below turns to those Union veterans who migrated to the South after the Civil War, setting up fragile but ultimately enduring Grand Army networks. Their long-term legacy of upholding an unabashed, GAR-endorsed memory of the war, however, is mostly a failure and inextricably linked to the difficulties of living among their onetime enemies and to the vexing question of race. While helping usher in a modern New South, many Union veterans here cultivated accord with white southerners and drove a wedge between themselves and many northern GAR members (white and Black) who refused to concede the importance of Union victory. It was in fact all-Black southern posts that audaciously asserted an emancipationist memory of the war in a region otherwise given over to Lost Cause mythology. The second section examines those veterans who populated the Great Plains and converted the nation's heartland into a GAR Zion. Union veterans farmed the sprawling prairies, planted prosperous communities, dominated regional politics, established hundreds of posts, and successfully imprinted Grand Army values over the nonveteran population. Interacting with a more homogeneous and less urban society, GAR members here proved successful in transplanting the public outreach and reform activities that eastern posts had perfected. The final section investigates the endeavors of Union veterans in the Far West, many of whom arrived in the region at the end of a long search for contentment and a sense of community unfulfilled in the East. The posts on the Pacific coast present a mixed legacy. On the one hand, they successfully promulgated many of the civic and educational reform interests important to their eastern comrades. On the other hand, regional issues surrounding labor, immigration, and race prompted some veterans to retreat into a reactionary posture that diminished some of their Progressive Era accomplishments.

On the Skirmish Line of the Organization

Alongside a modest number of native Black and white southerners who served in federal units during the Civil War, the states of the former Confederacy attracted some northern-born Union veterans after the war—typically those who were young, resourceful, and eager to take advantage of commercial opportunities in the reconstructing South. Of course, to hostile southerners, these transplanted Yankees were regarded as little more than insidious "carpetbaggers," keen to profit off their defeated foes and align themselves with newly empowered African Americans. These fresh arrivals were in fact reformers in their own right, using their economic investments and democratic outlook to modernize a New South. As the GAR's *National Tribune* boasted, these Union veterans "were enterprising men, who saw the great commercial and industrial possibilities of the South, and went there to develop them. . . . It is they who have made Florida a great orange grove, who have lighted furnace fires in Virginia, Tennessee, Georgia and Alabama, and developed thrifty farms in Arkansas and Texas." During Reconstruction, some of these Union veterans espoused genuine interest in aiding formerly enslaved persons, assisting the freedmen as teachers or lawyers, or becoming agents of the Freedmen's Bureau. Still others leveraged their relationship with African Americans and southern-born white Republicans into a political career.[3]

Nevertheless, the number of Union veterans who migrated southward remained comparatively low and, especially with the rise of southern "redeemer" governments in the 1870s, their effect on the region's cultural development was subsequently limited. One demographic estimate highlights the overall paucity of northern transplants to the South, suggesting that only 2 percent of all Union veterans ultimately immigrated to the region by 1880. Still, for those who did settle in the former Confederate states, the bonds of comradeship remained strong enough to organize GAR posts and state departments, even while surrounded by their former foes. The immediate postwar years witnessed a brief flourishing of southern posts, largely comprised of African American veterans or whites associated with federal agencies or Reconstruction governments. Indeed, the nascent Ku Klux Klan must have deemed the GAR to be a large enough threat to white southern interests that it compelled prospective members to pledge that they had never joined "the Radical Republican party, or either of the organizations known as the 'Loyal League' and the 'Grand Army of the Republic.'" The GAR, however, mostly died out in the South during the 1870s (paralleling the membership decline experienced nationally that decade), and although a lasting Department of Virginia and North Carolina was established in 1871, most other southern departments did not revive and achieve permanent status until the 1880s.[4]

Even then, GAR membership in the South remained fairly anemic and coffers frequently empty, limiting the civic activism and public outreach that characterized posts elsewhere. Indeed, surviving records intimate the tenuous nature of merely sustaining the fraternity's presence in the region. When the city of Galveston was struck by a catastrophic hurricane in 1900, the GAR's Department of Texas felt helpless in aiding Union veterans and other victims there. Estimating "between 100 and 200 ex-Federal soldiers" who had settled in the area "mostly on account of impaired health and to escape the rigors of a Northern climate," state officials urged the national organization not to "forget their comrades in south Texas." Finding themselves "weak numerically and financially to accomplish what should be done," the state's GAR and Woman's Relief Corps (WRC) members implored posts nationwide "to aid this Department in the performance of the duty which it owes these comrades." Three years later in Tallapoosa, Georgia, the local WRC auxiliary made its own donation request to aid the aging veterans of the James B. Steedman Post. Noting the "adverse surroundings" associated with being "on the skirmish line of the organizations, away down in 'Dixie,'" the women appealed "to the loyal and liberal hearted brothers and sisters in the more favored sections of the North" to help the veterans collect funds to procure a proper space for their fraternal meetings.[5]

Many southern posts also struggled to fulfill the basic commemorative tasks that their northern counterparts took for granted. Perhaps most onerous was the Memorial Day obligation to plant flags and strew flowers on the graves of those Union soldiers who had died on southern battlefields. An ambitious postwar program by the federal government reinterred some 300,000 Union soldiers under the so-called National Cemetery System that by 1870 included seventy-three burial grounds (forty-six of which were located in states of the former Confederacy). Grand Army officials, meanwhile, declared it one of the duties of the order to care for these sites, regardless of their location. In his 1882 Memorial Day circular, for instance, Commander in Chief George Sargent Merrill directed all members to "search out every one of [the] known resting places [of the Union dead], so that in all our broad land, wherever exists a Post of the Grand Army, not a single grave of a Union soldier or sailor shall be unvisited." Consequently, for those GAR veterans who hailed from or settled in the cemetery-strewn South, the care of these hallowed places became their special—though onerous—charge. In 1890, veterans in the Department of Georgia and South Carolina, for example, felt overwhelmed by the responsibility. Between Marietta National Cemetery, the Andersonville prison site, and other cemeteries in the region, the small department estimated that 40,000 graves required attention. Because membership in the entire department did "not equal that of many of the [northern] Posts," officers explained that "the burden has heretofore fallen heavily on our scattered Comrades in the South." Therefore, the department appealed to northern members' comparatively deeper pockets and the memory of their fallen friends whose graves might otherwise remain undecorated. "[F]eeling that in every community there are many Grand Army men who have comrades, file-leaders and bunk-mates lying in these cemeteries," entreated the department officials, "[w]e ask but a trifle—15, 25 or 50 cents—from each of the members present when this [appeal] is read."[6]

When southern GAR veterans sent overtures like these across the North asking for small donations, national-level officers did their best to assist. In 1894, Commander in Chief John G. B. Adams lectured his northern comrades that they did not "fully appreciate the work of our comrades in the South" and urged more financial assistance for the arduous task. Adams further illustrated the challenges of decorating graves in hostile territory, stating that "[i]n the South, Posts have neither moral nor financial assistance. Take, for instance, the day in Richmond, Va., this year. Everything possible was done to turn the day and the occasion into a glorification of the lost cause; but our comrades of that city, loyal and true to those who died for the right, marched to Seven Pines and other battle-fields and laid their garlands of love upon the graves." After the turn of the twentieth century, GAR and WRC officials frequently cajoled their members to donate generously to what became known as the "Southern Memorial Fund" and to aid their southern comrades "where the Departments and Posts are relatively few in numbers and poor in purse." In 1907, then-Commander Robert B. Brown sought to shift some of the burden from the aging veterans to the federal government and proposed the "modest suggestion that this great government might properly assume the expense of purchasing the small flags and through the Superintendents of National Cemeteries with the employes [sic] at their command, plant them on the graves before Memorial Day." Allies in Congress successfully appended an amendment to an army appropriation bill approving $2,000 in federal funding for flags to decorate the national cemetery graves. Even with this governmental assistance, however, southern GAR veterans and their auxiliaries were still responsible for organizing Memorial Day ceremonies at the cemeteries and strewing flowers on the graves. By 1918, GAR officials estimated that only 2,500 comrades remained in the eight southern departments to carry on the task and continued to plead with northern posts to send more donations to their overworked comrades.[7]

More than their northern counterparts, Union veterans in the South also faced the difficulties of deciding if and how they would cultivate reconciliation with the southern populace. On these questions, the region's GAR departments faced a challenging negotiation: how to maintain the goodwill of their white southern neighbors while assuring their northern comrades that they exulted the virtues of the Union Cause for which they all sacrificed. This was no easy task, as GAR veterans frequently reported examples of white southern resentment and ill-treatment leveled against them. One officer in Louisiana, for example, recollected that the organization of his New Orleans post required "a supreme test of moral and physical courage and loyalty to principle to avow oneself a 'Yankee.'" Similarly, Alabama GAR officer A. P. Stone complained that membership in the GAR remained weak in the state because "social and business ostracism is the weapon still used to pay off grudges and keep alive animosities of the late war." Other veterans objected to the incongruity of onetime rebels controlling their access to federal benefits won by fighting for the Union. In Texas, veterans complained to national headquarters when ex-Confederates were placed on their local pension boards. Although admitting that these examiners were "most meritorious of their profession," the Union veterans hoped "to save our comrades from asking the opinion of any person who was formerly opposed to him."[8]

At other times, however, southern GAR veterans were admonished for cultivating too much fellowship with former rebels, particularly if Lost Cause symbolism overshadowed the sacrifices for which Union soldiers fought and died. In 1887, for example, some northern veterans objected to their southern comrades "bringing flowers and offerings of peace" to the unveiling dedication of an equestrian statue to Confederate General Albert Sidney Johnston in New Orleans. One California member, particularly incensed at Union veterans' participation in the ceremony (while African American veterans in some parts of the South were simultaneously being barred from GAR membership), proclaimed that he "would rather shake hands with the blackest n----- in the land if he was a true, honest man, than with a traitor." Two years later, Department of Louisiana and Mississippi Commander Jacob Gray barely evaded expulsion from the order for serving as a pallbearer at Jefferson Davis's funeral. In 1891, Georgia's O. M. Mitchel Post received scathing rebukes from national headquarters for their participation in a parade and monument unveiling (complete with Confederate flag waving) to Atlanta journalist and white supremacist advocate Henry W. Grady. The post defended itself by stating that they lived "in a section of [the] country where our numbers are few" and that they did their best to hasten "the honorable part which [southerners] are now taking . . . in obliterating animosities of the past."[9]

Adding further confusion to these postwar interactions were influential national-level GAR officers who each had their own distinct views on the degree to which the southern posts should serve as ambassadors of reconciliation to their erstwhile foes. Some officials, for instance, used their powerful positions to minimize sectionalism and encouraged southern comrades to foster camaraderie with former Confederates. During his travels through the South in 1901, Commander in Chief Albert Shaw was pleased to see "harmony now existing" between the Yankee transplants and Dixie natives. "Northern men have married Southern women, and Southern men have married Northern women," Shaw observed, "and there have been many branches of industry established in the South that never were there before; all working and living together in perfect harmony under the protection of the same old flag." During his own tour of the South the following year, the new commander, Eliakim "Ell" Torrance (see Figure 6), wrote that although he "met about ten Confederates for one Union man," they were all "pretty much alike." Further, Torrance estimated "that the day of reconciliation has come, at least as far as the old soldiers are concerned and that we are all brothers."[10]

These rosy assessments were constantly tested and sometimes resisted by the North's GAR rank and file. This was especially true during the turn-of-the-century movement to establish Confederate soldiers' homes in the South. Beginning in the 1880s, southerners rallied to create institutions for disabled or destitute Confederate veterans and their dependents. However, unlike similar institutions created for Union veterans in the North (often with GAR backing), these southern homes lacked the federal government's financial support. An early example stemmed from the efforts of the Robert E. Lee Camp of Richmond, Virginia, a Confederate veteran association organized in 1883 in part to establish a home for needy comrades. Many Union veterans in the South enthusiastically supported the call for assistance, even though it directly benefited their former enemies. Members of Lee Camp and Richmond's Philip Kearney GAR Post issued a joint circular urging "liberal charity" for the "helpless and pitiable" ex-Confederates and assured prospective contributors that the two sides "live in harmony and act in accord in this section." However, this spirit of reconciliation on behalf of the Confederate destitute did not fully pervade the GAR. Ohio officer T. D. McGil-

Figure 6 Eliakim "Ell" Torrance of Minneapolis, Minnesota, was a prominent national-level GAR officer. While serving as the organization's commander in chief in 1902, Torrance unleashed indignation among many GAR members by encouraging charity for destitute Confederate veterans and expressing other reconciliationist views. Courtesy of Prints and Photographs Division, Library of Congress.

licuddy, for instance, sternly admonished his comrades in the South for acting solely on the GAR principle of "charity" while ignoring "the crowning principle of loyalty." The *National Tribune* ultimately agreed, warning that such actions would mar the GAR's reputation by appearing "more solicitous for the welfare of those who once fought to destroy the Union than of those who shed their blood to preserve it." Ultimately, even without the full support of the GAR's charitable network, the Lee Camp Soldiers' Home opened in Richmond in 1885.[11]

Several years later, a similar debate divided the GAR across sectional lines as proponents sought to establish a soldiers' home in Alabama. Returning from his 1902 tour of the South, Commander in Chief Torrance remarked on the "cordial good feeling I found existing between the Union and Confederate soldiers" and urged all comrades to donate money to the project "to assist in making their last days comfortable." The magnanimous message, however, stirred up a fierce debate among the posts. Strikingly, the South's Union veterans largely supported assistance for the institution, consciously choosing to privilege reconciliation over devotion to their own Union victory. Former Virginia Department Commander Edgar Allen praised Torrance for "strik[ing] the right keynote" and promised to get all the state's GAR posts "to make a liberal donation in the same direction." Similarly, a Union veteran in Mississippi complimented the "old Johnnies" as the region's "best citizens" and pledged to send a dollar in support of the Confederate home.[12]

Reactions to Torrance's directive generally proved far different among northern comrades who maintained a distinct conviction that traitors did not deserve their generosity. They flooded Torrance's headquarters with angry missives suggesting that the commander had misread the GAR's obligations to ex-Confederates, perverting the meaning of the war itself. For some, resentment stemmed from Torrance's implicit erasure of the line between loyalty and treason. "[D]o we want to see a disposition to allow . . . those who were our ennimies [sic] treated the same as our friends," asked Nathan B. Easton, whose post gave "an emphatic refusal to do anything in that line." Others pointed out that the GAR had not completed its mission to offer charity to those loyal Union veterans in need. "Your motive I do not criticize," wrote one GAR officer to Torrance, "but while so many of our own comrades are dependent and in need, it does seem to me that our resources should not be drawn on to provide for the men who fought to destroy our country." Still others notably resisted any form of reconciliation with southerners, on the grounds that they had done little since the war to reaffirm their devotion to the nation, its laws, and its principles. As one Kansas veteran argued, southerners "are in open defiance of the Constitution, violating the 14th and 15th amendments with disregardful impunity, and, with immunity. This is in fact, strictly speaking, more violative of Constitutional Law, than was their Rebellion." Whatever the disharmony among Union veterans, the Alabama Confederate Soldiers Home ultimately opened and accommodated some 800 veterans and their dependents between 1902 and 1939.[13]

Questions on race posed an even thornier challenge to GAR departments in the South as they struggled to negotiate intensifying postwar segregation and discriminatory policies there. Many Union veterans in the South were African American—soldiers of the United States Colored Troops (USCT) who returned to or remained in the region after the war. Indeed, a majority of the members in some departments in the Deep South were Black. Even so, the South's white GAR members left behind an undistinguished legacy on race. Despite a national GAR directive against race-based membership discrimination, departments in Texas and Alabama successfully barred prospective African American members from joining. Similarly, the Department of Louisiana and Mississippi in 1890 sought to establish two separate divisions—one for whites and one for Blacks—within its organization (predating the US Supreme Court's ruling on the legality of the "separate but equal" doctrine by six years). At the 1891 national encampment in Detroit, however, delegates rejected the proposal and Commander in Chief John Palmer coerced the wayward department into integrating Black posts. These directives from national headquarters, however, did not eradicate later discriminative tendencies among some white southern Union veterans. When, for instance, the 1895 national encampment was planned for the border city of Louisville, Kentucky, northern veterans bristled at reports that their African American comrades might be denied accommodations in the city and that "Southern posts would refuse to go in the parade if colored men marched." The president of the city's encampment committee assured concerned veterans that "if your post visits our city and brings along two or three or half a dozen colored veterans . . . there will be no objection." The publicity was nonetheless troublesome.[14]

Still, racial discord was not ubiquitous in southern departments and there were genuine displays of interracial harmony and comradeship. When, in 1894, the Department of Louisiana and Mississippi sought to elevate one of its comrades to GAR national-level office, white and Black veterans rallied in support of New Hampshire-born Charles H. Shute (see Figure 7). A banker by profession who settled in New Orleans at the close of the war, Shute—a white man—helped steer the state's turbulent integration of white and Black posts after the 1891 directive from national headquarters. Further, he gained the respect of the Black community for using his professional expertise to teach financial literacy to African Americans. All told, Louisiana's Union veterans asserted that Shute was "among those who proved steadfast and loyal to the Order and to all who were entitled to become members thereof, regardless of race or color." By 1902, the department's commander reported to national headquarters that there was "the greatest harmony and best of good feeling . . . among all the comrades" and that Black and white veterans were establishing new posts. Meanwhile, some Black comrades in southern GAR departments had success in securing important officers' and staff positions—occasionally with greater frequency than even some northern states.[15]

Indeed, the region accommodated a sizeable number of all-Black posts whose members used their GAR affiliation to not only empower African American communities across the segregationist South but also assert their memory of the Civil War that celebrated emancipation and the Union Cause. Although finding surviving southern Black post records is exceedingly difficult, even the perusal of

Figure 7 New Hampshire-born Charles H. Shute became a prosperous banker in New Orleans, Louisiana, after the Civil War and was recognized as one of the city's prominent GAR members. Shute successfully navigated the tumultuous integration of white and Black posts within the GAR Department of Louisiana and Mississippi and was a notable backer of African American higher education and financial literacy programs. Courtesy of Augustus Weissert Collection, Wisconsin Veterans Museum.

white-owned southern newspapers uncovers a surprisingly active, even daring, alliance of Black veterans and their supporters using the power of their associations to stand up to Lost Cause mythology. The Ransom Post of Natchez, Mississippi, for instance, brazenly led "Federal Decoration Day" ceremonies deep in the heart of the Old Confederacy, parading through the streets of the town and strewing flowers at the nearby graves of the Union dead. Although weakened by low membership and empty coffers through the years, the post nonetheless persisted until at least well into the second decade of the twentieth century. The post in Beaufort, South Carolina, spearheaded well-attended Emancipation Day ceremonies each January followed by Memorial Day programs in the spring at the neighboring national cemetery. For the latter event, Beaufort's Black veterans sometimes called on their comrades in the region, inviting a network of all-Black posts from Charleston and Hilton Head, South Carolina, and Savannah and Brunswick, Georgia, to assist with the strenuous task. Black posts in the coastal North Carolina communities of Elizabeth City, New Bern, and Wilmington, also developed an informal regional bond whose members similarly hosted Emancipation Day and Memorial Day ceremonies. Further, these posts apparently collaborated with each other in organizing other events that symbolically centered Unionist personages and principles including memorial ceremonies after the death of Ulysses S. Grant in 1885, centennial celebrations of Abraham Lincoln's birth in 1909, frequent reunions of USCT units, and entertainments during the integrated encampments of the Department of Virginia and North Carolina. Collectively, all-Black posts throughout the former Confederacy became tenacious hubs of emancipationist memory activism in a section of the country particularly hostile to political and civic assertiveness exercised by African Americans.[16]

Even so, the GAR in the South (despite many indomitable Black posts and a few clear examples of genuine Black-white comradeship) simply had neither the numbers nor the wherewithal to reconfigure the region's legacy of racial discrimination and deep-seated hostility toward African American civil rights. Many transplanted Union veterans did not exhibit much inclination or fortitude to disturb the white populace with progressive entreaties about race. All told, white southern posts tacitly adopted the segregationist principles of their native-born white neighbors, a blot on the national GAR's otherwise reasonably enlightened stance on race relations and efforts to maintain Black and white comradeship in the local posts.[17]

Amid these challenges and controversies, another wave of Union veterans invaded the South around the turn of the century. Different from earlier migrants, these men, older and more frequently with wives and families in tow, viewed the region as a place to bask in warm weather, exploit new economic opportunities, and, for some, commune almost exclusively with like-minded Yankees. Strewn throughout the former Confederate states were self-isolating soldiers' colonies where Union veterans and their loved ones gathered to start a new life among sympathetic companions. Perhaps most notable was Fitzgerald, Georgia, eponymously named for Indiana veteran, newspaper editor, and town founder Philander Fitzgerald. After the Panic of 1893 and a concurrent drought struck the Midwest, Fitzgerald pondered ways to alleviate his fellow comrades' distress. By 1895, Fitzgerald established a stock company and with the proceeds purchased thousands of acres in the heart of south central Georgia's pine forests. Soon, veterans from across the North claimed the colony's newly platted commercial lots and agricultural tracts. Within three years, some 7,000 people had made Fitzgerald home, erecting "[t]hree banks, a score of pretentious blocks for stores, several office buildings of brick and stone, a hospital, churches and a hall for G. A. R. posts."[18]

Many of these soldiers' communities cropping up in Dixie, however, were far less successful and GAR officials reminded the comrades to take care in avoiding harebrained colonization schemes. Noting that "[o]ld soldiers cannot afford to make a mistake," national headquarters alerted the rank and file to "the traffic in these fraudulent titles, and . . . the efforts to unload them upon innocent and unadvised purchasers." There was no shortage of shady ventures. In 1896, Iowa comrade J. R. Martin advertised his interest in organizing a "Soldier Colony Association" that would transplant Union veterans to the Texas Gulf Coast "where the climate is described as one of perpetual spring." Martin admitted that he felt pressure from disingenuous "land sharks," but felt that if interested comrades went "a little slow, raise all the capital we can, and secure our tract so as to controll [sic] it ourselves, then the Comrades instead of speculators can profit from the legitimate profits of their own labor in developing the country." Although Martin appears to have formally chartered his colony association and staked out land in aptly chosen Liberty County, no indication exists that Union veterans followed him to the state. Another suspicious undertaking in Archer County, Texas, lured some 500 Indiana families to the arid plains between 1901 and 1903 with the promise "to give old soldiers an opportunity to get a home cheaply." Drought and internal dissension plagued the fledgling community and by 1904, the colonists of the short-lived town of Geraldine "scattered to the four winds."[19]

The rapid postwar development and sunny skies of Florida beckoned other Union veterans in their declining years. Whether relocating to the state full time or merely wintering there, aging Union veterans developed a modest GAR network. Indeed, stemming from the immigration of elderly veterans to the state, the GAR's Department of Florida was one of the few to see membership growth through the early years of the twentieth century. In 1900, for instance, Florida was home to 352 GAR veterans meeting in nineteen posts. Fifteen years later, the department tallied 812 members in twenty-six posts. One of the permanent transplants was William S. Siggins, "an old Michigan man," who resettled in the

Sunshine State and became department commander in 1913. Returning to Lansing for a visit with his comrades at the Michigan state encampment that year, Siggins boasted that membership in Florida was "increasing rapidly" because "[t]he opportunities are good, the land is cheap, [and] the climate is fine." Similarly, Ransom C. Luther reported in 1916 to his comrades in Wisconsin's Lucius Fairchild Post of his winter spent in St. Petersburg, Florida. Luther enjoyed the "genial climate" and the city's population, which remained "quite active." However, Luther was troubled by at least two characteristics of the southern city. First, although admitting his Florida GAR post had good relations with the local United Confederate Veterans camp, he questioned their patriotism because they had "no flag of any kind in their camp room." Second, he lamented the poorer educational opportunities available for the city's African American children. Noting that "[t]he public schools for colored children are two months shorter than those for the children from white families," Luther observed that Blacks were "much handicapped in getting our education." Still, he noted they were adamant about learning. "The colored children and young people used to come sometimes and sing for us," Luther recalled, "and then take a collection for money to be used to continue their schools. In their school work they are doing their best to learn how to become good citizens."[20]

Spurring the old soldiers into retirement in Florida was the GAR's own organ, the *National Tribune*. The publication established the Seminole Land and Investment Company to purchase tracts for a soldiers' colony, deciding on 35,000 acres in central Florida upon which the community of St. Cloud was built in 1909. The *Tribune* promised that for those veterans who purchased lots and retired to the nascent colony, they would "note the flowers blooming, hear the birds singing, see the waters of the mirror-like lakes softly shimmering in the sunshine, and find everywhere around you men wearing the G. A. R. badge and basking in the air of a perfect day." Just two years after its settlement, St. Cloud already attracted some 500 Union veterans and their families who, in a short time, established a GAR memorial hall, the Veterans Memorial Library, and other civic structures providing "nearly every modern improvement and convenience." Around the same time, the *Tribune* established a second colony at St. Andrews Bay on Florida's panhandle. Named Lynn Haven for the newspaper's editor, William H. Lynn, the community similarly attracted many veteran-retirees who, notably, donated portions of their pension payments to establish one of the few Union soldiers' memorials in the Deep South in 1920.[21]

Few in number and surrounded by native whites opposed, or even hostile, to celebration of Union victory, GAR members in the South's posts generally possessed neither the resources nor the mettle to confront the region's firm embrace of Lost Cause mythology and espousal of a white supremacist memory of the Civil War. Although many Yankee migrants played an important role in modernizing and revitalizing the reconstructing South, few were willing to sacrifice their social or economic gains by publicly praising their sacrifices for liberty and democracy or brandishing the honorable nature of their Union Cause. Civic activity remained either modest in scope (as with the decoration of Union soldiers' graves) or performed in conjunction with Confederate veterans' organizations and their auxiliaries (as with the establishment of Confederate soldiers' homes). These activities better assured the diffusion of reconciliationist sentiment in the region, but at the cost of truly close and sophisticated comradeship between the South's white and Black GAR veterans. Despite some audacious all-Black posts and a few sincere examples of integrationist principles in the southern GAR departments, the challenges of creating island posts in a sea of Confederate nostalgia guaranteed the eclipse of the most important race-related outcomes and promises of Union victory. The South's posts largely failed to demonstrate the robust spirit of community reform and progressive activism that the bonds of GAR membership unleashed elsewhere.

The Great Soldier States of the Union

Far more than their outnumbered comrades in the South, Union soldiers flooded the Great Plains after the Civil War, conspicuously shaping both the landscape and community development of the region. The demobilization of the northern armies occurred just as new ventures opened up beyond the Mississippi River. Chief among these were settlement opportunities under the Homestead Act, the law granting a deed of title to public lands (usually 160 acres) for any US citizen who agreed to live on and improve the tract for a period of five years. Passing the Republican-led Congress in May 1862, the act had already garnered some 15,000 applications by war's end. Eager to participate in the land rush, many intrepid soldiers sought to stake claims upon their return to civilian life. Although the federal government never awarded bounty lands to Union veterans as it had to those of earlier wars, it did offer them preferential considerations. An 1872 amendment to the original act stipulated that veterans could subtract their term of Civil War service from the required five-year residency to "prove up" on their land claim. One hopeful homesteader, responding to these generous laws, appreciatively declared that "uncle sam [sic] has been mindful of those who stood by the country in her hour of Peril." Perpetuating this reciprocal relationship, these prospective freeholders augmented the power of the state whose government they had recently saved during the Civil War, now helping to extend its sovereignty westward.[22]

For many plucky veterans, carving out a life on the plains brought satisfaction after military adventure or a chance to rebuild their lives after the disruptions caused by war. If fortunate, a soldier's homestead provided not only a living, but also a springboard to wealth and stature in a newly settled land. After serving in an Illinois cavalry unit, the German-born Charles Roberts spent time working at the John Deere plow manufacturer in Moline before trying his luck on a Howard County, Nebraska, homestead in 1871. Roberts (who later joined the local GAR post at Grand Island) quickly proved up on his land, leveraging those initial holdings to ultimately own some 1,200 acres and a "handsome dwelling, with all improvements and substantial farm buildings of every kind." Fellow Grand Army comrade Rufus J. Collins initially endured drought, hailstorms, and plagues of grasshoppers after claiming his central Nebraska homestead in 1872. Collins persevered, however, claiming title to his land and becoming a "prosperous man of affairs" who owned "good city property" and speculative land holdings in Kansas. The Irish-born Patrick Kilfoil spent the years after his war service restlessly, "travel[ing] in many parts of the country, working and taking in the sites" before settling on a homestead in Custer County, Nebraska. Successfully proving up on his land, Kilfoil became a civic leader in the area (with a township even eponymously named for him), proudly joined his local GAR chapter, and helped establish the county's first Catholic church.[23]

Of course, not every adventurous homesteader carved out a productive farm and failure was a common occurrence. Poor soil, extreme weather conditions, plagues, scarce resources, and the agricultural inexperience of some settlers were just a few of the factors that contributed to tens of thousands of surrendered claims. Early Nebraska migrant and prominent GAR officer Addison Wait (who avoided the homesteaders' plight by instead taking a job as a telegraph operator after the war) admitted that the early years on the prairies saw many luckless settlers "in [a] very bad condition. . . . Potatoes could not be sold at any price, while corn was selling for 10 cents a bushel." To be sure, Union veterans were no less likely to face hardship or insolvency than other prospective homesteaders. For instance, Jarvis Dean, who served in a Wisconsin battery for three years, relocated his family to a Pierce County, Nebraska, tract and struggled for years to eke out a living. The luckless Dean clan "went through every form of pioneer life—having narrow escapes from danger on account of wild beasts and Indians, and suffering failure of crops and all discouragements." Paul Herman Fiebig, a

German-born immigrant who served in an Indiana regiment, moved his family to Sherman County, Nebraska, in 1872 to take up a homestead. Grasshoppers ravaged their crops on two occasions, a prairie fire destroyed their barn, and more than once "they were forced to make their main article of diet common field corn and a little wheat, which was ground in the coffee mill." Worse, an 1881 diphtheria outbreak took five of Fiebig's children. Nonetheless, the family continued to toil away at their homestead until selling out in 1904.[24]

Late in life, GAR veteran Henry V. Hoagland of the Farragut Post in Lincoln, Nebraska, provided a particularly candid reminiscence about his arrival to homestead in the state, several years after his Illinois regiment disbanded. Toiling with three other comrades, Hoagland described how they "planted corn but the grass-hopper took it. We sowed wheat but the dry weather and hot winds killed it. The cattle men on Ranches in the Valley did everything to get us to abandon our claims, let their cattle run on our crops, told me that the grass hoppers came every year.... Starvation seemed to stare us in the face, I was so discouraged that I sat down and cried." Hoagland was lucky. He eventually proved up on his land, although he had to make extra money gathering dried buffalo bones on the prairies until his fortunes improved. Meanwhile, hapless homesteaders seeking relief frequently turned to rapacious speculators and land jobbers, who exploited a loophole in the Homestead Act that permitted the sale or transfer of land patents. One particularly audacious GAR veteran, for instance, sent circulars to posts across the country seeking to buy up his fellow comrades' unfulfilled homestead rights. "I am in the business of buying these rights," Henry N. Copp frankly admitted, "which I sell to cattlemen and others out west."[25]

Whatever the challenges migrating veterans faced, enough found success on the plains to remain, build up new communities, and develop healthy and active GAR posts and state departments. Nebraska veterans, for instance, established a permanent department in 1877, ultimately encompassing over 350 individual posts in every corner of the state. Although peak membership in the department never exceeded 10,000 members, this modest host nonetheless enjoyed a disproportionate influence in Nebraska politics. Between 1873 and 1907, Grand Army voters had a hand in elevating seven comrades to the governorship. Veteran lobbying brought about state assumption of destitute veterans' funeral and headstone-placement expenses; tax exemptions on soldiers' pensions; punishment for fraudulently wearing a GAR badge; and recognition of Memorial Day as a state holiday. Further legislation in 1887 and 1895 established state soldiers' homes at Grand Island and Milford, respectively. Even into the twentieth century, the aged veterans' shrinking ranks exercised political clout. In 1913, the state's Department of Public Instruction sought the GAR's assistance in revising the school codes, asking the "honorable organization" to present their "help and suggestions" in the important task. The following year, the state superintendent of public schools authorized the annual observance of "Nebraska Patriotic Day" each October—a proposal introduced by the state's GAR and WRC departments. Over the next several years, veterans and their auxiliaries across the state delivered school and community programs designed "to interest and instruct the young" that revolved around fundamental American creeds such as opposition to "tyranny and unjust privilege" and appreciation for a "land of opportunity for all, regardless of birth or circumstance."[26]

Much like their eastern counterparts, GAR veterans on the Great Plains often became prominent local- and state-level figures. The Nebraska Department's chief founder (and, later, national GAR commander in chief) Paul Vandervoort, for example, became a leader in the region's Populist Party, supporting agrarian reforms and heading the National Reform Press Association. The once illfated Henry V. Hoagland, after securing his homestead, became a civic leader in Phelps County, serving as the county sheriff, chief of police, justice of the peace, and state senator. "In every school district, in every township, in every county and district, and the state at large," boasted Nebraska GAR official Isaiah D. Evans, "wherever men and women were gathered together to consider the welfare of the commonwealth, there the Civil War soldier was found presiding, directing, guiding and in large part controlling the destinies of the state." Evans's own biography matched this declaration. Since his arrival to the state in 1871, the Pennsylvania-born veteran had founded newspapers, platted towns, sat on his community's school board, and served in the state legislature as an avowed prohibitionist, antimonopolist, direct democracy advocate, and overall "progressive republican." Emphasizing his comrades' visibility in settling the region, Evans concluded that "Nebraska has been properly called the Soldier State."[27]

Of course, Nebraskans' neighbors to the south likely took exception to that characterization, as it was GAR veteran and Kansas Governor John A. Martin who declared his adopted home "the great 'Soldier State' of the Union." Although Nebraska's GAR department was organized three years earlier, Kansas's grew larger, comprising some 500 posts and reaching a peak membership in 1890 of over 18,000. As early as the 1880s, the state's Grand Army presence was sufficient to make a notable impact on Kansas politics and society, prompting the department commander to remark that "the Grand Army of the Republic is a power in this State, and, if so disposed, can make its influence felt." Indeed, in the quarter century after the Civil War, nine of the state's ten governors and five of eight senators were Union army officers and GAR members. Meanwhile, political pressure by veterans (and, after its 1888 creation, a formal GAR lobbying committee) had extracted a number of favorable laws from the state legislature, including the creation of soldiers' homes at Leavenworth and Fort Dodge; a soldiers' orphans' home at Atchison; recognition of Memorial Day as a legal holiday; preferential consideration in political patronage and public employment posts; and criminalization of fraudulently wearing the GAR button.[28]

Meanwhile, Governor Martin proved especially eager to extol the contributions of Union veterans in Kansas's development and fought passionately for veterans' rights during his tenure in office. Born in Pennsylvania, Martin arrived in the territory in 1857, just as violence peaked between pro and antislavery forces. A rabid Free-Soiler himself, Martin established an abolitionist newspaper, joined the state's nascent Republican Party, and sat in on proceedings of the so-called Wyandotte Constitution that, ultimately, brought Kansas into the Union as a free state in 1861. Serving in the 8th Kansas Volunteers for many of the Western Theater's prominent battles, Martin returned to the state after the war and helped organize the Kansas GAR department. As governor, Martin oversaw the implementation of several veterans' welfare policies and frequently congratulated his comrades for their positive influence on the state. Thanks to the prewar arrival of Free State Jayhawkers and the postwar settlement of veteran-homesteaders, Martin proclaimed that the state attracted "a host of bright and generous men, to oppose the aggression of slavery; and when the Civil War was over, a hundred thousand soldiers of the Union established homes on our broad prairies. No State in the Union can boast of a braver or more intelligent, enterprising, sober and law-respecting population; and no country in the world can point to achievements or results rivaling those wrought by the citizens of Kansas."[29]

Not to be overlooked among these migrants were the tens of thousands of African Americans seeking hope and opportunity on the state's wide plains. Bearing new understandings of freedom in the wake of the Civil War, a stream of southern Blacks fled the disfranchisement, violence, repression, and economic victimization that marked the "redeemed" South of the late 1870s and early 1880s. For many, the destination was Kansas—attractive not only for the opportunity to farm its prairies, but also for the sacredness derived from the state's antislavery legacy. Some of these migrants were veterans of the USCT, emboldened by the empowerment and sense of manhood acquired while fighting for the Union and emancipation. To be sure, many of these so-called Exodusters met with failure and disappointment—the victims of continued discrimination, false promises of free land and supplies, and inferior tracts passed over by earlier arrivals. Still, many succeeded in carving out a better life, particularly those that abandoned dreams of landholding and opted instead to labor in the state's burgeoning industries. For those African American veterans who persisted in Kansas, some sought camaraderie in the GAR. At least five Kansas posts were comprised exclusively of Black veterans, while dozens of other predominantly white posts welcomed Black comrades. For his part, Governor Martin endorsed the presence of the African American migrants in the state. He observed "that the 48,000 people of color in Kansas . . . have done their full share, with their strong arms, toward the upbuilding of the State, which has been the scene of the first successful occupation and settlement of public lands by persons of African descent."[30]

Like the parallel migration that established northern veterans in their own soldiers' colonies in the South, the Great Plains also hosted a number of these exclusive settlements. The small, central Nebraska communities of Comstock and Wescott originated from a tight-knit community of transplanted Wisconsin soldiers in the mid-1870s. Many of these original homesteaders formed the Crittenden Post whose comrades "helped to make this a community of loyal and progressive people." With the piecemeal opening of the Oklahoma Territory to non-Native American settlement (and its attendant exploitation) beginning in 1889, Union veterans banded together to stake their claims. One early community was the village of Frisco where one visitor commented that "the vets made no mistake as their location in lands and town site is excellent." The all-Black Sumner Post of Kansas City, Kansas, caught "Oklahoma fever" as well and ostensibly facilitated the migration of at least some veterans seeking to "better their condition in this world" in self-segregating African American colonies in the territory. Perhaps the most famous Union veteran colony in the country, however, was in the Dakota Territory (now South Dakota). Here, Captain James Bryson, head of a joint-stock company, guided a group of veterans to Potter County in 1883 and established the aptly christened Gettysburg (with nearby sister communities of Appomattox and Lincoln). Shortly thereafter, the veterans organized the Meade Post, while their female relations established a WRC auxiliary and their own meeting hall in 1901.[31]

Despite a potent GAR presence on the Great Plains, the region's veterans oddly had little success in luring the national encampment, along with the prestige and financial perks that accompanied it. Despite many attempts, none of the eighty-three annual gatherings between 1866 and 1949 was ever held between Kansas City, Missouri, and Denver. To be sure, comrades frequently promoted the region as a logical host site, citing the many veterans who migrated there after the war and the special legacy these states exemplified in ushering in the fight for freedom. Conjuring their state's emancipationist heritage, Kansas veterans proposed Topeka as the site for the 1887 national encampment since it was "the home of old John Brown; we do not want you to go by the place where the war began five years before 1861, and where the blood which was there shed dedicated the State to freedom." The effort failed, but a new one emerged with the bid to bring the 1892 national encampment to Lincoln—"the heart of old soldier country." Paul Vandervoort and other Nebraska boosters, seeking to unseat Washington, D.C., as the top contender admitted that "[w]e have not got the battle-fields, but we have 250,000 old soldiers within a radius of 300 miles of Lincoln that have conquered homesteads from the great American desert, and are feeding you your beef and your corn to-day." Further, Vandervoort criticized the nation's capital for its citizens' alleged southern sympathies. Instead of selecting a city whose people "do not believe in the cause for which [we] fought," he urged GAR delegates to select the humble Nebraska city "where every man, woman and child is loyal, devoted and true." Despite the Nebraska delegates' entreaties, however, Washington edged out a slim victory.[32]

Nevertheless, the Grand Army of the Great Plains proved as influential in instilling its notions of patriotism, loyalty, and civic engagement there as much as any part of the country. Arriving in numbers far greater than their comrades in the South, GAR veterans successfully expanded their Unionist vision and devotion to the burgeoning US nation-state over the very territory whose free-soil promise sparked the Civil War years before. By homesteading the land, developing prosperous new communities, influencing local and state politics, and using their newly formed posts to engage their nonveteran neighbors, GAR members replicated and, in their minds, improved upon the communities they left behind in the East. These veterans, many of whom became influential in the region's populist and progressive movements, firmly fastened the settlers of the nation's heartland to an allegiance to a restored and consolidated nation. All told, development on the Great Plains—comparatively undisturbed by the challenges of urbanization and industrialization—proved especially amenable to Grand Army activism.

That Great Western Empire

From the Rockies to the Pacific, Union veterans affiliated enthusiastically with the Grand Army, whose influence was unmistakable in the developing region. Even before the postwar flood of transcontinental migrants brought tens of thousands of Union veterans to the West, GAR recruiters already had a base from which to draw members. The 1860 US census counted nearly 400,000 individuals in California, with another 52,000 in Oregon, 12,000 in Washington Territory, and 7,000 in Nevada Territory. These early settlers provided the Union army with a modest but vital force to maintain federal control of the region and curb the Confederacy's aspirations to extend its influence to the Pacific coast. California fielded eight full infantry regiments and a handful of cavalry units throughout the course of the war, while a jumble of units came from other far western territories. As US Army regulars stationed in the West redeployed to critical points in the East, volunteer units like these assumed important roles—constructing and garrisoning fortifications, protecting overland trade and mail routes, building roads in the western interior, escorting migrant caravans across hazardous trails, and defending against both Confederate and Native American attacks. As one chronicler of GAR activities in the West wrote, California "promptly sent out her quota of nearly sixteen thousand" many of whom "loyally defended an important country . . . and by wearisome marches patrolled this great territory."[33]

For some of these veterans in the Far West, their ties to the region extended back to the antebellum period. One of California's defenders, for example, was Theodore H. Goodman, who would later serve as the state's GAR department commander. A New Yorker by birth, Goodman arrived in California in 1859 and took a job with an express company. Upon the outbreak of the war, he enlisted in the 2nd California Cavalry and served in the southern part of the state, "scouting after hostile Indians [and] protecting public property and that of the settlers." A number of Oregon GAR veterans likewise migrated to the state before the war, a few even arriving as early pioneers along the Oregon Trail. George W. Davis of McMinnville's Custer Post was born in Tennessee but moved to Missouri as a boy. In 1848, Davis "crossed the plains by ox team," settling briefly in Salem before journeying to California at the peak of the gold rush. Returning to Missouri before the outbreak of hostilities, Davis served out the war, "recrossed the plains" with a family in tow, and lived out his days in Yamhill County, Oregon. Similarly, the Indiana-born John W. Cullen accompanied his family on their migration west in 1847. The boy "walked to The Dalles, all the way from the starting point, more than 2000 miles," helping to "drive the cows attached to the caravan." Taking a number of odd jobs in Oregon's maturing settlements—herding, waiting tables, operating a ferry, and making saddles and harnesses—Cullen later served in the Yakima War in the 1850s. With the onset of the Civil War a few years later, he enlisted in the 1st Oregon Volunteer Infantry and served on frontier duty with the regiment.[34]

Grand Army officials identified in veterans like these a core of western recruits to begin forging transcontinental camaraderie. Veteran fraternalism in the region began almost immediately after the war when several army officers organized the Society of California Volunteers in November 1865. Two years later, Sacramento native Thomas J. Blakeney, returning from a visit to the East, carried with him authorization from GAR officers in Washington, D.C., "to establish posts of the Grand Army of the Republic within the Department of California." In a matter of months, the new department claimed four posts—two in San Francisco and one apiece in Sacramento and Vallejo—and hosted its first state encampment in 1868. Like its eastern counterparts, California's posts suffered deterioration through much of the 1870s until finally rebounding the following decade. By the time of the 1884 national encampment, eastern officers marveled at the membership growth on the West Coast, commending the California department's one hundred posts whose members "made up . . . the rank and file of nearly all the regiments and commands of the war, that have gone over the Rocky Mountains and have carried the flag of our Empire down on the shores of the Pacific Ocean."[35]

Indeed, steady streams of Union veterans migrated to the West after the war, furthering GAR reach as pockets of settlers came together to form their own posts. For many years, these fledgling units in the region's states and territories adhered to the California Department until sufficient numbers allowed the formation of the permanent departments of Colorado and Wyoming (1879); Oregon (1882); New Mexico (1883); Utah (1883); Washington and Alaska (1883); Montana (1885); Arizona (1888); and Idaho (1888). Energetic officials whipped up fraternal enthusiasm in these areas, calling on prospective recruits to crown their war service by banding together in posts across the West's wide expanses. One GAR officer in Las Vegas, New Mexico, for example, sent circulars across the territory goading "comrades residing in Raton, Albuquerque, Socorro, Silver City and Deming" to "fall into line at once and emulate the example of their comrades in Santa Fé and this city." National-level officers noted the surge in many of the western departments by the 1880s, rewarding the region several times with national encampment selections. Out of the GAR's eighty-three annual encampments, the West hosted eight: Denver (1883, 1905, and 1928); San Francisco (1886 and 1903); Salt Lake City (1909); Los Angeles (1912); and Portland (1918). After attending the Portland encampment, Commander in Chief Daniel M. Hall was amazed that two-thirds of the comrades he met while there "came originally from Ohio, Pennsylvania, [and] New York, but went West after the war. It is a fact, we have a great empire out there, that western empire. . . . You are to be congratulated, my comrades, on what you have accomplished."[36]

For many Union veterans who joined the GAR in the West, their settlement in the region came years after the war and often after a long, itinerant journey. Of the 165 members who joined Portland's George Wright Post, for instance, only ten had enlisted in Oregon-based regiments, nine in California units, and one in the 1st Washington Territory Infantry Regiment. The rest served in a hodgepodge of eastern units, led by New York (28), Illinois (18), Ohio (16), Minnesota (11), Wisconsin (11), Pennsylvania (10), Indiana (10), and Missouri (10). In 1931, then-nonagenarian Gideon Stolz of Salem's Sedgwick Post reported that out of the 508 veterans who were members of his post, only three had served in an Oregon regiment during the Civil War, most of the rest representing "different services or regiments in states east of the 'Rockies.'" For many of these western GAR veterans, their postwar odysseys were circuitous. Captain James P. Shaw, for instance, was Virginia-born, but being a "firm believer in the Union," left the state and enlisted in an Ohio regiment. After the war, he returned to Ohio but then "kept moving westward," ending up in California by 1874. Seven years later, Shaw settled in Portland after securing a job with the Oregon Railroad and Navigation Company. Often, migrants took advantage of the fluid state of the West's social stratification and rose to become respected civic leaders. When the aged Gideon Stolz died in 1938, the Salem newspapers praised him as crucial to the "civic and business development" of the city, serving as a councilman who had helped develop the community's road, water, and sewage systems. Similarly, the New York-born George A. Prentiss found his way to Oregon after the war, becoming a respected schoolteacher in the Willamette Valley and rising to the school superintendency of Yamhill County.[37]

Examining biographies like these reveals two key reasons to account for the substantial number of veterans who migrated west of the Rockies after the war. First, feelings of wanderlust affected many men upon mustering out of the military. As Union soldiers often discovered, no other experience for the remainder of their lives would compare with the adventure and exhilaration of their Civil War service. Some constantly relocated after the war, seeking opportunities to recapture the excitement they had experienced while campaigning. Second, returning soldiers frequently experienced socioeconomic push and pull factors that made immigration to the Pacific coast an attractive option. Scholars have reported economic slowing caused by the Civil War, especially in the long-settled sections of the North. Opportunity, for some, lay in migrating westward to reclaim the life they had before enlisting or securing a new life of greater prosperity. Burgeoning towns in the West provided a chance for Union veterans to develop new communities along similar economic, social, and cultural lines as antebellum eastern towns. Meanwhile, the revered status that Union veterans typically enjoyed provided them with a pedestal on which to claim status as civic leaders in western towns where social hierarchies were still in flux. Along these lines, a *National Tribune* editorial claimed that many men "who would have remained a clerk or small-salaried employee of some kind all his life had he stayed in the East, becomes, amid the larger opportunities of the West, a 'leading citizen,' and the owner of a fine farm or a prosperous business." In this context, the speed and completeness in which Grand Army posts proliferated across the region is logical. As in the East, membership in the GAR typically offered social networking opportunities, identification with the middle class, civic prestige, and greater influence in community reform and upbuilding efforts.[38]

Western posts subsequently shared with their eastern counterparts many of the same interests and advocacies. For example, patriotic instruction in public schools and institutions of higher education was as strongly advocated there as elsewhere. In California, one officer urged his comrades to "furnish living history" to the state's children by visiting schools in person. "Those children," declared Vallejo veteran John Spellman, "will wonder and think that the men standing before them took part in that war mentioned in the history they are now reading. . . . I tell you you have no idea as to the effect it has on the school children." Members of Portland's Lincoln-Garfield Post lamented the financial straits of Oregon's colleges and universities at the conclusion of World War I. Citing a need for strong postsecondary education opportunities for returning doughboys who were "learn[ing] the wonderful value of a college education," the post passed resolutions favoring the Higher Educational Tax Act then before the state's legislators. Although never as numerous or grandiose as examples in the East, Grand Army veterans in the region also planted memorial halls for the educational and civic benefit of their communities. The local post in Boise, Idaho, for example, after "rustling for cash," established a modest structure in the center of town in 1892, later utilized by the state university.[39]

Still, a variety of unique, regional issues compelled GAR posts in the West to undertake initiatives and reform activities less familiar to their comrades in the East. For instance, resistance to Grand Army influence occurred in Utah where veteran-migrants clashed with the embedded traditions of Mormonism. The rugged territory attracted few demobilized soldiers after the war, with most arrivals filling administrative government offices or laboring in the region's extractive industries. When the GAR reached its peak membership nationwide in 1890, Utah still mustered only three posts with fewer than 150 comrades. Nevertheless, these few along with their WRC allies exercised their reformist bent to correct

Mormons' alleged disloyalty to the federal government and the elimination of, in their minds, the group's most deviant social practice—polygamy. Local posts frequently forwarded resolutions to top GAR officials urging suppression of Mormon control of the territory, while WRC members filed complaints "against the vile practices and the continued disloyalty of Mormonism" in order to preserve "the purity of the ideal of the American home." Due in part to Utah's GAR and WRC objections, posts across the country mobilized with resolutions of their own, aiding in the 1887 passage of the antipolygamy Edmunds-Tucker Act. The law pressured LDS Church president Wilford Woodruff to issue an 1890 manifesto advising his followers "to refrain from contracting any marriage forbidden by the law of the land," an action that diminished veterans' antagonism. Still, hostility to polygamy remained and some veterans advocated reformers' efforts to amend the US Constitution to ban the practice forever. One post in 1915, for instance, endorsed a resolution in support of such an amendment, directed at those "prophets and priests [who] continue to practice polygamy, in defiance of the Law of Christ and . . . the Law of the Land."[40]

Elsewhere, GAR members in the West took an interest in populating the region with upright, hardworking migrants. In 1888, California official Robert C. J. Adley indicated his pleasure with the "tide of immigration from the Eastern States," particularly those comrades who arrived "to build up and strengthen [the] Posts." Many Union veterans actively promoted this immigration to the West. Ahead of the 1886 national encampment in San Francisco, the Department of Oregon sensed an opportunity to tout the advantages of their state for the many visitors they were expecting from the East. Officer Frank H. Lamb urged his comrades to act as members of an impromptu "immigration agency" at the encampment to "attract people to our state and . . . make a fine exhibit of Oregon products to [show] the Eastern visitors." Similarly, Augustus S. Hopkins of Sacramento's Sumner Post merged his membership in the GAR with an executive position in the Northern California Immigration Society. The latter organization pledged "to disseminate reliable information respecting the climate, resources, capabilities and opportunities which exist in northern California" and attract a "desirable class of people" to "add to our population, increase our taxable wealth, stimulate all the trades and industries, and increase our educational, religious, and society advantages."[41]

Of course, there was considerable disagreement among western GAR posts about who exactly constituted a "desirable" settler, and veterans left behind a mixed legacy on their tolerance to nonwhite newcomers. Particularly during times of crisis, xenophobia and bigoted comments were not uncommon. At the height of the Spanish-American War, Lyon Post members in Oakland, California, erupted when they learned that "sweat-shop contractors and their coolie operatives" were making uniforms for US soldiers, displacing the wives and widows of Union veterans who sought this employment. Pressuring the local commissary department "to consider the rights of the white people who need work, as against the Chinese . . . who are doing a 'skinning' business on the soldiers' garments," the post displayed the same hostility to Asian immigrant labor that many white Californians had broadly exhibited for decades. Twenty years later, anti-immigrant fervor flared up during World War I, when one GAR post in Salem, Oregon, passed resolutions demanding "the exclusion of all foreign[er]s from exercising the right of political suffrage, and the deportation of all disloyal subjects of foreign countrys [sic] from the United States."[42]

Still, virulent nativism was not the norm for western veterans and GAR post rooms were generally not strongholds of outspoken prejudice. Although few members actively praised cultural heterogeneity or immigrant heritage, many nonetheless believed that they possessed a special expertise to train "Americans-in-the-making." The Department of Oregon, for instance, proudly touted the Union veteran's instructional role to provide an "object lesson to the hordes of foreign born who are flocking to our shores—a lesson which they are learning rapidly." Occasionally, veterans' expressions were even emphatically *pro-immigrant*. One Portland post relished the address of one invited speaker who modernized iconic words from the veterans' past, praising the United States as a nation indicative of "something new under the sun, by establishing a Union of people from all quarters of the globe in a melting pot, to a great nation, as the immortal Lincoln said, of the people, by the people and for the people, which shall never pass from the face of the Earth." Little evidence suggests that the region's GAR posts actively lobbied for anti-immigration policies or that veterans used membership in the order to amplify bigotry—even against Asian migrants on the West Coast. Granted, the era's most significant pieces of federal legislation curtailing Asian immigration—the 1882 Chinese Exclusion Act and the 1924 National Origins Act—fell on either end of the GAR's most influential years and western veterans' prevailing reticence on the subject may be attributable to this fact. Nevertheless, the overall paucity of GAR petitions or resolutions against Asian immigrants in minute books and state-level circulars is striking.[43]

Much like their comrades in the East, western members were generally tolerant of those newcomers devoted to making good-faith efforts at acculturation in their adopted country, regardless of ethnic, racial, or religious background. During World War I, for instance, comrades in a Portland post applauded a Japanese

American graduate of the state university who expressed that "his heart was with America in her present war strife, and, if need be, would gladly fight for the stars and stripes, even if against his beloved country." At the Oregon soldiers' home in Roseburg, the GAR commandant and veteran inmates stood firmly in support of their diligent Chinese American cook, "Chow Sing," who became ill and was threatened with expulsion by the state inspector. Seventy-four comrades signed a petition lauding the cook's nineteen years of faithful service and insisted that he remain with the veterans in the home with "provision . . . made for him during his few remaining years." For many white veterans, the triumph of the Union assumed the triumph to tolerate differences, even with nonwhites. "We were made free and equal in this country," averred GAR Commander in Chief David J. Palmer with a healthy dose of paternalistic sentiment. "This country was made so free that the Chinaman can come in here and set up his wooden god and worship him. No one dare molest him or make him afraid. That . . . is what the boys in blue brought forth in 1861–1865."[44]

Causing far greater aggravation to the West's GAR posts was the region's growing association with socialist, anarchist, and radical labor movements—a trend that veterans frequently likened to the South's disruption to the Union decades earlier. To be sure, many members did not consider labor complaints to be wholly unfounded and occasionally critiqued capitalist excesses. One Portland post, for instance, believed it was the responsibility of employers to be "open to unselfish improvement of the masses." However, veterans rarely tolerated vigorous worker protests and their perceived threat to national stability. In the wake of the Homestead steel strike in 1894, for instance, Oregon's GAR department pledged to protect "the country for which he [the veteran] once periled so much," and promised to "oppose all violent, anarchical and revolutionary movements tending to the subversion of our free institutions." A mounting source of irritation for the region's veterans was the burgeoning strength of the Industrial Workers of the World (IWW, or "Wobblies"). Founded in 1905, the labor union pledged to organize workers across a host of industries and proudly aimed "to do away with capitalism." The IWW garnered particular strength in the Far West where discontented workers in the mining, lumber, and fishing industries sought redress. For Grand Army veterans, a radical organization that sought to form "the structure of [a] new society within the shell of the old" sounded too reminiscent of the Confederacy's rebellion.[45]

As IWW demonstrations proliferated across the West Coast during the early twentieth century, the GAR vehemently voiced their opposition. Responding to IWW protests in Spokane in 1909, local posts urged city authorities to "maintain peace and good government," decried the "horde of aliens, anarchists and hoboes" in the city, and pledged the same "readiness that we did to that of our beloved and honored President Lincoln, and that we favor ridding our fair city of this disorderly alien and anarchistic element." Another post in San Diego proposed a merciless solution on how to dispense with these elements, urging Congress "to establish upon one of the United States island possessions a penal colony and deport anarchists to it." Weeks later in Oakland, California, three area posts, unwilling to watch certain elements "degrade and trample upon the American flag," passed joint resolutions declaring IWW activities "treasonable and all propagators of such sentiments as unworthy of the privileges they enjoy." On the streets of Portland, self-proclaimed anarchists reportedly insulted the memory of Abraham Lincoln, an action that prompted the local post to lament the "misguided people" who failed to understand that Lincoln's "very soul went out in sympathy for the oppressed."[46]

Western veterans proved equally intolerant of civilians' revisionist interpretations of the Civil War, particularly as they related to questions of race and the emancipationist memory of the conflict. Portland's Lincoln-Garfield Post provides a good case study. During the early twentieth century, the post's members recorded a number of activities that characterize a remarkably consistent concern for both their African American comrades and the Black community broadly. In 1915, the veterans mimicked other GAR posts across the country by endorsing resolutions that condemned *The Birth of a Nation*, charging the film with a "wanton perversion of history." Comrades subsequently formed a committee to meet with the mayor and have the film banned from all city theaters. After the death of Booker T. Washington later that year, the post accepted an invitation from civic leaders to attend integrated memorial services honoring the esteemed educator. At a post meeting five years later, several white comrades commented on African Americans' role during the war and the challenges that they faced afterward. One veteran remembered that southern Blacks "were true good Union soldiers" while another applauded them for setting up their own "cotton compress, banks, [and] stores" even while under discriminatory laws forcing them to "read and write and pay [a] poll tax before they can vote—whites only necessary for [their] Grandfather[s] to have fought for the south in [the] Civil War." By that time, Oregon was becoming a bastion for a resurgent Ku Klux Klan movement in the early 1920s. GAR veterans, however, refused to abide this latest version of Klanism, remembering the hateful legacy it forged decades before. At the 1921 state GAR encampment, aged delegates vilified the Klan as "unAmerican [sic] and unpatriotic" and urged all Oregon veterans to "strongly oppose the revival of this relic of the Southern Confederacy in our state."[47]

As the postwar United States became an interconnected, transcontinental nation, so too did the Grand Army become an interconnected, transcontinental network of local posts. Drawing on a core of demobilized soldiers who had defended the Union's distant borders, the organization rapidly encompassed the many veteran-migrants who sought opportunity and community in the Far West. Here, GAR members promoted civic engagement and inculcated many of the same lessons of the Civil War—devotion to Union, commitment to service, and even, at times, defense of the war's emancipationist legacy—that their comrades in the East instilled. Far more than veterans in the South, those out West enjoyed greater freedom to exalt their Union victory and exercise moral authority among their fellow citizens. Nonetheless, unique regional trends confronted GAR members on the Pacific coast—labor radicalism, Asian immigration, and a rapidly diversifying and restless population—that even the most enlightened old soldiers found, at best, disconcerting and, at worst, disruptive. The reactionary responses that many veterans displayed indicate how much the nation had changed since Appomattox and how their civic-minded and community-building solutions to presumed social disorders did not always triumph.

As the postwar United States reaffirmed its jurisdiction over the defeated South and pushed its sovereignty beyond the boundaries of the 1865 Union, Grand Army posts cropped up and provided both nascent and reconstructing communities with centers of civic outreach and activism. The veterans that belonged to them shared a common interest in demonstrating to their nonveteran neighbors their understanding of the meaning of Union triumph. Further, they invested in reforming their communities, a desire that—depending on the region—shows the strengths and limitations of GAR activism within the larger history of southern and western progressivism. Southern posts faced the greatest obstacles in teaching loyalty, patriotism, and improvement, plagued as they were by low membership and native whites averse to Yankee commemoration and assertive Black posts. On the other hand, the largely homogeneous and northern-bred population of the Great Plains proved largely receptive to GAR influence and placed veteran-migrants in political and civic authority over their new communities. Veterans in the Far West fared less well, although better than their comrades in the South. GAR civic and educational activism made important strides there but was occasionally stymied by the region's confounding labor, immigration, and race issues. Meanwhile, as the United States consolidated its lands from coast-to-coast, Americans increasingly looked beyond the nation's borders and considered their standing in the world. "The imperial projects of the 1890s and early twentieth century," one scholar argues, "plainly owed to experiences in the South, the West, and the southwestern borderlands." As it happened, GAR veterans were at the vanguard of all these projects—seamlessly linking the dissemination of their Union victory's significance across the continental United States to an expansive new interest in doing the same internationally in the realm of foreign affairs.[48]

4 Clasping Hands Across the Sea

The lessons of patriotism taught by the boys of 1861 and 1865 to their offspring have not been lost, and to-day the grand old banner of liberty and freedom, the emblem of humanity and equality floats over the isles of Cuba, Porto Rico and the Philippines; [it] is respected by all the Nations of the world.

—Pennsylvania GAR Department Commander
James F. Morrison, 1899

On May 25, 1884, twenty-six members of Honolulu's George W. De Long Post filed soberly into Fort Street Church. Awaiting them were King David Kalākaua, his cabinet, US diplomats, visiting comrades from the mainland, and a large body of Native Hawaiians. All had gathered for memorial services to do "fitting honor to the memory of the brave men who periled their lives in defence [sic] of country, liberty and equality." Speaking before the assembled, comrade John A. Cruzan boldly proclaimed that "[t]he Union Army did not fight for America only, nor for the deliverance of slaves on our own soil alone, but, for Liberty everywhere. That every bondman on the globe might have hope! That every patriot might rejoice. That every traitor, and every oppressor on the whole earth and in all coming time might tremble and be ashamed." Five days later, beneath palm fronds and sunny skies, many of the same attendees marched to Nuuanu Cemetery, where six GAR comrades lay buried, and sanctified "the last resting place for the patriotic soldiers and sailors who may 'fall on sleep' in this distant land." In the evening, post member Alfred S. Hartwell delivered an emancipationist address about the Civil War's legacy. "What the South wanted was certainly a separate government in order to perpetuate their institution of Negro slaves," he confirmed. "Their leaders knew that if they stayed in the Union, slavery was doomed." Although Hartwell admitted the war began as a fight to halt southern secession, he rejoiced that "[i]t resulted at last in a war for freedom, as well as for Union." Since then, the United States had fulfilled its lofty claims to liberty and now stood strengthened in the eyes of the world. "The flag of the Union," he concluded, "now as never before the war—commands respect the world over."[1]

Grand Army veterans became eager advocates of turn-of-the-century US imperial and commercial expansion abroad, perceiving America's increasingly assertive standing in the world as the consummation of their Union victory. Members trusted that their GAR-endorsed memory of the Civil War, grounded in the principles for which they fought a generation earlier—democratic government, representative institutions, free labor ideology, and universal freedom—was widely applicable to foreign lands and peoples (with appropriate US guidance and edification). Meanwhile, they believed that this interventionist objective to recreate the world in America's image simultaneously bolstered these important doctrines at home, safeguarding social order and progress, while resisting an unwelcome descent to sectional reconciliationism. GAR comrades were often in the vanguard of US expansionism themselves, arriving in extracontinental territories and foreign countries as missionaries of democracy and transplanting the chief venue of veterans' outreach and activism—the Grand Army post—internationally. As the GAR forged a global network of interconnected posts, members back home observed a range of freedom struggles in Latin America with interest and often advocated US humanitarian and military intervention to promote these efforts. By the time the Spanish-American War broke out in 1898, many Union veterans construed the conflict as the culmination of a hemispheric struggle for liberty and self-determination rather than (as it became for many white Americans) the fulfillment of post–Civil War North-South reconciliation.

Understanding the Grand Army's role at the turn of the century requires examination of the group's community activism alongside its members' attitudes toward foreign interventionism. Progressive Era reform, in other words, occurred within the context of an imperial age and it is vital to consider how each influenced the other. Scholars have long portrayed the progressive movement as expansive enough to include activists with a wide variety of beliefs about US imperialism. In the mid-twentieth century, William E. Leuchtenburg contended that imperialism and progressivism in fact thrived symbiotically because each embodied "a worship of definitive action for action's sake" in the "overarching democratic mission of America." More recently, historians have shown how pro-imperial sentiments furthered the aims of an eclectic range of progressive activists and that war and intervention abroad provided a distinct opportunity to fast-track reform efforts at home. Along these lines, imperialism offered a chance for many US progressives to legitimize and execute domestic social improvement aims by encouraging similar reform, "civilization," and moral uplift efforts (with all their attendant racist and paternalist implications) around the world. As one scholar has argued, progressives sought to globally institutionalize the "principles of democracy and republican government" as a way of "regenerating the world." As it happens, there were few better candidates than GAR veterans—the very men who regenerated the United States by reaffirming liberty, order, and democracy in the 1860s—to support the same in American interventionist activities abroad at the turn of the twentieth century. By disseminating what they viewed as the benefits of Union victory internationally, these proselytizers of patriotism expressed the complementary nature of Progressive Era community reform and muscular foreign policy—even as this impulse furthered imperial America's culpability in race-based inequities, economic coercion, and the denial of sovereignty in its relationships with nations and peoples in the Caribbean, Latin America, and the Pacific.[2]

The first section below analyzes the largely forgotten Grand Army activities outside the continental United States and the ways in which Union veterans implicitly and explicitly facilitated the commercial, cultural, and geopolitical objectives of the aggressively expanding United States. Spurred by restlessness, adventure, and the prospect of wealth, these veterans sought postwar opportunities outside the nation they had saved. Nevertheless, they carried with them the lessons learned in war, often promulgating to the native-born population of these lands what they viewed as the universally applicable interpretations of Union victory. Here, the GAR's most distant posts became the social centers of expatriate American communities from which US norms, values, and traditions emanated—and, more invasively, from which imperial-minded commercial exploitation and territorial annexation found a foothold. The second section investigates GAR members' attitudes and activities surrounding America's growing presence in the Western Hemisphere as late century conflicts in Latin America convinced many veterans to view their own wartime sacrifices as the inspiration for a new round of freedom and self-determination struggles in neighboring countries. Culminating with the Spanish-American War, many Union veterans employed Civil War–era rhetoric to drum up support for "enslaved" Cubans against their colonial Spanish overlords—a tactic at odds with some of the nation's wider reconciliationist symbolism shared between white northerners and white southerners who were then going off together to fight a new war. The conflict also provided the veterans with their first significant opportunity to inspire the next generation of citizen-soldiers and fulfill the role of their communities' patriotic paragons. The final section examines the interaction between the GAR and returning Spanish-American War veterans. Although the relationship was often cordial, serious debate ensued over the appropriateness of incorporating the young men (and their reconciliationist inclinations) into a fraternity stubbornly insistent on upholding Union victory as the worthiest US military honor.

Carrying the Flag of Progress

By the time Grand Army rolls peaked circa 1890, Union veterans had grown accustomed to hearing how their sacrifices preserved a nation whose might and influence only accelerated after Appomattox. At encampments, rallies, and commemorative events, veterans and nonveterans alike praised GAR members for their role in enabling the United States to stand among the great powers of the world. "Whatever our nation has since enjoyed in its growth and prosperity, is the fruit of your labor," commended Minneapolis Mayor George A. Pillsbury at the 1884 national encampment. "Without your efforts free Government would have been a failure, and we could not have . . . gazed on a rapidly growing and extending nation." Four years later, California GAR officer Edward S. Salomon, concluded that his comrades were "entirely different from the soldiers and sailors of any other country in the world" and praised them for fighting "to keep together the grandest Union ever devised by human brains, and in order that the down-trodden and oppressed of all nations could find an asylum and escape from the terror of tyranny and oppression."[3]

Paeans like these were noteworthy, as they bound together Grand Army veterans' Union victory with the nation's late century expansionist currents—not only across the continent, but also, increasingly, around the world. In the quarter century after the war's end, the surge of western homesteaders (many of whom were veterans) and the intensified investment in ranching, lumbering, mining, and other extractive industries firmly knit the West into an integrated, continent-spanning US commercial powerhouse. Meanwhile, the Census Bureau declared in 1890 that the frontier was closed, alarming many who viewed westward migration as the key to the nation's strength and vitality. When added to the era's myriad social and economic pressures—financial panics, a widening wealth gap, labor strikes, agrarian unrest, an influx of immigrants, and more—Americans grew worried about the stagnation of the country's dynamism and the erosion of its democratic institutions.

To remedy these concerns, a host of policymakers, industrialists, and intellectuals asserted that the nation's continued wellbeing required muscular foreign policy, an aggressive stance with roots going back decades. Just two years after the Civil War, Secretary of State William Seward acquired Alaska from the Russian Empire, raising the prospect that now-enveloped western Canada might someday fall to American takeover. Republican veteran-presidents Grant, Hayes, and Garfield maneuvered to either develop trade with or even annex regions in the Caribbean, Latin America, and the Pacific, and assertively pursued favorable commercial ties in the Far East. Meanwhile, many American entrepreneurs and business leaders considered these peripheral regions to be untapped frontiers for new ventures and markets to unload growing surpluses. With US continental development matured and industrial output booming, Americans now turned to international expansion, particularly in the realms of investment and trade, to augment the nation's prosperity.[4]

Union veterans often stood at the forefront of postwar US contact with foreign lands and peoples, laying the groundwork for new social, cultural, and commercial relationships. Concurrently, they transplanted the GAR post—with its attendant traditions and activities—abroad, just as their comrades back home were tending to the sophisticated network of posts already affixed across the continental United States. For instance, the allure of opportunity, adventure, and gold attracted a few Union veterans to Alaska after its acquisition. In 1889, thirteen charter members established the first post in the territory—Juneau's Seward Post—followed by two other short-lived posts in Sitka and Nome. Particularly around the turn of the century, GAR officers heralded the Alaskan posts for the good effect they had in Americanizing what they viewed as a virgin and underdeveloped land. At the 1902 national encampment, for example, attendees boasted that "in the territory of Alaska the seeds of loyalty are being planted by the scattering hands of the G.A.R." Indeed, newspaper reports frequently mentioned Seward Post's Memorial Day exercises and the patriotic instruction it offered Alaska's schoolchildren. Meanwhile, when the wives and daughters of Juneau's veterans organized a Woman's Relief Corps (WRC) auxiliary, their civic and charitable activities earned praiseworthy coverage. Formed in 1897 to alleviate the "great suffering among the gold miners" in the region, the corps received plaudits the following year for raising one hundred dollars and forwarding it to California's Red Cross Society during the Spanish-American War. Although Alaska veterans were always small in number, local newspapers continued to report on their activities well into the twentieth century.[5]

Grand Army members proved more numerous, active, and influential in Hawaii, becoming key collaborators in cementing the islands' ever-tightening political and commercial bonds with the United States. Evidence suggests that many veterans there thrived financially and became part of Hawaii's American elite. Often, they had colorful histories themselves. The globetrotting, one-armed veteran James D. Arnold mustered out of Civil War service in Pittsburgh, then spent time in Montana prospecting for precious metals. Later, he voyaged regularly between Honolulu and Queensland, where he was employed by the Australian government in drilling artesian wells to irrigate the continent's arid interior. Charles H. Dickey returned from the war to work initially as a telegraph operator in his native Illinois. Later settling in Honolulu, Dickey used his technical expertise to establish the first commercial telegraph line in 1875 and, four years later, the first telephone on the islands. Honored at the time of his death as "a progressive power in [Hawaii's] civic activities," Dickey served in the Hawaii senate and belonged to Honolulu's Mission Children's Society, Anti-Saloon League, and Civic Federation.[6]

These men, along with many of their comrades on the Hawaiian Islands, established in 1882 the George W. De Long Post—the GAR's first extracontinental chapter (see Figure 8). Named for a US Navy officer who died the previous year on an ill-fated voyage to the North Pole, the post and its roughly forty charter members received the enthusiastic sanction of veterans stateside. The *National Tribune* boasted that these men "are always to be found in the van, in the march of civilization, carrying the flag of progress as of old they bore the flag of freedom." For their part, De Long Post, at least initially, enjoyed the goodwill and cooperation of Hawaiian royalty, particularly King Kalākaua. It was Kalākaua, for instance, who authorized the formation of a GAR post in his realm ("a peculiarly American association in a foreign country" remarked a local newspaper) and donated cannons for placement in Nuuanu Cemetery's designated GAR plot. When Queen Emma (wife of the former King Kamehameha IV) died in 1885, De Long Post members occupied a conspicuous place in the funeral procession. The veterans in turn invited Hawaiian royals and their subjects to attend post events. When Robert Henry Hendershot—the so-called "Drummer Boy of the Rappahannock"—visited Honolulu to perform his rousing fife and drum concert, De Long Post veterans and Queen Kapiʻolani equally relished his playing of "A Life on the Ocean Wave." Meanwhile, post veterans encouraged Native Hawaiians' participation during annual Memorial Day ceremonies—a gesture that inherently involved an ulterior motive to use commemorative pageantry to help inculcate American values over the islands.[7]

Indeed, GAR veterans had a hand in consummating the decades-long move to forcibly bring Hawaii and its lucrative sugar industry under US control, simultaneously depriving Native Hawaiians of their rights, stripping the monarchy of

Figure 8 Members of the George W. De Long Post of Honolulu, Hawaii, pose among several American flags, not long after the 1898 US annexation of the Hawaiian Islands. Some of these Union veterans played a direct role in undermining the power of the Native Hawaiian monarchy and laying the groundwork for US takeover of the kingdom. *Pacific Commercial Advertiser* [Honolulu, Hawaiian Islands], 31 May 1909. Courtesy of Chronicling America, Historic American Newspapers, Library of Congress.

its power, and firmly sealing white business leaders' supremacy over the population. When a mostly white cabal coerced Kalākaua into signing the so-called "Bayonet Constitution" in 1887, limiting the king's authority and consolidating power behind the government's legislature and cabinet, several prominent Union veterans were behind the maneuver. At least two De Long Post members were involved in writing the constitution, while fellow comrade Volney V. Ashford led the all-white Honolulu Rifles company (thus providing the military coercion for Kalākaua to accede to the document). Similarly, Union veterans were among the conspirators in the 1893 overthrow of Kalākaua's sister and successor Liliʻuokalani. De Long Post member William C. Winder, for instance, joined Sanford B. Dole's American-led provisional government and participated in early annexation negotiations with the United States. Over the next few years, Grand Army veterans rallied to show US policymakers that annexation of the islands was the next logical step. In 1894, sixteen De Long Post comrades made the arduous trek to the GAR national encampment in Pittsburgh, with intent to "carry the flag of the Hawaiian republic alongside the folds of Old Glory"—doubtless attempting to solidify in observers' minds the closeness of the two nations' governments. Three years later, De Long Post added its name to a proclamation issued by Hawaii's Sons of the American Revolution, urging the United States "to secure this outpost of its western frontier . . . for the sake of maintaining and extending American principles at this central meeting place of races." Veterans achieved their goal with the elevation of fellow comrade William McKinley, whose administration formally annexed Hawaii in 1898—a prominent example of how GAR activists could deftly fuse the memory of Union victory, paternalistic interest in foreign peoples' edification, and rapacious commercial expansionism.[8]

More than any other region outside the continental United States, Canada boasted a prominent and active Grand Army membership that furthered postwar friendship between the two nations. This international accord was not necessarily inevitable. During the Civil War, relations with British Canada soured during a number of high-profile incidents that suggested the Crown's initial, tacit support for the Confederacy. Meanwhile, some areas in Canada and the Maritimes sympathized with southerners, providing a safe haven for the launch of rebel raids on US soil and conspiratorial schemes against the Lincoln government. By the end of the war, some US officials held their northern neighbor under suspicion, demanding purchase of all or part of Canadian territory to satisfy wartime affronts. Although voices supporting annexation diminished by the late nineteenth century, occasional utterances from jingoes flared up. One GAR officer, for instance, boldly insisted that "the part [of Canada] that is worth anything is ready to come to us whenever we want it, without any war." Despite the fraught relationship, the participation of Canadian citizens in the Union Cause was, in fact, significant. In the decade before the Civil War, some 100,000 Canadians crossed the permeable border for work and other opportunities. Many of these itinerants remained in the United States after war broke out and enlisted (the vast majority for the North, but a few for the Confederacy). Despite Parliament's passage of the Foreign Enlistment Act, which prohibited British citizens from joining militaries abroad, significant numbers left Canada after 1861 to join the US armed forces. All told, between 35,000 and 50,000 Canadians and Maritimers enlisted for Civil War service in at least 500 individual Union regiments (and nearly fifty Confederate regiments).[9]

It is little wonder then that Grand Army posts sprang up in the country, comprised of either Canadians who returned home after their service or Americans who sought postwar opportunities abroad. Between 1889 and 1896, Union veterans chartered at least six GAR posts in Canada—three in Ontario (Toronto, Hamilton, and London); two in Quebec (Montreal and Coaticook); and one in Manitoba (Winnipeg). Despite their establishment on foreign soil, these posts demonstrated many of the same functions and interests as their counterparts in the United States. Montreal's Hancock Post, for instance, maintained a relief fund for destitute veterans and their dependents "to alleviate their distress in the dominion of Canada" and transplanted US-inspired Memorial Day commemorations at local cemeteries. In 1896, the tiny post in Coaticook similarly conducted a memorial service despite having just two graves to decorate. Meanwhile, Canadian posts exhibited other fundamentally Americanized displays. In 1900, Hancock Post received government permission to host a public Fourth of July celebration, reportedly the first of its kind on Canadian soil. The following year, grieving comrades in Hamilton's William W. Cooke Post led a memorial program for slain president William McKinley at a local church. Besides offering camaraderie for veterans in a land that had not directly shared the experience of the Civil War, the posts nonetheless organized civic events that asserted veteran heroism and sacrifice for a cause naturally less meaningful to the general Canadian populace.[10]

The posts also provided the best means for veterans in Canada to obtain service pensions to which they were entitled but had difficulty securing. All Union veterans, whatever their US citizenship status, were eligible for these benefits. Nonetheless, they faced a number of predictable obstacles—less dissemination of pension law information, limited access to pension agents, and more arduous travel to appear before an examining board. Additionally, the Canadian veteran frequently had more difficulty tracking down fellow comrades in the United States who might supply affidavits on his behalf. Fortunately, Canada's Grand Army posts provided determined advocacy for their members. When Congress briefly prohibited pensions to non-US citizens in 1893, Canada's posts rallied in opposition. Hamilton's post decried the bill as "obnoxious" while Winnipeg's repeatedly forwarded resolutions to congressional pension committees to restore the benefits. Responding to this outcry, Congress rescinded the bill two years later, prompting Montreal's Hancock Post members to write their American counterparts that "[i]t would make your heart happy" to see "broken-down comrades being reinstated on the rolls after being suspended and wrongfully deprived of their pensions for nearly two years." In some posts, a well-connected member might advocate on behalf of his comrades, supplying knowledge about pension regulations, offering advice, and forwarding applications to pension committees in Washington, D.C. Harper Wilson, a GAR officer in Winnipeg, became a tireless supporter for veterans in Manitoba and western Canada. Local newspapers frequently reported how Wilson distributed information about the latest pension provisions, prepared pension applications for comrades free of charge, and even assured veterans considering settling in the country that there would "be no trouble about getting their pensions paid to them in Canada."[11]

More than a few of these Canadian GAR veterans were Black, demonstrating that the organization's integrationist principles even transcended US borders. Estimates suggest that around 2,500 Black men across Canada and the Maritimes served in the Union military. Although some of these individuals were native-born, many were fugitives from southern slavery or freeborn northern Blacks fleeing discrimination. Whatever their origins, a devotion to the Union Cause carried over into their postwar lives, as evidenced by Black membership in Canada's GAR posts. Although Canadian post records are scanty, enough evidence survives to prove the existence of not only integrated posts, but even Blacks holding leadership positions. The Virginia-born Oliver Fountain, for instance, enlisted in a United States Colored Troop (USCT) unit in July 1863, rising to the rank of sergeant. An early member of Hannibal Hamlin Post in London, Ontario, Fountain served for a time as the post's surgeon—an important role that often encompassed caring for sick and destitute comrades and their families. Anderson Abbott (see Figure 9), prominent as the first African Canadian to become a licensed physician, was born in Toronto to freeborn parents who had fled intolerable conditions in their native Alabama. After receiving his medical license, Abbott ultimately secured a position as a contracted civilian surgeon in 1863, resigning from US service three years later. He returned to Toronto after the war, occupying the position of surgeon in the city's local post and was later selected aide-de-camp to the New York Department commander. In a 1907 speech, Abbott affirmed the emancipatory aims of the Civil War, declaring that he and every comrade of the GAR had taken part in offering "to the humblest citizen . . . whether he lives under the protecting folds of the red cross of St. George, or the glorious star spangled banner, the blessings of peace, civil and religious liberty and in giving to the world a higher conception of the value of human liberty."[12]

The Canadian posts also shared occasional joint events with their US counterparts, fostering closer ties and friendship between the two nations. Members of Winnipeg's post attended the 1896 national encampment in St. Paul, Minnesota, flaunting a "Union Jack . . . carried along with the Stars and Stripes." Three years later, the Department of Vermont selected Montreal as the site of its annual state encampment, marking the first time that such an event was held

Figure 9 Reputedly the first African Canadian to become a licensed physician, Toronto-born Anderson Abbott served the Union Cause as a surgeon during the Civil War. Returning to Canada after the war and practicing medicine there, Abbott joined Toronto's James S. Knowlton Post in which he occupied the office of post surgeon. Courtesy of Baldwin Collection of Canadiana, Toronto Public Library.

on foreign soil. Serving as host was the city's Hancock Post who feted "a peaceful invasion" of several hundred Vermont veterans, their families, and British and Canadian military officers. Through the course of the affair, the veterans announced resolutions that hailed "the increasing friendliness between the two great English-speaking nations of the world," and closed with a military band playing the shared melody of "God Save the Queen" and "My Country, 'Tis of

Thee." Perhaps more than any other display of international goodwill between two posts was the affection between comrades of Cooke Post of Hamilton, Ontario, and Chapin Post of Buffalo, New York. The veterans, separated by fewer than a hundred miles, frequently traded invitations around the turn of the century to take part in important civic events. In 1898, at the invitation of Cooke Post, veterans of Chapin Post participated in the unveiling of a soldiers' and sailors' monument at Hamilton Cemetery. Returning the favor, Chapin Post invited the Canadian veterans to Buffalo the following year to celebrate Queen Victoria's eightieth birthday. The veterans marched together through the city streets, with "British and United States flags mingl[ing] in union, and everywhere the good feeling between Anglo-Saxons . . . visible." All told, displays like these contributed to the nurturing of peace between the two nations.[13]

Union veterans migrated across America's southern border as well, joining a US enclave in Mexico City that exercised substantial influence over the country's economic development. Of course, some of the first Civil War soldiers to migrate to Mexico were ex-Confederates—first, individuals fleeing the threat of federal prosecution, and then a more organized exodus of southerners seeking colonies to settle permanently. These migrants, however, were relatively few in number and had little long-term success sustaining their communities. More influential was the later movement of Union veterans alongside other American migrants attracted to business and investment opportunities in Mexico. The ensuing formation of a thriving American colony in Mexico City coincided with the latter years of Porfirio Díaz's regime (1876–1911). Díaz, whose presidency encouraged the infusion of American investment and capital, developed a warm regard for Union veterans. When several forwarded an appeal to Díaz in 1891 seeking authorization to charter a new GAR post, the president responded cordially. "It is a pleasure for me to answer you that the fundamental law of the nation expressly guarantees the right to foreigners to meet together and associate for every lawful purpose whatsoever," Díaz affirmed, adding that he "heartily congratulate[s] you on your purpose of inaugurating the beneficent organization."[14]

The result was the chartering of Edward O. C. Ord Post, which maintained a healthy membership in the American enclave and an amicable relationship with the Mexican government for many years. Typically, well-to-do colonists controlled the leadership of Ord Post, using their membership to advance their social and economic clout in a foreign land. Colonel William J. DeGress, for example, leveraged his conspicuous Civil War service into prominent positions in the transnational railroad and arms manufacturing industries (even supplying Díaz with matériel). By the 1880s, DeGress became superintendent of various

Mexican rail lines and was appointed consul to the then-kingdom of Hawaii. Similarly, John C. Mordough arrived in Mexico in 1881 to oversee the Mexican National Railroad's company stores, before branching out into finance and the country's extractive industries. By the early twentieth century, Mordough had acquired vast wealth while serving as an officer in the United States-Mexican Trust Company. Still, Ord Post's broader membership was by no means dominated by the American colony's business elites. Some veterans more closely qualified as part of the community's petty bourgeois, using the connections developed in civic organizations like the GAR to foster respectability in the enclave. One was Peter J. Rising, an Ord Post charter member, who died in 1893 while employed as a railway auditor. Another was Henry W. Howe, a dentist by profession, who arrived in Mexico City around 1891 and spent the remaining two decades of his life there.[15]

Despite the Díaz regime's notable achievements in modernization, the comparatively prosperous era was also marked by rural unrest, working-class grievances, and growing antipathy to foreigners' interventions. GAR veterans likely exacerbated tensions. For instance, Ord Post enjoyed the president's approval to observe Memorial Day at Mexico City's American Cemetery, with Díaz even providing a staff band to assist the post with their memorial services. In return, Union veterans fired salutes on Cinco de Mayo and laid a wreath each year at the monument to the Mexican cadets who fell in defense of the castle at Chapultepec in 1847. Although the gestures indicate the depth to which Díaz and the American colony fostered mutual accommodation in their respective commemorative objectives, to many Mexicans the curious comingling of memorial traditions highlighted the unwelcome invasion of parasitic *yanquis*. Meanwhile, most Ord Post veterans appeared to rally behind the increasingly embattled Díaz, even after the fraudulent election of 1910 that fomented the beginning of the Mexican Revolution. One veteran, J. J. Fitzgerrell, admonished the "yellow press" in the United States for exaggerating reports of uprisings throughout Mexico. Fitzgerrell claimed that there were only "a few rioters" who would be "promptly suppressed" and assured those stateside that "[a]ll the Americans doing business in Mexico...are attending to their business as usual." Although the fate of individual Ord Post members during the Mexican Revolution is difficult to determine, many Americans in the colony sought refuge in the United States during the chaotic 1910s. Some of the post's veterans fled Mexico and resettled in the western states, particularly California. Enough of the members lived around Los Angeles that they received a special permit to hold their meetings there—marking an effective end to the post's influence on affairs in the American enclave in Mexico City.[16]

Akin to Ord Post members in Mexico, commercial interests in Peru attracted Union veterans who established a Grand Army post in perhaps the most far-flung locale of all. Since the end of the Civil War, the United States steadily increased trade with the South American nation (importing Peruvian guano, nitrates, precious metals, and wool) while American entrepreneurs invested heavily in infrastructure and mining initiatives. During the War of the Pacific (1879–1883), the US sympathized with Peru (assigning former Union army General Stephen A. Hurlbut as minister in Lima). After its decisive defeat by Chile, the Peruvian government sought to stabilize its reeling economy with American capital—an opportunity that a number of adventurous Union veterans pursued. Jacob Backus, a New York veteran and nephew of prominent railroad promoter Henry Meiggs, arrived in Peru with his uncle soon after the war. After Meiggs's death in 1877, Backus struck out on his own, establishing with a business partner the Backus and Johnston Brewery in Lima in 1879. The entrepreneur next succeeded in planting a mining and smelting operation high in the Andes at Casapalca a decade later. Similarly, the Boston-born veteran Alfred F. Sears entered Peru's national corps of engineers, inspected fledgling railroads, and headed the country's irrigation commission.[17]

Backus, Sears, and a score of other American expatriates in Peru replicated the example of their compatriots in the United States and established a Grand Army post in their adopted land. The chief organizer was Pennsylvania-born Henry Carty who had lived in Peru for some twenty years, married a native-born woman, and sought "to bring these [Union veteran] exiles more closely together and to perpetuate in Peru the memory of the brave deeds of the Grand Army by organizing . . . a Post." Formally chartered in 1890 in Lima, this chapter "in the land of the Incas and of Pizarro" became known as Abraham Lincoln Post and affiliated with the Department of Pennsylvania. To be sure, the post was not as active as many of its stateside counterparts—some members did not live in the capital while others were frequently away on business. Formal meetings occurred just twice each year (although always, pointedly, on the Fourth of July). Still, the Lincoln Post's few surviving records suggest a proud and close-knit membership whose veterans persevered in remaining patriotic Americans in this distant land. The veterans published a post organ, the *Peruvian Outpost*; hosted a reception for officers of US battleships fresh off their 1898 victory at the Battle of Santiago de Cuba; and, despite one comrade's announcement that the veterans' wives were "mostly of this country and speak Spanish," nonetheless boasted a WRC auxiliary. As the Lincoln Post demonstrates, wherever the United States developed postwar commercial or territorial ambitions, Union veterans (and, subsequently, GAR posts) often followed.[18]

As the United States increasingly asserted its imperial and commercial aims across the Western Hemisphere during the late nineteenth and early twentieth centuries, ambitious and adventurous Union veterans were part of the migratory movement that brought Americans into direct contact with foreign governments and peoples. In some cases, the relationship was cordial, even deferent, especially in Canada where GAR veterans encountered other inhabitants of European descent. Elsewhere, particularly in Latin America and Hawaii, primarily Anglo veteran-migrants often exercised culturally and commercially exploitative relationships with Native populations, even as they proclaimed that their presence brought order, progress, and liberty to underdeveloped parts of the world. In a range of extracontinental locations, Union veterans transplanted their GAR posts that formed the basis of expatriates' social activity and the centers from which they diffused notions of Americanized values and traditions. All told, the GAR-endorsed memory of Union victory transcended national boundaries and proved a useful instrument when wielded on behalf of US imperial ambitions.

Liberty Will Be the Rule

As GAR clout extended internationally with the establishment of extracontinental posts, veterans back home closely observed the U.S. government's increasingly expansionist currents. By late century, American foreign policy assumed a more muscular bent, reasserting the intent of the 1823 Monroe Doctrine. Fortifying this age-old doctrine with a new combativeness, the United States staked out much of the Western Hemisphere as its sphere of influence, to remain unimpeded by European encroachment. For their part, many Grand Army members acceded to the nation's growing responsibilities and burgeoning status in the world, staying keenly aware of developments in foreign affairs. At a public event hosted by Minnesota's Acker Post in 1896, comrade Charles D. Kerr declared that if "Americans opposed to the Monroe doctrine…prevail, we should turn [the Statue of Liberty] face about and have it gazing in over the land instead of out over the sea, and inscribe on it: 'We have a good thing here. Let us keep it and let the rest of mankind go to the devil.' But I say to you this is not my kind of patriotism." The *National Tribune* also remained a staunch advocate of promoting US hegemony over the hemisphere. "Unless we want to see the European nations divide up South America among them as they have done Africa and a great part of Asia," the *Tribune* warned, "we will insist obstinately upon the Monroe Doctrine." Linking the doctrine to the nation's foundational principles, the organ added that it was "no more a subject of arbitration than the Declaration of Independence or the Constitutional Amendments."[19]

Meanwhile, rank-and-file Grand Army members—Black and white—remained well-informed about developments in Latin America, connecting the emancipationist outcome of the Civil War to freedom struggles emerging elsewhere in the Western Hemisphere. In 1887, the all-Black John A. Andrew Post and Thaddeus Stevens Post joined with other members of New York City's African American community in celebrating the recent abolition of slavery in Cuba. Marching alongside "colored Cubans" from the local Odd Fellows lodge, the veterans paraded into the Bethel A.M.E. Church where luminaries from the United States, Liberia, and the Caribbean presided over the event. Attendees passed resolutions celebrating "with the greatest possible appreciation and joy, the emancipation of our kinsmen of the Isle of Cuba." Still, the celebrants were not silent about the racial injustices that persisted in the United States, using the opportunity to declare "that there yet remains a pressing need of an emancipation for our brothers, in this, our own country."[20]

White veterans, too, rejoiced at the extension of liberty abroad, but demonstrated much less cognizance about enduring discrimination against Blacks at home. When Brazil at last abolished slavery in 1888 and its monarchy gave way to a republic the following year, GAR veterans in Michigan could not help but discern their own influence on the events. Department Commander Michael Brown cheered that Brazil had "emerged from her thralldom, and the people started on the road to freedom." Further, Brown credited the veterans before him for inspiring other peoples around the world to strike at despotism. "[I]f the glorious history of the United States of America had not been written," he averred, "the government of the United States of Brazil would never have been known. It may be that the influence of the example of the comrades . . . will go on and on, until sometime in the future liberty will be the rule." Meanwhile, some white comrades exhibited a fundamental misinterpretation of the inherent cruelty of slavery in the US South that perhaps contributed to a minimization of the postwar plight of African Americans compared with enslaved Blacks elsewhere. At an event held by an all-Black Philadelphia post, invited speaker and prominent white GAR officer St. Clair A. Mulholland claimed that southern slavery "was liberty as compared with slavery in Cuba." In the South, Mulholland alleged that a slave was "valued and cared for" whereas in Cuba he was "merely a beast of burden."[21]

As Black and white Union veterans observed and interpreted these late century freedom crusades, they discerned America's important role in preserving the self-determination of fellow republics in the hemisphere. Perhaps more than any event in the region predating the Spanish-American War, Grand Army members took particular interest in the boundary dispute between Venezuela and the British colony of Guiana (now Guyana). The quarrel tested US commitment to protecting the sovereignty of Latin American nations and fending off European intrusions. President Grover Cleveland and Secretary of State Richard Olney eyed arbitrating an agreement between the two aggrieved nations in 1895. When Britain initially declined interest in such a course, Cleveland moved to appoint a commission anyway to settle the boundary dispute, whose report the United States would uphold with force if necessary. The conflict provided Olney with an opportunity to reinforce the Monroe Doctrine, declaring that the United States had "made it clear to Great Britain and to the world that the controversy is one in which its honor and its interests are involved." Cleveland's tough stance resonated with Grand Army veterans, who provided the Democratic administration with their uncharacteristic praise. One Nebraska post "heartily indorse[d] the patriotic utterances of President Cleveland . . . regarding the enforcement of the Monroe doctrine . . . commending him for nobly standing up for Americanism, and assuring him that the Grand Army is with him in this matter." Elsewhere, GAR posts pledged their aging members' services to the president in the event of war against Britain.[22]

On the heels of Olney's decree, Minnesota senator and Grand Army veteran Cushman K. Davis issued his own resolution reaffirming the Monroe Doctrine, insisting that no European power could acquire territory in South America and that any such movement would be viewed as "an unfriendly disposition toward the United States." Further, Davis suggested that congressional legislation should firmly codify the doctrine's principles. GAR response was enthusiastic. The Culver Post members in Duluth drafted resolutions in support of their comrade. Agitated by the attempt of a "foreign power to extend a form of Government hereditary in its nature" over "our sister Republic Venezuela," the post promised Davis "unfaltering support in the position he has taken, to secure the enactment of the Monroe Doctrine into a fundamental law of the Republic." Iowa veterans similarly stood ready not only to preserve US foreign policy prowess, but also the independence of Latin American peoples. After commending policymakers for their "promulgation of the Monroe Doctrine" in recent affairs in the region, a committee of state-level officers also advocated "a broad and liberal view towards those who are struggling to rise above king, prince or potentate."

Even GAR Commander in Chief Ivan N. Walker rallied the organization in support of the nation's developing role as guardian of the hemisphere. "The world must understand," Walker stated, "that the flag of America is broad enough and long enough to wave, not only above the States, but above the republics of South America." Walker further warned that if Britain ever again sought "to set up her banner across the legitimate boundaries in Venezuela," it would find "our cannon [and] the brave old flag of America."[23]

As the Venezuelan boundary dispute went to arbitration, Americans' inflamed passions next turned to Cuba, whose people sought to throw off the shackles of Spanish colonialism. Since the 1860s, a series of liberation wars weakened Spain's hold over the island. By century's end, American investments in Cuba's sugar and tobacco industries intensified (as did some US expansionists' interests in annexing the island outright) just as Cuban-independence activists revived their revolutionary militancy. The rebels' stunning successes resulted in the elevation of Spanish General Valeriano Weyler y Nicolau to suppress the uprising. Weyler garnered notoriety for his methods, which included executions, scorched-earth techniques, and the creation of deadly concentration camps designed to separate noncombatants from insurgents. Enraged Grand Army veterans flooded their representatives with resolutions supporting "*Cuba Libre.*" Senator John T. Morgan reported in March 1896 that among the many Americans who "had expressed their views of Cuban belligerency and independence by a great deluge of petitions and memorials" were the nation's Grand Army posts. That same month, Minnesota politician and GAR officer Samuel R. Van Sant asserted before a veterans' campfire that although he did not foresee a war with Spain, Americans would nonetheless "break the yoke of slavery and oppression that the Spanish government had forged with Cuba." Even Cuba's own independence advocates perceived the GAR as an ally. Rafael Navarro, treasurer of the Cuban Army Sanitary Corps, flattered GAR veterans for "the returns of contributions from members of that organization in the different states," expecting that no other group would "respond more promptly than the patriotic body called the 'Grand Army of the Republic.'"[24]

As reports of violence and atrocities in Cuba filled US newspapers, GAR calls for intervention escalated. When news of the death of Cuban guerilla leader Antonio Maceo Grajales reached Pittsburgh's posts in December 1896, one steely veteran vowed that "[i]f this is true, we will all go to the aid of the Cubans." By the following year, GAR post meetings and state department events became wellsprings of support for Cuban independence. During a visit to San Francisco's Lincoln Post, California Department Commander T. C. Mastellar announced his sympathy for Cuba's fight and urged his fellow veterans to take a leading role in establishing a branch of the Cuban League in the city. "I sympathize heartily with the Cubans in their struggle," Mastellar proclaimed, "and believe that the moral support of this Government should be given them in their fight for freedom." At the 1897 department encampment in Nebraska, attendees passed "a resolution of sympathy" for the Cubans and requested their state's representatives "to favor any measure looking to their independence." At the Ohio encampment in Chillicothe, veterans declared a broad claim for the sovereign rights of all peoples in the Western Hemisphere. Endorsing the efforts of Cubans "to secure for themselves and their children the right of self-government," the veterans proclaimed that this was "a right inherited in all American countries."[25]

Even after the explosion of the USS *Maine* in Havana Harbor on February 15, 1898, many GAR veterans balanced their long-simmering animosity for Spain with more prudent calls to conduct a full inquiry into the tragedy before committing to hasty action—likely remembering firsthand the great costs of war. Commander in Chief John P. S. Gobin stated that during this time "when the sword is half out of the scabbard," the GAR preferred a thorough investigation into the matter. "If it was an accident," Gobin judged, "amends can be made, but if it is a crime, God help some one who will have to pay the penalty." In Pittsburgh, prominent veterans insisted that if Spanish treachery were the cause of the disaster, they would demand "ample reparation" but placed full confidence in President McKinley's "coolness and firmness" in the difficult days ahead. Elsewhere, rank-and-file GAR veterans refused to submit carelessly to war fever. One Illinois comrade feared "that there is too much of a spirit of revenge and hatred toward Spain by Senators, Congressmen and people. I see no reason why the Gospel of Love commanded us in the Bible should not be as applicable to a Nation as to any individual." Veterans in the nation's capital, meanwhile, verified their "abiding faith ... [in] the government for the prompt and wise action taken to thoroughly investigate and promptly determine the cause of the destruction of the Maine." Not to be taken for pacifists, however, the men added that if "treachery" were discovered, they stood "ready to aid in demanding immediate and unconditional reparation at whatever cost."[26]

Grand Army veterans, a generation removed from their own martial struggle, largely subscribed to a policy of preparedness in the weeks between the *Maine* explosion and the formal declaration of war nine weeks later. Still, some claimed readiness to take up arms again on behalf of the nation. At the New Hampshire encampment in April 1898, veterans cited the "cruel, barbarous, and inhuman manner" in which Spanish authorities were overseeing Cuban noncombatants and resolved "if need be" to "respond to the call of the government by personal service on land and sea, to vindicate its rights and support its demands against the government of Spain." In California, one post presented resolutions to Governor James H. Budd, "requesting a loan of fifty muskets, fifty cartridge boxes or belts, fifty canteens and fifty haversacks, for a period of ninety days, to be used in our Post room for the purpose of drilling the manual of arms, and otherwise fitting ourselves for any emergency that may arise." Fearful that they might "appear a little rusty," the veterans wanted "to burnish up the old drill so as to be able to come to a right-shoulder-shift with the snap of '61." An officer in Maine reportedly raised a regiment of heavy artillery drawn solely from the state's GAR ranks, tendering the veterans' services to the president. Others valued their own combat experience and saw themselves as uniquely suited to take on leadership roles in a new war. One comrade asserted that his California post "could supply a splendid lot of officers—men who have been tested under fire, and who are capable of commanding troops in battle."[27]

Amid this preparedness craze, both Union and Confederate veterans cooperated in mobilizing the nation's military-age men for possible service in the event of war. In late March, aged military heroes on both sides of the sectional divide (including John M. Schofield and Oliver O. Howard from the North and James Longstreet and Joseph Wheeler from the South) met in New York to organize the so-called National Volunteer Reserve, whose purpose was "to get together a reserve body of men to take up arms at a moment's notice without conscription or draft . . . [and] without entailing upon the Government or State the expense of maintaining such a large body of troops, and without drawing from their pursuits the young men of the Nation." Prospective reservists between eighteen and forty-five years of age signed an enrollment blank, pledging that at the call of the state or national government they would enlist in the National Guard, Naval Reserve, US Army, or US Navy. Pointedly referring to the Reserve as a "Grand Army of Individual Americans," the organization's executive committee requested "[t]he aid of the Grand Army of the Republic, of the Confederate and of all other veteran organizations, of the Sons of Veterans, and of all patriotic societies . . . to further the movement, and each is invited to become a recruiting office of the National Volunteer Reserve."[28]

Grand Army veterans responded to the summons promptly, using their revered community status to encourage enrollment. Michigan Department Commander Aaron T. Bliss supplied his state's posts with enrollment blanks and urged comrades to "advance the spirit of loyalty and patriotism" by encouraging young men to sign their names on the forms. In Asbury Park, New Jersey, members of the local post stood ready in city hall to circulate and collect enrollment blanks from interested men. Los Angeles veterans went a step further, not only registering younger men for the National Volunteer Reserve, but also spurring enrollment in a National *Veterans* Reserve, comprising a company of fifty Union and fifty Confederate veterans. Sentiment like this was not uncommon, as GAR veterans elsewhere self-recruited for reserve duty. Missouri's Department Commander John P. Platt knew that although "age and its attendant ills" would prevent most GAR veterans from enrolling in the Reserve, there were still-spry men who wanted to "make their influence felt in the direction of loyalty to the flag" and promptly enroll. One Vermonter expressed just this view. Writing to the GAR officer in charge of local Reserve recruiting, Robert Haskell asserted that he was "not so old and used up yet" and was "ready and willing to go again for my country's cause." Although the effect that National Volunteer Reserve enrollment might have had on eventual Spanish-American War enlistment is difficult to assess, it is clear that GAR veterans assumed it part of their patriotic duty to inspire fervor for the program as the nation faced the growing prospect of war.[29]

African American posts, too, rallied proudly on behalf of the mobilizing nation in the frenzied weeks surrounding the US war declaration. In Wilmington, Delaware, the local all-Black post endorsed a resolution offering the veterans' services in the event of war, while in Leavenworth, Kansas, the members of the Shaw Post did the same at an interracial campfire that they hosted, which "elicited prolonged cheers" as they pledged "sympathy for Cuba in her fight for freedom from Spanish rule." Detroit's John Brown Post, perhaps reluctant to promise its aging members' active participation in the strenuous war to come, instead had members man a recruitment station in the city and guaranteed the enlistment of a "large number" of volunteers. The zeal with which African American veterans channeled their activism to support US adventurism abroad may be unexpected given the intense discrimination and meager governmental protection that Blacks then faced domestically. However, evidence suggests at least two motivations for Black GAR posts' patriotic devotion during the crisis. First, these veterans clearly felt affinity for the Cuban people (many of whom were Blacks who had only recently broken free from enslavement) and likened their uprising to their own liberation struggle. The Delany Post members in Indianapolis, for instance, expressed "the profoundest sympathy for the oppressed and downtrodden Cubans" and believed "that a war, having for its purpose their emancipation, is a holy war." Second, African American veterans perceived military service as one of the primary ways for Blacks to challenge the political and social status quo and lay claim to unfulfilled rights, akin to how their own Civil War service had ushered in the abolition of US slavery and the Reconstruction-era amendments a generation earlier. During 1898 Memorial Day ceremonies in Washington, D.C., Black GAR members and their allies linked their desire for "caste prejudice [to] be buried" with a call for "every negro in the country to demand the creation of one or more negro regiments, not only composed of men in the ranks, but regiments officered from the highest place to the lowest by men of our race." For all of war's attendant hardships, many African American veterans distinctly recognized the opportunity for their descendants to inch Black civil rights forward through their loyalty and enlistment in the nation's latest conflict.[30]

Of course, once war was declared, a few gutsy Civil War veterans actually enlisted or accepted appointments in the armed forces, participating in military campaigns in the Caribbean and the Philippines. As one GAR member retrospectively touted, "the old veterans of '61 and '65 have borne an active and honorable part. Its officers and leaders have been largely our comrades, and . . . won glorious and decisive victories." The most publicized of these examples were veterans who had received commissions as generals of volunteers during the Civil War, remained with the regular army after Appomattox, and acquired high-ranking commands in 1898. Medal of Honor awardee Nelson A. Miles, for instance, was brevetted a young major general of volunteers during the Civil War and rose to become general-in-chief of the US Army by the outbreak of the Spanish-American War. Miles and another Union army general, John R. Brooke, proved vital to the success of the invasion of Puerto Rico. George Dewey, who saw action as a young naval officer outside Confederate strongholds at New Orleans and Port Hudson, commanded the naval forces that demolished the Spanish fleet at Manila Bay, while Wesley Merritt, a Union cavalry commander during the Civil War, led the ground forces in the capture of the Philippine city. With Russell A. Alger (the GAR's national commander in 1889) leading the War Department and McKinley as the country's commander in chief, Union veterans provided the leadership thrust for US victory in 1898. Given great hype, of course, were a number of ex-Confederate officers who donned the blue at the outbreak of war with Spain. McKinley, recognizing the need to curry the South's support for the war ahead, designated several old adversaries to positions of high command. Among these were Fitzhugh Lee, nephew of the Confederacy's beloved general, and Joseph "Fighting Joe" Wheeler, a Confederate cavalry commander who, as a then–Alabama congressman, whooped the rebel yell after passage of a March 1898 bill allocating funds for the US military buildup.[31]

The Spanish-American War service of former commanders of the "Blue and Gray" generated predictable sentimentality in the national media as the reuniting North and South turned their animosities toward a common foe. To be sure, many veterans on both sides celebrated the spirit of intersectional harmony. Particularly at the national level, high-ranking officers of veterans' fraternities gushed over the new accord. With war still raging, members of the United Confederate Veterans (UCV) convened in Atlanta for their annual meeting in July 1898 and hailed their northern counterparts. Commander in Chief John B. Gordon spoke with clear understanding that the war against a foreign enemy offered both the South and the nation broadly a singular opportunity. Predicting the "complete and permanent obliteration of all sectional distrusts," Gordon also contended that the war provided the chance for "our boys ... to bear, wrapped in the folds of the American flag, the light of American civilization and the boon of Republican liberty to the oppressed islands of both oceans." Two months later in Cincinnati, GAR veterans assembled at their own annual encampment. By then, a ceasefire had been arranged between the United States and Spain, and speakers acknowledged the war's great power in healing the sectional divide. Citing the "common rejoicing by all of the people, East and West—and North and South," officer Albert O. Marsh reported that the war "has had the effect of bringing the people of all sections of the country into the most harmonious relations, and, as we hope and believe, in obliterating every trace ... of resentment and ill will between the men who fought on opposite sides in the great civil conflict." Chaplain in Chief Frank C. Bruner even cautiously wondered if veterans North and South might be "on the eve of making a history of ourselves in a Grand Army which will 'include the boys in Blue and Gray.'"[32]

Whatever the sentimental outpouring emanating from these well-publicized fraternal events, rank-and-file GAR veterans at the local level rarely dwelled on these reconciliationist themes. Instead, typical post meetings devoted far more time tracking the Spanish-American War service of beloved hometown heroes and locally raised units than effusing praise for ex-Confederates like Lee and Wheeler. In northern communities across the country, veterans cheered those comrades who shouldered arms to defend the nation once more. Pennsylvania-born Alexander L. Hawkins, for instance, earned a commission as captain in a USCT regiment during the Civil War, after which he became colonel of the 10th Pennsylvania Regiment of the National Guard, a unit deployed for service in the Philippines. While he and his regiment were returning to the United States in July 1899, Hawkins—ill from tropical disease—died, leaving GAR veterans mournful and his troops' joyful homecoming "tinged with sadness" because of the loss of their "kind and considerate commander." The career of Owen Summers took a similar trajectory. After enlisting at fourteen in an Illinois cavalry regiment during the Civil War, Summers settled in Oregon in 1879. There, he got involved in state politics, became an officer in the Oregon National Guard, and served as GAR department commander in 1891. At the outbreak of the Spanish-American War, Summers was commissioned colonel of the 2nd Oregon Volunteer Infantry, seeing service in the Philippines. He was breveted brigadier general of volunteers "for gallant and meritorious services in the field," before mustering out the following year. At the time of his passing in 1911, Oregon's statehouse flag and those of all the GAR department posts were ordered flown at half-staff.[33]

Aiding the military effort in various combat support services proved less onerous for many aging Union veterans but generated similar admiration from their posts' comrades. The US quartermaster and ordnance departments attracted a number of GAR members who wished to satisfy the call of duty. Massachusetts GAR officer George L. Goodale received a captain's commission and acted as assistant quartermaster in the US Army's Seventh Corps. After accompanying the unit in the campaign to take Cuba, he remained in the army until his retirement from active service in 1908. Joab N. Patterson, after years commanding units in the post–Civil War New Hampshire National Guard, was appointed captain and division-level ordnance officer on the staff of another Union veteran, Colonel Joseph P. Sanger. After providing "good service during the war," Patterson remained in Cuba for several years as superintendent of public buildings in Havana. Other Union veterans provided spiritual solace to the next generation of soldier-heroes. Rhode Island's Joseph J. Woolley served in the Civil War as chaplain of the Eighth Connecticut Volunteer Infantry and, after the war, became a pastor in Pawtucket and a well-respected member of the city's GAR Tower Post. With the outbreak of war in 1898, Woolley again enlisted for service as chaplain, this time with the First Rhode Island Volunteer Regiment, and pledged "to try and teach the men to live up to high ideals as soldiers and as men." Although the unit did not see service abroad, Woolley became "one of the most popular men in the regiment" and provided memorial services for the several recruits who died as a result of sickness or accident.[34]

For many other Union veterans, providing support, comfort, and inspiration to the next generation of soldiers was a suitable alternative to active enlistment. To augment the small, prewar standing army, Congress and the McKinley administration coordinated in April 1898 to bolster the regular army to 65,000 and raise a volunteer force of 125,000. To fulfill their volunteer quotas, the states relied on their National Guard units, which, in turn, largely assented to a formal mustering into federal service. Locally raised companies of guardsmen became their communities' instant celebrities and the focal points of civic parades and banquets.

As the paragons of a previous era of wartime voluntarism, Grand Army members nationwide frequently became the young men's hometown mentors and models of heroism. For example, GAR posts in a range of small Ohio towns—Lancaster, Youngstown, Bucyrus, Urbana, Findlay, Delaware, Marion, and more—paraded with the communities' National Guard companies (complete with Weyler effigy and Spanish flag burnings in Marion) and escorted them to the trains bearing them to rendezvous points in Cleveland, Columbus, and Akron. In tiny Red Oak, Iowa, some 8,000 citizens—reportedly the "largest crowd ever assembled" there—lined the streets to witness the parade of Company M, Third Iowa Regiment. Accompanying the unit in the procession was the local GAR post who saw the young men off to the train station where they would be whisked away to a mobilization camp in Des Moines. Across the country in Stockton, California, GAR veterans similarly accompanied volunteers to the steamship that would bear them down the San Joaquin River to San Francisco Bay and their mustering in.[35]

As the nation's newest volunteers congregated in camps and awaited transport to staging areas, members of GAR posts located nearby often visited the young men—doubtless providing some distraction and excitement from the tedium of drill and physical exams. Delaware veterans from Wilmington's Thomas A. Smyth Post took the train to nearby Middletown to visit recruits stationed at Camp Tunnell. The post band provided the music for the recruits' dress parade— a stirring example of intergenerational militarism. Pleased with the progress, the post was reported to have been "interested spectators and the old veterans complimented the youthful soldiers." Several GAR posts were located near St. Paul's Camp Ramsey, where Minnesota's volunteer regiments mustered in. Members of the Acker Post frequently visited recruits there to observe their training and provide encouragement. Josiah P. Chaney reported that on one day, 400 members of his post thronged the camp. "We had a few short speeches at each regiment," Chaney wrote, "gave them three rousing cheers, which were reciprocated with a will, and, after staying awhile to see them drill, came home. They are progressing finely." The veterans returned a few days later with a drum corps to see the men off when their regiments had orders to concentrate at Chickamauga and San Francisco.[36]

Some posts took a particularly vested interest in their community's locally raised units, continuing to cultivate close bonds with the soldiers and monitoring their movements at home and deployments abroad. The veterans of Rutland's Roberts Post became informal mentors for their town's volunteers, organizing a farewell reception for the men of Company A, First Vermont Regiment. By late May, company captain H. Edward Dyer, then stationed with the regiment at Chickamauga's Camp George H. Thomas, wrote the Union veterans with thanks for the "many kindnesses shown us by the GAR" and for counting on the unit "to take the Flag from your care, and trust that no man shall ever say that it has suffered by the change." Although Company A never saw action abroad, the Roberts Post and its WRC auxiliary nonetheless organized a homecoming reception at the post hall in September where, reportedly, "a general good time was enjoyed by all." Similarly, the Sedgwick Post of Orange, Massachusetts, closely followed the exploits of the community's volunteer company. The comrades, along with their WRC and Sons of Veterans auxiliaries, escorted the recruits to the town hall in early May for a reception honoring their service "to fight the enemies of Liberty in Cuba." The veterans kept a close eye on the unit as it was deployed to the Caribbean and, in July, participated in the Battle of El Caney, praising them for fighting "as the sons of America always have fought as men to whom honor of country is dearer than life itself" even as they expressed the "sadness at the thought of the boys who will never come marching home again." One of the fallen was Sergeant Fred Rides, whose funeral the post attended in late August.[37]

Indeed, the most painful duty that many GAR posts assumed during the Spanish-American War was memorializing the death of local soldiers. As was the case in the Civil War, the vast majority of military deaths in 1898 were from illness, not combat. One Minnesota veteran complained that medical treatment in the latest war had not improved much from his experience a generation earlier. In both 1861 and 1898, explained Josiah B. Chaney, "a man . . . may have been a passable doctor in his city or country practice, but, as an army surgeon, might not be worth the powder to blow him up." Drawing further parallels between both wars, Chaney continued that "Congress was hounding the President to take immediate action, and the people were clamoring for precipitate action, without any adequate preparation, shouting 'On to Cuba,' as, in the early part of the Civil War, they cried: 'On to Richmond;' causing in both cases unnecessary loss of life." Communities, along with their GAR posts, experienced the tragedy of this unpreparedness firsthand. When Corporal William Gilmartin died from typhoid fever while stationed in Georgia, the GAR post in his hometown of Scranton, Pennsylvania, took part in providing military honors for the soldier. Similarly, when Private Frederick Angiers, one of the famed Rough Riders, died of illness in Newport, Rhode Island, members of the local post escorted the body from the hospital and offered military honors at the young man's burial. Having experienced massive death in their own war, Grand Army veterans reminded their fellow Americans how to cope with loss and properly venerate sacrifice.[38]

The Spanish-American War provided Grand Army members with what they saw as tangible evidence of the successful international expansion of their earlier fight for liberty and democracy at home. Witnessing freedom struggles in the Caribbean and Latin America, Union veterans (with some degree of hubris) congratulated themselves for inspiring subjugated peoples abroad to rise up to demand their own emancipation and self-determination. When Cubans sought to achieve this from their Spanish overlords, many GAR veterans believed it was in the humanitarian interests of the United States to intervene and guide the liberation process for a people whom they believed needed instruction to prepare for freedom's promises. Meanwhile, some veterans took up arms in America's latest struggle while many more remained behind to serve as their communities' patriotic boosters who encouraged and instructed the next generation of defenders. Avoiding the sectional lovefest that swept up many northerners and southerners during the heady days of the war, rank-and-file members in GAR posts across the country more often preferred to honor their local heroes while viewing the conflict as the global projection of their Union victory.

Let This Society Die with the Union Veterans

With the speedy end to America's "splendid little war," many US volunteers returned home just months after departing. By the fall of 1898, communities nationwide began holding lavish receptions for their heroes with Grand Army veterans often at the head of these homecoming ceremonies. Frequently, the aging defenders of the Union offered the hand of friendship to the young soldiers of America's latest exploits abroad. When companies of the Thirteenth New York Volunteers—some of the victors of San Juan Hill—returned home to Buffalo, hundreds of the city's GAR members came out to welcome them. Reviewing the parade of the youthful conquerors, their elders reportedly "were in battle again" and "cheered and screamed themselves hoarse, and . . . all around them waved the flag they had fought for and would fight for again if they could drag themselves into the fray." Other Grand Army veterans, while celebrating the homecoming of their communities' returning soldiers, also recognized the larger consequences of their victory over Spain. At an Iowa reception, Isaac N. Carr of the Ed Hamlin Post thanked the returning troops who "carried our flag to the Philippine Islands, and unfurled it in victory over the Island of Luzon." He added that the soldiers' sacrifices had carved out a new status for the United States. "Civilization and expansion is what has made us one of the foremost nations of the world," Carr declared, "and civilization and expansion will help us to retain this position."[39]

Of course, few of America's volunteers actually took part in combat, instead spending the bulk of the short war training in crowded and disease-ridden camps. Still, communities and their GAR posts often received the returning soldiers warmly and acknowledged their heroism despite never testing their mettle in battle. In Madison, one hundred Union veterans escorted the soldiers of Company G, First Wisconsin Volunteers from the train station to the armory where members of the local WRC served the tired but untested troops a hearty meal. When a Pennsylvania company returned home to Hollidaysburg after idling away the war at a camp on the old Chickamauga battlefield, a lively "public ovation" awaited them with the town's GAR members staked out at the train station to greet their arrival. One speaker, doubtless trying to assuage the men whose greatest wartime foe was disease, assured them that "[t]he soldier who, in the fever-stricken camp, faithfully performs his allotted duty is as true a hero as is his comrade who storms the battery or charges on the enemies' rifle pits." In Rochester, the local newspaper drew parallels between the homecoming of the Third New York Volunteers and that of Union soldiers more than thirty years earlier. The *Democrat and Chronicle* reprinted the June 1865 account of the Yankees' reception alongside columns describing the festivities planned for the Spanish-American War soldiers. Still, the newspaper hinted at a greater heroism of the "old and respected . . . members of the G.A.R." who were planning to "welcome home and do honor to the boys to-day who, though unlike themselves, have seen no baptism of shot and shell and blood in active battle, [but who] are none the less worthy a right royal reception, since they went forth as eagerly and as loyally to uphold the honor of their country."[40]

With the homecoming of the Spanish-American War soldiers and their return to civilian life, Union veterans faced a pivotal decision concerning the boundaries of GAR membership. Doubtless the young men, like their Union veteran forebears, would choose to organize fraternally and bond over their military service. Could the GAR evolve to encompass intergenerational camaraderie, characterized only by the shared experience of veteranhood? Or, would it remain solely the domain of those men who shared a specific experience and collective memory of Union victory in the Civil War? There was no shortage of Union veterans advocating a welcoming stance. Rhode Island's Tower Post—whose beloved member, Joseph J. Woolley, was even then catering to the spiritual needs of Spanish-American War recruits as a regimental chaplain—advocated that the GAR constitution be amended at the next national encampment so that "men who serve the United States honorably as soldiers and sailors in the present war against Spain shall be eligible to admission . . . in full comradeship." Similarly, comrades in a Pittsburgh post forwarded resolutions to the Department of Pennsylvania encampment "recommending the admission to our order of the gallant young men who are now battling to uphold the dignity of our flag." Joseph W. Kay of New York, while opposing the admission of former Confederates into the GAR, nonetheless believed it possible to welcome Spanish-American War veterans into the order. Embracing a spirit of "universal comradeship and fraternal regard," Kay argued "that the principles which the Grand Army of the Republic represents might well be perpetuated by taking in all who volunteered to serve under the flag." All told, proponents of open admission to the GAR tended to be rank-and-file members of local posts, veterans with close connections to Spanish-American War troops, or those who found it unlikely that a southerner would stumble into their northern post room or memorial hall seeking membership.[41]

Despite these magnanimous calls to welcome the new heroes into the fold, a vehement opposition nonetheless ensured that the GAR remained the exclusive realm of Union veterans. This outcome was often the result of efforts by well-placed department- and national-level officers who used their influence at GAR encampments to remind Union veterans of their organization's special heritage. Inundated with "letters and resolutions" from local posts in favor of open admittance was Commander in Chief John P. S. Gobin, who determined to provide finality on the subject at the 1898 national encampment in Cincinnati. In the annual address to the GAR delegates, Gobin applauded the soldiers even then still in the service who "contributed magnificently to the success of the operations which resulted in so glorious a peace." However, Gobin tacitly admitted to the different wartime experiences of the two generations of soldiers and asserted that "there can be no merit in their becoming members of our organization, founded under different auspices and based upon entirely different principles. When the Grand Army of the Republic has fulfilled its mission it should cease to exist." State departments largely fell into line behind the national headquarters' directive. In Pennsylvania, for instance, Department Commander William J. Patterson echoed Gobin's command. "We honor them for their patriotism and valor," assured Patterson, "but to make the soldiers of the Spanish War a part of an organization founded on the internecine struggle of the sixties, would not be, to my mind, conducive to the welfare of either." Wisconsin officer Jerome Watrous took a slightly different tack, arguing that the best thing for the Spanish-American War veterans was to organize their own association. Extolling the "same love in their hearts for the government and the flag," Watrous nonetheless thought they would be better off "earning their own place. . . . Do not let us forestall them by turning over to them that which we are nearly through with. Let this society die with the Union veterans of the War of the Rebellion."[42]

Watrous was prescient, as Spanish-American War veterans ultimately did chart their own path to fraternal organization. As early as 1899, a variety of new associations cropped up to provide demobilized soldiers with an opportunity to socialize under their newfound identity as veterans. This assortment of groups—including the Spanish War Veterans, Spanish-American War Veterans, the Legion of Spanish War Veterans, the Army of the Philippines, the American Veterans of Foreign Service, and more—reflected America's escalating military interventions in the Caribbean and Pacific. By 1904, many of these societies united under the umbrella of the more powerful United Spanish War Veterans (USWV). Barred from GAR membership, the USWV instead adopted many of the Union veterans' fraternal rituals, activities, and objectives. According to its constitution, the USWV accepted all men (and women nurses) who served honorably in the military during the war with Spain and "during the campaigns incidental to and growing out of that war." Further, it pledged "to honor the memories of the comrades who have answered the last roll call; to preach the spirit of patriotism; to gain honorable recognition for those who served faithfully and well; to aid weak and unfortunate comrades . . . [and] to carry the same spirit of sacrifice and service exercised in time of war into the less spectacular walks of daily life." Also akin to the GAR was the selection of a triad of foundational principles—"Freedom, Patriotism, and Humanity"—which mirrored the Union veterans' promotion of "Fraternity, Charity, and Loyalty."[43]

Despite many parallels between the GAR and USWV, a few antagonistic episodes indicated at least some incompatibility between the two generations of veterans. At times, GAR members demonstrated a belief in the superior worthiness of their service and sacrifice. When the GAR post in Duluth, Minnesota, insisted that a monument to Civil War hero and post namesake Joshua B. Culver top a soldiers' and sailors' monument intended to honor all war veterans, the local USWV camp refused to donate to the project. "The proposal is like buying a medal for yourself," complained USWV officer C. J. Sherman. "The Spanish-American War Veterans were not represented on the monument committee and the camp . . . refuses to give to a one-man memorial." In Pittsburgh, GAR comrades erupted when they learned that the warden at the Western State Penitentiary dismissed aging Union-veteran employees and replaced them with convict labor (including, notably, an inmate who had served in the Spanish-American War). The GAR men charged that the warden "is partial to those of that service, to the disadvantage of the civil war [sic] veterans." Further, the USWV broadly subscribed to reconciliationist rhetoric and symbols that inherently minimized the significance of Union victory. In its constitution, the USWV asserted that because of its members' military service, "sectional lines are obliterated, and our people are welded together as one great nation." Fraternity members even sported a two-hued uniform, "indicative of the final peace between the former wearers of the northern blue and the southern gray."⁴⁴

Nevertheless, local-level cooperation between GAR and USWV members was not uncommon. Particularly during Memorial Day ceremonies, soldiers of both generations commiserated over the loss of their comrades. In Menominee, Michigan, veterans of both wars came together in 1902 to decorate the graves of forty-two Union veterans and one Spanish-American War soldier. Relinquishing some of the day's duties, the Lyon Post permitted the young veterans to supply the firing squad and music for the event. Still, with a bit of bluster, forty-eight of the post veterans journeyed to the cemetery on foot "and part of the way doubled quick to show how they did it 40 years ago." In 1905, Oklahoma GAR officer W. B. Herod reported that the state's Spanish-American War veterans had helped keep Memorial Day "sacred, and paid due reverence to the memory of departed soldiers and proudly stood by and assisted the living soldiers." Meanwhile, Grand Army veterans occasionally utilized their fine-tuned lobbying machine to assist the younger veterans. When opponents attacked legislation that would have opened up preferential hiring to Spanish-American War veterans applying for New York's civil service positions, the GAR stepped in to ensure the benefit was extended. The state's USWV thanked the GAR for "guid[ing] our steps by the light of its larger experience" and pledged "to keep fragrant forever the lessons of their lives and to perpetuate the principles of their Order."⁴⁵

Despite the emergence of a new generation of American heroes, the GAR stood firm as an organization dedicated exclusively to Union veterans. Ultimately unwilling to cede their fraternity to what some felt was a lesser cause (not to mention the disagreeable prospect of accepting reconciliationist-minded young members), a decisive number of Union veterans successfully defended the boundaries of their order. Further, the small membership of the USWV (that even as late as World War I did not exceed GAR numbers) ensured that veterans' community presence and civic activism remained dominated by Grand Army comrades and their vision for many years to come. Even though most members at the turn of the century were then entering their twilight years, they nonetheless maintained their beloved organization's reformist potential as the United States opened a new chapter as a modern, imperial power.⁴⁶

As the United States evolved to become one of the world's great powers, Grand Army members keenly understood that the nation's imperial expansion not only promised the dissemination of their cherished democratic and emancipationist values abroad, but also the continuation of social order, patriotism, and progress at home. By regenerating the world under the same principles that imbued the Yankee soldier of 1861, Union veterans recognized that the reform and perfection of US society had an even greater chance of success in 1898 and beyond. In this way, progressivism and imperialism were complementary, if problematic, GAR doctrines. The commingling of these processes—despite the veterans' humanitarian-inflected declarations—was by no means wholly, or even mostly, altruistic, and white supremacy consciously and subconsciously infused veterans' thoughts about and interactions with peoples abroad. Whether exploiting business opportunities in Mexico, indoctrinating Hawaiian children to the meaning of Union victory, or gauging the capacity of Cubans to exercise sovereignty, many GAR veterans paternalistically viewed nonwhite foreigners as underdeveloped and helpless, more akin to children in need of their civic and moral instruction. Moreover, as the Spanish-American War unfolded, Union veterans often perceived the next generation of soldiers as their martial descendants, carrying the torch of liberty and the superiority of American institutions to deprived and culturally void peoples. All told, Grand Army veterans were surprisingly well-informed about US foreign affairs and attuned to advancing American interests abroad alongside the nation's policymakers and proimperialist reformers. This engagement with the world, and America's place within it, remained a staple of GAR posts' activities and advocacies for many years to come, particularly as the nation marched toward a much larger conflict with an even greater bearing on the trajectory of US progressivism.

5   Rally Once Again

The world war teaches the same civic lessons as the civil war. Behind the man in khaki stands the man in blue.

—RHODE ISLAND GRAND ARMY FLAG DAY PROGRAM, 1919

On September 1, 1917, some 1,200 army draftees joined another 3,000 enlisted soldiers in a patriotic parade through the streets of Minneapolis. Escorting democracy's newest defenders were its oldest defenders—one hundred of the city's Grand Army veterans—leading the procession. After the demonstration, former GAR Commander in Chief Eliakim "Ell" Torrance spoke before the draftees and praised them as the "selected soldiers of liberty." The seventy-three-year-old veteran's valedictory to the doughboys echoed famous words from his own youth: "With malice toward none and charity for all you will take up the mighty task assigned to you." He impressed upon the next generation of freedom fighters that they would "blaze a new path to glory and will write upon the page of history that governments 'of the people, by the people and for the people' have triumphed throughout the earth." Thus, blessed by ancients who had lived to tell about making the Union safe for democracy, the boys moved out to training camps and troop ships, crossing the ocean to make the world safe for it, too.[1]

As the United States entered World War I, grizzled Union veterans mobilized once again to play more than merely ceremonial roles. Nationwide, local GAR posts responded overwhelmingly to America's wartime needs. Torrance, for instance, reported in 1918 that his Minnesota post had aided the city's Red Cross work and sold Liberty Bonds (with post members investing some $1,200). In Portland, Oregon, GAR members bought one hundred dollars in war bonds and organized an informational session on gas attack defense in Europe's trenches. Other posts sent their comrades out into the community to serve as patriotic organizers and educators. The veterans' drum corps attached to Indiana's all-Black Martin R. Delany Post, for example, reportedly "played so hard in the interests of recruiting that it is a wonder they have any breath left." In Philadelphia's Manayunk neighborhood, two GAR posts joined with children of the local parochial schools to take part in demonstrations, recitations, and a flag raising that steeled the neighborhood's Catholic community to the sacrifices to come. Meanwhile, newspapers across the country featured headlines about the assistance Union veterans provided in the nation's mobilization efforts. "G.A.R. Aids Recruiting" and "G.A.R. Secure 19 recruits," blazoned the organs in Harrisburg, Pennsylvania, and Davenport, Iowa.[2]

As the GAR entered its supposed twilight period during the years surrounding the Civil War's golden jubilee, a close examination of rank-and-file member activity reveals the fraternity's continued importance as a decentralized civic organization during the waning years of the nation's Progressive Era and the onset of World War I. Leveraging their status as beloved community patriarchs, aging veterans remained active civic elders, whose network of local posts stood ready and willing to rouse themselves once more in support of the US home front and national mobilization efforts. Although most of the youngest surviving Civil War veterans were septuagenarians as the Great War dawned, many rallied as energetic, engaged citizens uniquely experienced in the transition to a war footing. Although they lacked the organizational power they once mustered, Grand Army members maintained full awareness of the national and international issues that affected American peace and security. Meanwhile, they continued to perform an important service, both as symbols of sacrifice and civic duty to younger generations and as the moral and patriotic authorities for the country at large. Having witnessed the ill effects of military unpreparedness and home front disengagement during the Civil War, GAR veterans deployed their organization and status to serve in this new conflict as advocates for military reform, enthusiasts for domestic war work, and watchdogs for full-throated loyalty and Americanism in a time of national emergency. Understanding that few Americans still lived who had a *direct* memory of the Civil War, Union veterans continued to shape the *historical* memory of their Union victory and deftly linked its patriotic and nationalistic meanings to bestir new generations to the latest crisis at hand. To guarantee the survival of the reforms for which they had long fought and sacrificed, GAR members took active measures to ensure that their vision of democracy and freedom survived this latest test.

Tracking the Grand Army's Progressive Era civic engagement through World War I requires a reassessment of senior citizens' capacity to participate in community activism. GAR scholarship often overstates contemporary depictions of veterans as antiques of a bygone age, perpetuating the myth that the last GAR members were little more than their towns' curiosities—gawked at for their advanced age and trotted out for commemorative events and observances. To be sure, the GAR of the 1910s was a fraction of its peak strength from a quarter century earlier. From a high in 1890 of roughly 409,000, membership had fallen to 160,000 by 1915 and dwindled further to just 100,000 by 1920. Nevertheless, many spry Union veterans remained highly engaged citizens through the World War I era, forcing a reassessment of just when the Grand Army old-timer passed from a status of active reformer to that of docile relic. Similarly, the limited scholarship on age consciousness and geriatrics in US history has focused less on elder activism and more on the turn-of-the-century acceleration of "gerontophobia" and Americans' simultaneous move to embrace a "cult of youth." Certainly, shifting cultural views toward agedness in the early twentieth century hastened old-age policies like pension plans, retirement enforcement, and social security. However, painting the era's Union veterans as little more than wards of the state does them a disservice, as it ignores ample evidence of seniors fighting both on their own and on the nation's behalf during the turbulent World War I years.[3]

The first section below examines the Grand Army's involvement with the so-called "preparedness movement" and veterans' efforts to set the country on a path of prudent military readiness in a chaotic and war-torn world. Resurrecting a defense of the US volunteer citizen-soldier (a role they had played a half century before), GAR members advocated the democratic, reformist idea of universal military training that they believed would cultivate a sense of civic obligation and responsible citizenship among America's young men. Concluding that military unpreparedness had led to the unparalleled loss and destruction of the Civil War, veterans largely agreed that practical military instruction and modernized defense capabilities were the surest deterrents to war. The second section argues that despite their advanced age, GAR veterans engaged tirelessly in wartime defense activities and became useful contributors on the US home front. After the April 1917 war declaration, Grand Army members viewed the global conflict as the latest opportunity for the United States to transmit the principles of democracy and liberty, this time to European peoples "enslaved" by oppressive and authoritarian governments. Meanwhile, Union veterans became dutiful soldiers for the federal government's interventionist efforts to mobilize the country's military-age men and to incentivize, discipline, and inspire civilians for war work. The final section assesses the GAR response to the vital decisions concerning the reconstruction of the postwar world. Like many Americans exhausted by the war's demands and fearful of new threats to social order, members often shed their enthusiasm for reform in favor of more conservative and isolationist principles. Nearing the end of their fraternity's effective life (not to mention, for most, their own lives), many Union veterans acquiesced to US society's prevailing reactionary posture as the nation's next generation of soldier-heroes returned home.

Advance the Cause of Preparedness Now

On July 5, 1913, the front page of the *Gettysburg Times* featured two articles side by side in compelling juxtaposition. The first reported on the departure of the last of the roughly 50,000 aged Union and Confederate veterans who had gathered on the battlefield to commemorate the fiftieth anniversary of the nation's bloodiest battle. Over the previous four days, the old fellows had swapped war stories, toured the grounds, and taken meals around the campfires. Political luminaries provided commentary—heavy on themes of reconciliation and shared heroism—during the course of the celebrations, culminating with an Independence Day address by President Woodrow Wilson. Remaining in town after the last of the veterans departed were regular army troops of the Fifth Infantry, tasked with preparing for Gettysburg's next (albeit less heralded) event and the subject of the newspaper's other front-page story. Readers learned that scores of college students from across the country were arriving on July 7 to participate in a six-week course on military training. The experimental camp was the brainchild of US Army Chief of Staff Leonard Wood and Secretary of War Lindley M. Garrison. Participants, under the guidance of the regulars, would "receive instructions in camp sanitation, military training, personal hygiene and the principles of military art, including advance and rear guards, outposts, marches, orders and combats." Ultimately, the camp's organizers hoped that attendees would not only receive the training needed to serve as noncommissioned army officers in the event of war, but also to awaken the country's youth to a renewed appreciation of each citizen's obligations to defend the nation—what Wood designated as "a policy which means reasonable military preparedness." For Wood, Garrison, and like-minded military reform advocates, there were few better locations than the hallowed grounds of Gettysburg and few better times than upon the departure of the Civil War heroes to inculcate the values of military preparedness in the nation's rising generation.[4]

In the years preceding the United States' entry into World War I, many Americans developed a keen interest in the nation's military and defense capacities. With US commitments abroad steadily expanding after the Spanish-American War and international crises seemingly mushrooming in size and scope, supporters argued that a modern nation required a modern military. Those in favor of measures such as the strengthening of the armed forces, the expansion of a rigorously trained reserve of volunteer citizen-soldiers, and compulsory military training and service for young men, gave voice to the era's so-called "preparedness movement." Although more frequently associated with the Republican

Party, preparedness advocates never fit conveniently into a single party ideology. Instead, supporters of all political stripes frequently associated military expansion with the preservation of US security and neutrality, and drew firm links between military service, civic duty, and the perpetuation of democratic rights.[5]

Indeed, preparedness was not at odds with many of the objectives of the era's reform-minded activism, and proponents of military expansion often fit comfortably into the disparate mosaic comprising the progressives. Historian David M. Kennedy, for instance, argues that "[m]any progressives yearned for some experience that would heighten social consciousness and tighten social bonds" and that war might serve as "the forge in whose fires they might shape a new ethos of social duty and civic responsibility." Granted, some reformers worried that issues of preparedness only served to preoccupy the nation with dangerous militarism at the expense of social justice advocacy. However, many others noted a democratic and just element to military preparedness—particularly the universal military training of the nation's young men. As the nation drew closer to war, preparedness steadily crept into progressive ideology and leading activists more frequently linked military service with civic obligation. In 1916, the Progressive Party supported strong preparedness planks in its national convention platform including a restored and strengthened navy, a regular army enlarged to 250,000 troops, and a "system of military training adequate to organize with promptness . . . a citizen soldiery supplied, armed and controlled by the national government." Even the onetime preparedness foe Woodrow Wilson ultimately converted to the tenets of "reasonable preparedness" and signed into law the National Defense Act in June 1916, which increased the regular army to 175,000 (298,000 in wartime), expanded the National Guard to 400,000 and intensified guardsmen's training, made possible the federalization of the Guard for foreign service in cases of national emergency, and established the Reserve Officers' Training Corps for college men.[6]

For many years before the preparedness movement won wide support, Grand Army veterans had been sounding the call for military reform, targeting the nation's youth as prime candidates to help accomplish the objective. GAR cofounder John A. Logan, for example, supported a comprehensive plan to provide students with military instruction and thereby perpetuate the type of citizen-soldier that had preserved the Union. In his *The Volunteer Soldier of America* (1887), Logan urged the federal government to establish "a military department in every State university," in which students would be taught "the rudiments of a military education, to include a thorough gymnastic training, the elementary and higher mathematics, drawing, natural and experimental philosophy, military and civil engineering, ancient and modern history, infantry tactics . . . etc., etc." Logan's prescription also involved reforming the nation's public schools to include athletics, drill, and hygiene instruction in the hopes that "every youth of the country could be instructed in the elementary training of the soldier." Meanwhile, at state and national encampments, GAR officers frequently endorsed proposals to institute military training for schoolboys and college students. In 1900, for instance, Commander in Chief Albert D. Shaw—echoing the proposals of the then-deceased Logan—insisted that school military drill "develop[ed] both mind and body in a desirable way" and cultivated "national strength of the most desirable sort in times of peace." In the years surrounding Shaw's endorsement, Grand Army officials at the state and national levels even assigned so-called "aides on military instruction in the public schools" to drum up support and push legislation for student training.[7]

In these ways, Grand Army veterans' advocacy for the military instruction of America's youth presaged the efforts of a younger generation of reformers born during the Civil War era—Wood, Garrison, Theodore Roosevelt, and others—to take up the cause. The 1913 Gettysburg summer training camp had been well received and encouraged Wood to expand the program the following summer (incidentally, at a time the nation faced a new military crisis with Mexico), establishing camps in Vermont, Michigan, North Carolina, and California that attracted nearly a thousand college students. By 1915, with Europe now engulfed in war, preparedness advocates clamored for more training camps (particularly after the sinking of the *Lusitania*) open to all interested men, irrespective of college enrollment. The demand persuaded Wood and his allies to establish the so-called Plattsburg camp in Upstate New York, drawing some 1,800 mostly East Coast elites for four weeks of summer training. The War Department expanded the program further still the following year, establishing camps across the country and garnering some 16,000 participants. These camps, explained one journal, often attracted businessmen and other young professionals "who are unable, for business or family reasons, to devote years of time or to tie themselves down to fixed periods of drill, as required by the National Guard, yet are willing and ready to arrange their affairs so that they can take a month in the summer and go through intensive field training at a military camp."[8]

Grand Army members took note of the burgeoning military training movement and largely voiced their support, citing the need for the nation's young men to understand the obligations of democratic citizenship. At the 1915 national encampment, attendees passed resolutions in "favor [of] such military training of the rising generation as will inure to both their physical and mental culture with a teaching of the responsibility and duties of future citizens of the Republic to whom will be confided its safe-keeping." The following year, Nebraska veterans praised those businesses that encouraged their employees to either attend the War Department's summer camps or participate in National Guard training. At the state encampment, GAR delegates "approve[d] and commend[ed] the action of some of the larger interests, especially the Nebraska Telephone Company, by which their employees are encouraged to attend Military training camps without loss of pay, and that we feel that this patriotic attitude should become that of all corporations and business firms." The training camps had a few detractors as well. Of these, many questioned the ability of such brief programs to suitably prepare trainees to lead other men in battle and gird themselves for the rigors of war. One New Hampshire comrade, for example, asked, "[w]hat sane person can think for a minute that thirty days at Plattsburg is sufficient to give a man a commission and to be entrusted with the lives of our sons in battle or even to simply guard their rations and health in camp?"9

By and large, however, Union veterans remained enthusiastic about the nation's escalating interest in preparedness, a sentiment that also extended to the GAR's Sons of Veterans (SV) auxiliary. Spurred into action by dint of its relationship to the older generation of soldier-heroes, the order added a military wing at its 1903 national encampment called the Sons of Veterans Reserves (SVR). Arranged into companies attached to individual SV camps, the SVR functioned as a paramilitary organization in support of the GAR veterans. Wearing the "dark blue blouse [and] light blue pantaloons" of their fathers, SVR members frequently served as honor guards during civic parades, Memorial Day events, or GAR comrades' funerals. Proponents commended the healthful benefits membership in the SVR would have on America's young men. "Round shoulders are cured or prevented," asserted one SVR advocate. "Chests are rounded out, muscles are builded [sic] up. In fact the members of the Reserve are taught what goes most to make perfect manhood." To be sure, enlistment in the SVR assumed no obligation of service at the state or federal level. Still, the SVR mimicked other functions akin to the era's National Guard—requiring members to enlist for an extended term of service, take part in regular drills, and participate in dress parades and sham battles. Moreover, the SVR instilled in a new generation of young men an affinity for the citizen-soldier of the 1860s. As one early supporter noted, the SVR would serve the dual function of assuring "confidence in the effectiveness of the American volunteer soldier" while diminishing the "necessity to maintain a large and expensive standing army."10

In many northern communities, the SVR became a popular and highly visible organization before American entry into World War I. As early as 1910, for instance, the Pennsylvania Sons of Veterans boasted that they could "furnish upwards of 7,230 fully equipped, thoroughly disciplined troops in defense of the country, without a dollar of expense to the State or Government." In Ohio, the state's SVR commander called on "the youth of our Order [to] receive a Military training, so that if our Glorious Old Nation ever find [sic] the need to call for support as it did in '61, it will not take a year to whip an army into shape." The state's SV members responded. Just weeks before World War I began in Europe in 1914, Ohio SVR membership numbered thirty-three officers and 432 men in fourteen companies. By 1916, the numbers had grown to sixty-five officers and 853 men in twenty-five companies. Meanwhile, SV camps sought legitimacy for their reserves by appealing to the government for arms and supplies. Despite a failed resolution offered in 1916 by then-Senator Warren G. Harding (himself the son of a Union veteran) to authorize the secretary of war "to grant the free use for military drill, of any discarded rifles to any duly accredited camps of the Sons of Veterans Reserves," the SVR had better luck at the state level. Some states sold arms and other supplies to SVR companies. Others, including Minnesota and Rhode Island, furnished equipment without cost.[11]

With many Americans investing in the doctrine of preparedness and greater numbers of young men receiving military training, Grand Army veterans closely monitored world events and responded to the prospect of the United States' entry into the war in Europe with a wide range of opinions. For a few particularly zealous comrades, anticipation for war aroused excitement. Wisconsin member Jerome A. Watrous, for instance, decried those peace advocates who sought "the suppression of the military spirit" fearing that if it "were . . . totally smothered, men would be molly-coddles and women nonentities." Most, however, maintained a measured response, earnestly believing that military preparedness remained the best way to diminish the prospect of war or, at worst, to minimize the damage caused by it. Former GAR Commander in Chief Ell Torrance came out against "what might be termed frenzied preparedness," warning that, on the one hand, the United States could "never become Prussianized." On the other hand, he cautioned Americans not to "become Chinafied by reason of not being able to rouse the necessary military spirit to insure [sic] our safety and protection." James F. Connelly of New Jersey, another comrade who supported reasonable preparedness, nonetheless decried the tragedy unfolding across the Atlantic. "[B]oys that should be enjoying home life and being prepared to accept the duties of manhood are to-day filling the trenches in that great holocaust," he lamented.

"That war, my friends, shows that the boasted civilization of the twentieth century is simply a veneer on the savagery of old."[12]

Preparedness proponents in the GAR frequently invoked their own war experiences to straddle the line between pacifism and militarism, carving out a prudent middle ground. Veterans resurrected William T. Sherman's blunt definition of war after the outbreak of the European conflict. "None know better than members of the Grand Army of the Republic that 'War is Hell,'" proclaimed Duluth's J. B. Culver Post before accepting an invitation to attend a sermon coinciding with President Wilson's designation of October 4, 1914, as "Peace Sunday." New Hampshire's patriotic instructor, David E. Proctor, also conjured up Sherman's declaration in his 1916 report. "We have heard of Sherman's definition [of war] and believe in its truth," Proctor announced. "While we believe in preparedness we have no desire for war for conquest." At other GAR demonstrations, veterans linked the nation's unpreparedness in past wars to offer a warning about future military action. "You all suffered through the lack of preparedness during the Civil war [sic]," uttered Commander in Chief David J. Palmer at a Grand Army event in Chicago, "and it is your duty to your country and to your fellowmen [sic] to use every effort to advance the cause of preparedness now." At the 1916 Iowa state encampment, Albert Head proclaimed that "[t]here is not a comrade within the sound of my voice that does not know that if the North had been as well prepared as the South there would have been no war."[13]

As Europe plunged into its own war, GAR veterans continued to use their post rooms as educational venues, this time to stay informed about the conflict and issues surrounding military preparedness. Charles W. Gerwig of Pittsburgh's Lysle Post delivered a lecture at nearly every post meeting between the outbreak of war in 1914 until American intervention nearly three years later. Gerwig designed his well-received talks to educate listeners about many of the European nations at war on subjects ranging from "an account of the manner and details of mobilization of the German Army," "Serbia and its situation & condition in the European War," and a "description of the Swiss Army and its preparedness." Another Pennsylvania post holding a public banquet to celebrate the forty-eighth anniversary of its founding lent much of the evening to guest speakers discussing preparedness. One lecturer, linking past and present, "quoted the example of the Civil War, saying that lack of preparation had a great deal to do with the awful loss of life, and that with that example . . . they could not long postpone some adequate arrangement for national defense." Similarly, SV camps used their fraternal space to inform members and guests of their duties in the event of national emergency. At one Connecticut camp's meeting, a speaker reminded his fellows of their fraternal oath to defend the nation and that there was an "imminent possibility" that they would be compelled to fulfill that pledge. "I know of no better organization to strive toward the end of adequate national preparedness than this one," declared SV member Lucien F. Burpee, "composed of the sons and grandsons of soldiers who offered their lives for the preservation of our country."[14]

Keeping well-apprised of war news from across the Atlantic, Grand Army members became early critics of imperial Germany's conduct. Veterans and their women's auxiliaries proved particularly sympathetic to the plight of the Belgian people and the violation of their sovereignty at the hands of the German army. In Kansas, for example, the state's local GAR and Woman's Relief Corps (WRC) units gave generously to relief efforts for the suffering nation. Emporia's Plumb Post canceled a planned banquet, instead opting to donate their entertainment funds to the town's Belgian relief fund. Across the state in Fort Dodge, veteran inmates at the Kansas State Soldiers' Home collected an admirable $106.65 for the same purpose. Members of the state's WRC also contributed generously, prompting officials to congratulate the women for offering "willing heart and hand" for "a worthy cause to feed and clothe the people of a stricken country." Elsewhere, Grand Army posts responded to the needs of the starving Belgians, remembering the European nation's magnanimity in years past. Wisconsin's Lucius Fairchild Post recollected their state's deadly 1871 Peshtigo wildfire and the Belgians' response to the disaster. After one veteran reminded his comrades that "Belgium had sent to our state $1,000 for aid to those suffering from the great conflagration," the post agreed to appropriate twenty-five dollars to the local Belgian relief efforts. Although GAR veterans remained largely neutral during the early stages of the European war, the desecration of the vulnerable country inclined them to a later anti-German position.[15]

As escalation of the war in Europe edged the United States closer to involvement, Grand Army predisposition for military readiness found an outlet in the various preparedness lobbies that emerged. From September 27 to October 2, 1915, for instance, some 20,000 GAR veterans converged on Washington, D.C., for the annual national encampment and celebration of the semicentennial of the 1865 Grand Review. A significant number of these participants extended their stay in the nation's capital to attend the four-day conference of the National Defense League, an organization founded to support preparedness and the strengthening of the US Army, US Navy, and National Guard. David J. Palmer, who had just ended his term as GAR commander in chief at the conclusion of the Washington encampment, spoke at the League event and reminded the audience of the importance "to care for and safeguard the government and our rights as a nation." Grand Army veterans also threw their support behind the similarly named but more influential

National Security League (NSL)—one of America's strongest preparedness organizations. Founded in December 1914 by Leonard Wood and New York attorney S. Stanwood Menken, the NSL advocated a reform platform that included "the adoption of a definite military policy; a stronger, better balanced Navy; an effective mobile Army; a larger and better equipped national guard; [and] the creation of an organized reserve for each branch of our military service." Within eighteen months of its founding, the organization boasted 50,000 members in 155 branches across the country. Its bylaws—"to promote patriotic education and national sentiment and service among the people of the United States"—also mirrored key objectives for which Grand Army veterans had been striving for decades.[16]

It was hardly surprising, then, that the NSL and the aging ranks of Union veterans fostered a close relationship during the period before the United States' entry into World War I. Indeed, NSL promoters immediately recognized the vaunted civic status of the GAR and devised ways to make the presence of the veterans at local NSL events a symbol of the new organization's legitimacy. In July 1915, for instance, NSL president Menken—seeking ways to "put dynamite into the organization"—advocated a "visualization" plan to invite Grand Army veterans to man NSL recruitment tents that would supplant less effective methods such as "mere education by circularization." At NSL branch meetings across the country, organizers made a point to invite the local GAR posts and reserve prime seating for the veterans. Doubtless done out of deference to the aged men, the spectacle of a bloc of uniformed national defenders of yore nonetheless added to the respectability and seriousness of the affair. At one April 1916 meeting in Pittsburgh, for example, the audience of 2,500 beheld the city's GAR invitees as Menken honored the "fighting forefathers [who] bequeathed to us, the richest empire in the world"—one now requiring security from the world's "great mobile armies and narrow oceans." At a similar NSL meeting in Manhattan that same month, the press reported that the presence of the old GAR heroes "recalled the glorious past of the nation and served to bring into great contrast the uncertain future which the advocates of preparedness see if the nation pursues its present policy."[17]

NSL leaders also identified GAR-led Memorial Day ceremonies as especially revelatory events when communities were already prone to consider the sacrifices of past wars and more receptive to admonitions about unpreparedness. Particularly during the 1916 observance, it was a common sight to see Grand Army veterans and NSL members marching together in the holiday parade. In Westfield, New Jersey, the local NSL branch (joined by Boy Scouts and other schoolchildren) escorted the town's tottering veterans to the cemetery to strew flowers on their comrades' graves. In Philadelphia, hundreds of the city's GAR veterans shared their annual Memorial Day visitations at the public schools with NSL members to impart lessons of patriotism and civic duty on the students. The two organizations, according to the *Philadelphia Inquirer,* "co-operated to make the exercises for the children as entertaining, instructive, [and] thrilling as possible," informing the youths "that the armies which saved the Union were indeed mainly composed of boys, millions of them being of twenty-two years of age, and under, and nearly a million of twenty years and under."[18]

At the same time, GAR members became revered fixtures in the rash of so-called preparedness parades that peaked during the spring and summer of 1916. Organized by civic and business leaders in communities of all sizes, these parades attracted an outpouring of support and participation from a wide variety of citizens, including war veterans who lent an air of authority to the events. For the June 3, 1916 preparedness parade in Providence, Rhode Island, Grand Army men were assigned to form a "guard of honor" for the living flag—a coordinated collection "composed of 1,560 school girls, dressed in red, white and blue . . . who filled a large stand erected in front of the City Hall." That same day in Chicago, a huge procession of some 130,000 citizens also included a small group of GAR veterans. Although the old men marched only for a short time during the eleven-and-a-half-hour event, the press reported that these men "who went into the Civil War unprepared and came out the most formidable military body then on earth, were cheered to the echo all along the line." Arguably the most famous preparedness parade, however, was marred by tragedy later that summer in San Francisco. On July 22, 1916, with over 50,000 marchers participating, a suitcase bomb exploded just as the city's Grand Army veterans swung into line along the parade route. The blast killed ten and injured forty more. Among the dead was seventy-two-year-old GAR veteran Adam Fox who reportedly "died from shock of [the] explosion." In a bizarre show of fortitude, however, the parade continued because of "the lot of the Grand Army men, who, years ago, faced exploding shells in the trenches of Vicksburg, Gettysburg and Grant's campaign for Richmond." Unperturbed by the bombing, GAR veterans and their fellow San Franciscans completed the parade, doubtless hardening their views on preparedness and their opposition to antimilitarist agitators.[19]

Union veterans also participated in the burgeoning motion picture craze that preparedness supporters harnessed for use in their propaganda films. Defense advocate J. Stuart Blackton produced two epic pictures—*Battle Cry of Peace* (1915) and *Womanhood, the Glory of the Nation* (1917)—both presenting a fictionalized chronicle of a foreign invasion of New York City due to the nation's military unpreparedness. Of unusual interest in the films was the presence of hundreds of aged Grand Army veterans portrayed in key moments of the plot. These veterans-turned-actors served as filmic symbols of an era more duty bound and a cohort more heroic than the peace advocates Blackton repeatedly disparaged in his screenplays. Although the films have not survived, contemporary reviews allow some reconstruction of the veterans' roles and the impact they may have had on the silver screen. Each centered on charismatic GAR comrade John Wallace "Captain Jack" Crawford whose post–Civil War exploits as an adventurer and scout during the Great Sioux Wars leveraged a career as a professional entertainer and lecturer on the American Wild West during the 1890s. In *Battle Cry*, Crawford leads a patriotic rally, surrounded by GAR veterans (most likely from Brooklyn's U.S. Grant Post [see Figure 10]) standing solemnly at attention.

Figure 10 Members of the U.S. Grant Post of Brooklyn, New York, stand at attention along with active military officers in a still of J. Stuart Blackton's preparedness film, *Battle Cry of Peace* (1915). Flamboyant GAR comrade John Wallace "Captain Jack" Crawford stands on the raised dais, second from the right, clutching an American flag. "Vitagraph's Patriotic Picture," *Moving Picture World*, 31 July 1915.

"The veterans present a pathetic sight," reported *Moving Picture World*, "their ranks thinned by the ravages of time, but their patriotism undaunted." Another reviewer espied a clear link between the Civil War generation and the present age by declaring that the film was "doing for preparedness against war what 'Uncle Tom's Cabin' did to arouse the sentiment of the nation against the evils of slavery." "Captain Jack" and his fellows reprised their role in Blackton's sequel, proving their mettle again in a "last stand of a group of devoted Grand Army men who make a fight against the invaders of America."[20]

Besides their portrayal in Blackton's films, GAR veterans also became enthusiastic moviegoers and some of the preparedness films' biggest backers. For several weeks after *Battle Cry*'s premiere, Crawford reproduced for theater audiences a spirited patriotic oration akin to that he was seen delivering in the film. After viewing the movie, crowds in New York, Boston, Philadelphia, and Washington (reportedly up to 100,000 over a two-week period in the latter's Strand Theater) heard Crawford defend military preparedness and intone his own lyrics arranged especially for the event:

> My mother raised her boy to be a soldier!
> My mother raised a patriotic boy!
> My mother placed a musket on his shoulder,
> The enemies of freedom to destroy!

So popular was the film that officers of the 1915 GAR national encampment in Washington, D.C., sanctioned that it be shown during the week of festivities. Meanwhile, GAR posts across the country swarmed their local theaters to see the production. When *Battle Cry* first opened in Houston, Texas, members of the city's GAR, United Confederate Veterans, local US Navy recruiters, and Boy Scouts (a collection of "soldiers of the past, present and future" as the *Houston Post* described) gathered in a parade of 400 and marched down Main Street to the city's Prince Theater. Judging by "the repeated applause which, several times grew to . . . an ovation," the *Post* concluded that the viewers "went away deeply impressed by the message of preparedness, which the silent drama carries." Massachusetts GAR veteran Frederick G. Kinsman, who had never before seen a moving picture, came away "astounded at the realistic manner in which the scenes of war, peace and industry were shown," and quipped that "he used to think he was in a pitiful condition because he didn't have the free use of his limbs, but he was glad he had been spared the use of his eyes in order to witness such a wonderful spectacle."[21]

As the United States faced the growing prospect of intervening in Europe's Great War, Grand Army members intensified their long-standing advocacy of military preparedness. They and their auxiliaries urged various reforms to ensure that the tragedy and hardships they had once endured never took the nation by surprise again and encouraged younger generations to recognize a firm commitment between military training, citizenship, and civic duty. Supporting the democratic, reformist notion that this training was a universal obligation for the nation's young men, GAR veterans resurrected their belief in the volunteer citizen-soldier whose service would quell any national emergency. Despite members' advanced age, they became some of the nation's most assertive and visible activists, endorsing military reform, training camps, preparedness groups, parades, and propaganda films. Assuming the venerable role of America's patriotic elders, Union veterans successfully deployed their beloved status as the nation's onetime saviors to instruct rising cohorts how to do the same.

Some Vim Left in the Old Boys Yet

In the early years of his administration, President Woodrow Wilson developed a rocky relationship with the Grand Army of the Republic. Wilson, a Democrat, garnered little enthusiasm among Union veterans who still largely adhered to the Party of Lincoln. During the election of 1912, most GAR members (like Republicans broadly) divided their support between incumbent William Howard Taft and challenger Theodore Roosevelt, whose "Bull Moose" third-party bid caught fire around Roosevelt's charisma and pledge to eliminate corruption from politics and business. Many veterans remembered Roosevelt's earlier tenure in office fondly, appreciating his frequent visits to speak at GAR events, support for GAR-backed reform measures, and the feelings of comradeship with a fellow war veteran. Indeed, when Roosevelt telegraphed his intentions to run for president again by delivering his iconic New Nationalism speech at Osawatomie, Kansas, in August 1910, Grand Army veterans stood prominently in the crowd to hear the address. "As for the veterans of the Grand Army of the Republic," Roosevelt acknowledged before the appreciative comrades, "they deserve honor and recognition such as is paid to no other citizens of the Republic; for to them the Republic owes it all; for to them it owes its very existence." After Roosevelt secured the Progressive Party's nomination two years later, many veterans' political allegiances shifted to him. The ultimate election of Wilson—a southern-born nonveteran with states' rights sympathies—was for many GAR veterans a disagreeable outcome.[22]

Unlike his predecessors, Wilson initially struggled to foster goodwill with the GAR and appeared tone-deaf when called upon to keynote all-important Civil War commemorative events. Months after his inauguration, Wilson blundered by nearly declining an invitation to speak at the 1913 Blue-Gray Reunion at Gettysburg in favor of vacationing with his family. The president ultimately relented but scored bad marks from some Union veterans by leaning into reconciliationism and speaking of "battles long past" and a "quarrel forgotten." The *New York Times*, reporting that Wilson stayed in Gettysburg a mere forty-six minutes before leaving for his summer retreat, noted that the crowd thought Wilson "had not been in camp long enough to catch the sentiment that prevailed" and claimed that his speech was "interrupted only once or twice with cheering... that seemed perfunctory." In the months ahead, Wilson compounded his issues with Union veterans. In November 1913, a GAR delegation descended upon the White House to protest the supplanting of veterans in government service with loyal Democrats. Although the practice was typical after a party's electoral takeover, the sacking of aged Union veterans produced bad optics. The following May, Wilson further offended the GAR by declining an invitation to deliver a Memorial Day address at Arlington National Cemetery, while accepting one to speak five days later at the unveiling of the United Daughters of the Confederacy's Arlington Confederate Memorial. Again, Wilson relented and ultimately spoke at both events, but many veterans scorned the president's affront.[23]

Over time, Wilson gradually cultivated a better relationship with what he must have realized was a still-influential Union veterans' bloc. At the next GAR invitation to attend Memorial Day ceremonies in 1915, Wilson agreed to deliver the keynote address without hesitation. The following autumn, he was an active participant throughout the GAR's multiday national encampment, which was held in Washington, D.C. On the first day, the president had his welcome message to the veterans "wig-wagged"—sent around the city by surviving veterans of the Union army's Signal Corps. That evening, Wilson flattered GAR attendees for "set[ting] the nation free for that great career of development, of unhampered development, which the world has witnessed since the civil war [sic]." The following day, 20,000 veterans marched before a crowd of 100,000 through the streets of the capital. Wilson stood on the reviewing stand near the White House, at the same spot President Andrew Johnson reviewed many of these same men a half century earlier. "Tears gathered in [Wilson's] eyes time and again," the newspapers reported, "and, unashamed, he brushed them away." The president received widespread plaudits by the GAR veterans for his participation and speechmaking during the encampment, prompting former Commander in Chief

James Tanner to utter that "President Wilson can rely on the fact that the Grand Army of the Republic is just as loyal to him as it was to Lincoln and Johnson fifty years ago." Wilson cultivated such positive feelings from one elderly New England veteran that he reportedly told the president that "I have never voted for a Democrat for President since the war, but I am for you, and if I die before I vote next year I will ask my sons and grandsons to support you."[24]

With his standing among GAR veterans improving, Wilson also received their praise for his leadership and prudent foreign policy maneuvers as Europe descended into war. In the early months after combat began, many gave him credit for charting a path of US neutrality and reasonable military preparedness. A collection of Grand Army veterans at the 1915 national encampment lauded Wilson for standing "against those who would push us into a useless war" and "winning by bloodless battles everything that battles ever won." In Vermont, veterans admitted that "while we do not want our country at war, it would be better to spend a billion in preparedness than run the risk of losing a million American lives. . . . We must be prepared, and we must stand by our President and help him face this situation." At the February 1916 encampment for the GAR's Potomac Department, Wilson delivered brief remarks touching on democracy, the war in Europe, and the powers of the executive office. "[B]ut what I think of more often than the [executive] powers is the difficulty of knowing the right use to which to put those powers," Wilson reflected. At the close of his address, Commander in Chief Elias R. Monfort—evidently moved by Wilson's frank admission of the great weight of the presidency in a time of global war—said, "you are my President, you are the President of the Grand Army of the Republic, you are the President of every true American in this country—I pledge you the allegiance and support of whatever measures you may deem proper in the measure of your ability to preserve this Nation in prosperity and unity, for which these men have fought for their country."[25]

The following year, GAR veterans confirmed that allegiance when the Wilson administration, under great strain to maintain neutrality while facing increasingly hostile German actions and U-boat attacks, took steps to ready the nation for war. From all across the country, Wilson received assurances of GAR members' unwavering support. In February 1917, GAR Commander in Chief William J. Patterson personally visited the president to offer his comrades' services to the government. Patterson subsequently informed all comrades that Wilson "knew in advance that he could count on their loyalties." During the annual encampment of the GAR Arkansas Department held the following month, the scant veterans there similarly pledged their loyalty to the president. Asserting their understanding of "the blessing of American citizenship," they promised their "unswerving support in [Wilson's] effort to protect the rights and lives of American citizens irrespective of race, color or nationality." Wisconsin's Fairchild Post, admitting that they were "not as nimble now in body" as they had been a half century earlier, drew on Civil War–era imagery to nonetheless pledge their readiness for the upcoming fight. "[W]e are even more patriotic in spirit than then, if that is possible," the members claimed, "and, in case of need, we will 'rally round the flag, boys, rally once again, shouting the battle cry of freedom.'" Even the surviving members of distant Honolulu's George W. De Long Post offered their services to the country "in any manner or form which may be required of us and which we are able to perform."[26]

GAR veterans closely followed the events that drove the nation further toward confrontation with Germany and largely favored the president's actions to defend American rights and security. When Wilson severed diplomatic relations with the German government in February 1917 (on the same day as the sinking of the US cargo ship *Housatonic*), Duluth's Culver Post immediately voiced its support. Commending Wilson's action, the post sent a letter to the president declaring that "[t]he Veterans of '61–'65 deny the right of any nation to dictate or make innovations that jeopardize the rights of neutrals on land or sea." Weeks later, Wilson sought congressional support to arm merchant ships to counter the increasingly hostile affronts by German U-boats. Although the House of Representatives overwhelmingly approved the request, Ohio Congressman Isaac R. Sherwood—a Union veteran and member of Toledo's Forsyth Post—voted against the so-called armed neutrality bill. Sherwood's veteran-constituents, shocked at their comrade's decision, adopted resolutions censuring him, charging that he "did not represent patriotic sentiment in his district." Just days after the United States declared war in April 1917, Wisconsin GAR veterans paid Wilson one of the highest compliments, comparing him to a previous war chief. "President Wilson, as our great leader, is much like President Lincoln," they said. "He has the highest of ideals and is wholly unselfish. We may not all agree with every policy of his, as many of the best people did not agree with Lincoln, yet we have reason to believe him as honest as Abraham Lincoln was."[27]

The war declaration unleashed among some Grand Army veterans hostile anti-German prejudices that characterized the response of many native-born citizens. One Delaware comrade, for example, denounced Germany as "a cruel country . . . so wicked and without any pity for innocent people." This sentiment at times manifested itself in examples of intolerance for German Americans or, at least, impatience with the insufficiency of their proper Americanization. One

Wisconsin veteran patronizingly reminded the state's large contingent of German immigrants about the implication of naturalization. "[The German American] has chosen of his own notion to adjure allegiance to the land from which he came," lectured Hosea W. Rood, "and has sworn such allegiance to his adopted country as demands of him, if necessary, to go to war side by side with those who were born into citizenship here." In Duluth, the Culver Post appointed a committee to investigate reports that a high school teacher (with the suspect Germanic surname "Zeigler") had placed a German flag above the American flag in her classroom. "[W]e resent," wrote the post to school Superintendent W. J. Hoke, "the spectacle of any flag raised above the Stars and Stripes and particularly the flag which symbolizes the nation with which our President and Government has deemed necessary to sever relations." Hoke, claiming this was an unfortunate oversight, assured the veterans that the teacher did not mean "to commit an act of disloyalty" and that he "desire[d] to see nothing but americanism [sic] in our public schools." Meanwhile, other posts remained discreet about Germans generally and instead directed their hostility at Kaiser Wilhelm II. At meetings of Pittsburgh's O. H. Rippey Post, members periodically read "ludicrous" poems about the German emperor, mocking his claims to rule by divine right. One New Hampshire comrade, knowing the coming combat would not "be boys play," still relished the thought of Granite Staters "lick[ing] the old villain."[28]

Of course, many Grand Army veterans were German-born or had German ancestry and refused to abide their countrymen's accusations of disloyalty. When President Wilson disparaged so-called "hyphenated Americans" before the United States' entry into the war, New Jersey comrade Ernest C. Stahl took exception to the slight and endeavored to teach his comrades that pride in one's homeland did not equate to treachery against his adopted country. "I cannot forget the love I bear to the land that gave me birth," Stahl conceded, but reminded his comrades that for those tens of thousands of Germans "who joined the Union army and shed their blood for the stars and stripes . . . let me tell you that, like me to-day, these hyphenated Americans that our good President has such a grudge against are just as loyal to Columbia and the United States and its banner as any man born here ever dared to be." Other German American veterans worked hard to allay any charges of indifference to their adopted country's war effort in its conflict with the land of their birth. Minnesota veteran Peter Shippman called his comrades' attention to the four and a half years he served in the US Army "and though born in Germany . . . considers himself 100 per cent American and thoroughly loyal to his adopted country." In Rochester, New York, the twenty-six surviving members of the Peissner Post (who were almost all of German birth or ancestry) proved their loyalty at one October 1917 meeting when they, as the local newspaper succinctly reported, "[d]irected quartermaster to buy a $100 Liberty Bond. Gave three cheers for America. Saluted the flag. Sang 'My Country, Tis of Thee.'"[29]

After Congress declared war, a rash of GAR post resolutions streamed into the offices of not only the president, but also mayors, governors, and other public officials, who received assurances of Union veterans' support during this time of national emergency. To be sure, many of these resolutions remained fairly perfunctory and unspecific, issued symbolically at a large number of local post meetings in the days and weeks after the declaration. Still, the resolutions illustrated that Union veterans would not use the excuse of age to sit idly by as the nation mobilized for war. One post in Mt. Carmel, Pennsylvania, for example, sent a telegram to President Wilson pledging that they were "ready and willing to serve in any capacity where we can be used." Veterans in Concord, Massachusetts, similarly wrote the town's board of selectmen with a promise to serve in any capacity "useful to town, State or nation." Even military officials and National Guardsmen were targets for GAR members' offers to serve. In Iowa, for instance, the adjutant general of the state's National Guard was reportedly swamped with "innumerable offers of services" from Grand Army men during the heady early days of the war when the Guard was seeking recruits to fill up its ranks.[30]

Meanwhile, individual GAR veterans—frequently spurred by a mix of pride, patriotism, and nostalgia for their past war service—announced their intentions to bear arms in the latest conflict. One Pittsburgh veteran boasted to his post's comrades that he had passed a physical examination before a recruitment board but was ultimately turned down because of his age. Perhaps smarting from the snub, the veteran intended to walk to Virginia's Camp Lee "to show them that there was some vim left in the old boys yet." The press relished printing stories about gray-haired GAR veterans declaring their intentions to defend the nation again. Seventy-seven-year-old William B. Draper of Long Island made a stir when he proclaimed his readiness to serve in the US Navy as he had during the Civil War over a half century before. "Any kind of a boat I'd like to see service on, submarine chaser or anything," Draper stated, adding that he found the Germans to be "a cowardly and contemptible race." Fellow Grand Army man George W. Perkins of Houston, Pennsylvania, wrote Secretary of War Newton D. Baker, offering his services. In response, Baker advised Perkins to aid his local recruiting office. At once, Perkins (who had served in the US Military Telegraph Corps during the Civil War) reported to the nearest US Army Signal Corps recruiting station and, presumably, assisted with local enlistment efforts. Prominent Washington, D.C. jurist and GAR veteran Hosea B. Moulton wrote President Wilson just days after the war declaration with a proposal to establish and command a volunteer infantry regiment. Having served in the Civil War in a New Hampshire regiment and been twice wounded, the local papers marveled that the septuagenarian's health was "excellent," and the judge remained "active and strong." Although many of these veterans' pledges were unrealistic given the advanced age of these would-be volunteers, they were still admirable and demonstrated a lasting commitment to the nation into which they had already invested so much.[31]

Some GAR offers to serve were in fact quite farsighted and more than mere token responses to a nation now at war. This was especially true for posts comprised of racial minorities who seized the occasion of the war emergency to reaffirm their loyalty and simultaneously strive for fairer treatment and civil rights. For instance, members of the Joseph Ledergerber Post of Keshena, Wisconsin—comprised solely of Native Americans of the Menominee tribe—pledged their services to the federal government and encouraged younger tribal members to aid the war effort, thereby soliciting better conduct by the Bureau of Indian Affairs. Influenced by the Menominee reservation's Union veterans, the tribe pledged all its "eligible men to prepare themselves by such home training as may be possible in preparing them for the call to arms" and "to utilize their property and their tribal funds and develop the natural resources of the reservation along any and all lines which may be beneficial to the government in carrying on the war." One admiring local newspaper reported that it was "doubtful if any white community in the land" demonstrated "more unselfish devotion to the country." African American veterans, too, linked their professed devotion to the nation at war with demands for the fulfillment of equitable interracial citizenship. The Fort Pillow Post of Topeka, Kansas, forwarded resolutions to the state's governor pledging their "aid in every way in our power to win the war against Germany" with an accompanying insistence "that all classes be equal before the law." Interestingly, the veterans also took the opportunity to defend women's suffrage, which had been adopted in the state a few years earlier, announcing that they endorsed the reform and would "stand for it first, last and all the time."[32]

Another useful effect of the outpouring of veterans' service pledges that flooded in from across the country was that it cajoled younger generations to match the commitment of these civic elders. Days after the war declaration, Nebraska GAR officer W. H. Stewart admitted that although his comrades were "past the age for active service," they still could "show the spirit of true patriotism in urging the young men of the country to 'rally round the flag' as we did from 1861 to 1865." In neighboring Iowa, one post circulated eight separate resolutions designed to resolve the nation's war crisis. These included advocating universal and compulsory military service, displaying the American flag widely, and pledging loyalty to the president and Congress. Further, the post vowed to shame shirkers of military age who planned to use "the subterfuge of marriage and other means to escape military and naval service in defense of their homes, firesides and country." The press, meanwhile, recognized the influence that GAR advocacy had on spurring the nation's younger generations to enlist. One Ohio newspaper noted that when the local GAR post offered up its 250 members for service to the government, it had the effect of "stimulating recruiting in Akron." Young readers of the local organ in Burlington, Vermont, may have felt shame to hear of GAR officer J. B. Lewis's intent to enroll at least 1,500 Union veterans for service to the state in any capacity they might be needed. Arguing that the GAR members should only be called upon "in a remote contingency of invasion," the paper chided that "[t]he present generation should not allow these grand men to do double duty in this way."[33]

To be sure, political and military officials recognized that it was the most appropriate use of the GAR's limited potency to inspire the younger generations to enlist in the fight ahead. In response to one Wisconsin post offering its services to the state's Council of Defense, Governor Emanuel L. Philipp personally wrote that the aged veterans' "only labor should consist of giving inspiration to the young men who will be called upon to render the service that is demanded of the people of their generation, as it was demanded of you." Meanwhile in Congress, just days after the war declaration, Representative Everis A. Hayes of California introduced House Bill 2775, "authorizing the employment of Grand Army veterans for recruiting purposes." Veterans needed no legislative spur to aid the country's recruitment efforts, however. In communities across the country, Grand Army veterans were a highly visible force whose presence was frequently cited as a reason for compliance with selective service registration and healthy enlistment efforts. GAR Adjutant General Herbert H. Bengough urged comrades across the country to offer their services—free of charge—as conscription clerks in the registration offices. The rank and file responded. For example, Alfred E. Stacey of Elbridge, New York, complimented by his comrades as "energetic and faithful in every position . . . he has been placed," served as the chairman of his town's draft board. Similarly, Captain Robert M. Painter was not only an active organizer for his community's food conservation efforts but also served on the Meade County, Kansas, draft board.[34]

Grand Army members, though, remained particularly fond of the National Guard, as it represented the spirit of voluntarism and selfless duty that led many of them to enlist in the Civil War decades before. "[L]et us get behind our National Guard and assist them in filling up their ranks!" cheered one Nebraska officer. "It typifies the volunteer system and should have the support of every comrade." Adjutants general working to fill the ranks of their states' National Guard units frequently welcomed the activism of Grand Army veterans to spur recruitment. While cajoling his state's civic and business leaders to "become a part of the movement" to encourage young men to join the Guard, Iowa's Adjutant General, Guy E. Logan, lauded the GAR's department officers for "issu[ing] orders for their men to aid in this recruiting work." Similarly, when Lansing, Michigan, endeavored to fill the ranks of its two locally raised artillery batteries, recruiting officers were pleased that the aging veterans of the Charles T. Foster Post arrived "in force" to encourage the city's youth to join up. "Lansing's share in the defense of the nation from Prussian militarism is personified in the two batteries," asserted one veteran. "Can the youth of the city do less than to offer their services in enlistment?"[35]

With the federal government's controversial call for conscription to fill out its armed forces, however, Grand Army veterans plunged into contentious debate about the meaning of military service, civic duty, and the appropriate motivations behind enlistment. For some veterans, a spirit of voluntarism was the only correct incentive to serve the nation, as this best characterized an earnest inner patriotism and the surest guarantee of victory in a time of crisis. The majority of Grand Army men volunteered for Civil War service and remembered the unfair, and even dishonorable, legacy of the era's conscription measures, bounties, and substitutes. In an editorial, New York GAR officer George B. Loud asked "[w]hy does not everybody respect the memory at least of the glorious result that came to our country through the achievement of the men—volunteers all—who have done all the war fighting—fighting I saw—for our country in the last fifty-six years?.... When, where and by whom other than volunteers was any war victory won?" For other veterans, the conscription law was not shameful and in fact was a just way to identify those young men who would best serve in a time of national crisis. Eschewing the term "draft law," Wisconsin's Jerome A. Watrous preferred to call it a "selective law" as the policy reached those men "because of their fitness in health, in habits, in morals, in all of the things necessary to make them valuable and valiant soldiers of the nation." Commander in Chief William J. Patterson agreed and thought the policy "splendid" and best "show[ed] how we stand on the question of volunteering the entire population, if need be, in the defense of human liberty all over the world, and the suppression of imperialism." Still, for many veterans, it was likely the case that although they came to terms with the necessity of a conscription law, it was far better to rally to the colors voluntarily and prove one's patriotic worth before being compelled to do so by government decree. "Every patriotic young man" reasoned Nebraska's W. H. Stewart, "should place his services at the disposal of the government, instead of waiting for a compulsatory [sic] call to protect the honor of our great and beloved country."[36]

However the next generation of America's defenders entered the Great War, Grand Army men stood ready to encourage their enlistment, inspire devotion to duty, and offer the hand of friendship to the young men about to embark for Europe (see Figure 11). Veterans frequently participated in community parades and

Figure 11 An unidentified Union veteran, wearing his GAR badge, sits for a photograph beside a World War I soldier. The pair—likely from Moscow, Pennsylvania, and possibly grandfather and grandson—exemplify the intergenerational affinity between many aging GAR members and young American doughboys and the similarities they believed their respective causes shared. Courtesy of Prints and Photographs Division, Library of Congress.

demonstrations designed both to cultivate patriotic spirit and, more practically, spur enlistments. One Kansas post claimed they were not averse "to take up our guns again to guard . . . Old Glory," but ultimately thought it more prudent to help the state by "guiding the plow, chopping weeds with the hoe, to grow more grain to feed the people of the world in this time of need, [and] in marching along the streets to show to the younger men that our loyalty and nerve are still with us." Similarly in Wausau, Wisconsin, local post members were the most venerable participants in a patriotic parade that wended its way through the town's streets. Alongside Wausau's Grand Army veterans, GAR auxiliary members, Spanish-American War veterans, police officers, and some 2,000 schoolchildren marched the community's newly enlisted army and navy recruits. Several months later in Harrisburg, Pennsylvania, 6,000 citizens took part in the city's "recruiting demonstration" to help add to the roughly 1,000 young men of the community who had already enlisted in the military. In a show of thanks for the local GAR posts' participation in the parade and for encouraging enlistment among Harrisburg's citizens, Lieutenant R. W. Lesher of the city's recruiting district lauded the aging veterans' commitment. "The name of your organization and the fact of your membership," Lesher asserted, "should acquire a new value for you from the fact that it stands for its share of support of this Country during the time of National stress."[37]

As the nation's enlistees began consolidating in camps across the country and shipping out to Europe, Grand Army veterans played another important role—fortifying the young generation with their support and pride. Common were GAR posts that accompanied recruits to the embarkation points. In Salem, Oregon, forty members of the GAR escorted the city's eleven draftees from the courthouse to the train station where they were to be transported to Camp Lewis. Two African American draftees in Carlisle, Pennsylvania, were feted with a reception by members of the Black community, given comfort kits, and urged "to be true to their race and country." Present were members of the all-Black J. G. Thompson Post, who formed in line of march to parade alongside the young men to the train station and their departure to Camp Meade. Meanwhile, at the annual state encampment in Des Moines, Iowa, young men training at nearby Camp Dodge paraded alongside the GAR attendees. The press delighted in the image of soldiers past and present sharing the experience and comparing the two cohorts' parallel missions. "Khaki clad troops, training for participation in the present great war," reported one local newspaper, "served as escort yesterday to the thousand or more 'boys in blue,' veterans of that other great struggle for human liberty of a half century ago, in their parade."[38]

Meanwhile, evidence suggests that although the Sons of Veterans Reserves never received formal recognition from the US government as a reserve force, the organization's training efforts had a notable effect on both home front service and overseas recruitment for the Great War. "It is of record," claimed one Indiana newspaper, "that . . . entire regiments of drilled, uniformed and properly equipped Sons of Veterans of the civil war [sic] (known as Sons of Veterans Reserves), offered their services to fight for America and for American homes." This may have been some exaggeration, yet SV and SVR members were noted for their service at home and abroad. The SVR company in Allentown, Pennsylvania, provides a good case study. By the fall of 1917, forty-six members of the company had enlisted in the armed forces. Another 150 members of the city—many with dependents—elected to stay home. But intent on "doing their bit for the country in the war with Germany," they nonetheless offered their services to the commonwealth and reorganized as a company of Home Defense Guards, "subject to call by the state and local authorities at any time lives and or property are placed in jeopardy." SV and SVR members across the country had a respectable rate of service in the World War I–era armed forces, particularly in the eastern states where the organization was strongest. In his 1919–1920 reports, the SV's national patriotic instructor detailed the number of Sons in the service by state, led by Massachusetts (1,000 enlisted men and 117 commissioned officers); Pennsylvania (748 and 85); New York (185 and 66); Connecticut (171 and 22); Ohio (132 and 22); and New Jersey (123 and 2).[39]

Besides offering pride and comfort to the departing doughboys, Grand Army veterans also proved active in their communities' efforts to discipline the nation's home front to the sacrifices required for victory. Equal to any other group in wartime America, the GAR captured the spirit of voluntarism and self-sacrifice that the Wilson administration hoped to cultivate on behalf of the nation's war mobilization needs. With the naming of Herbert Hoover as the country's food administrator in May 1917 (and the subsequent establishment of the US Food Administration three months later), the GAR and its auxiliaries wholeheartedly tendered their support for food conservation efforts to feed the mobilizing American army and its European allies. The members of Duluth's Culver Post recognized the wastefulness of slaughtering immature cows, pigs, and chickens and urged citizens to "[c]ontribute their bit" by "refrain[ing] from buying or consuming any Veal or products thereof or 'chicken fries' or 'Little pigs,'" through the course of the war. In neighboring Wisconsin, veterans prided themselves on "learning how to make the most of what we have" and spurred themselves and their neighbors to create Victory gardens to the point that they were "pretty nearly living off those gardens." Meanwhile at the 1917 Fourth of July celebration in Berkeley, California, members of the local WRC joined with other women's associations to supply homemakers with Hoover Pledge Cards—tokens of a woman's personal oath to encourage their families to avoid wasting food and disciplining them to observe "Meatless Mondays" and "Wheatless Wednesdays."[40]

Similarly, the GAR mobilized on behalf of Treasury Secretary William G. McAdoo's efforts to finance the war by appealing to Americans' economic patriotism and self-sacrifice. For example, Pittsburgh's J. B. McPherson Post saw that—barring actual combat service—their proper duty was the support of the government's Liberty Loan efforts. "Those of us who are not called to go [to] the front," post members recorded, "can render most effective service by contributing to the new Liberty Loan. . . . Every Liberty Bond purchased . . . will be a guarantee of victory—a reassurance to our boys in the trenches that the nation is back of them, not only with our hopes and our prayers, but with our entire resources down to the last dollar." Indeed, local post support for Liberty Bonds was often stunningly generous, with many posts nearly exhausting the contents of their post funds to support the effort. GAR minute books are strewn with recordings of post officers authorizing their quartermasters or finance committees to purchase bonds. The amount of post funds dedicated to Liberty Loan purchases largely depended on the health and membership strength of the post. Not unusual, however, were purchases like those made by the Alfred G. Reed Post of Butler, Pennsylvania ($100); the Farragut Post of Lincoln, Nebraska ($150); the Gen. Sedgwick Post of Orange, Massachusetts ($300); or Pittsburgh's Duquesne Post ($1,000). Common, too, was GAR participation in Liberty Loan parades or solicitation drives. In 1918, comrade Edward A. Weed of California dedicated so much time to selling Liberty Bonds and War Savings Stamps (in addition to volunteering for the Red Cross and giving speeches as a "four-minute man" for the Wilson administration's Committee on Public Information) that he "collapsed from overwork for Uncle Sam." In sum, McAdoo's financial strategy clearly flourished thanks in part to the Civil War generation's ardent patriotism.[41]

Meanwhile, GAR women's auxiliaries were particularly preoccupied with the proper comportment of the male relations they sent off to war, advocating for government assistance in keeping their loved ones pure and unharmed by the salacious behaviors long attributed to soldiering. Less than a month after the war declaration, for example, one Kansas congressman received a petition from Topeka's Ladies of the Grand Army of the Republic "praying for the enactment of legislation to protect military camps from vice." The Wilson administration, however, had preempted the women's pleas. Citing a desire to return the US recruit to his home "with no scars except those won in honorable conflict," Wilson established the Commission on Training Camp Activities (CTCA) in April 1917. The commission, charged with eliminating soldier immorality in training camps and the communities surrounding them, distributed literature on social hygiene, organized healthful recreational programs, administered chemical prophylaxis, and provided a range of other services. Aiding the CTCA, women's groups such as the WRC wrote their sons in the service and urged them to "respect the womanhood in the countries to which they are going," while also encouraging young women drawn to the training camps or surrounding communities for work to avoid defiling themselves through inappropriate sexual encounters with the soldiers. Wisconsin's WRC department urged its local chapters to donate money for the construction of proper housing for young women working near the camps, which would mean "safeguarding . . . the health and morals of thousands of our women and girls and will indirectly benefit our enlisted men." Even the GAR—normally reticent on matters of soldier purity—occasionally assessed the role that vice suppression played in the military training of the nation's doughboys. In 1919, for instance, GAR Medical Director Egbert T. Andrews of Maine extolled the sex education offered in part by the efforts of the CTCA. "The wide prevalence of venereal disease among our young men was a revelation to the people at home," Andrews reported, "and probably from now on, the campaign against venereal disease will be one of the good results of the war."[42]

All told, Grand Army veterans proved to be among the wartime nation's most devoted home front contributors, recognizing the Great War as perhaps their last chance to affirm the principles for which they fought as youths. This commitment came despite the veterans' initial aversion to Woodrow Wilson, whom they ultimately came to view as an effective administrator and war leader. With the entry of the United States into World War I, GAR members embraced an activist role, reminding Americans of the nation's heritage of preserving democracy and liberty in the face of subjugation, while inspiring younger generations to enlist in the latest conflict. Meanwhile, Union veterans became avid supporters of the Wilson administration's expansion of the federal government's powers to manage and fight the war effectively. From food conservation to war bond drives, Grand Army posts in communities across the nation assumed many of the burdens of disciplining civilians to the pursuit of victory. Too old for service abroad, GAR veterans understood that in this new war they would earn their plaudits as senior commanders of the home front.

To Work for the Salvation of the World

As an armistice quieted the guns in Europe in November 1918, Grand Army members back home concentrated their sage thoughts on the meaning of this latest conflict. GAR meditations on the war frequently centered upon the values that Union veterans had cherished since their fraternity's inception—the familiar lexicon of freedom, liberty, and democracy—and compared the achievements of the nation's returning soldiers with their own. For most, the Civil War and the Great War were inextricably linked—the latter merely the logical, global culmination of what they had begun in 1861. "Lincoln declared in his day that slavery and freedom could not exist side by side in the same nation," reasoned Wisconsin GAR veteran Hosea W. Rood (see Figure 12). "Since then the world conscience

Figure 12 Hosea W. Rood of Madison, Wisconsin, was an energetic member of the city's Lucius Fairchild Post and a prolific chronicler of the post's civic activities. Like many surviving GAR members at the end of World War I, Rood believed the aim to liberate Europe from autocracy to be the logical culmination of the Union Cause to expunge slavery from the United States. Courtesy of GAR Memorial Hall Collection, Wisconsin Veterans Museum.

has come up to the point when it can no longer tolerate side by side autocracy and democracy." Indeed, for many veterans, the emancipationist meaning of the Civil War lived on through the heroic service of the American doughboy. One Rhode Island veteran, recalling the "grievous menace" of "African slavery in this country," equated the German kaiser's similar "unholy doctrine" that "subject[ed] all peoples to abject slavery. It was this doctrine, this slavery, this autocracy, that our boys in France have been fighting." Similarly, at the 1919 state encampment in Vermont, one officer perceived the consummation of the Union veterans' divine sacrifice by their descendants who fought and bled across the Atlantic. "You, my Comrades, went to liberate the slaves and you liberated them forever, you cemented our country," preached Edwin J. Foster. "You, my Comrades, made it possible for these young Comrades of today who are coming home to us to go forth to work for the salvation of the world. You made it possible for them to go across and help to liberate all of these people in bondage across the water and to save democracy."[43]

To commend this noble cause, timeworn Union veterans drummed up all the vim they could muster to provide a worthy homecoming for the young crusaders who spread GAR values abroad. State-level officers set the tone, insisting that the local posts do all they could to provide the boys with a hearty welcome. Massachusetts Department Commander Edwin P. Stanley, for example, encouraged every post in the state to "arrange in its hall a welcome to the Boys in such form as may be acceptable to them. In this way they will be assured that the old Veterans have a warm place in their hearts for those who have made democracy possible in the Old World." GAR members in communities nationwide hardly needed the cajoling, proudly throwing open their post rooms and memorial halls to the returning troops. In New Castle, Pennsylvania, the local post prepared an open meeting at their headquarters to simultaneously commemorate Washington's birthday and hail the returning soldiers, arranging a rousing performance by the local drum corps. Veterans in Brandon, Vermont, lent their memorial hall to a town celebration honoring the scores of returning troops, many of whom received medals from Governor Percival W. Clement. In Port Huron, Michigan, members of the William Sanborn Post, assisted by their women's auxiliary, prepared a series of entertainments throughout the spring of 1919 for some 150 World War I soldiers in the area, serving them supper, hearing their stories from abroad, and providing them with warm comradeship. In Topeka, Kansas, the 92nd Infantry Division—the sole African American division to fight in Europe—returned home to an integrated community reception and a special welcome by the aged members of the all-Black Fort Pillow Post who proudly served as the event's color bearers.[44]

Although all GAR veterans could agree to commend the returning doughboys, President Wilson's bid for the United States' participation in his League of Nations proposal (an addendum to the larger Treaty of Versailles) proved a thornier issue. Grand Army veterans, like Americans broadly, debated the merits of the League and the degree to which the United States should engage with the postwar world. For some, the promise of an international body charged with arbitrating peace was a cause worthy of support. Even before the United States' entry into the war, GAR members looked with horror upon the unparalleled death and destruction occurring in Europe and some proved sympathetic to the idea of a global peace organization. In June 1915, under the guidance of former President William H. Taft, concerned Americans formed the League to Enforce Peace (LEP) with aims to work with other nations in the interest of collective security. Although GAR veterans did not flock to peace groups as robustly as the competing preparedness organizations, some did express interest in the LEP. The George A. McCall Post of West Chester, Pennsylvania, citing that they knew "in measure the horrors of war with modern weapons," stated that the LEP "commends itself to our judgment because it is international in scope, most likely to be effective when passion is subsiding, and the world can calmly consider the immeasurable calamity of modern war." After the armistice, some veterans maintained an interest in Wilson's call for an international body to arbitrate future peace. Ohio GAR Chaplain Edmund Burdsall believed joining such an order in peacetime to be as patriotic as the organization's home front efforts during the war. Burdsall congratulated his comrades and all Americans for "obtain[ing] money for the Liberty Loans, for the Red Cross, to sell War Saving Stamps, and now to secure the best 'League of Nations' that war may never come again in wanton greed, and murderous crime and waste." Others lent their participation to the civic expressions of support for Wilson's League. In Duluth, members of the Culver Post attended a "Patriotic Pagent [sic] of the League of Nations" organized by advocates of the alliance.[45]

But many veterans, paralleling the loss of support the League of Nations underwent as a result of Republican attacks throughout 1919, objected to American ratification of the Treaty of Versailles with the stipulation of League membership attached. Like Wilson's political opponents, these Grand Army veterans distrusted Article X of the League's covenant. The article, which bound members to act in support of a fellow member nation under attack, contradicted a long tradition of US diplomatic isolationism. Going back to George Washington's call to avoid "entangling alliances," veterans frequently invoked this admonition in their opposition to the League. In a set of resolutions, the GAR Department of

Colorado and Wyoming believed that ratification of the Treaty of Versailles did "not safeguard the constitutional rights and interests of our country" and withheld support "unless the interests of our government are securely protected and safeguarded by proper restrictions." At the Pennsylvania encampment that same year, one speaker received the audience's hearty applause for his assertion that the veterans themselves had "saved this great big temple under God, this great big United States that today stands forth so big, so powerful, that we can stand and say—we need no league of nations, no European entanglements, we are great and big and powerful enough to stand alone as the savior of the world."[46]

Moreover, the Wilson administration's diplomatic efforts to secure the League of Nations too frequently met with bad political optics that offended a veteran cohort already predisposed to opposition. One target of the GAR's wrath was Texas-born Edward M. House, Wilson's close friend and foreign policy advisor, charged as one of the chief negotiators in Europe during the Paris Peace Conference. House, who helped Wilson outline his famous Fourteen Points and the League covenant, used the moniker "Colonel" despite having no military service to his name. House's unearned rank and southern roots annoyed members of the GAR. "[I]t is a matter of contemplation to me now," criticized Commander in Chief Clarendon F. Adams, "why those splendid men, two million in numbers, should have been entirely overlooked and it seemed to have become necessary that our government should go down in to the State of Texas and select a man and politician who never had done any military service, make him a colonel and place him at the peace table." In another imbroglio, Grand Army veterans became irked when former President Taft planned a speech to tout the League of Nations on Memorial Day 1919—violating the commemoration of their hallowed day.[47]

For other pensive veterans who had participated in one costly war and lived through two others in their long lives, the prospect of a League of Nations seemed naïve and its objectives impossible to fulfill. Having seen war and its destruction time and again, some veterans simply assumed it was human nature and something tragic but ultimately unavoidable. GAR patriotic instructor David E. Proctor considered the words of nineteenth-century preacher Henry Ward Beecher who said "I have made up my mind as long as God has made man as he is there will be wars. It has been the history since the beginning of the world." Proctor agreed, admitting that he had "but little faith in any league of nations to stand the test of passion, injury and misrule." For evidence, he pointed to feelings of enmity that remained between North and South, citing a friend living in Kentucky who reported "it beat all, the secesh talk I have heard while there." For prominent GAR member James Tanner, the botched denouement of the Great War convinced him that peace would not last long. He complained that Germany was being pardoned too easily and that the Allies should have demanded German peace in the kaiser's palace in Berlin. "If President Wilson's dream of a League of Nations and Universal Peace in the future can be accomplished, why, we will all be mighty glad of it," Tanner said. But with a striking degree of prescience, he predicted that war would come again when "the Huns can gather power enough, if it takes twenty years, to make another strike at liberty."[48]

Others simply found membership in the League of Nations to be superfluous to what GAR members—expressing a sentiment likely only understandable to veterans—found to be more lasting ties of international comradeship than the peace perfunctorily gained by signing a treaty. This shared experience of combat was deemed a stronger assurance of peace than any diplomatic efforts ongoing in France. Commander in Chief Adams expressed these sentiments to the comrades at the Department of the Potomac encampment in Washington, D.C., in 1919. Admitting that a League of Nations was "[p]ossibly . . . the best thing to be done," Adams went on to identify a stronger league. "[T]he League I am thinking about over there is the League that binds you all together, the League that was formed on the battle line of Europe. This League is not the League of Nations that is written out on parchments of paper, but is the unwritten League of Friendship. . . . The man that went forth with his Comrades to battle . . . will hold a memory that no thirty-six documents or another constitution on that light can ever subsert." For Adams, the peace and friendship that pervaded the Grand Army's ranks would undoubtedly be reproduced among the soldiers of all nations who fought in the Great War. One newspaper agreed, wondering if the Grand Army of the Republic might be replaced by a "Grand Army of the World, with reunions in London, Paris, Rome and Washington." For another GAR officer in Colorado, the shared experience of death and mourning would be a more powerful guarantor of peace than any document. Reminding the comrades before him of the powerful effect that shared mourning on Memorial Day had in removing "the old bitterness between the North and South," Carroll M. Bills predicted that "[o]ver these uncounted millions of graves the people of alien tongues will speak to each other in the universal language of flowers and tears. . . . An international Memorial Day may well become the real heart of a league of nations." Ultimately, faith in the shared experience of combat and loss would not be enough to sustain peace. Although by no means the fulcrum upon which the League of Nations' survival depended, Grand Army veterans' largely oppositional stance against the body delivered another blow preventing US participation in the organization and, arguably, America's investment in stopping the next global struggle through international arbitration.[49]

Grand Army veterans' retreat from the League of Nations and the internationalist foreign policy it represented was not entirely unique as it coincided with most Americans' embrace of isolationist tendencies and their abandonment of the activist government that had navigated the United States to victory in the Great War. The nation was exhausted by the discipline and demands required by the conflict just as the postwar period ushered in new emphases on consumerism, pursuit of pleasure, and individual freedom that derailed much of the Progressive Era reform energy of the past few decades. What was unusual, however, was how thoroughly the GAR seemed to vacate its support for government interventionism at home and abroad after the 1918 Armistice, given that Union veterans had been among the Wilson administration's most ardent devotees during the war. Harnessing progressivism's activism, efficiency, and vigor, the war government had fundamentally remade US society through mobilization, conscription, conservation, and the forging of a patriotic and cooperative populace. At the center of this transformation stood GAR veterans, duty bound to enforce the loyalty and sacrifice needed to win the war and guide the perpetuation of their Union victory through this latest crisis. Even so, as the GAR shuffled into the 1920s, the reform-minded spirit that had long informed its members' civic activism appeared all but used up and acquiescent to the nation's reactionary turn. Perhaps this is not surprising at all. Surviving Union veterans—most now well into their seventies and eighties—had been leading members of their communities for a half century or more. As the American doughboy returned home, they along with the other rising members of their cohort firmly supplanted the Civil War generation and steered the post–World War I nation through opportunities and challenges that looked so much different than the ones that existed before.[50]

Spurning their advanced age, Grand Army veterans during the second decade of the twentieth century were in fact still active and patriotic community elders. Instead of merely reminiscing on their war service from half a century earlier, they instead drew lessons from the Civil War to instruct the modernizing nation about the dangers of military unpreparedness in a disorderly world. Restoring the honor of the volunteer citizen-soldier and advocating the extension of universal military training, Union veterans endeavored to leave their lasting mark on the nation's armed forces and younger generations' understanding of civic duty. After the United States entered World War I, GAR posts and their auxiliaries were among their communities' most fervent home front organizers, helping the Wilson administration steel young men to enlist and prepare civilians at home for the sacrifices to come. Meanwhile, not far from many comrades' thoughts was a belief that victory in this latest war was an extension of their own Union victory—a new, victorious chapter in the struggle of democracy, liberty, and freedom over the forces of authoritarianism, oppression, and slavery. "[T]he principles for which the Grand Army contended," assured one veteran, "have sunk into the hearts of the rising generation, and that is why, when the call came, so many of them were willing to give their lives if it were necessary that the flag might float free and the union be still a union of liberty and democracy." As living testaments of sacrifice and patriotism for their communities, these aged veterans sought to "rally 'round the flag," one last time, for the principles for which they fought so many years before. By the end of the war, however, the civic influence of the GAR was almost used up and a young cohort of soldiers returned home to find unfamiliar political, economic, and social challenges awaiting them. America's Progressive Era was coming to an end and the nation's newest veterans would chart their own path and their own breed of organizational activism upon their return to civilian life.[51]

Conclusion: From Their Battlements in Heaven

One by one the old men went up to that sun-swept hilltop to sleep beneath the lilacs, and as they departed we began to lose more than we knew we were losing. For these old soldiers, simply by existing, had unfailingly expressed the faith we lived by. . . . It was a faith in the continuity of human experience, in the progress of the nation toward an ideal, in the ability of men to come triumphantly through any challenge. That faith lived, and we lived by it. Now it is under the lilacs.

—Bruce Catton, Waiting for the Morning Train (1972)

Service was in the blood of Lieutenant Colonel Loren C. Grieves. His father, an artilleryman during the Civil War, was a proud GAR member in Michigan until his death in 1907. The younger Grieves was born in 1877, graduated from West Point with Douglas MacArthur in 1903, and began his military career as a talented cartographic officer in the Philippines. After serving in France during the First World War, Grieves pondered how four million demobilizing US troops might benefit from an organization like that which he had known from boyhood, as the son of a GAR veteran. Imagining "a great soldier and sailor organization the most significant of its kind," he published the pamphlet, *The New Grand Army of the Republic* (1919), that laid out his vision. Like its exemplar, this prospective fraternity of doughboys would include "every man, regardless of his previous environments" (just as the GAR had welcomed all honorably discharged soldiers); supportive auxiliaries (akin to the Woman's Relief Corps and Sons of Veterans); and an official publication (like the GAR's *National Tribune*) for the "communication and dissemination of ideas." In short, Grieves called for a new national association of men "who have experienced the thrill of patriotism, and have identified themselves with their country's flag in the hour of peril."[1]

It did not take long for the veterans of the Great War to imitate those of the Civil War in devising fraternal bonds of camaraderie. Within one year of the publication of Grieves's pamphlet, the American Legion had already accumulated over 800,000 members—more than twice the membership that the GAR claimed at its 1890 peak—to become the most significant World War I veterans' organization. And yet, the doughboys did not adopt the same ideological strain of veteran-led activism that had marked the GAR's community involvement of the previous thirty years. The politics and priorities of the 1920s meant that the American Legion would not be the fraternity of its members' fathers and grandfathers. If the Grand Army in the Progressive Era had worked to *perfect* society through its local-level reforms, its successors (particularly the Legion) during the interwar years worked to *protect* it from threats—real and imagined. This important distinction reflected a new age marked by labor strikes, race riots, rising unemployment and inflation, and fear of Bolshevism and the accompanying Red Scare. Politically, after the death of Theodore Roosevelt in 1919 and debility of the ailing Woodrow Wilson, Progressives lost their most high-profile champions, replaced by conservatives like Warren G. Harding who pledged a return to "normalcy" and "equipoise" during the presidential campaign of 1920. The progressivism that had dominated the last three decades yielded to a new adherence to "Roaring Twenties" individualism and a growing mistrust of government intervention. To the degree that World War I veterans took up the mantle of GAR civic activism, they did so by redirecting it toward reactionary objectives more suited to the temperament of a postwar nation exhausted by progressivism.[2]

At war's end, Grand Army veterans—only 100,000 remaining by the Armistice—stood at a fateful crossroads. The return of the young soldiers from Europe offered one final opportunity for the GAR to revise its constitution and admit new generations of servicemen or, otherwise, acknowledge their extinction with the death of the last Union veteran. As had occurred after the Spanish-American War, many continued to tout their order's selectiveness and the unique glory of their sacrifices. "With the proclamation of peace that followed the surrender of the Confederate armies," boasted one Iowa veteran just before Europe's descent into war, "the door of admission to the Grand Army of the Republic was forever closed, and since that day no proclamation of a president, no edict of a king or czar has been able to gain admission into our ranks." Similar sentiments persisted through 1919 and beyond. Pittsburgh officer William J. Patterson, for example, warned his fellows "that when these men come back from over there [it would be expected] that we old Soldiers would have to take a back seat." Instead, Patterson "wanted the Comrade to be imbued with the idea that we would not take a back seat because it was our service that made it possible for our Country to hold the place which she holds in the world today."[3]

Nevertheless, some Union veterans proved unwilling to concede the GAR's demise and pondered how rigid the boundaries of their fraternity actually were. Pennsylvania's Samuel E. Gill circulated resolutions throughout the commonwealth's posts advocating looser eligibility. "Are we so jealous of our own achievements and honor," the resolutions queried, "as to be insensible of the honor due our sons and grandsons now offering their lives in this great World War for humanity . . . to carry down to future generations the story of sacrifice and the practise [sic] of fraternity, charity and loyalty among those who offer the supreme sacrifice of life that liberty and freedom and civilization may live?" Although more than one hundred posts adopted the resolutions, the proposal faced stiff headwinds and was defeated at the next department encampment. Others dabbled with forming loose leagues of veterans' and other patriotic groups that allowed the GAR to maintain its exclusivity even while extending the hand of friendship to younger generations. Along these lines, some communities formed "federated patriotic societies" comprised of the local Civil War, Spanish-American War, and World War I veterans, along with their auxiliaries. Ultimately though, many Union veterans seemed to agree with Herbert H. Bengough, who firmly stated that he did not "want any new men coming in and telling us what to do," while also contending that it would be unfair to the returning soldiers to sap their organizational potential by inviting them into a long-established fraternity. Arguing that for "those men who did such great work on foreign shores," Bengough thought it would be an insult for GAR veterans to say "[y]ou are not able and you are not competent to form an organization; now we will take you and teach you how to do it."[4]

The old veteran was right, for the young ones organized their own fraternities even before formal peace was ratified. One choice was the World War Veterans (WWV), officially incorporated in February 1919. Perhaps capturing some of the residual activist spirit of the GAR, the WWV established a reasonably progressive and labor-friendly platform, demanding federal distribution of jobs, land, and generous bonuses to returning soldiers. It also showed antipathy to officers by admitting only private soldiers (the WWV's alternate name was, in fact, the Private Soldiers and Sailors Legion). Claiming a membership of at least 100,000 before its collapse during the Red Scare, the WWV gained sympathy from some Union veterans. Congressman and GAR veteran Isaac R. Sherwood, for instance, noted that although he held officers' commissions during the Civil War, he "look[ed] back with more self-satisfying pride to my service as a private soldier" and gave the WWV his "most fervent prayers for a successful mission to make fraternity and real comradeship a living vital element in their future lives."

Conclusion: From Their Battlements in Heaven

The Veterans of Foreign Wars (VFW), which assumed its modern form in 1913 after the merger of separate societies for veterans of the Spanish-American and Philippine-American wars, was another option for Great War veterans. Still, the VFW only accepted those men who served abroad, excluding the millions of soldiers who never left the United States before the Armistice. Specialized veterans' groups existed, too, some serving religious groups, officers, or the disabled.[5]

The nascent American Legion, however, attracted the widest following of Great War veterans and ultimately assumed the GAR's long-held role as the most assertive of all US veterans' groups. With the Armistice in place in November 1918, officers worried about the depressed morale of their soldiers in the American Expeditionary Force (AEF) who foresaw months of idleness before transport home. Lieutenant Colonel Theodore Roosevelt Jr. and a band of compatriots (receiving the tacit approval of AEF Commander John J. Pershing) set to work in the early months of 1919 to organize a veterans' association spanning both the US servicemen abroad and those still stationed stateside. Quickly consolidating and exploding in membership, the Legion consistently looked to the GAR's successes to chart its own future. As early as March 1919, observers predicted that "it is fairly to be expected that their influence on public affairs will be as great as was that of their predecessors of a half century ago." At a Minnesota GAR encampment in 1922, one legionnaire invitee applauded the "great things" Union veterans had done "for the world and humanity" and pledged that his society would execute "a movement in Americanization which will enable us to carry on that work which you started." Others touted the influence that fraternal membership would hold for soldiers returning to civilian life. As one Michigan officer asked at an early American Legion event, "[w]ho knows of a Civil War veteran of much public recognition unless he be a member of the G.A.R.?"[6]

Even as the new fraternity quickly out-recruited competitors, many individual legionnaires remained deferent to the Grand Army. Ahead of the GAR's 1920 national encampment in Indianapolis, the Legion and the United Spanish War Veterans circulated a joint message informing Union veterans that they "recognize[d] their seniority, and hold the Grand Army, composed as it is of our fathers and grandfathers, in reverent affection" and pledged that "when the Grand Army shall be no more, to . . . continue the customs and honor the memory of the Grand Army as we will our own." As a show of this affection, committees from the three groups prepared resolutions that would ease the aging GAR's burdens and bring all the martial generations into closer accord. One set of resolutions sought to federate the three groups nationally while another endeavored to transfer the bulk of the nation's memorialization responsibilities to the younger veterans. When these proposals were presented at the GAR's national encampment, however, many delegates balked at the anticipated loss of their organization's autonomy and the assertion of shared heroism between the three groups. Moreover, GAR officials remained sensitive to their Sons of Veterans (SV) auxiliary, which charged that the American Legion was faithlessly conspiring to inherit the traditions of the Civil War generation. In Minnesota, GAR officials noted that "there was a little bit of jealousy" between the Sons and the Legion and that the former were "a little afraid that the American Legion will do the work they expect to do when we are done." The SV, meanwhile, insisted that they would best carry on the legacy of the fading Grand Army. Boasting that their organization comprised "many of the most loyal and public spirited men of our country," officials declared that only they perpetuated "the sacrifices of our fathers, and their services, for the maintenance of the Union, and to promote the spirit of patriotism throughout our nation."7

But if stubborn pride typically characterized state and national GAR officials after the First World War, rank-and-file members in the local posts demonstrated few qualms about welcoming and celebrating their communities' younger veterans. For example, the post in Menominee, Michigan, "unanimously voted to make all honorably discharged ex-service men of the World War residing in the city . . . honorary members." The town's American Legion post responded in kind. In Wisconsin, local posts acknowledged the great aid the legionnaires provided on Memorial Day. Kenosha's Union veterans graciously recognized that the local Legion "offered to place flowers on the graves of Grand Army comrades," while the post at Manitowoc reported similar assistance and felt at ease that "the torch from our failing hands will pass to able successors, those who upheld the flag 'on Flanders fields.'" Expressions like these are fairly common in the final pages of GAR post minute books, with Union veterans conveying genuine solace that the nation was in good hands under the tutelage of the legionnaires whom they felt had the nation's interests at heart. "I sort of feel as though the American Legion are to be our successors when the time comes," admitted Minnesota's GAR patriotic instructor Levi Longfellow. "I heard a number of addresses from young fellows that only a few years ago were here in the high school, and it was remarkable; their addresses were so pathetic and so intelligent and of such a high grade. And so I look for a great future for our continuation."8

In many ways, the American Legion did become the natural successor to the GAR, although the substance of its veteran activism was markedly different than that which Union veterans had advocated during the Progressive Era. Much of this likely had to do with the post–World War I environment in which the Legion matured, a period of wrenching economic and political upheaval. Aiming to uphold what its constitution dubbed "one hundred percent Americanism," the legionnaires typically directed their civic engagement toward law-and-order principles (to a more militant degree than the GAR ever expressed) and against what it deemed to be radical and disruptive ideologies. Some of their animus was leveled at the Industrial Workers of the World (IWW) and similar groups. In Centralia, Washington, for instance, legionnaires parading on Armistice Day 1919 infamously clashed with IWW members—ending with six deaths and the lynching of "Wobbly" adherent Wesley Everest. The Legion's suspicion of socialism and labor militancy extended to the WWV and its progressive (opponents said "radical") agenda. Under the tacit direction of the newly established Federal Bureau of Investigation, legionnaire-informants had a hand in discrediting and undermining the WWV as a radical organization, which paved the way for the more conservative Legion to control Great War veterans' fraternal enrollment. For the next decade, many American Legion posts supported suppressive policies in the pursuit of national security, including free speech curtailments, antisyndicalism laws, and immigration restriction. By 1927, the American Civil Liberties Union declared openly that the Legion had "replaced the [Ku Klux] Klan as the most active agency of intolerance and repression in the country."[9]

Indeed, perhaps more than in any other measure, the Legion stood in starkest contrast with the GAR on the issue of race. Despite nonsegregationist directives in both orders' membership policies, the GAR more consistently and explicitly welcomed African American comrades into their fraternity and acknowledged their equality, at least within the walls of the post room. The GAR thwarted its southern departments' attempts to establish separate white and Black divisions, while hundreds of integrated GAR posts existed at the local level. African Americans held officers' positions in many posts and state departments and majority-white and all-Black posts held joint commemorative, patriotic, and community events. The early American Legion, by contrast, deferred to white southern veterans on questions surrounding post membership policies and, unsurprisingly, enrolled relatively few African Americans overall. Many Black World War I veterans instead joined the League for Democracy or Lincoln Legion fraternities throughout the 1920s. Others joined the so-called Grand Army of Americans—perhaps a nod to the historically tolerant GAR—whose African American founders insisted that the United States' involvement in the Great War "was not simply for white humanity and for white freedom . . . but for us all, irrespective of race, color or condition. Let America be friendly and free." Conversely, some early legionnaires were, in fact, also Klansmen, burdening the national organization to reach conciliation with such members even as it claimed that individuals or groups that stirred up "racial . . . strife among our people" were "un-American, a menace to our liberties."[10]

As the American Legion solidified its status as the most prominent US veterans' organization and even welcomed a new generation of soldiers after the Second World War, the GAR continued its steady march toward extinction. Even so, glimmers of its Progressive Era interests periodically resurfaced. Many Union veterans, mindful of the day when the organization would cease to exist, pushed for the proper housing of the fraternity's records and relics. One GAR-circulated petition in the late 1920s asked Congress to transform Robert E. Lee's Arlington House into a repository in which GAR posts and departments might transfer their belongings—a subtle nod privileging Union victory over the Confederacy's Lost Cause. Indeed, perpetuation of the GAR's memory of the war over the nation's reconciliationist tendencies remained a lasting objective of the aged comrades. Posts across the country protested the 1924 congressional approval of a commemorative half dollar (featuring Lee and Stonewall Jackson) designed to raise money for the carving of Georgia's Stone Mountain Memorial. GAR veterans in Nebraska objected to "any appropriation of funds of this government" benefiting "this rebellious project," while others in Illinois protested the memorial that "honored and commemorated . . . leaders in the endeavor to destroy our government in order that human slavery might be perpetuated." When, four years later, Congress considered a bill to house records of the Confederate dead in the War Department, a New York post protested that "no rebels who fought to destroy the Union are entitled to have a record of their treason placed in the archives of the United States War Department." GAR intolerance for the Confederacy's glorification extended to American popular culture as well. Just as Union veterans had rallied to denounce *The Birth of a Nation* in 1915, they did so again in 1939 with the release of *Gone with the Wind*. At their national encampment in Pittsburgh that year, 200 grizzled survivors endorsed resolutions demanding that the Pennsylvania Board of Motion Picture Censors ban the film, calling it "an affront to all who wear our country's uniform." The board disagreed. In response to the veterans' complaint that Union soldiers were portrayed in the film as unsavory marauders, one chairperson simply replied: "that's history."[11]

By the 1930s and 1940s, Grand Army members—the last of a generation long since supplanted by the next and the next—exercised little remaining clout to shape the historical memory of their Civil War. Now they more often made headlines in the local newspapers when being chauffeured down city streets for patriotic parades or through the obituaries proclaiming their deaths. In interviews, journalists repeatedly treated their GAR subjects as curious antiques and pumped them for romantic stories about camp life and battlefield exploits, often ignoring their once-powerful fraternal activism. Despite quixotic calls to "hold ... as long as there is a man left," state and national encampments became smaller and smaller affairs as posts began disbanding for want of members. By August 1949, only six wrinkled heroes assembled at the last national encampment of the GAR in Indianapolis, the site of the first such event held eighty-three years before. Led by the US Marine Band and escorted by Sons of Veterans, the men motored around the city, before they were driven back for a final campfire. There, one-hundred-year-old Commander in Chief Theodore A. Penland mused, "I am so thankful that I have a few comrades, that we can be together and visit. It won't be very long until we will all be gone." That day finally came when 105-year-old Albert Woolson of Duluth, Minnesota, answered "the last roll call" on August 2, 1956. The Sons of Veterans, marking the poignant occasion, hoped that the generation of Grand Army veterans was even then peering down "from their battlements in heaven" to "salute with loving hands this proud Republic."[12]

Forgotten in the inundation of loving eulogies to the GAR was the role that the Union veteran had played, not in the Civil War itself, but much later, in the era of progressive reform. It was then that the Grand Army member, in concert with his comrades in the local post, fundamentally reshaped the community and the nation through his activism and provided a model for every US veteran thereafter to seize a prominent role in civic affairs. For at least thirty years, as Americans came to terms with a modernizing nation under strain, GAR veterans stood ready with prescriptions to direct the United States toward their vision of national strength and harmony. This vision, although guided by and grounded in old lessons learned in war—lessons about freedom, democracy, sacrifice, loyalty, and humanity—was nonetheless well-suited for community-level application around the turn of the twentieth century, a time when the veterans and many younger citizens were hungry for reform. Members, then, were effective but overlooked participants among the sundry alliance of Americans who deployed public-spirited citizenship in the effort to advance the country's welfare. In a way, this makes perfect sense. Having, in their youth, given so much to save the Union and liberate a race, few Americans had more incentive than Grand Army veterans to pacify and improve a restless and disorderly nation. Armed this time with sage wisdom and unwavering principles, they mobilized again to consummate their wartime victory with reform-minded activism on behalf of establishing an even more perfect Union. Compared with the reactionary agenda of its veteran-successors, the GAR's civic legacy was the product of a specially equipped cohort living in an era uniquely receptive to progressive change. Speaking before some of his venerable comrades in 1924, Josephus C. Plank conceded that although they were destined to soon "drop out one by one" from the ranks of the GAR, they all could rest assured that behind them was erected "a monument of achievement."[13]

Acknowledgments

A book like this one that is firmly rooted in the idea of "community" encourages me to reflect on the community of family, friends, and scholars that made its completion possible. Without the collective efforts and sacrifices of so many, I never would have had the deeply fulfilling opportunity to study these Union veterans whose life stories it has been my honor to relate. The work that follows has come about because of a community of people that I have been so fortunate to know over the course of many years.

When this project first took shape as a doctoral dissertation, it benefited from research grants that made my exhilarating cross-country road trips to visit dozens of museums, archives, and historical societies more feasible. I am extremely grateful to the Wisconsin Veterans Museum for the funding to research in their incredibly rich collections and, in particular, to Russ Horton, for making the trip so productive. Further thanks go to the State Historical Society of Iowa for its financial support, and to Marvin Bergman, Andrew Klumpp, and the archival staff in Des Moines and Iowa City for their hospitable assistance and for permission to reprint portions of an article published in the society's journal. Additional funds and research support came from the US Army Heritage and Education Center's General and Mrs. Matthew B. Ridgway Research Grant; the Bordin-Gillette Researcher Travel Fellowship from the Bentley Historical Library at the University of Michigan; and Carnegie Mellon University's Graduate Student Small Project Help (GuSH). I must also thank the Graduate Studies Committee of Carnegie Mellon's Department of History for its generous accommodation when I regularly came calling for more funds. Deserving of special praise are Michael Kraus, Lisa Petitta, and Tim Neff at Soldiers and Sailors Memorial Hall and Museum in Pittsburgh, who helped facilitate a yearlong internship, entrusted me with processing the institution's precious Grand Army records, and provided cheerful comradeship. Access to this one of a kind collection (along with Michael's formidable knowledge of all things Civil War) has enhanced this project immensely. I thank CMU's Department of History for releasing me from teaching obligations so I could pursue this incredibly fruitful internship.

I have had the good fortune to visit so many unique and interesting places in pursuit of my research and the archivists and librarians who lent me their professional expertise along the way are too many to name individually. I offer my gratitude to the staff at the Andrew Carnegie Free Library and Music Hall; the Archives of Michigan; the Butler Area [Pennsylvania] Public Library; the Delaware Historical Society; the Detre Library and Archives at the Heinz History Center; the Filson Historical Society; the Lyon County [Kansas] History Center and Museum; the Grand Army of the Republic Museum and Library; the Livingston County [New York] Office of the County Historian; the Mason City [Iowa] Public Library; the Massachusetts Historical Society; the Minnesota Historical Society; the Nebraska State Historical Society; the New England Civil War Museum; the New Hampshire Historical Society; the New York State Archives; the Oregon Historical Society; the Pennsylvania State Archives; the Rhode Island Historical Society; Syracuse University's Bird Library; the Toledo-Lucas County Public Library; the Tulane University Archives; the University of Minnesota Duluth's Northeast Minnesota Historical Center; the University of Pittsburgh's Archives Service Center; the Vermont Historical Society; the Western Michigan University Archives; and the Wisconsin Historical Society.

Once I had amassed a vast and unwieldy collection of archival findings from these places, I relied on many brilliant scholars to help bring order out of the chaos. I owe an enormous debt of gratitude to my advisor, Scott Sandage, who provided a constant source of wisdom, encouragement, and compassion, and who fiercely believed in me and in this project at times when I faltered. Thank you for everything, Scott. I gratefully acknowledge the mentorship of my committee members, Lisa Tetrault and Joe Trotter, whose guidance and keen revision comments made this work a better product. I was very fortunate to receive valuable input from Barbara Gannon, who provided insightful thoughts about race and memory that greatly improved my manuscript. Brian Matthew Jordan offered kind collegial interest in my work and an opportunity to publish in an edited volume with LSU Press (to which I owe thanks for permission to reprint portions of a chapter). A number of other scholars fundamentally shaped my training as a historian, including Kate Lynch, Paul Eiss, Doug Coulson, Perry Blatz, Jay Dwyer, Joseph Rishel, Allen Guelzo, Michael Birkner, Laurel Cohen, and Michael Ritterson. I was also fortunate to have shared the rigors of doctoral pursuit with many gifted individuals. Mark Hauser, Amanda Katz, Bennett Koerber, Matthew McGrath, Matthew Nielsen, and Amund Tallaksen deserve a special salute.

The team at Fordham University Press has been a reliable source of support and professionalism. Andrew Slap, editor of the press's "Reconstructing America" series, championed this project years ago and waited patiently as I finally determined to transform a sprawling dissertation into a more tightly focused book. Andy's excellent editorial suggestions and generous guidance to a first-time author have made the end result so much better. Fredric Nachbaur, Kem Crimmins, William Cerbone, Eric Newman, and the rest of the Fordham University Press staff have made the publication process a delight to undertake. I am also deeply grateful to Lis Pearson for her expert copyediting.

Rewarding and stabilizing companionship outside the business of research and writing has proven just as important to finishing this project as relationships within it. Longtime friendships with Lauren DePoy and Jonathan DePoy, Gretchen L. Carlson and Andrew Carlson, Amy Michelson and Jay Michelson, Erika McAfee and Sean McAfee, Anna Curtis and Brad Curtis, Carla Maiolini, Leslie Velgach and Filipp Velgach, Michael Solomon and Greg Lutz, Bre Timko and Dan Timko, Tracy Coleman and Nick Pascuzzi, MK Baker, and Rachel McCool have been my good fortune and source of many good times. My in-laws, Susan Hewitt and Charles Hewitt, as well as Patricia Felske, Anna Hewitt and Chris Hewitt, and Finnian Hewitt have been my Michigan boosters and provided kind reassurance and frequent respite through the years.

My parents, Marilyn Neu and David Neu, offered me the foundation upon which to grow, learn, and thrive. I can never thank them enough for the love and encouragement they have provided me from the very beginning and the impact they have had on my educational and personal development. I carry with me forever your examples, Mom and Dad. This book is very much a reflection of the belief you have always had in me. My grandparents, Rose Neu and Herbert Neu, as well as David Friday have always provided support and pride. Vickie Neu has offered companionship and a source of comfort through many of life's challenges. My grandmother, Gloria Friday, and grandfather, Paul Friday, are not here to see the completion of this project, but their spirit is all through these pages. Their eclectic interests and the zest for life that they shared with me continue to have an enormous effect.

Finally, there is Margaret, to whom I could never offer exactly the right words of thanks to acknowledge how loving and supportive a partner she has been for nearly the entirety of our adult lives. A talented scholar and researcher in her own right, her dogged pursuit of many of the sources and subjects mentioned in *Our Onward March* has made this a far better piece of work. She has accompanied me to archives to root out caches of veterans' materials, joined in on hunts for obscure GAR memorial halls, shared impromptu wanders through battlefields and cemeteries, and cheerfully endured the hijacking of our dining room table for interminable writing pursuits. She has been the ultimate companion in so many ways. We have had great fun in life—and I look forward to more to come.

Notes

Introduction: Our Onward March

1. "James Whitehead Dead," *Emporia Gazette* [Emporia, KS], 20 November 1920, 8; W. L. Gaston and A. R. Humphrey, *History of Custer County, Nebraska* (Lincoln, NE: Western Publishing and Engraving Company, 1919), 845.

2. Speech of James Whitehead at Broken Bow, Nebraska, 25 May 1902, box 2, volume 7, James Whitehead Papers, Wisconsin Historical Society, Madison, WI (hereafter WHS); Speech of James Whitehead at College of Emporia, 26 May 1916, box 1, folder: Articles, Speeches, and Miscellaneous Writings, 1901–1918, James Whitehead Papers, WHS. For a sampling of Plumb Post's civic activities, see "The G.A.R. at Home," *Emporia Gazette* [Emporia, KS], 13 April 1907, 4; "Against Discharge of Negro Soldiers," *Topeka Daily Capital* [Topeka, KS], 18 February 1908, 3; "G.A.R. Lincoln Day," *Emporia Gazette*, 13 February 1909, 2; "The Old Boys Entertain," *Emporia Weekly Gazette*, 23 March 1911, 4; "Grand Army Affairs," *Emporia Gazette*, 12 November 1915, 5; "The Old Boys Speak," *Emporia Weekly Gazette*, 2 December 1915, 1; "The President Appreciative," *Emporia Weekly Gazette*, 2 March 1916, 6; and "Old Boys—and Girls—Frolic," *Emporia Gazette*, 22 March 1916, 8.

3. This book seeks to refine or build on several valuable studies whose emphases may miss or obscure the continued potency, visibility, and activism of the Progressive Era GAR. See, for instance, Mary R. Dearing, *Veterans in Politics: The Story of the G.A.R.* (Baton Rouge: Louisiana State University Press, 1952); Stuart McConnell, *Glorious Contentment: The Grand Army of the Republic, 1865–1900* (Chapel Hill: University of North Carolina Press, 1992); Theda Skocpol, *Protecting Soldiers and Mothers: The Political Origins of Social Policy in the United States* (Cambridge, MA: Harvard University Press, 1992); David W. Blight, *Race and Reunion: The Civil War in American Memory* (Cambridge, MA: Harvard University Press, 2001); and Brian Matthew Jordan, *Marching Home: Union Veterans and Their Unending Civil War* (New York: W.W. Norton, 2014).

4. For frustrations with the concept of progressivism, see Peter G. Filene, "An Obituary for 'The Progressive Movement,'" *American Quarterly* 22, no. 1 (Spring 1970): 20–34; and Robert D. Johnston, "The Possibilities of Politics: Democracy in America, 1877 to 1917," in *American History Now*, ed. Eric Foner and Lisa McGirr (Philadelphia: Temple University Press, 2011), 100. For the notion of plural "progressivisms," see Daniel T. Rodgers, "In Search of Progressivism," *Reviews in American History* 10, no. 4 (December 1982): 113–32. For reasonable attempts to identify the progressives and pin down the elusiveness of their agenda, see Nell Irvin Painter,

Standing at Armageddon: The United States, 1877-1919 (New York: W. W. Norton, 1987), xii, 216; Richard L. McCormick, "Public Life in Industrial America, 1877–1917," in *The New American History*, ed. Eric Foner (Philadelphia: Temple University Press, 1997), 121–29; and Michael McGerr, *A Fierce Discontent: The Rise and Fall of the Progressive Movement in America* (New York: Oxford University Press, 2003), xiii-xvi. On expanding the temporal boundaries of the Progressive Era and viewing the Gilded Age period as the "seedbed" for progressive ideas and community engagement, see Rebecca Edwards, *New Spirits: Americans in the "Gilded Age," 1865–1905* (New York: Oxford University Press, 2006), esp. 5.

5. Rayford W. Logan, *The Betrayal of the Negro: From Rutherford B. Hayes to Woodrow Wilson* (1954; reprint, New York: Da Capo Press, 1997), 62, 88; Barbara A. Gannon, *The Won Cause: Black and White Comradeship in the Grand Army of the Republic* (Chapel Hill: University of North Carolina Press, 2011), 8.

6. Larry M. Logue, *To Appomattox and Beyond: The Civil War Soldier in War and Peace* (Chicago: Ivan R. Dee, 1996), 87; Gannon, *The Won Cause*, 16. For more on the early blossoming of Civil War veterans' organizations, see James Marten, *Sing Not War: The Lives of Union and Confederate Veterans in Gilded Age America* (Chapel Hill: University of North Carolina Press, 2011), 11–12; and Caroline E. Janney, *Remembering the Civil War: Reunion and the Limits of Reconciliation* (Chapel Hill: University of North Carolina Press, 2013), 107–8. On the GAR's early years, see McConnell, *Glorious Contentment*, 24–52.

7. United States Census Office, *Report on Population of the United States at the Eleventh Census: 1890*, vol. 2 (Washington, D.C.: Government Printing Office, 1897), clxxii.

8. Dearing, *Veterans in Politics*, vii, 117; Skocpol, *Protecting Soldiers and Mothers*, viii; Larry M. Logue, "Union Veterans and Their Government: The Effects of Public Policies on Private Lives," *Journal of Interdisciplinary History* 22, no. 3 (Winter 1992): 411–34; Megan J. McClintock, "Civil War Pensions and the Reconstruction of Union Families," *Journal of American History* 83, no. 2 (September 1996): 456–80; Dora L. Costa, "Displacing the Family: Union Army Pensions and Elderly Living Arrangements," *Journal of Political Economy* 105, no. 6 (December 1997): 1269–92; Peter Blanck and Chen Song, "'Never Forget What They Did Here': Civil War Pensions for Gettysburg Union Army Veterans and Disability in Nineteenth-Century America," *William and Mary Law Review* 44, no. 3 (February 2003): 1109–71; Larry M. Logue and Peter Blanck, "'There is Nothing That Promotes Longevity Like a Pension': Disability Policy and Mortality of Civil War Union Army Veterans," *Wake Forest Law Review* 39, no. 1 (2004): 49–67. On race and pensions, see Sven Wilson, "Prejudice and Policy: Racial Discrimination in the Union Army Disability Pension System, 1865–1906," *American Journal of Public Health* 100, S1 (April 2010): S56–S65; Dora L. Costa, "Pensions and Retirement Among Black Union Army Veterans," *Journal of Economic History* 70, no. 3 (September 2010): 567–92.

9. McConnell, *Glorious Contentment*, xiii.

10. Paul A. Cimbala, *Veterans North and South: The Transition from Soldier to Civilian After the American Civil War* (Santa Barbara, CA: Praeger, 2015), xvii. For more on the so-called "dark turn" in Civil War and post–Civil War scholarship that tends to deromanticize the war and focus on the death, debility, and destruction it caused, see for

instance, Eric T. Dean Jr., *Shook Over Hell: Post-Traumatic Stress, Vietnam, and the Civil War* (Cambridge, MA: Harvard University Press, 1997); Marten, *Sing Not War*; Jordan, *Marching Home*; Diane Miller Sommerville, *Aberration of Mind: Suicide and Suffering in the Civil War-Era South* (Chapel Hill: University of North Carolina Press, 2018); and Sarah Handley-Cousins, *Bodies in Blue: Disability in the Civil War North* (Athens: University of Georgia Press, 2019). On the risks of taking the "dark turn" too far, see Gary W. Gallagher and Kathryn Shively Meier, "Coming to Terms with Civil War Military History," *Journal of the Civil War Era* 4, no. 4 (December 2014): 492.

11. See Blight, *Race and Reunion*, esp. 2–3.

12. James E. Young, *The Texture of Memory: Holocaust Memorials and Meaning* (New Haven, CT: Yale University Press, 1993), 2; Barbara A. Gannon, *Americans Remember Their Civil War* (Santa Barbara, CA: Praeger, 2017), xiv. Important challenges and refinements to Blight's reconciliationist paradigm include William A. Blair, *Cities of the Dead: Contesting the Memory of the Civil War in the South, 1865–1914* (Chapel Hill: University of North Carolina Press, 2004); John R. Neff, *Honoring the Civil War Dead: Commemoration and the Problem of Reconciliation* (Lawrence: University Press of Kansas, 2005); Gannon, *The Won Cause*; Janney, *Remembering the Civil War*; and M. Keith Harris, *Across the Bloody Chasm: The Culture of Commemoration Among Civil War Veterans* (Baton Rouge: Louisiana State University Press, 2014).

13. *Journal of the Thirty-First National Encampment of the Grand Army of the Republic, Buffalo, New York, August 25th, 26th, and 27th, 1897* (Lincoln, NE: State Journal Company, 1897), 228.

1. Practical Monuments

1. "Most Records Saved," *Oshkosh Daily Northwestern* [Oshkosh, WI], 29 February 1904, 7; Paul F. Hunter, ed., *Wisconsin Blue Book, 1919* (Madison, WI: Democrat Printing Company, 1919), 294; "Great Loss of Grand Army," *The Daily Telegram* [Eau Claire, WI], 29 February 1904, 3; GAR Department of Wisconsin circular, 6 February 1917, box 6, folder 7, Grand Army of the Republic, Department of Wisconsin Records, Wisconsin Veterans Museum, Madison, WI (hereafter WVM); Report of Hosea W. Rood, 1919, box 54, folder 15, Grand Army of the Republic, Department of Wisconsin Records, WVM. Today, many of the items donated to the memorial hall are stored at the Wisconsin Veterans Museum in Madison where researchers and visitors even today fulfill the civic legacy that the state's veterans intended.

2. Robert D. Putnam, *Bowling Alone: The Collapse and Revival of American Community* (New York: Simon & Schuster, 2000), 399; Theda Skocpol, *Diminished Democracy: From Membership to Management in American Civic Life* (Norman: University of Oklahoma Press, 2003), 20.

3. Thomas C. Fletcher et al., *Life and Reminiscences of General William T. Sherman by Distinguished Men of His Time* (Baltimore, MD: R. H. Woodward Co., 1891), 467; Wallace Evan Davies, *Patriotism on Parade: The Story of Veterans' and Hereditary Organizations in America, 1783–1900* (Cambridge, MA: Harvard University Press, 1955), 119; Stuart McConnell, "Who Joined the Grand Army?: Three Case Studies in the Construction of Union Veteranhood, 1866–1900," in *Toward a Social History of the American Civil War:*

Exploratory Essays, ed. Maris A. Vinovskis (New York: Cambridge University Press, 1990), 169; Caroline E. Janney, *Remembering the Civil War: Reunion and the Limits of Reconciliation* (Chapel Hill: University of North Carolina Press, 2013), 110; Patrick J. Kelly, *Creating a National Home: Building the Veterans' Welfare State, 1860-1900* (Cambridge, MA: Harvard University Press, 1997); Stuart McConnell, *Glorious Contentment: The Grand Army of the Republic, 1865-1900* (Chapel Hill: University of North Carolina Press, 1992), 115, 141; Theda Skocpol, *Protecting Soldiers and Mothers: The Political Origins of Social Policy in the United States* (Cambridge, MA: Harvard University Press, 2001); Brian Matthew Jordan, *Marching Home: Union Veterans and Their Unending Civil War* (New York: W.W. Norton, 2014), 151–69.

4. "Albert C. Leonard," *Harrisburg Telegraph*, 20 December 1915, 13; "A. C. Leonard, Veteran, Is Dead," *Harrisburg Daily Independent*, 21 December 1915, 4; A. C. Leonard, *The Boys in Blue of 1861-1865: A Condensed History Worth Preserving* (Lancaster, PA: New Era Printing Company, 1904); A. C. Leonard, *Grand Army of the Republic Hand Book* (n.p., 1884), preface (unpaginated) and 22.

5. W. S. Harwood, "Secret Societies in America," *North American Review* 164, no. 486 (May 1897): 623. On the era's increase in fraternity membership, its causes, and its consequences, see Lynn Dumenil, *Freemasonry and American Culture, 1880-1930* (Princeton, NJ: Princeton University Press, 1984), 18–19, 221; Mark C. Carnes, *Secret Ritual and Manhood in Victorian America* (New Haven, CT: Yale University Press, 1989), 81–89; Mary Ann Clawson, *Constructing Brotherhood: Class, Gender, and Fraternalism* (Princeton. NJ: Princeton University Press, 1989), 178–80; Christopher J. Kauffman, *Faith and Fraternalism: The History of the Knights of Columbus, 1882-1982* (New York: Harper & Row, 1982); Putnam, *Bowling Alone*, chapter 23; Skocpol, *Diminished Democracy*; and Jason Kaufman, *For the Common Good? American Civic Life and the Golden Age of Fraternity* (New York: Oxford University Press, 2002).

6. Dumenil, *Freemasonry and American Culture*, 80–87. For more on the GAR's foundational principles, post room arrangement, and the organization's replication of Masonic example, see McConnell, *Glorious Contentment*, 87–93.

7. "G.A.R.," *Pittsburgh Press* [Pittsburgh, PA], 14 January 1900, 7; Ellen Carol DuBois, *Feminism and Suffrage: The Emergence of an Independent Women's Movement in America, 1848-1869* (Ithaca, NY: Cornell University Press, 1978), 181; Jeanie Attie, *Patriotic Toil: Northern Women and the American Civil War* (Ithaca, NY: Cornell University Press, 1998); Nina Silber, *Gender and the Sectional Conflict* (Chapel Hill: University of North Carolina Press, 2008), 85–86. As historian John Pettegrew explains, Union veterans found in their war service "a heroic identity that transcended ordinary ways of being a man." For quote, see Pettegrew, "'The Soldier's Faith': Turn-of-the-Century Memory of the Civil War and the Emergence of Modern American Nationalism," *Journal of Contemporary History* 31, no. 1 (January 1996): 58.

8. Washington Davis, *Camp-Fire Chats of the Civil War; Being the Incident, Adventure and Wayside Exploit of the Bivouac and Battle Field, as Related by Veteran Soldiers Themselves* (Chicago: Lewis Publishing Company, 1888), 241. On the GAR grade system, see McConnell, *Glorious Contentment*, 30–38.

NOTES TO PAGES 18–22

9. T. D. McGillicuddy, ed., *Proceedings of the Annual and Semi-Annual Encampments of the Department of Ohio, Grand Army of the Republic, for the First Fourteen Years of Its Existence* (Columbus, OH: F. J. Heer Printing, Co., 1912), 74; *Early History of the Department of Massachusetts, G.A.R., from 1866 to 1880 Inclusive* (Boston: E. B. Stillings and Co., 1895), 153.

10. "Politics and Candidates," *New York Times*, 15 August 1884, 2; Pennsylvania GAR Department circular, December 1899, box 4, folder 18, Thomas Espy Post Collection, Andrew Carnegie Free Library and Music Hall, Carnegie, PA; Oliver M. Wilson, *The Grand Army of the Republic Under Its First Constitution and Ritual. Its Birth and Organization* (Kansas City, MO: Franklin Hudson Publishing Co., 1905), 205. For more on Logan's machinations to use the GAR for political gain, see Mary R. Dearing, *Veterans in Politics: The Story of the G.A.R.* (Baton Rouge: Louisiana State University Press, 1952); and McConnell, *Glorious Contentment*, 23–30.

11. *Proceedings of the Ninth Annual Meeting of the National Encampment, Grand Army of the Republic. Held at Chicago, Illinois, May 12 and 13, 1875* (Boston: n.p., 1875), 11; "The Silver Anniversary of the G.A.R.," *Clare Democrat and Press* [Clare, MI], 17 April 1891, 7; *Journal of the Twenty-Fifth Annual Session of the Encampment of the Department of the Potomac, Grand Army of the Republic, Washington, D.C., January 25, 26, 27, 28, 31, and February 6, 1893, and Special Encampment, September 15, 1892* (Washington, D.C.: Gibson Bros., 1893), 120. To compare other contemporary fraternities' moves toward service, see Dumenil, *Freemasonry and American Culture*, chapters 4 and 5; and Putnam, *Bowling Alone*, chapter 23.

12. Joseph F. Lovering, *Services for the Use of the Grand Army of the Republic* (Boston: E. B. Stillings and Co., 1881), 58.

13. *Journal of the Nineteenth Annual Session of the National Encampment, Grand Army of the Republic, Portland, Maine, June 24th and 25th, 1885* (Toledo, OH: Montgomery and Vrooman, 1885), 168; *Proceedings of the Twentieth Annual Encampment of the Department of California, Grand Army of the Republic. Held at Los Angeles, February 21st, 23^{d}, and 24th, 1887* (San Francisco, CA: George Spaulding and Co., 1887), 258; *Journal of the Thirty-Fifth Annual Encampment, Department of Michigan, Grand Army of the Republic, held at Lansing, Mich., June 18, 19, 20, 1913* (Lansing, MI: Wynkoop, Hallenbeck, Crawford Co., 1913), 169; J. Worth Carnahan, *Manual of the Civil War and Key to the Grand Army of the Republic and Kindred Societies* (Chicago: Easel Monument Association, 1897), 36; "Grand Army Bugle Notes," *New York Tribune*, 1 January 1894, 3. To be sure, directives from national headquarters to open up post rooms to the public were likely a response derived from local post pressure. Examples of public installations in local posts can be found even before the 1885 directive.

14. "Grand Army Bugle-Notes," *New York Tribune*, 5 January 1891, 4; "Grand Army of the Republic," *Pittsburgh Press*, 6 January 1895, 15; "The Grand Army," *Leavenworth Times*, 5 January 1889, 4.

15. John Hay, *Pike County Ballads and Other Pieces* (Boston: James R. Osgood and Co., 1871), 24; John Taliaferro, *All the Great Prizes: The Life of John Hay, from Lincoln to Roosevelt* (New York: Simon & Schuster, 2013), chapter 6. For the proceedings of the Lyon Post's installation, see minute book entry, 7 January 1898, box 1, volume 1: Lyon

Post 266 Minute Book, 1895–1929, Jean Worth Papers, Bentley Historical Library, Ann Arbor, MI (hereafter BHL).

16. Barbara A. Gannon, *The Won Cause: Black and White Comradeship in the Grand Army of the Republic* (Chapel Hill: University of North Carolina Press, 2011), 35; *Providence News*, 2 December 1892 and 23 December 1892; "To Install Officers," *Sunday Leader* [Lexington, KY], 1 January 1899, 3; "Lodge News," *Indianapolis Recorder*, 15 January 1910, 2; "Garrison Post," *Daily Standard Union* [Brooklyn, NY], 18 January 1895, 7; "Installation of the Wm. Lloyd Garrison Post and Corps," *The Chat* [Brooklyn, NY], 2 February 1907, 16; "Brooklyn Notes," *New York Age*, 3 February 1910, 7. Of course, it is important to remember that this "spirit of equality and brotherhood" often remained confined within the post room walls and rarely prompted white veterans to act on behalf of their Black comrades' social or political equality outside the fraternity. See Gannon, *The Won Cause*, chapter 12.

17. GAR state circular, 22 September 1891, GAR Sheridan Post No. 14, box 1, book 1 (General Orders, Department Headquarters), New Hampshire Historical Society, Concord, NH; *Journal of Proceedings of the Fortieth Annual Encampment of the Department of Minnesota, Grand Army of the Republic, Held at McKinley Hall, Minneapolis, March 21 and 22, 1906* (St. Paul, MN: Pioneer Press, 1906), 54.

18. "Washington's Birthday," *Reading Times*, 22 February 1897, 1; "Hold an Open Meeting," *Nebraska State Journal* [Lincoln, NE], 16 February 1902, 15; "George Washington," *West Bay City Times-Press* [West Bay City, MI], 19 February 1900, 3.

19. *Indiana Gazette* [Indiana, PA], 5 April 1893, 14; "Grand Army Men Celebrate," *Chicago Tribune*, 12 August 1893, 7; "Morgan's Celebrated Raid," *Daily Nebraska State Journal* [Lincoln, NE], 25 August 1889, 5; *Topeka Daily Capital*, 1 October 1892, 4; Minute book entry, 9 April 1910, box 1, folder 2, Grand Army of the Republic records, Northeast Minnesota Historical Center, University of Minnesota Duluth, Duluth, MN; "Open Meeting Tonight," *Scranton Republican*, 28 October 1910, 3; "Crown City Notes," *Los Angeles Herald*, 25 May 1906, 9. On the era's profusion of written regimental histories, see Alice Fahs, *The Imagined Civil War: Popular Literature of the North and South, 1861–1865* (Chapel Hill: University of North Carolina Press, 2001), 313–14; and Jordan, *Marching Home*, 83–91. Oral battlefield testimony that GAR veterans shared at their open meetings reflects a similar need to record and communicate their memories with typically well-researched and compelling narratives.

20. "Grand Army of the Republic," *Pittsburgh Press*, 4 February 1894, 13; "Open Meeting, G.A.R.," *Newton Daily Republican* [Newton, KS], 17 February 1887, 1; Ivy G. Wilson, ed., *At the Dusk of Dawn: Selected Poetry and Prose of Albery Allson Whitman* (Boston: Northeastern University Press, 2009), 259; "Ex-Slave to Lecture," *Oregon Daily Journal* [Portland, OR], 17 November 1902, 7; Minute book entry, Lincoln-Garfield Post No. 3, 21 May 1918, box 3, folder 7, Grand Army of the Republic Collection, Oregon Historical Society, Portland, OR (hereafter OHS); Minute book entry, Lincoln-Garfield Post No. 3, 5 March 1920, box 3, folder 8, Grand Army of the Republic Collection, OHS. For more on Drew's remarkable life, see "Bethel A. M. E. Church," *Oregon Daily Journal* [Portland, OR], 26 May 1917, 16; Henry J. Cadbury, "Negro Membership in the Society of Friends," *Journal of Negro History* 21, no. 2 (April 1936): 206–7; and Thomas Kennedy, *A History of*

Southland College: The Society of Friends and Black Education in Arkansas (Fayetteville: University of Arkansas Press, 2009), 38–39, 58, 303 n. 76. Examples of interracial public post events strengthen recent scholarly arguments that Black and white GAR veterans shared a postwar comradeship that often transcended the reconciliationist mood of the nation as a whole. See Gannon, *The Won Cause*, esp. 6–7, 60–61.

21. "Emancipation Day," *Topeka State Journal*, 22 September 1894, 8; "Glad They Are Free," *Topeka State Press*, 29 August 1895, 1; "Union Celebration," *Topeka Daily Capital*, 20 September 1900, 6; "Dawn of Freedom," *Topeka Daily Capital*, 23 September 1903, 8; "Emancipation Proclamation Celebration," *Standard Union* [Brooklyn, NY], 27 December 1907, 11; "Colored Folks Celebrate," *Brooklyn Daily Eagle*, 2 January 1909, 11; "Emancipation," *National Republican* [Washington, D.C.], 12 April 1884, 2; "Emancipation Day," *Evening Star* [Washington, D.C.], 16 April 1897, 1; "Dr. Monroe on the 54th Massachusetts," *Providence News*, 12 March 1892, 8; "Notice," *Indianapolis Recorder*, 7 May 1910, 2; "A Lincoln Birthday Observance," *Daily New Era* [Lancaster, PA], 10 February 1902, 1; "Sergeant Benn Post," *Morning News* [Lancaster, PA], 31 May 1897, 3; "At the Grave of Stevens," *Lancaster Examiner* [Lancaster, PA], 2 June 1900, 2.

22. Newspaper clipping pasted in minute book, 16 January 1911, box 16, folder 2, Grand Army of the Republic, Department of Wisconsin records, WVM.

23. An early version of this section was published as "A Building Very Useful: The Grand Army Memorial Hall in U.S. Civic Life, 1880–1920," in *The War Went On: Reconsidering the Lives of Civil War Veterans*, ed. Brian Matthew Jordan and Evan C. Rothera (Baton Rouge: Louisiana State University Press, 2020): 173–90. "Rockville Memorial Hall," *Springfield Republican* [Springfield, MA], 18 November 1888, 6; Burpee Post resolutions, 24 September 1890, box 7, folder 9, Thomas F. Burpee Post No. 71 Collection, New England Civil War Museum and Research Center, Rockville, CT. On Burpee Post, see Harry Conklin Smith, ed., *A Century of Vernon, Connecticut, 1808–1908* (Rockville, CT: T. F. Rady and Co., 1911), 19–20.

24. Kirk Savage addresses the proliferation of the common-soldier monument in the postwar United States. Little attention, however, has been paid to the commemorative trend or function of the memorial hall. See Savage, *Standing Soldiers, Kneeling Slaves: Race, War, and Monument in Nineteenth-Century America* (Princeton, NJ: Princeton University Press, 1997), esp. chapter 6.

25. *History of Mason County, Michigan, with Illustrations and Biographical Sketches of Some of Its Prominent Men and Pioneers* (Chicago: H. R. Page and Co., 1882), 41; "Mere Mention," *Washington Standard* [Olympia, WA], 5 September 1890, 3; "Woman's Relief of Blair Will Enter the Bee's Contest," *Omaha Daily Bee*, 29 December 1913, 2.

26. Gannon, *The Won Cause*, 40–41; "Sergeant Benn Post," *New Era* [Lancaster, PA], 3 June 1903, 3; "Peter Woods Dead," *Lancaster Examiner* [Lancaster, PA], 5 September 1917, 5; Leroy T. Hopkins, "No Balm in Gilead: Lancaster's African American Population and the Civil War Era," in *African Americans in Pennsylvania: Shifting Historical Perspectives*, ed. Joe William Trotter Jr. and Eric Ledell Smith (University Park: Pennsylvania State University Press, 1997), 186–88; "Colored Men's G. and A. Club No. 2," *Wyandotte Gazette* [Kansas City, KS], 13 August 1880, 3; "Grand Army of the Republic," *Weekly Press* [Kansas City, KS], 24 December 1890, 1; "Tabernacles," *Topeka Plaindealer*, 2 January

1903, 4; "Can We Succeed Without Efforts?" *Kansas City Advocate* [Kansas City, KS], 25 March 1921, 1; "Charles Sumner Post, G.A.R.," *Daily Leader* [Lexington, KY], 4 January 1899, 7; Marion B. Lucas, *A History of Blacks in Kentucky: From Slavery to Segregation, 1760–1891* (Frankfort: Kentucky Historical Society, 2003), 239–40. For African American mutual aid societies and institution-building groups in the late nineteenth and early twentieth centuries, see for instance, Tera W. Hunter, *To 'Joy My Freedom: Southern Black Women's Lives and Labors After the Civil War* (Cambridge, MA: Harvard University Press, 1997), chapter 6; Steven J. Diner, *A Very Different Age: Americans of the Progressive Era* (New York: Hill and Wang, 1998), chapter 5; and Anne S. Butler, "Black Fraternal and Benevolent Societies in Nineteenth-Century America," in *African American Fraternities and Sororities: The Legacy and the Vision*, 2nd ed., ed. Tamara L. Brown, Gregory S. Parks, and Clarenda M. Phillips (Lexington: University Press of Kentucky, 2012).

27. Quoted in McGillicuddy, *Proceedings of the Annual and Semi-Annual Encampments*, 75; *National Tribune* [Washington, D.C.], 26 January 1888, 6.

28. *Ordinances of the City of Philadelphia, from January 1 to December 31, 1906 and Opinions of the City Solicitor* (Philadelphia: Dunlap Printing Company, 1907), 236; Newton Bateman and Paul Selby, eds., *Historical Encyclopedia of Illinois and History of Kendall County*, vol. 2 (Chicago: Munsell Publishing Company, 1914), 790.

29. "A Memorial Building," *New Haven Evening Register* [New Haven, CT], 14 April 1884, 4; *Democrat and Chronicle* [Rochester, NY], 1 January 1886, 4; *Huntington Democrat* [Huntington, IN], 20 June 1895, 2.

30. "The Iowa Soldier's Monument," *Grand Army Advocate* [Des Moines, IA], 2 May 1889; *Journal of the House of Representatives of the Twenty-Fourth General Assembly of the State of Iowa, Which Convened at the Capitol in Des Moines, Iowa, January 11, 1892* (Des Moines, IA: G. H. Ragsdale, 1892), 197; "Want Cottages for the Veterans," *Postville Graphic* [Postville, IA], 14 January 1892, 2; On the dedication of Iowa's Soldiers' and Sailors' Monument, see Cora Chaplin Weed, *Hand Book for Iowa Soldiers' and Sailors' Monument* (n.p., 1897).

31. "Galesburg Objects to Grand Army Memorial Hall in Kalamazoo," *Grand Rapids Press*, 11 January 1904, 5; "Honor Bestowed on War Veterans," *Kalamazoo Gazette*, 10 April 1908, 5. For New York memorial hall quotes, see "Portage," *Livingston Republican* [Geneseo, NY], 11 March 1880, 3; and "Another View of the Soldier's Monument or Memorial Hall in Portage," *Nunda News* [Nunda, NY], 10 April 1880, 3, accessed in compiled documents folder entitled, Livingston County Military; Monuments, Memorials, and Organizations, vol. 2, Office of the Livingston County Historian, Mt. Morris, NY (hereafter LCH).

32. I. L. Stuart, ed., *History of Franklin County, Iowa: A Record of Settlement, Organization, Progress and Achievement*, vol. 1 (Chicago: S. J. Clarke, 1914), 167–68.

33. "In Memory of Heroes," *Chicago Tribune*, 27 November 1893, 3; *History of Porter County, Indiana: A Narrative Account of Its Historical Progress, Its People and Its Principal Interests*, vol. 1 (Chicago: Lewis Publishing Company, 1912), 124–25.

34. *Nunda News* [New York], 13 March 1880, 27 March 1880, 20 April 1888, 5 May 1888, accessed in compiled documents folder entitled, Livingston County Military; Monuments, Memorials, and Organizations, vol. 2, LCH. For further history of the construction of Portage's memorial hall, see James H. Smith, *History of Livingston County,*

NOTES TO PAGES 33–37   193

New York with Illustrations and Biographical Sketches of Some of Its Prominent Men and Pioneers, 1687–1881 (Syracuse, NY: D. Mason and Co., 1881), 272–73.

35. *Nunda News* [Nunda, NY], 4 February 1888, 4 July 1908, accessed in compiled documents folder entitled, Livingston County Military; Monuments, Memorials, and Organizations, vol. 2, LCH. On the Carter Memorial Hall and the military career of John J. Carter, see H. Wells Hand, ed., *Centennial History of the Town of Nunda, 1808–1908* (Rochester, NY: Rochester Herald Press, 1908), 606–10.

36. *Dalton Enterprise* [Dalton, NY], 15 March 1895, 18 October 1895, 15 November 1895, 10 April 1896; "Tonight Is the Big Night," *Nunda News* [Nunda, NY], 6 December 1929, 1; "Briefs from Rochester Neighbors," *Rochester Times-Union* [Rochester, NY], 5 July 1938, 3; "Not Ready to Give Up Identity," *Genesee County Express* [Dansville, NY], 9 May 2002, accessed in compiled documents folder entitled, Livingston County Military; Monuments, Memorials, and Organizations, vol. 2, LCH.

37. Miles Orvell, *The Death and Life of Main Street: Small Towns in American Memory, Space, and Community* (Chapel Hill: University of North Carolina Press, 2012), chapter 3; Kirin J. Makker, "Village Improvement and the Development of Small Town America, 1853–1893," *Journal of Planning History* 13 (February 2014): 68–87; "New Memorial Hall Nearing Completion," *Kalamazoo Gazette*, 6 December 1912, 10; *The True Northerner* [Paw Paw, MI], 17 January 1913, 19 February 1915, 26 February 1915, 5 March 1915, 6 August 1915; "Paw Paw G.A.R. Men Provide Rest Room in Memorial Hall," *Kalamazoo Gazette*, 15 February 1913, 2.

38. "The Grand Army Memorial Hall," *Springfield Republican* [Springfield, MA], 14 February 1890, 3; "Dedication at Windsor Locks," *Springfield Republican* [Springfield, MA], 11 June 1891, 4; "Thompsonville Needs a Hall," *Springfield Republican* [Springfield, MA], 14 June 1891, 2. On the construction of Windsor Locks's memorial hall, see Henry R. Stiles, *The History and Genealogies of Ancient Windsor, Connecticut; Including East Windsor, South Windsor, Bloomfield, Windsor Locks, and Ellington, 1635–1891*, vol. 1 (Hartford, CT: Case, Lockwood, and Brainard, 1891), 528–31.

39. Petition quote from digitized page of the 1903 minutes of the Winnebago County Board, courtesy of and in possession of the curator of Rockford's Veterans Memorial Hall; "Memorial Hall History," *Rockford Republic* [Rockford, IL], 3 June 1903, 2; "Post Meets in New Home," *Rockford Daily Register-Gazette* [Rockford, IL], 9 June 1903, 8. For more on urban building projects in modest-sized cities, see Maureen Ogle, "Beyond the Great City: Finding and Defining the Small City in Nineteenth Century America," in *American Cities and Towns: Historical Perspectives*, ed. Joseph F. Rishel (Pittsburgh, PA: Duquesne University Press, 1992), 48–66.

40. John R. Osborn, *An Historical Sketch of the Rise and Progress of the Toledo Soldiers Memorial Association* (Toledo, OH: Barkdull Printing, 1883), 8, in box 1, folder 19, Toledo Soldiers Memorial Association collection, Toledo-Lucas County Public Library, Toledo, OH; *Soldiers' Memorial Building, Toledo, Ohio, in Honor and in Memory of Those Who Fought and Those Who Fell in Defense of Our Country During the War of the Rebellion* (Toledo: B. F. Wade Co., 1886), 46.

41. Report of Committee on ex-Senator Palmer's Proposition, June 1892, William Herbert Withington Papers, microfilm reel 1, BHL; "Realty and Building," *Detroit Free Press*, 5 July 1896, 19; "History of Memorial Hall," *Detroit Free Press*, 12 December 1900, 8.

42. Minute book entry with resolutions to Allegheny County Grand Army Association, 14 June 1902, box 1, folder 7, Major William G. Lowry Post No. 548 Records, Detre Library and Archives, Heinz History Center, Pittsburgh, PA; Allegheny County Grand Army Association minute book entry, 26 July 1902, Allegheny County Grand Army Association Records, 1898–1940, microfilm reel 1, Archives of Industrial Society, University of Pittsburgh, Pittsburgh, PA.

43. Jon A. Peterson, "The City Beautiful Movement: Forgotten Origins and Lost Meanings," *Journal of Urban History* 2, no. 4 (August 1976): 415–34; William H. Wilson, "The Ideology, Aesthetics and Politics of the City Beautiful Movement," in *The Rise of Modern Urban Planning*, ed. Anthony Sutcliffe (New York: St. Martin's Press, 1980), esp. 165–66; William H. Wilson, *The City Beautiful Movement* (Baltimore, MD: Johns Hopkins University Press, 1989); Montgomery Schuyler, "The Building of Pittsburgh," *Architectural Record* 30, no. 3 (September 1911): 230. In 1907 and 1908, New York's philanthropic Russell Sage Foundation funded the so-called Pittsburgh Survey, a sociological investigation of the city designed to call awareness to the city's labor exploitation, political corruption, and unhealthful conditions. Harnessing the newfound power of applied scientific study, researchers proposed progressive reforms to redress Pittsburgh's "bitter human waste and rankling injustices." See Paul Underwood Kellogg, ed., *The Pittsburgh Survey: Wage-Earning Pittsburgh* (New York: Survey Associates, 1914), iii.

44. Report of the Allegheny County Grand Army Association Monument and Memorial Committee, 25 November 1905, pasted in minute book, box 3, Allegheny County Grand Army Association Collection, Soldiers and Sailors Memorial Hall, Pittsburgh, PA (hereafter SSMH).

45. H. H. Bengough to North Side Board of School Controllers, 5 October 1910, record and minute book of the Soldiers' Memorial Hall Committee, Soldiers' Memorial Hall Committee Collection, SSMH; "Veterans of the Civil War March to Memorial Erected in Their Honor," *Pittsburgh Press*, 11 October 1910, 1; "Memorial Hall Thrown Open to People," *Pittsburgh Gazette Times*, 10 October 1910, 1. M. Christine Boyer notes that turn-of-the-century aesthetic reforms, particularly the erection of commemorative monumental structures, could serve as "community educators" by instilling the people with civic pride. This, in turn, fostered greater commitment to public life, good citizenship, and social order. See Boyer, *Dreaming the Rational City: The Myth of American City Planning* (Cambridge, MA: MIT Press, 1983), 44–46. See also Richard E. Foglesong, *Planning the Capitalist City: The Colonial Era to the 1920s* (Princeton, NJ: Princeton University Press, 1986), 141.

46. On the civic activities of Pittsburgh's Robert G. Shaw Post, see Diane Ragan, *Grand Army of the Republic, Department of Pennsylvania, Personal War Sketches of the African American Members of Col. Robert G. Shaw Post No. 206, Pittsburgh* (Pittsburgh: Western Pennsylvania Genealogical Society, 2003); Donald R. Shaffer, *After the Glory: The Struggles of Black Civil War Veterans* (Lawrence: University Press of Kansas, 2004), 152–53; and Barbara A. Gannon, "Sites of Memory, Sites of Glory: African-American Grand Army of the Republic Posts in Pennsylvania," in *Making and Remaking Pennsylvania's Civil War*, ed. William Blair and William Pencak (University Park: Pennsylvania State University Press, 2001), 172–73. For the civic activities of Pittsburgh's Black veterans more generally, see Laurence A. Glasco, "Optimism, Dilemmas, and Progress:

The Pittsburgh Survey and Black Americans," in *Pittsburgh Surveyed: Social Science and Social Reform in the Early Twentieth Century*, ed. Maurine W. Greenwald and Margo Anderson (Pittsburgh, PA: University of Pittsburgh Press, 1996), 218.

47. Report of H. H. Bengough, 24 August 1910, record and minute book of the Soldiers' Memorial Hall Committee, Soldiers' Memorial Hall Committee Collection, SSMH; "Negro Preacher Speaks," *Pittsburgh Post*, 10 October 1910, 6; Gannon, *The Won Cause*, esp. 7–8. For coverage of the Shaw Post's first use of Soldiers and Sailors Memorial Hall to hold its meetings, see "G.A.R. to Meet," *Pittsburgh Press*, 6 November 1910, 27.

48. Rules of Government for Hall, October 1910, record and minute book of the Soldiers' Memorial Hall Committee, Soldiers' Memorial Hall Committee Collection, SSMH; Guest register entry of John T. Roberts, October 19, 1915, Soldiers and Sailors Memorial Hall visitor's register (February 1915–May 1917), SSMH.

49. *Report of the Proceedings of the Society of the Army of the Tennessee at the Fourteenth Annual Meeting, Held at Cincinnati, Ohio, April 6th and 7th, 1881* (Cincinnati, OH: Society of the Army of the Tennessee, 1885), 518.

2. A Grand Army of Scholars

1. George W. Martin, ed., *Collections of the Kansas State Historical Society, 1909–1910*, vol. 11 (Topeka, KS: State Printing Office, 1910), 269–70; "H. B. No. 313 by Mr. Rankin," *Lawrence Daily Journal* [Lawrence, KS], 31 January 1889, 2; "The House," *Topeka Capital-Commonwealth* [Topeka, KS], 23 February 1889, 3; *House Journal. Proceedings of the House of Representatives of the State of Kansas. Sixth Biennial Session, Begun at Topeka, January 8, 1889* (Topeka: Kansas Publishing House, 1889), 260; "Kansas Editors Spoke First," *Belleville Telescope* [Belleville, KS], 7 May 1914, 6; "Memorial Hall Edition," *Topeka Daily Capital* [Topeka, KS], 26 May 1914, 17; D. O. McCray, "A Kansas War-Time Story," in *Journal of the Thirty-Third Annual Encampment of the Grand Army of the Republic, Department of Kansas and Dedication of Memorial Hall, Held at Topeka, May 26, 27, and 28, 1914* (Topeka: Kansas State Printing Office, 1914), 103; Kyle S. Sinisi, "Veterans as Political Activists: The Kansas Grand Army of the Republic, 1880–1893," *Kansas History: A Journal of the Central Plains* 14, no. 2 (Summer 1991): 89–99. The Kansas Historical Society operated out of the memorial hall until 1995. The building continues to serve a public purpose, housing the offices of the state's attorney general and secretary of state.

2. Robert H. Wiebe, *The Search for Order, 1877–1920* (New York: Hill and Wang, 1967), 57; Cecilia Elizabeth O'Leary, *To Die For: The Paradox of American Patriotism* (Princeton, NJ: Princeton University Press, 1999), 190; Stuart McConnell, *Glorious Contentment: The Grand Army of the Republic, 1865–1900* (Chapel Hill: University of North Carolina Press, 1992), 224–32; David W. Blight, *Race and Reunion: The Civil War in American Memory* (Cambridge, MA: Harvard University Press, 2001), 277–81; Karen L. Cox, *Dixie's Daughters: The United Daughters of the Confederacy and the Preservation of Confederate Culture* (Gainesville: University Press of Florida, 2003), 1; Caroline E. Janney, *Remembering the Civil War: Reunion and the Limits of Reconciliation* (Chapel Hill: University of North Carolina Press, 2013), 184; Barbara A. Gannon, *The Won Cause: Black and White Comradeship in the Grand Army of the Republic* (Chapel Hill: University of North Carolina Press, 2011), 148; M. Keith Harris, *Across the Bloody Chasm: The*

Culture of Commemoration Among Civil War Veterans (Baton Rouge: Louisiana State University Press, 2014), 123–25; James M. McPherson, *For Cause and Comrades: Why Men Fought in the Civil War* (New York: Oxford University Press, 1997), 11. Julie A. Mujic also discusses the various motivations of those Midwestern college students who left their institutions to enlist in the military and those who stayed behind to complete their studies. A small number completed their education after their military service ended. See Mujic, "Between Campus and War: Students, Patriotism, and Education at Midwestern Universities During the American Civil War," PhD diss. (Kent State University, 2012).

3. Steven J. Diner, *Universities and Their Cities: Urban Higher Education in America* (Baltimore, MD: Johns Hopkins University Press, 2017), 18–20, 35; Rosemary Ruhig Du Mont, *Reform and Reaction: The Big City Public Library in American Life* (Westport, CT: Greenwood Press, 1977); Dee Garrison, *Apostles of Culture: The Public Librarian and American Society, 1876–1920* (New York: The Free Press, 1979).

4. "Miss Templeton Leaves," *The Daily Northwestern* [Oshkosh, WI], 2 June 1906, 4; Charlotte Templeton speech to Nebraska GAR department encampment, May 1913, series 1, box 1, folder 8, Grand Army of the Republic, Department of Nebraska Records, Nebraska State Historical Society, Lincoln, NE. Librarians like Templeton occupied a key node in the turn-of-the-century network of women reformers—settlement workers, schoolteachers, and others—who devised progressive solutions to their communities' social ills. Garrison, *Apostles of Culture*, chapter 11; Abigail A. Van Slyck, *Free to All: Carnegie Libraries and American Culture, 1890–1920* (Chicago: University of Chicago Press, 1995), chapter 5.

5. Sidney Ditzion, *Arsenals of a Democratic Culture: A Social History of the American Public Library in New England and the Middle States from 1850 to 1900* (Chicago: American Library Association, 1947); Du Mont, *Reform and Reaction*, chapter 1; Garrison, *Apostles of Culture*, chapter 14; and Wayne A. Wiegand, *Part of Our Lives: A People's History of the American Public Library* (New York: Oxford University Press, 2015), chapters 2–4. For the professionalization of the library field, see Garrison, *Apostles of Culture*, chapters 1–2; and Marion Casey, "Efficiency, Taylorism, and Libraries in Progressive America," *Journal of Library History* 16, no. 2 (Spring 1981): 265–79. For Carnegie quote, see Ellen Condliffe Lagemann, *The Politics of Knowledge: The Carnegie Corporation, Philanthropy, and Public Policy* (Chicago: University of Chicago Press, 1989), 17.

6. *Ninth Report of the Free Public Library Commission of Massachusetts* (Boston: Wright and Potter, 1899), 444.

Drew Gilpin Faust discusses the ways in which the nation's staggering loss sustained during the war required new outlets to honor the dead. Megan Kate Nelson reflects on the ways in which war compels survivors to create and rebuild as a way to come to terms with death and loss. Meanwhile, John R. Neff indicates that commemoration of the Civil War dead is one of the strongest indications that northerners' reconciliation with ex-Confederates—especially for Union veterans—was not as pervasive as suggested in some literature. The establishment of memorial libraries throughout the postwar North fits this assertion. See Faust, *This Republic of Suffering: Death and the American Civil War* (New York: Vintage, 2008), 268; Nelson, *Ruin Nation: Destruction and the American Civil War* (Athens: University of Georgia Press, 2012), 4; and Neff, *Honoring the Civil*

War Dead: Commemoration and the Problem of Reconciliation (Lawrence: University Press of Kansas, 2005). On garden cemeteries, see David Charles Sloane, *The Last Great Necessity: Cemeteries in American History* (Baltimore, MD: Johns Hopkins University Press, 1991). On libraries and memorialization, see Kenneth A. Breisch, *Henry Hobson Richardson and the Small Public Library in America: A Study in Typology* (Cambridge, MA: MIT Press, 1997), 46.

7. Christopher T. Thayer, *Address Delivered at the Dedication of Memorial Hall, Lancaster, June 17, 1868* (Boston: Nichols and Noyes, 1868), 10, 39; "Report of the Committee on Soldiers' Monument" (Foxboro, MA: William H. Thomas, Printer, 1867), 1, 6, in compiled volume, *Civil War Pamphlets: Massachusetts Monuments and Memorials*, U.S. Army Heritage and Education Center, Carlisle, PA. It is important to note that some communities had prewar library clubs or library collections housed provisionally in town halls or other public buildings. Lancaster, Massachusetts, for instance, had a long history of library culture, but its first freestanding, permanent library building was that dedicated as a memorial hall in 1868.

8. *Ninth Report of the Free Public Library Commission of Massachusetts* (Boston: Wright and Potter Printing Co., 1899), 68; *Dedication Services of the Memorial Library and Grand Army Hall at Manchester-by-the-Sea, Massachusetts, October 13, 1887* (Boston: Rand Avery Company, the Franklin Press, 1888), 22; "M'Kinley at Adams," *North Adams Transcript* [North Adams, MA], 27 September 1897, 1.

9. For Rutland's library and memorial hall, see *National Tribune* [Washington, D.C.], 27 April 1893, 6; *Vermont Phoenix* [Brattleboro, VT], 2 June 1893, 1; George Haddad, *Mt. Lebanon to Vermont: Autobiography of George Haddad, Taken Down by His Daughter Emily Marie Haddad with the Assistance of Berenice Rachel Tuttle* (Rutland, VT: Tuttle Company, 1916), 123, 125; Jacob Sherman, "Lost Buildings of Old Rutland: A Calendar," *Rutland Historical Society Quarterly* 33, no. 4 (2003): 4–5; and Robert Ranftle, "Rutland in the Civil War (Part 1)," *Rutland Historical Society Quarterly* 41, no. 2 (2011): 8–10. For Rockland Public Library, see "Maine Melange," *Bangor Daily Whig and Courier* [Bangor, ME], 6 April 1893, 1; and "By Telegraph," *Bangor Daily Whig and Courier* [Bangor, ME], 20 May 1893, 3. Kenneth Alan Breisch notes that it was Massachusetts that led the nation's public library movement and that from there, public library buildings "spread almost concentrically outward." This observation holds true with public libraries created with GAR influence. Massachusetts GAR posts led the way, followed by the rest of New England, and then other northern states. See Breisch, "Small Public Libraries in America, 1850–1890: The Invention and Evolution of a Building Type," PhD diss. (University of Michigan, 1982), 10.

10. "The Aurora Public Library," *Aurora Beacon News* [Aurora, IL], 10 December 1884; "Public Library," *Aurora Beacon News* [Aurora, IL], 10 July 1886.

11. "Post Libraries," *National Tribune* [Washington, D.C.], 1 March 1883, 4; Joseph Ripley Chandler Ward, *History of George G. Meade Post No. One, Department of Pennsylvania Grand Army of the Republic* (Philadelphia: n.p., 1889), 51; "Grand Army Library," *Bangor Daily Whig and Courier* [Bangor, ME], 15 April 1887, 3 June 1887, and 13 April 1888. The *National Tribune* changed over time from an organ created primarily to advocate pension rights to one that devoted a great deal of its space to the interests and civic activities

of local posts and rank-and-file members nationwide. The newspaper thus evolved in a similar way to the organization as a whole. For more, see Steven E. Sodergren, "'Exposing False History': The Voice of the Union Veteran in the Pages of the *National Tribune*," in *The War Went On: Reconsidering the Lives of Civil War Veterans*, ed. Brian Matthew Jordan and Evan C. Rothera (Baton Rouge: Louisiana State University Press, 2020), 137–56.

12. John A. Rawlins Post war library circular, 5 May 1890, box 1, folder 19, Henry A. Castle Papers, Minnesota Historical Society, St. Paul, MN (hereafter MinnHS); Culver Post minute book entries, 26 March 1910 and 27 August 1910, box 1, folder 2, Grand Army of the Republic records, Northeast Minnesota Historical Center, University of Minnesota Duluth, Duluth, MN.

13. *National Tribune* [Washington, D.C.], 29 March 1883, 15 November 1883, 10 May 1894. In 1895, the Massachusetts GAR endorsed Apsley's effort and urged its members to write their representatives in Congress to support the resolution. See *Journal of the Twenty-Eighth Annual Encampment, Department of Massachusetts, Grand Army of the Republic, held in Springfield, Feb. 13 and 14, 1895* (Boston: E. B. Stillings, 1895), 163.

14. Elizabeth B. Custer, *"Boots and Saddles": or, Life in Dakota with General Custer* (New York: Harper & Brothers, 1885), and *Tenting on the Plains; or, General Custer in Kansas and Texas* (New York: Charles L. Webster & Company, 1887); *National Tribune* [Washington, D.C.], 19 April 1888 and 19 September 1907; Clara Barton, *The Story of My Childhood* (New York: The Baker & Taylor Co., 1907); Janet Jennings, *The Blue and the Gray* (Madison, WI: Cantwell Printing Co., 1910), 6; GAR Department of Wisconsin circular, 27 March 1911, box 6, folder 7, Grand Army of the Republic, Department of Wisconsin Records, Wisconsin Veterans Museum, Madison, WI (hereafter WVM). Alice Fahs calls attention to a "feminized war literature" that emerged in the immediate postwar years and generally heralded the domestic war work that women shouldered. Elizabeth Bacon Custer's writings confirm historian Kathryn Kish Sklar's argument that women writers and historians born during the antebellum period generally "gave considerable attention in their writings to…domestic life." See Fahs, "The Feminized Civil War: Gender, Northern Popular Literature, and the Memory of the War, 1861–1900," *Journal of American History* 85, no. 4 (March 1999): 1461–94; and Sklar, "American Female Historians in Context, 1770–1930," *Feminist Studies* 3, no. 1/2 (Autumn 1975): 171–84.

15. N. P. Chipman, *The Tragedy of Andersonville: Trial of Captain Henry Wirz, the Prison Keeper* (San Francisco: Blair Murdock Company, 1911), 9–10; *Journal of the Thirty-Third Annual Convention of the Department of Massachusetts Woman's Relief Corps, Auxiliary to the Grand Army of the Republic, Shawmut Congregational Church, Boston, Mass., April 2 and 3, 1912* (Boston: Griffith-Stillings Press, 1912), 318. For more on the importance of Civil War memory as it relates to ex-prisoners, see Angela M. Riotto, "Remembering 'That Dark Episode': Union and Confederate Ex-Prisoners of War and Their Captivity Narratives," in *The War Went On: Reconsidering the Lives of Civil War Veterans*, ed. Brian Matthew Jordan and Evan C. Rothera (Baton Rouge: Louisiana State University Press, 2020), 121–36.

16. Report of Headquarters Committee, 12 March 1906, series 4, box 4, folder 9, Thomas Espy Post Collection, Andrew Carnegie Free Library and Music Hall, Carnegie,

PA (hereafter ACFL); Minute book entry, 30 May 1923, box 1, Lyon Post No. 266 minute book, Jean Worth Papers, Bentley Historical Library, Ann Arbor, MI (hereafter BHL); Newspaper clipping, 9 December 1925, box 1, folder: Lyon Post 266, Record Book, 1934 Compilation, Jean Worth Papers, BHL. Fascinatingly, the Espy Post's quarters remained closed off for decades after the members stopped meeting. When the room was reopened in the 1980s, a veritable time capsule of the veterans' possessions remained. The Andrew Carnegie Free Library and Music Hall still tends to the Espy Post meeting room and invites visitors inside, fulfilling the members' desire for the space to remain the "GAR Memorial Room for all time." For more recent coverage of the Espy Post meeting room, see "'Ten-shun! Civil War Mini-Museum Offers a Journey into Past," *Pittsburgh Press*, 8 November 1984, S11; and "Civil War Treasures Rescued from Time," *Pittsburgh Post-Gazette*, 8 December 2000, B1, B10.

17. Report of Weissert, Bell, and Merrick in *Journal of the Thirty-Ninth National Encampment of the Grand Army of the Republic, Denver, Colorado, September 7th and 8th, 1905* (Boston: Griffith-Stillings Press, 1905), 321. For the postwar careers of these men, see Andrew Jackson Aikens and Lewis A. Proctor, eds., *Wisconsin Men of Progress in 1897: A Selected List of Biographical Sketches and Portraits of the Leaders in Business, Professional and Official Life, Together with Short Notes on the History and Character of Wisconsin* (Milwaukee: The Evening Wisconsin Company, 1897), 397; "Col. A. Weissert, Milwaukee, Dies," *Eau Claire Leader* [Eau Claire, WI], 26 April 1923, 6; "Judges and Lawyers Join in Memorial Tribute to Col. Bell," *Brooklyn Daily Eagle*, 12 December 1919, 22; Gillis J. Harp, *Positivist Republic: Auguste Comte and the Reconstruction of American Liberalism* (University Park: Pennsylvania State University Press, 1995), 65–68; Edwin Carey Whittemore, *The Centennial History of Waterville, Kennebec County, Maine* (Waterville, ME: Executive Committee of the Centennial Celebration, 1902), 527–28.

18. Text of Morrill Act, quoted in William M. McKinney, *Federal Statutes Annotated: Second Edition, Containing All the Laws of the United States of a General, Permanent and Public Nature in Force on the First Day of January, 1916*, vol. 3 (Northport, NY: Edward Thompson Co., 1917), 100. For statistics, see Thomas D. Snyder, ed., *120 Years of American Education: A Statistical Portrait* (Washington, D.C.: US Department of Education, 1993), 63, 75, 76. On antebellum higher education, see Frederick Rudolph, *The American College and University: A History* (Athens: University of Georgia Press, 1962), chapters 9–11; and Michael David Cohen, *Reconstructing the Campus: Higher Education and the American Civil War* (Charlottesville: University of Virginia Press, 2012), 2–11. On the ways that the Civil War opened up higher educational opportunities for women at some institutions, see Mujic, "Between Campus and War," 292–95.

19. *Presentation of a National Flag to the College of the City of New York on Friday Evening, June 8, 1888 in the Academy of Music by Lafayette Post, No. 140, Department of New York, Grand Army of the Republic* (New York: J. J. Little, 1888), 7, 11, 12. For more on post–Civil War colleges as useful progenitors of middle-class, Protestant values, see W. Bruce Leslie, *Gentlemen and Scholars: College and Community in the "Age of the University," 1865–1917* (University Park: Pennsylvania State University Press, 1992), 1. For a discussion on the GAR's role in promulgating a "cult of the flag" in the late nineteenth century, derived in part from the Union soldier's devotion afforded the Stars and Stripes during

battle, see Scot M. Guenter, *The American Flag, 1777–1924: Cultural Shifts from Creation to Codification* (Rutherford, NJ: Farleigh Dickinson University Press, 1990), chapter 5. In the postwar years, a common trend in higher education was the hiring of former Union officers as professors at, or even presidents of, colleges and universities. See Cohen, *Reconstructing the Campus*, 61–65; and Kanisorn Wongsrichanalai, "Lessons of War: Three Civil War Veterans and the Goals of Postwar Education," in *So Conceived and So Dedicated: Intellectual Life in the Civil War-Era North*, ed. Lorien Foote and Kanisorn Wongsrichanalai (New York: Fordham University Press, 2015), 129–52.

20. "Grand Army Bugle Notes," *New York Tribune*, 23 March 1896, 10; *Ceremony of Flag Presentation to Columbia University of the City of New York, May Second, 1896, and May Seventh, 1898 by Lafayette Post, No. 140, Department of New York, Grand Army of the Republic* (New York: n.p., 1899), 48, 87, 88; Theodore Roosevelt, *The Rough Riders* (New York: Charles Scribner's Sons, 1899), 15. For Seth Low's tenure at Columbia, see Roger L. Geiger, *The History of American Higher Education: Learning and Culture from the Founding to World War II* (Princeton, NJ: Princeton University Press, 2015), 351–52. For discussion on college students and the Spanish-American War, see Kristin L. Hoganson, *Fighting for American Manhood: How Gender Politics Provoked the Spanish-American and Philippine-American Wars* (New Haven, CT: Yale University Press, 1998), 119–20.

21. Minute book entry, 15 April 1910, box 16, folder 1, Grand Army of the Republic, Department of Wisconsin Records, WVM. The Fairchild Post's minute books speak to a range of events hosted by the veterans for the benefit of university scholars as well as university events to which veterans were invited. See for instance, minute book entries, 15 April 1910 and 19 September 1910, box 16, folders 1 and 2, Grand Army of the Republic, Department of Wisconsin Records, WVM. For more on the University of Wisconsin, the "Wisconsin Idea," and the development of a healthy partnership between campus and community, see Rudolph, *The American College and University*, 363; John S. Brubacher and Willis Rudy, *Higher Education in Transition: A History of American Colleges and Universities*, 4th ed. (New Brunswick, NJ: Transaction Publishers, 1997), 161; John R. Thelin, *A History of American Higher Education*, 2nd ed. (Baltimore, MD: Johns Hopkins University Press, 2011), 137–38; and Geiger, *History of American Higher Education*, 358–59. On college outreach to their communities and the "service ideal" of American higher education, see Rudolph, *American College*, chapter 17; and Cohen, *Reconstructing the Campus*, chapter 5.

22. "That G.A.R. Surplus," *Pittsburgh Commercial Gazette*, 29 September 1894, 2; "Dr. Holland's Proud of It," *Pittsburgh Commercial Gazette*, 17 September 1895, 3; Allegheny County Grand Army Association to Thomas Espy Post, 30 April 1901, Thomas Espy Post Collection, series 4, box 4, folder 5, ACFL; Allegheny County Grand Army Association minute book entry, 22 March 1902, Allegheny County Grand Army Association Records, 1898–1940, microfilm reel 1, Archives of Industrial Society, University of Pittsburgh, Pittsburgh PA; "University of Pittsburgh Bulletin: General Catalog," 18, no. 23 (June 1923): 60. With the encampment surplus funds, three scholarships were created and named for Pittsburghers with Civil War–era connections—Secretary of War Edwin M. Stanton; General Alexander Hays; and Colonel Samuel H. Black. For more on the wider postwar activism that reduced the financial burden on college enrollment for many low-income scholars of

the era, see Thelin, *American Higher Education*, 100–101; and Merle Curti and Roderick Nash, *Philanthropy in the Shaping of American Higher Education* (New Brunswick, NJ: Rutgers University Press, 1965). For the commercialization involved in the Grand Army encampments and the great lengths to which civic and business leaders went to have their cities selected for the often-lucrative events, see O'Leary, *To Die For*, 41–44; and James Marten, *Sing Not War: The Lives of Union and Confederate Veterans in Gilded Age America* (Chapel Hill: University of North Carolina Press, 2011), 126–33. For biography of Curry, see *The Successful American: A Magazine Devoted to the Achievements of, and Containing Biographical and Character Sketches, Together with Portraits of Representative 'Successful Americans'* 1, no. 6 (June 1900): 8, 12.

23. Certificate of contribution to Brown University's G.A.R. scholarship fund, 1891, Elisha Hunt Rhodes Papers (MSS 1089), Box 4, Folder 6, Rhode Island Historical Society, Providence, RI; "The Catalogue of Brown University, One Hundred and Fifty-Sixth Year, 1919–1920" (Providence, RI: Brown University, 1919), 178; *Journal of the Twenty-Fifth Annual Encampment of the Department of Rhode Island, Grand Army of the Republic, January 20, 1892"* (Providence: Rhode Island Printing Company, 1892), 22, 106. For recipients of the fellowship and their fields, see for example, *Annual Report of the President to the Corporation of Brown University, October 13, 1909* (Providence, RI: Brown University, 1909); the annual issues of "The Catalogue of Brown University"; and "Wins Fellowship at Brown," *Wilkes-Barre Record* [Wilkes-Barre, PA], 24 May 1923, 4. On the creation of graduate programs in the late nineteenth-century United States, see Geiger, *History of American Higher Education*, chapter 8. On Williams's military and professional career, see William Richard Cutter, ed., *New England Families, Genealogical and Memorial: A Record of the Achievements of Her People in the Making of Commonwealths and the Founding of a Nation*, vol. 2 (New York: Lewis Historical Publishing Co., 1914), 980–81.

24. Patriotic instructor's report in *Journal of the Twenty-Eighth Annual Encampment, Department of New Hampshire*, 1895, Journal of the Encampments, Department of New Hampshire Records, Grand Army of the Republic, New Hampshire Historical Society, Concord, NH; "To Promote Patriotic Study in the Public Schools, Report of Special Committee Appointed by Col. Albert D. Shaw, Department Commander of the Department of New York, Grand Army of the Republic, in General Orders No. 6, Issued August 9, 1897" (New York: Department of Public Instruction, 1897), 8, located in box 94, folder 5, New York State Historian Grand Army of the Republic Records, New York State Archives, Albany, NY; Minnesota state normal school board report of Ell Torrance, 1908, box 34, folder 1, Ell Torrance Papers, MinnHS. Christine A. Ogren dubs the period between 1870 and 1910 the "heyday" of the state normal school. See Ogren, *The American State Normal School: "An Instrument of Great Good"* (New York: Palgrave Macmillan, 2005), esp. 1–5, 55–83; and Jurgen Herbst, *And Sadly Teach: Teacher Education and Professionalization in American Culture* (Madison: University of Wisconsin Press, 1989).

25. James C. Klotter, "The Black South and White Appalachia," *Journal of American History* 66, no. 4 (March 1980): 832–33; *The Houston Post*, 31 December 1908, 7. Michael David Cohen argues that as a result of postwar rebuilding and a need to boost enrollments, southern colleges remade themselves into comprehensive universities in the

pattern of their northern counterparts and diversified their student bodies to include the poor, women, and occasionally, African Americans. Christine A. Ogren notes the postwar explosion of state normal schools in the South as legislatures and private citizens (including African American communities) opened a profusion of teaching colleges through the 1910s, at times outpacing all other regions of the country. Cohen, *Reconstructing the Campus*, 16; Ogren, *American State Normal School*, 59–61.

26. "Catalogue, Grant Memorial University, 1887–1888" (Athens, TN: Grant Memorial University, 1887), 35; "Yearbook, U.S. Grant University, Athens and Chattanooga, Tenn., 1891–1892" (Athens, TN: Grant Memorial University, 1891), 45; "Annual Catalogue of Grant University, Chattanooga and Athens, Tenn., 1902, with Announcements for 1902–1903" (Athens, TN: Grant Memorial University, 1902), 9.

27. Major General Oliver O. Howard, "Lincoln's Monument in the Mountains," *The National Magazine: An Illustrated American Monthly* 22 (April–September 1905): 299, 300; *Journal of the 29th Encampment, Department of Tennessee, Grand Army of the Republic, National Soldiers' Home, Tennessee, May 16th and 17th, 1912* (Greeneville, TN: J. R. Self and Co., 1912), 28; *Journal of the Forty-Sixth National Encampment, Grand Army of the Republic, Los Angeles, California, September 12th and 13th, Including Semi-Official Meeting, Tuesday, September 10, 1912* (N.P., 1912), 263; Lincoln University Endowment Association to Capt. Freas Post No. 163 (Beaver City, NE), 16 November 1912, series 9, box 12, folder 90, Grand Army of the Republic, Department of Nebraska Records, Nebraska State Historical Society, Lincoln, NE. For Howard, the use of Lincoln's name had a twofold purpose. First, it was a way to fulfill a desire that Lincoln expressed to Howard in 1863 to reward the wartime loyalty of the people of East Tennessee. Second, Howard recognized that the very name Lincoln would serve as a powerful fundraising tool among northern donors, including Grand Army veterans. The 1909 centennial of Lincoln's birth and the years immediately preceding it were a particularly heady time for the memory of the war president. A slew of counties and towns were named for Lincoln; his birthday was decreed a holiday by many state legislatures; and a mania to collect Lincoln memorabilia—that is, "Lincolniana"—swept the nation. The establishment of Lincoln Memorial University and the subsequent efforts to fundraise for the institution during the era fit this trend. See Earl J. Hess, *Lincoln Memorial University and the Shaping of Appalachia* (Knoxville: University of Tennessee Press, 2011), xiii–xix, 225; and Merrill D. Peterson, *Lincoln in American Memory* (New York: Oxford University Press, 1994), chapter 4.

28. Department commander's address, May 1904, manuscript book 4, box 11, GAR Records, Department of Delaware Encampments, Journal of Records, 1899–1907, 233, Delaware Historical Society, Wilmington, DE; Relief aid circular, 9 October 1895, box 2, folder 16, Henry A. Castle Papers, MinnHS; "Virginia and North Carolina," *National Tribune* [Washington, D.C.], 24 March 1910, 6; Gannon, *The Won Cause*, 170.

29. Booker T. Washington, "Industrial Education for Negroes," in *The Negro Problem: A Series of Articles by Representative American Negroes of To-Day* (New York: James Pott & Company, 1903), 25; Blight, *Race and Reunion*, 331–32; "The Slater Fund," *National Tribune* [Washington, D.C.], 22 April 1882, 4.

30. Samuel Chapman Armstrong, *Ideas on Education Expressed by Samuel Chapman Armstrong* (Hampton, VA: Hampton Institute Press, 1908), 8, 9; James D. Anderson, *The*

Education of Blacks in the South, 1860–1935 (Chapel Hill: University of North Carolina Press, 1988), chapter 2; Eric Foner, *Reconstruction: America's Unfinished Revolution, 1863–1877* (New York: Harper & Row, 1988), 142–53.

31. "Who Founded Fisk University?," *Daily American* [Nashville, TN], 29 November 1888, 3; "Services Over Remains of President E. M. Cravath," *Nashville American*, 10 September 1900, 10; *Erastus Milo Cravath* (New York: Devinne Press, 1900), 3; "High Honor to a Worthy Colored Man," *The Commercial Herald* [Vicksburg, MS], 3 June 1886, 4; "Flag Presentation," *National Tribune* [Washington, D.C.], 18 June 1896, 6; "Bequests for New Orleans," *The Times Democrat* [New Orleans, LA], 12 December 1907, 2; "Lincoln University," *Philadelphia Inquirer*, 7 June 1882, 8; "General Beaver at Oxford," *Lancaster Weekly Examiner* [Lancaster, PA], 14 June 1882, 6.

32. Joseph T. Glatthaar, *Forged in Battle: The Civil War Alliance of Black Soldiers and White Officers* (Baton Rouge: Louisiana State University Press, 1990), 245–46; Donald R. Shaffer, *After the Glory: The Struggles of Black Civil War Veterans* (Lawrence: University Press of Kansas, 2004), 123–26, 172; Gannon, *The Won Cause*, 42–43; "Past Commander Wolff of Massachusetts G.A.R. Dead," *Boston Globe*, 5 May 1913, 4; W. N. Hartshorn, ed., *An Era of Progress and Promise, 1863–1910: The Religious, Moral, and Educational Development of the American Negro Since His Emancipation* (Boston: Priscilla Publishing Company, 1910), 490; John David Smith, "'A Credit to the Author and an Honor to the Dead Heroes': George Washington Williams's A History of the Negro Troops in the War of the Rebellion, 1861–1865," in George Washington Williams, *A History of the Negro Troops in the War of the Rebellion, 1861–1865* (New York: Fordham University Press, 2012), ix-xxxvi; "Flag May Rest in Museum of State," *Charleston Daily Mail* [Charleston, WV], 11 November 1929, 8; "Educator Passes," *Hinton Daily News* [Hinton, WV], 25 March 1938, 8; C. G. Woodson, "Early Negro Education in West Virginia," *Journal of Negro History* 7, no. 1 (January 1922): 46–48.

33. "Death of David E. Small," *Evening Dispatch* [York, PA], 26 March 1883, 1; "Will of David E. Small," *York Democratic Press* [York, PA], 6 April 1883, 2; "The Boys Who Fought Bravely for the Union," *The Age* [York, PA], 24 August 1883, 4; ACGAA minute book entry, 27 October 1923, letterbook 3, Allegheny County Grand Army Association Collection, Soldiers and Sailors Memorial Hall, Pittsburgh, PA; Minute book entry, Lincoln-Garfield Post No. 3, 5 March 1920, box 3, folder 8, Grand Army of the Republic Collection, Oregon Historical Society, Portland, OR; "At the Front," *Buffalo Commercial*, 25 August 1897, 8; "Mrs. William Scott," *Buffalo Evening Times*, 2 September 1897, 3; "A Talented Woman," *Buffalo Commercial*, 3 September 1897, 8.

34. An early version of this section was published as "'Produce Patriots As Well As Scholars': GAR Educational Reform and the Establishment of Mason City's Memorial University," *The Annals of Iowa* 79, no. 3 (Summer 2020): 211–46. Jared Sparks, *The Writings of George Washington*, vol. 11 (Boston: Russell, Shattuck, and Williams, 1838), 3. For criticisms of the national university vision before the Civil War, see George Thomas, *The Founders and the Idea of a National University: Constituting the American Mind* (New York: Cambridge University Press, 2015), chapter 2.

35. *Letters and Messages of Rutherford B. Hayes, President of the United States, Together with Letter of Acceptance and Inaugural Address* (Washington, D.C.: n.p., 1881), 98;

John W. Hoyt, *Memorial in Regard to a National University* (Washington, D.C.: Government Printing Office, 1892), 23. On post–Civil War state formation and its obstacles, see Richard Franklin Bensel, *Yankee Leviathan: The Origins of Central State Authority in America, 1859–1877* (New York: Cambridge University Press, 1990).

36. *National Tribune* [Washington, D.C.], 7 October 1897, 5; *Journal of the Thirty-Second Annual Encampment, Department of Massachusetts, Grand Army of the Republic, Tremont Temple, Boston, Mass., February 8 and 9, 1898* (Boston: E. B. Stillings and Co., 1898), 56; Charles W. Eliot, *A National University. Report Made by Charles W. Eliot, President of Harvard University, to the National Educational Association, (Department of Higher Instruction), August 5, 1873* (Cambridge, MA: Charles W. Sever, 1874), 23. Besides the GAR, the national university venture attracted support from a host of hereditary and patriotic societies. The WRC was another vocal advocate for a national university. See Wallace Evan Davies, *Patriotism on Parade: The Story of Veterans' and Hereditary Organizations in America, 1783–1900* (Cambridge, MA: Harvard University Press, 1955), 245.

37. "G.A.R. Memorial College," *National Tribune* [Washington, D.C.], 5 May 1892, 10. Equating the danger of mid-nineteenth-century Confederate secession with the supposed threat of turn-of-the-century anarchism was common among Union veterans. See Harris, *Across the Bloody Chasm*, 58–59.

38. Charles Sumner Nicholls, "A Patriotic Ideal," *The National Magazine: An Illustrated American Monthly* 14 (April–September 1901): 445–47; "Al Sortor, Originator of Memorial University, Dies," *Mason City Globe-Gazette* [Mason City, IA], 7 February 1944; "Memorial University," *Mason City Globe-Gazette* [Mason City, IA], 19 August 1942, 10; "The Day of Jubilee Is Here," *Mason City Globe-Gazette* [Mason City, IA], 26 June 1901; "Memorial to the Grand Army," *Minneapolis Journal*, 30 March 1901, 9. For more on the SV's early planning for the institution, see *Journal of Proceedings of the Sixteenth Annual Encampment of the Sons of Veterans, U.S.A., Held in Indianapolis, Indiana, September 9th, 10th, and 11th, 1897* (Reading, PA: Press Reading Eagle, 1897), 210. For the SV's debate about and decision on the location of the institution, see *Journal of Proceedings of the Nineteenth Annual Encampment of the Sons of Veterans, U.S.A., Held in Syracuse, New York, September 11th, 12th and 13th, 1900* (Boston: E. B. Stillings and Company, 1900), 113–28.

39. Minute book entry, 23 November 1901, box 63, Grand Army of the Republic Post Records, State Historical Society of Iowa, Des Moines, IA (hereafter cited as SHSI); "Bulletin of Memorial University, Mason City, Iowa," 6, no. 1 (September 1907): 19; Minute book entry, 15 December 1900, box 108, Grand Army of the Republic Post Records, SHSI; WRC Department of Iowa circulars, 1 October 1901 and 15 April 1902, box 1, Grand Army of the Republic, Woman's Relief Corps Records, General Orders and Circular Letters from State Headquarters, SHSI; "Memorial University," *Mason City Globe-Gazette* [Mason City, IA], 19 August 1942, 10; Ell Torrance address delivered at cornerstone-laying ceremony of Memorial University, 26 June 1901, box 34, folder 5: speeches (dated); 1862–1916, Ell Torrance Papers, MinnHS.

40. George F. Parker, ed., *The Writings and Speeches of Grover Cleveland* (New York: Cassell Publishing Company, 1892), 354; "Oration on the Political Mission of the United States," in John Denison Champlin, ed., *Orations, Addresses and Speeches of Chauncey*

M. DePew, vol. 1 (New York: n.p., 1910), 33. In some ways, the insistence on training patriotic scholars at the turn of the twentieth century echoed the Civil War–era ideology of college students who opted to complete their education instead of enlist in the Union army. This earlier generation of scholars maintained that a college degree would provide them with the leadership skills to guide a reconstructing postwar society. See Mujic, "Between Campus and War," 18, 20, 159–60.

41. *Journal of the Thirty-Fourth Annual Encampment of the Grand Army of the Republic, August 29th and 30th, 1900, Chicago, Illinois* (Philadelphia: Town Printing Company, 1900), 254; Report of the American History Curriculum Committee to Alexander L. Sortor, Jr., 1 August 1902, box 36, folder 5, Ell Torrance Papers, MinnHS; American History Curriculum Committee's College of American History, Manual of Study, 1 August 1902, box 36, folder 5, Ell Torrance Papers, MinnHS; "Memorial to the Grand Army," *Minneapolis Journal*, 30 March 1901, 19; "Bulletin of Memorial University, Mason City, Iowa," 6, no. 2 (December 1907): 6–7; "Memorial University," *Mason City Globe-Gazette* [Mason City, IA], 11 September 1902, 3. On Union veterans' education-related efforts to defeat "national amnesia" about their sacrifices on behalf of the Union, see Harris, *Across the Bloody Chasm*, 38–40. In 1907, the university maintained a rigorous four-year program in US history that provided survey courses for freshmen and emphasized the Civil War and constitutional history for more advanced students. Interestingly, an entire semester in the junior year dealt with "The Rise and Fall of the Slave Power" and used as its chief text the antislavery politician Henry Wilson's three-volume *History of the Rise and Fall of the Slave Power in America*. See "Bulletin of Memorial University, Mason City, Iowa," 6, no. 1 (September 1907): 10–11. For Wilson's *History*, see John L. Myers, "The Writing of *History of the Rise and Fall of the Slave Power in America*," *Civil War History* 31, no. 2 (June 1985): 144–62. See also Henry Wilson, *History of the Rise and Fall of the Slave Power in America*, 3 vols. (Boston: Houghton, Mifflin and Co., 1872). Meanwhile, Memorial University's development of "applied patriotism" is akin to the rise of "applied sciences" more broadly affecting Progressive Era education and the pragmatic pedagogy of reformers like John Dewey. Applied patriotism, like applied science, was designed to be more practical and utilitarian in solving social problems. On applied science in Progressive Era US colleges and universities, see Laurence R. Veysey, *The Emergence of the American University* (Chicago: University of Chicago Press, 1965), chapter 3.

42. "Memorial University," *Mason City Globe-Gazette* [Mason City, IA], 11 September 1902, 3; "Aid for Memorial University Asked," *Des Moines Register*, 29 January 1903, 2. Consistent with many Progressive Era educational reformers, Memorial University's founders harbored no qualms about coeducation. Reformer John Dewey proclaimed that coeducation in high schools and colleges was "an intellectual and moral necessity in a democracy." Because GAR, WRC, and SV members readily acknowledged the service and sacrifices of men *and* women on behalf of the Union and democracy during the Civil War, it stands to reason they also understood the importance of coeducation to groom good citizens for the twentieth century at Memorial University. See Steven C. Rockefeller, *John Dewey: Religious Faith and Democratic Humanism* (New York: Columbia University Press, 1991), 256. On the "collegiate revolution" that witnessed the proliferation of student-led activities on campus, see Roger L. Geiger, *History of American Higher Education*, 365–80; and Leslie, *Gentlemen and Scholars*, chapter 9.

43. Gannon, *The Won Cause*, 7. For proceedings of Leggett's ceremony, see "A Colored Man," *Minneapolis Journal*, 23 June 1903, 13. For more on Leggett, see also, "At Memorial University," *Mason City Globe-Gazette* [Mason City, IA], 18 September 1902, 11; "First Graduate a Colored Man," *Indianapolis Journal*, 18 June 1903, 7; and "May 26, 1903," *Mason City Globe-Gazette* [Mason City, IA], 26 May 1933, 3. Unfortunately, Leggett's later career remains obscure in the historical record.

44. "Memorial University," *National Tribune* [Washington, D.C.], 28 June 1906, 6; "Bulletin of Memorial University, Mason City, Iowa," 6, no. 1 (September 1907): 25; *Journal of the Twenty-Eighth National Convention of the Woman's Relief Corps, Auxiliary to the Grand Army of the Republic, Atlantic City, New Jersey, September 21, 22 and 23, 1910* (Boston: Griffith-Stillings Press, 1910), 373. Within six months of its demise, the building and grounds were sold and converted for use by the Mason City school district. Memorial University's sole academic building later hosted the town's junior college and was unceremoniously razed in 1979. See "Memorial University Sold," *Oshkosh Daily Northwestern* [Oshkosh, WI], 19 February 1912, 9; and "Plan to Enlarge Building," *The Bystander* [Des Moines, IA], 12 April 1912, 3.

45. "Bulletin of Memorial University, Mason City, Iowa," 7, no. 4 (June 1909): 14, in Memorial University Collection, Mason City Public Library, Lee P. Loomis Archive, Mason City, IA.

46. *Journal of the Twenty-Ninth Annual Convention of the Woman's Relief Corps, Auxiliary to the Grand Army of the Republic, Department of South Dakota, Mitchell, S.D., June Sixth, Seventh and Eighth, 1912* (Mitchell, SD: Educator School Supply Co., 1912), 58.

3. West of Appomattox, South of Richmond

1. "The Same Old Tune," *Salt Lake Herald* [Salt Lake City, UT], 28 July 1886, 8; Robert B. Beath, *History of the Grand Army of the Republic* (New York: Bryan, Taylor and Co., 1889), 256; *Journal of the Forty-First National Encampment of the Grand Army of the Republic, Saratoga Springs, N.Y., September 11th and 12th, 1907* (Zanesville, OH: Courier Company, 1907), 178–79; *Journal of the Forty-Second National Encampment of the Grand Army of the Republic, at Toledo, Ohio, September 3rd and 4th, Including Semi-Official Meeting, September 1st, 1908* (Kansas City, MO: John C. Bovard Press, 1908), 240, 241; "Veterans of Civil War in an Inspiring Parade," *Salt Lake Tribune* [Salt Lake City, UT], 12 August 1909, 1; *Journal of the Forty-Third National Encampment of the Grand Army of the Republic at Salt Lake City, Utah, August 12th and 13th, Including Semi-Official Meeting, August 10th, 1909* (n.p., 1909), 14; Minute book entry, Lucius Fairchild Post No. 11, 18 October 1909, box 16, folder 1, Grand Army of the Republic, Department of Wisconsin Records, Wisconsin Veterans Museum, Madison, WI (hereafter WVM). On the Mormon rebellion, see Donald R. Moorman, *Camp Floyd and the Mormons: The Utah War* (Salt Lake City: University of Utah Press, 1992); and David L. Bigler and Will Bagley, *The Mormon Rebellion: America's First Civil War, 1857–1858* (Norman: University of Oklahoma Press, 2011).

2. Wallace Evan Davies, *Patriotism on Parade: The Story of Veterans' and Hereditary Organizations in America, 1783–1900* (Cambridge, MA: Harvard University Press, 1955), 36; Stuart McConnell, *Glorious Contentment: The Grand Army of the Republic, 1865–1900*

(Chapel Hill: University of North Carolina Press, 1992), 28–29; James Marten, *Sing Not War: The Lives of Union and Confederate Veterans in Gilded Age America* (Chapel Hill: University of North Carolina Press, 2011), 270–72; Brian Matthew Jordan, *Marching Home: Union Veterans and Their Unending Civil War* (New York: W.W. Norton, 2014), 181–82. For statistics, see *Journal of the Twenty-Fourth Annual Session of the National Encampment, Grand Army of the Republic, Boston, Mass., August 13th and 14th, 1890* (Detroit, MI: Richmond and Backus Co., 1890), 18; and *Journal of the Fifty-Fourth National Encampment, Grand Army of the Republic, Indianapolis, Ind., September 19 to 25, 1920* (Washington, D.C., Government Printing Office, 1921), 187. For studies emphasizing southern progressivism and community reform, see Dewey W. Grantham, *Southern Progressivism: The Reconciliation of Progress and Tradition* (Knoxville: University of Tennessee Press, 1983); William A. Link, *The Paradox of Southern Progressivism, 1880–1930* (Chapel Hill: University of North Carolina Press, 1992); John Dittmer, *Black Georgia in the Progressive Era, 1900–1920* (Urbana: University of Illinois Press, 1980); and Glenda Elizabeth Gilmore, *Gender and Jim Crow: Women and the Politics of White Supremacy in North Carolina, 1896–1920* (Chapel Hill: University of North Carolina Press, 1996). For studies emphasizing progressivism and community reform in western regions, see Lawrence Goodwyn, *The Populist Moment: A Short History of the Agrarian Revolt in America* (New York: Oxford University Press, 1978); Robert W. Cherny, *Populism, Progressivism, and the Transformation of Nebraska Politics, 1885–1915* (Lincoln: University of Nebraska Press, 1981); Robert D. Johnston, *The Radical Middle Class: Populist Democracy and the Question of Capitalism in Progressive Era Portland, Oregon* (Princeton, NJ: Princeton University Press, 2003); and John C. Putnam, *Class and Gender Politics in Progressive-Era Seattle* (Reno: University of Nevada Press, 2008). For recent scholarship that encourages geographical "peripheries" of the Civil War–era United States to be brought to the center, see Megan Kate Nelson, *The Three-Cornered War: The Union, the Confederacy, and Native Peoples in the Fight for the West* (New York: Scribner, 2020); and Steven Hahn, "The United States from the Inside Out and the Southside North," in *Remaking North American Sovereignty: State Transformation in the 1860s*, ed. Jewel L. Spangler and Frank Towers (New York: Fordham University Press, 2020), 25–35.

3. "Union Veterans in the South," *National Tribune* [Washington, D.C.], 21 March 1889, 4. For more on the identities of Union veterans in the South, see Barbara A. Gannon, *The Won Cause: Black and White Comradeship in the Grand Army of the Republic* (Chapel Hill: University of North Carolina Press, 2011), 28; and Rebecca Howard, "Lost to the Lost Cause: Arkansas's Union Veterans," in *The War Went On: Reconsidering the Lives of Civil War Veterans*, ed. Brian Matthew Jordan and Evan C. Rothera (Baton Rouge: Louisiana State University Press, 2020), 263–66. On the New South, see Edward L. Ayers, *The Promise of the New South: Life After Reconstruction* (New York: Oxford University Press, 1992). Eric Foner notes that carpetbagger politicians did particularly well in the South's Black Belt districts. Between them, southern-born "scalawag" white Republicans, and intrepid African American politicians, many southern states for a time fell under a uniquely diverse and effectual form of southern Republicanism. See Eric Foner, *Reconstruction: America's Unfinished Revolution, 1863–1877* (New York: Harper & Row, 1988), 294–307.

4. Chulhee Lee, "Health, Information, and Migration: Geographic Mobility of Union Army Veterans, 1860–1880," *Journal of Economic History* 68, no. 3 (September 2008): 869, 873–74; McConnell, *Glorious Contentment*, 278 n. 14; Howard, "Lost to the Lost Cause," 270–71; John C. Lester and D. L. Wilson, *Ku Klux Klan: Its Origin, Growth and Disbandment* (New York: Neale Publishing Company, 1905), 171. The chronology of established GAR departments in former Confederate states reads as follows: Arkansas, 1883; Tennessee, 1884; Louisiana and Mississippi, 1884; Florida, 1884; Texas, 1885; Georgia and South Carolina, 1889; Alabama, 1889. Many of these departments comprised only a handful of posts. In 1900, for example, the Department of Arkansas included only twenty-nine posts with 566 members. Alabama fielded merely thirteen posts and 123 members. For membership statistics, see *Journal of the Thirty-Fourth National Encampment of the Grand Army of the Republic, Chicago, Illinois, August 29th and 30th, 1900* (Philadelphia: Town Printing Co., 1900), 84.

5. "The Texas Catastrophe," *National Tribune* [Washington, D.C.], 8 November 1900, 6; Relief request letter of GAR Department of Texas to Willis A. Gorman Post No. 13, 24 September 1900, box 1, folder 21, Grand Army of the Republic Records, Northeast Minnesota Historical Center, University of Minnesota Duluth, Duluth, MN (hereafter NMHC); Relief request letter of James B. Steedman WRC to William I. Brown Post No. 31, 31 March 1903, box 3A, folder 1, Concord Public Library Historical Materials, New Hampshire Historical Society, Concord, NH (hereafter NHHS).

6. Beath, *History of the Grand Army of the Republic*, 235–36; Relief request letter of GAR Department of Georgia to Sheridan Post No. 14, box 1, book 1, GAR Sheridan Post No. 14 Records, NHHS. For the National Cemetery System, see John R. Neff, *Honoring the Civil War Dead: Commemoration and the Problem of Reconciliation* (Lawrence: University Press of Kansas, 2005), chapter 3 and appendix A; Drew Gilpin Faust, *This Republic of Suffering: Death and the American Civil War* (New York: Vintage, 2008), chapter 7; Caroline E. Janney, *Remembering the Civil War: Reunion and the Limits of Reconciliation* (Chapel Hill: University of North Carolina Press, 2013), 77–78; Timothy B. Smith, *Altogether Fitting and Proper: Civil War Battlefield Preservation in History, Memory, and Policy, 1861–2015* (Knoxville: University of Tennessee Press, 2017), 16–21; and Howard, "Lost to the Lost Cause," 273.

7. *Journal of the Twenty-Eighth National Encampment of the Grand Army of the Republic, Pittsburgh, PA., September 12th and 13th, 1894* (Boston: E. B. Stillings and Co., 1894), 55; GAR national headquarters circular, 22 February 1904, box 94, folder 4, New York State Historian, Grand Army of the Republic Records, New York State Archives, Albany, NY; *Journal of the Forty-First National Encampment of the Grand Army of the Republic, Saratoga Springs, N. Y., September 11th and 12th, 1907* (Zanesville, OH: Courier Company, 1907), 70; United States Congress, *Congressional Record: Containing the Proceedings and Debates of the Fifty-Ninth Congress, Second Session*, vol. 41 (Washington, D.C.: Government Printing Office, 1907), 1484. A 1918 circular distributed to Nebraska posts, for instance, urged that the entire state department should raise seventy-five dollars to assist the South's Union veterans in their Memorial Day duties. See Nebraska state department circular, 25 March 1918, box 1, folder 6, Grand Army of the Republic,

Department of Nebraska Records, Nebraska State Historical Society, Lincoln, NE (hereafter NSHS).

8. Gannon, *The Won Cause*, 29; Howard, "Lost to the Lost Cause," 274; Letter of P. H. Boyle to Charles H. Shute, 4 August 1906, box 1, folder 14, Grand Army of the Republic, Joseph A. Mower Post No. 1 Records, Howard-Tilton Memorial Library, Tulane University, New Orleans, LA; *Journal of the Thirty-Second National Encampment of the Grand Army of the Republic, Cincinnati, Ohio, September 8th and 9th, 1898* (Philadelphia: Town Printing Co., 1898), 118–19; Letter of C. C. Haskell to Ell Torrance, 6 August 1902, box 13, folder 2, Ell Torrance Papers, Minnesota Historical Society, St. Paul, MN (hereafter MinnHS).

9. *Journal of the Twenty-First Annual Session of the National Encampment, Grand Army of the Republic, St. Louis, Missouri, September 28th, 29th, 30th, 1887* (Milwaukee: Burdick and Armitage, 1887), 255; "A Grand Army Row," *New York Times*, 9 August 1890, 1; O. M. Mitchel Post No. 1 circular, 19 November 1891, box 4, folder 3, Thomas Espy Post Collection, Andrew Carnegie Free Library and Music Hall, Carnegie, PA (hereafter ACFL). For coverage of the Johnston statue and GAR participation at the unveiling, see "Johnston," *Daily Picayune* [New Orleans, LA], 7 April 1887, 1–3.

10. *Journal of the Twentieth Annual Encampment, Department of Delaware, Grand Army of the Republic, Held at the Rooms of Admiral S. F. DuPont Post No. 2, 504 Market Street, Wilmington, Del.* (Wilmington, DE: Wilmington Freie Presse, 1901), 30–31, in box 1, folder 3, Ada Anderson Collection, Delaware Historical Society, Wilmington, DE (hereafter DHS); Letter of Ell Torrance to Richard Gray, 16 July 1902, box 13, folder 1, Ell Torrance Papers, MinnHS.

11. "Grand Army of the Republic," *San Francisco Chronicle*, 22 April 1884, 3; "Confederate Veterans," *National Tribune* [Washington, D.C.], 3 April 1884, 2; "Charity Begins at Home," *National Tribune* [Washington, D.C.], 3 April 1884, 4. For reports of southern GAR posts donating money to the venture, see "Virginia," *National Tribune* [Washington, D.C.], 24 April 1884, 6; and "Florida," *National Tribune* [Washington, D.C.], 20 March 1884, 6. Disabled and destitute Union veterans frequently found refuge under the federally sponsored National Home for Disabled Volunteer Soldiers system, established in 1865. For more, see Patrick J. Kelly, *Creating a National Home: Building the Veterans' Welfare State, 1860–1900* (Cambridge, MA: Harvard University Press, 1997); and Jordan, *Marching Home*, 170–91. For the Lee Camp Soldiers' Home, see Gaines M. Foster, *Ghosts of the Confederacy: Defeat, the Lost Cause, and the Emergence of the New South, 1865–1913* (New York: Oxford University Press, 1987), 93–94; and R. B. Rosenburg, *Living Monuments: Confederate Soldiers' Homes in the New South* (Chapel Hill: University of North Carolina Press, 1993), 26–28.

12. National headquarters circular, 1 September 1902, box 13, folder 3, Ell Torrance Papers, MinnHS; "Torrance's Letter and the Response," *Minneapolis Journal*, 10 September 1902, 2; Letter of T. C. Murphy to Ell Torrance, 25 September 1902, box 13, folder 5, Ell Torrance Papers, MinnHS. Murphy's comments support many historians' claims suggesting Union and Confederate veterans occasionally fostered amity through the shared experience of their war service. For more on Union and Confederate veterans' shared experience of combat, see Nina Silber, *The Romance of Reunion: Northerners and the*

South, 1865–1900 (Chapel Hill: University of North Carolina Press, 1993), 97–98; Marten, *Sing Not War*, 245–49; and Janney, *Remembering the Civil War*, 249.

13. Letter of N. B. Easton to Ell Torrance, 16 September 1902, box 13, folder 4, Ell Torrance Papers, MinnHS; Letter of O. H. Coulter to Ell Torrance, 29 October 1902, box 13, folder 7, Ell Torrance Papers, MinnHS; Letter of P. H. Coney to Ell Torrance, 6 September 1902, box 13, folder 3, Ell Torrance Papers, MinnHS. For more on the Alabama Confederate Soldiers Home, see Rosenburg, *Living Monuments*, 69–70, 74, 149–50.

14. Gannon, *The Won Cause*, 29–30, 34; Letter of R. M. Smock to Albert Scott, 20 July 1895, folder 13, Grand Army of the Republic, 1895 Encampment Records, Filson Historical Society, Louisville, KY (hereafter FHS); Newspaper clipping pasted in scrapbook, 27 July 1895, folder 224, Grand Army of the Republic, 1895 Encampment Records, FHS. Palmer's order led to a mass departure of white veterans from the department in the ensuing months. Out of 345 white members in the department before the Detroit encampment, only 114 maintained their allegiance to the GAR by 1892. Donald R. Shaffer and Barbara A. Gannon argue how extraordinary it was for Palmer and other GAR veterans outside the Deep South to sacrifice white members for the purpose of integrating the southern department. See Shaffer, *After the Glory: The Struggles of Black Civil War Veterans* (Lawrence: University Press of Kansas, 2004), 149; and Gannon, *The Won Cause*, 28–29.

15. "Grand Army," *Times-Democrat* [New Orleans, LA], 14 September 1894, 9; "The Colored Race," *Times-Democrat* [New Orleans, LA], 11 May 1897, 7; "Annual Installation of Officers of Joseph A. Mower Post," *Times-Democrat* [New Orleans, LA], 6 January 1900, 3; Letter of Charles W. Keeting to Ell Torrance, 15 August 1902, box 13, folder 2, Ell Torrance Papers, MinnHS; Department of Louisiana and Mississippi circular, 1 August 1894, box 2, folder 12, Henry A. Castle Papers, MinnHS. Thanks in part to his comrades' testimony, Charles H. Shute did win election in 1894 to become junior vice commander in chief of the GAR. Oddly, Wallace Evan Davies in his *Patriotism on Parade* claims that Shute was African American. Examining census records, there is no indication that the state identified Shute as Black or mixed-race. Instead, it seems that Shute was a white veteran with a genuine interest in improving the condition of Louisiana's African Americans. In 1897, for instance, Shute participated in a New Orleans lecture series entitled "Industrial Condition and Progress of the Colored People," for the benefit of an apparently Black-majority audience. Shute gave a talk designed to help African Americans understand how to deploy the values of "industry, economy and perseverance" toward their personal savings and investment strategies. See Davies, *Patriotism on Parade*, 270. For African American comrades in GAR leadership positions, see Gannon, *The Won Cause*, 32–34.

16. "Federal Decoration Day," *Weekly Democrat* [Natchez, MS], 3 June 1891, 5; "Memorial Day," *Weekly Democrat* [Natchez, MS], 6 June 1900, 2; *Natchez Democrat* [Natchez, MS], 6 September 1917, 5; "Negro Day at Beaufort," *The State* [Columbia, SC], 4 January 1902, 6; "Down in Old Beaufort," *The State* [Columbia, SC], 3 January 1903, 2; "Memorial Day at Beaufort," *County Record* [Kingstree, SC], 11 June 1903, 3; "Ex-President Grant," *Weekly Star* [Wilmington, NC], 14 August 1885, 1; "Local Mention," *North Carolinian* [Elizabeth City, NC], 1 January 1890, 3; "Reunion of the Old 37th Regiment

U.S.C.T.," *New Berne Daily Journal* [New Bern, NC], 22 August 1895, 1; "Emancipation Day," *Wilmington Messenger* [Wilmington, NC], 2 January 1903, 8; *New Bern Weekly Journal* [New Bern, NC], 9 February 1909, 2; "39th Encampment GAR of Virginia and North Carolina," *New Bern Weekly Journal* [New Bern, NC], 8 April 1910, 3; "Notice G.A.R.," *The Sun* [New Bern, NC], 15 April 1914, 5. For more on the emerging concept of "memory activism" and how collective memory can be deployed as a "weapon of the weak," see Yifat Gutman and Jenny Wüstenberg, eds., *The Routledge Handbook of Memory Activism* (New York: Routledge, 2023), esp. 1–15. Although outside the scope of this study, memory activism as a theoretical and analytical approach could provide future researchers with a unique lens by which to examine how various groups (e.g., African American veterans, the United Daughters of the Confederacy, etc.) developed a collective memory of the Civil War and wielded it strategically in advance of their particular aims.

17. Barbara A. Gannon rightly argues that the very fact that there *was* controversy over including Black veterans in southern departments was in fact radical for the time (especially since many nineteenth-century organizations, particularly in the South, simply barred Blacks from membership without a second thought). For an illuminating assessment of the GAR in the South, see Gannon, *The Won Cause*, chapter 2.

18. "Grand Army Colony," *North Adams Evening Transcript* [North Adams, MA], 6 April 1898, 2. See also Corinne Stocker, "Northern Veterans Making Southern Homes," *The Illustrated American* 19, no. 318 (21 March 1896): 368; Fussell M. Chalker, "Fitzgerald: Place of Reconciliation," *Georgia Historical Quarterly* 55, no. 3 (Fall 1971): 397–405; Tony Horwitz, *Confederates in the Attic: Dispatches from the Unfinished Civil War* (New York: Vintage, 1998), 331–35; Marten, *Sing Not War*, 271; Janney, *Remembering the Civil War*, 187–88; and Brian Matthew Jordan, *A Thousand May Fall: Life, Death, and Survival in the Union Army* (New York: W.W. Norton, 2021), 207.

19. National headquarters circular, 25 May 1895, box 1, folder 2, Ada Anderson Collection, DHS; Letter of J. R. Martin to Josiah Given, 9 May 1896, box 2, folder: Veterans Associations—Iowa, Grand Army of the Republic correspondence records, State Historical Society of Iowa, Des Moines, IA; "Answers to the Call," *National Tribune* [Washington, D.C.], 25 June 1896, 3; "Colony of Old Soldiers," *Albuquerque Daily Citizen* [Albuquerque, NM], 21 February 1902, 7; "Hoosier's Colony Failed in Texas," *Muncie Morning Star* [Muncie, IN], 28 June 1907, 3.

20. *Journal of the Thirty-Fifth National Encampment of the Grand Army of the Republic, Cleveland, Ohio, September 12th and 13th, 1901* (St. Louis: A. Whipple, 1901), 113; *Journal of the Forty-Ninth National Encampment of the Grand Army of the Republic, Washington, D. C., Sept. 27 to Oct. 2, 1915* (Washington, D.C.: Government Printing Office, 1916), 167; *Journal of the Thirty-Fifth Annual Encampment, Department of Michigan, Grand Army of the Republic, Held at Lansing, Mich., June 18, 19, 20, 1913* (Lansing: Wynkoop, Hallenbeck Crawford Co., 1913), 70–71, at Bentley Historical Library, Ann Arbor, MI; Minute book entry, Lucius Fairchild Post No. 11, 3 April 1916, box 16, folder 4, Grand Army of the Republic, Department of Wisconsin Records, WVM.

21. "Haven of Health and Happiness," *National Tribune* [Washington, D.C.], 27 April 1911, 4; "Veterans in the South," *National Tribune* [Washington, D.C.], 27 April 1911, 4.

For more on the Lynn Haven colony, see Glenda Jane Walters, "Union Colony in the Confederate South: Lynn Haven, Florida, 1910–1920," PhD diss. (Florida State University, 1995).

22. Kurt Hackemer, "Civil War Veteran Colonies on the Western Frontier," in *The War Went On: Reconsidering the Lives of Civil War Veterans*, ed. Brian Matthew Jordan and Evan C. Rothera (Baton Rouge: Louisiana State University Press, 2020), 65; Letter of Uriah W. Oblinger to Mattie V. Thomas and Ella Oblinger, 1 December 1872, from Library of Congress (partnership with Nebraska State Historical Society), Uriah W. Oblinger Collection, https://memory.loc.gov/ammem/award98/nbhihtml/aboutoblinger .html (accessed 29 July 2022). The federal government had offered land grants to veterans of the Revolutionary War, War of 1812, Mexican-American War, and the antebellum Indian Wars. Bounty lands for military service ended after 1855. For more, see Malcolm J. Rohrbough, *The Land Office Business: The Settlement and Administration of American Public Lands, 1789–1837* (New York: Oxford University Press, 1968), esp. chapter 4. For more on the 1862 Homestead Act's subsequent amendments, including the Soldiers and Sailors Homestead Act of June 8, 1872, see Thomas Donaldson, *The Public Domain: Its History, with Statistics* (Washington, D.C.: Government Printing Office, 1884), 349. On western freeholders extending state power, see Christopher Clark, "State, Market, and Popular Sovereignty in Agrarian North America: The United States, 1850–1920," in *Remaking North American Sovereignty: State Transformation in the 1860s*, ed. Jewel L. Spangler and Frank Towers (New York: Fordham University Press, 2020), 177–99.

23. Paul A. Cimbala, *Veterans North and South: The Transition from Soldier to Civilian after the American Civil War* (Santa Barbara, CA: Praeger, 2015), 74–77; *Compendium of History, Reminiscence, and Biography of Nebraska Containing a History of the State of Nebraska* (Chicago: Alden Publishing Company, 1912), 788, 809; W. L. Gaston and A. R. Humphrey, *History of Custer County, Nebraska* (Lincoln, NE: Western Publishing and Engraving Company, 1919), 1025.

24. Newspaper clipping pasted in scrapbook, "Wait an Old-Timer," 13 September 1910, series 14, box 2, volume 1, Grand Army of the Republic, Department of Nebraska Records, NSHS; *Compendium of History*, 450, 802.

25. Account of H. V. Hoagland to Comrade Bross, 14 January 1920, series 1, box 1, folder 8, Grand Army of the Republic, Department of Nebraska Records, NSHS; Andrew C. Isenberg, *The Destruction of the Bison: An Environmental History, 1750–1920* (New York: Cambridge University Press, 2000), 160; Steven Rinella, *American Buffalo: In Search of a Lost Icon* (New York: Spiegel and Grau, 2008), 178–79; Henry N. Copp circular to Thomas Espy Post No. 153, 10 October 1899, series 4, box 4, folder 26, Thomas Espy Post Collection, ACFL; and Henry N. Copp circular, ca. 1890s, series 1, box 1, folder 1, Grand Army of the Republic, Department of Nebraska Records, NSHS.

26. Letter of the School Law Revision Commission to the GAR Department of Nebraska, 5 December 1913, series 1, box 1, folder 3, Grand Army of the Republic, Department of Nebraska Records, NSHS; GAR State Department of Nebraska circular, 13 September 1918, series 3, box 5, folder 7, Grand Army of the Republic, Department of Nebraska Records, NSHS; "Patriotic Day," *Evening State Journal* [Lincoln, NE], 19 September 1918, 3. For more on the Nebraska GAR department's influence on state policy,

see Albert Watkins, ed., *History of Nebraska: From the Earliest Explorations to the Present Time with Portraits, Maps, and Tables*, vol. 3 (Lincoln, NE: Western Publishing and Engraving Company, 1913), 438–40.

27. "Paralysis Caused His Death," *The Nebraska State Journal* [Lincoln, NE], 31 July 1902, 8; *Portrait and Biographical Album of Lancaster, County, Nebraska, Containing Full Page Portraits and Biographical Sketches of Prominent and Representative Citizens of the County* (Chicago: Chapman Brothers, 1888), 452–53; "Henry V. Hoagland, Public Figure, Dies," *Nebraska State Journal* [Lincoln, NE], 15 February 1930, 1; I. D. Evans editorial, n.d., series 1, box 1, folder 8, Grand Army of the Republic, Department of Nebraska Records, NSHS. On the National Reform Press Association as the "propaganda arm of the People's Party" and backer of the progressive-minded Omaha Platform of 1892, see Goodwyn, *The Populist Moment*, 116, 242–45. On Evans, see *Past and Present of Adams County, Nebraska*, vol. 2 (Chicago: S. J. Clarke Publishing Co., 1916), 52–54. Evans's biography labeled him a "progressive republican" for "being a strong believer in the rule of the people and in the strict regulation of big business. He recognizes that adjustment must be made…to bring about a more exact social justice." Evans's wide-ranging, progressive interests that met with mixed success in the state legislature included support for initiative and referendum amendments; regulatory banking reforms; prohibition and antiliquor traffic efforts; and bills proposing an inheritance tax and a traveling library. For more, see Watkins, *History of Nebraska*, 490–92; and "Isaiah D. Evans, 90, Former State G.A.R. Commander and Picturesque Nebraskan, Dies at His Home Here," *Lincoln Star* [Lincoln, NE], 10 January 1935, 1, 4.

28. John A. Martin, *Addresses: By John A. Martin, Delivered in Kansas* (Topeka: Kansas Publishing House, 1888), 104. There were upward of 50,000 Union veterans—both in and outside the GAR—in Kansas by the 1890s, representing one out of eight eligible voters in the state. For quote, statistics, and a fuller list of the Kansas GAR's many legislative victories, see Kyle S. Sinisi, "Veterans as Political Activists: The Kansas Grand Army of the Republic, 1880–1893," *Kansas History: A Journal of the Central Plains* 14, no. 2 (Summer 1991): 90–93. Historian Bruce R. Kahler, meanwhile, suggests that Kansas—with its significant ratio of veterans to civilians—understood more than other states a special duty to care for its defenders. See Kahler, "John A. Martin, Soldier State Visionary," *Kansas History: A Journal of the Central Plains* 34 (Spring 2011): 59.

29. John A. Martin, "The Progress of Kansas," *The North American Review* 142, no. 353 (April 1886): 355. For the pre–Civil War clash in Kansas, see Nicole Etcheson, *Bleeding Kansas: Contested Liberty in the Civil War Era* (Lawrence: University Press of Kansas, 2004). For biography of Martin, see Kahler, "John A. Martin," 50–59.

30. Martin, "Progress of Kansas," 352. Randall B. Woods suggests that a draw for Black migrants was the state's reputation as the onetime home of John Brown and the fact that Kansas had never legalized slavery. See Woods, "Integration, Exclusion, or Segregation? The 'Color Line' in Kansas, 1878–1900," *Western Historical Quarterly* 14, no. 2 (April 1983): 184. For more on African American migration to Kansas as a story of Black empowerment and courage, despite the many obstacles the migrants still faced outside the Deep South, see Nell Irvin Painter, *Exodusters: Black Migration to Kansas After Reconstruction* (New York: Alfred A. Knopf, 1977). Meanwhile, Barbara A. Gannon's careful

investigation delineates both all-Black and integrated GAR posts in Kansas. The all-Black posts include Kansas City's Sumner Post; Leavenworth's Shaw Post; Topeka's Fort Pillow Post; Lawrence's Walker Post; and Fort Scott's Steele Post. Gannon identifies more than sixty other integrated Kansas GAR posts. As was common among African American GAR veterans, members frequently named their posts after antislavery politicians (e.g., Charles Sumner) or USCT officers (e.g., Robert Gould Shaw and Frederick Steele). The Fort Pillow Post was named for the infamous Civil War battle in which Confederate forces massacred surrendering African American soldiers. For more, see Gannon, *The Won Cause*, 203, 214–15.

31. Gaston and Humphrey, *History of Custer County*, 323; "A Pilgrim in the Promised Land," *Wichita Daily Eagle* [Wichita, KS], 18 June 1889, 4; "On to Oklahoma," *Kansas City Gazette* [Kansas City, KS], 3 September 1891, 6. For more on African American self-segregating colonization endeavors, see Norman L. Crockett, *The Black Towns* (Lawrence: Regents Press of Kansas, 1979). On Gettysburg, South Dakota, and the influence of the GAR on the state, see Stephen T. Morgan, "Fellow Comrades: The Grand Army of the Republic in South Dakota," *South Dakota History* 36, no. 3 (Fall 2006): 229–59; and Jordan, *Marching Home*, 182. For an illuminating analysis of soldiers' colonies in the region and the motivation for veterans to seek out these collective communities, see Hackemer, "Civil War Veteran Colonies," 61–80.

32. William H. Ward, ed., *Records of Members of the Grand Army of the Republic with a Complete Account of the Twentieth National Encampment* (San Francisco: H. S. Crocker and Co., 1886), 129, 130; Lincoln promotional circular, 1891, box 1, folder 16, Henry A. Castle Papers, MinnHS; *Journal of the Twenty-Fifth National Encampment, (Silver Anniversary) Grand Army of the Republic, Detroit, Mich., August 5th, 6th and 7th, 1891* (Rutland, VT: Tuttle Company, 1891), 193–95.

33. Joseph C. G. Kennedy, *Population of the United States in 1860; Compiled from the Original Returns of the Eighth Census, Under the Direction of the Secretary of the Interior* (Washington, D.C.: Government Printing Office, 1864), iv; Frank Elliot Myers, "Defenders of the Union: Grand Army of the Republic on the Pacific Coast," *Overland Monthly* 27 (March 1896): 437–38. For more on western volunteer units and their wartime activities, see Andrew E. Masich, *The Civil War in Arizona: The Story of the California Volunteers, 1861–1865* (Norman: University of Oklahoma Press, 2006), chapter 1; and Nelson, *The Three-Cornered War*. On proslavery interests' designs on California, see Ward M. McAfee, "California's House Divided," *Civil War History* 33, no. 2 (June 1987): 115–30.

34. Frank Elliot Myers, "Defenders of the Union," *Overland Monthly* 28 (July 1896): 81; Newspaper obituary pasted in minute book, Custer Post No. 9, 25 November 1911, box 2, volume 5, Grand Army of the Republic Collection, Custer Post No. 9 Records, Oregon Historical Society, Portland, OR (hereafter OHS); Newspaper clipping pasted in scrapbook, 18 August 1931, box 1, book 1, Grand Army of the Republic Collection, OHS.

35. "The Growth of the Order in the Golden State," *San Francisco Chronicle*, 2 August 1886, 10; *Journal of the Eighteenth Annual Session, of the National Encampment, Grand Army of the Republic. Minneapolis, Minn., July 23, 24 and 25, 1884* (Philadelphia: Town Book and Job Printing House, 1884), 203. For more on the early history of the GAR's Department of California, see Beath, *History of the Grand Army of the Republic*, 589–91.

36. Circular of J. J. Fitzgerald, Thomas Post No. 21, 16 April 1883, box 3, folder 9, Grand Army of the Republic Records, NMHC; *Proceedings of the 54th Annual Encampment, Department of Pennsylvania, Grand Army of the Republic, Indiana, [PA,] June 9th and 10th, 1920* (Harrisburg, PA: J. L. L. Kuhn, 1920), 157. Only Nevada's posts remained permanently attached to the California department throughout the GAR's entire existence.

37. Roster of George Wright Post No. 1 in scrapbook, January 1889, box 1, book 2, Grand Army of the Republic Collection, OHS; Gideon Stolz, *Memoirs of Sedgwick Post No. 10 G.A.R.* (Salem, OR: n.p., 1931), 13, in box 5, folder 19, Grand Army of the Republic Collection, OHS; Newspaper clipping pasted in scrapbook, 25 August 1934, box 5, book 1, Grand Army of the Republic Collection, OHS; "Gideon S. Stolz Dies; in Salem Over 60 Years," *Oregon Statesman* [Salem, OR], 11 January 1938, 1; Newspaper clipping pasted in scrapbook, 18 August 1931, box 5, book 1, Grand Army of the Republic Collection, OHS. Although writing about mid-nineteenth-century settlement in the Old Northwest, Don Harrison Doyle's conceptualization of social order in frontier regions seems to apply elsewhere. He argues that in newly established communities, early settlers "fought to seize a leading place in an open, rapidly developing, and as yet unfixed region." Many Union veteran-migrants exhibited these tendencies in the Far West. See Doyle, *The Social Order of a Frontier Community: Jacksonville, Illinois, 1825–1870* (Urbana: University of Illinois Press, 1978), 3.

38. Maris A. Vinovskis, "Have Social Historians Lost the Civil War? Some Preliminary Demographic Speculations," *Journal of American History* 76, no. 1 (June 1989): 43; Brenda K. Jackson, *Domesticating the West: The Re-creation of the Nineteenth-Century American Middle Class* (Lincoln: University of Nebraska Press, 2005), 48; and Thomas R. Bright, "Yankees in Arms: The Civil War as a Personal Experience," *Civil War History* 19, no. 3 (September 1973): 215; "Shall I Go West?" *National Tribune* [Washington, D.C.], 28 December 1882, 5. For Union soldiers' return to civilian life and the lifelong quest some veterans undertook to recapture the thrill of army service, see for instance, Bright, "Yankees in Arms": 218; Eric T. Dean Jr., *Shook Over Hell: Post-Traumatic Stress, Vietnam, and the Civil War* (Cambridge, MA: Harvard University Press, 1997), 169; Jackson, *Domesticating the West*, 64; and Cimbala, *Veterans North and South*, 24. Brenda K. Jackson also argues that many Union veterans and their families who occupied middle-class status "were eager to re-create in the West the familiar trappings of antebellum commerce and society that they had known in the East." She notes that many Union army veterans who migrated West sought a town "to grow with" that would allow them "occupational status, community position, and wealth." Jackson, *Domesticating the West*, 62, 85. For more on middle-class experience and expectations, see also Stuart M. Blumin, *The Emergence of the Middle Class: Social Experience in the American City, 1760–1900* (New York: Cambridge University Press, 1989), 297.

39. *Proceedings of the Thirty-Ninth Annual Encampment of the Department of California and Nevada, Grand Army of the Republic, Held at Redding, California, May 17, 18 and 19, 1906* (San Francisco: C. W. Gordon, 1906), 120; Minute book entry, Lincoln-Garfield Post No. 3, 30 April 1920, box 3, folder 8, Grand Army of the Republic Collection, OHS; "Boise City News Items," *Morning Oregonian* [Portland, OR], 4 November 1889, 2.

40. *Journal of the Twenty-Fourth Annual Session of the National Encampment, Grand Army of the Republic, Boston, Mass., August 13th and 14th, 1890* (Detroit, MI: Richmond and Backus Co., 1890), 18; *Proceedings of the Fourth National Convention, Woman's Relief Corps, Auxiliary to the Grand Army of the Republic, San Francisco, California, August 4, 5, 6, and 7, 1886* (Boston: E. B. Stillings and Co., 1886), 154; *Journal of the Twenty-First Annual Session of the National Encampment, Grand Army of the Republic, St. Louis, Missouri, September 28th, 29th, 30th, 1887* (Milwaukee: Burdick and Armitage, 1887), 279, 281; *The Deseret Weekly: Pioneer Publication of the Rocky Mountain Region* 45, no. 22 (19 November 1892): 678; Minute book entry, Colonel John B. Clark Post No. 162, 4 March 1915, oversize box 6, Grand Army of the Republic Collection, Soldiers and Sailors Memorial Hall, Pittsburgh, PA. The Edmunds-Tucker Act sought to make polygamy untenable by punishing violators with fines, imprisonment, and disfranchisement, while threatening the LDS Church with financial disincentives. On just one day in February 1887, Congress received six separate petitions from GAR posts in four different states. The bill became law the following month. See *Journal of the House of Representatives of the United States, Being the Second Session of the Forty-Ninth Congress Begun and Held at the City of Washington, December 6, 1886, in the One Hundred and Eleventh Year of the Independence of the United States* (Washington, D.C.: Government Printing Office, 1886), 542–43.

41. *Proceedings of the Twenty-First Annual Encampment of the Department of California, Grand Army of the Republic, Held at Santa Rosa, March 14th, 15th and 16th, 1888* (San Francisco: George Spaulding and Co., 1888), 58; Letter of F. H. Lamb to W. C. Gray, 12 July 1886, box 4, folder 1, Grand Army of the Republic Collection, OHS; "Immigration Work," *Sacramento Daily Record-Union*, 18 December 1884, 4. For biography of Hopkins, see Ward, *Records of Members*, 305.

42. "White Women Demand Work," *San Francisco Call*, 13 July 1898, 8; Minute book entry, resolutions of Sedgwick Post No. 10 read at meeting of Lincoln-Garfield Post No. 3, 5 April 1918, box 3, folder 7, Grand Army of the Republic Collection, OHS. For an insightful analysis of how white Californians manipulated antislavery sentiment to raise questions about the purported unfree status of Chinese "coolie" labor (which led to enactment of anti-Chinese immigration laws), see Stacey L. Smith, *Freedom's Frontier: California and the Struggle over Unfree Labor, Emancipation, and Reconstruction* (Chapel Hill: University of North Carolina Press, 2013), chapter 7.

43. Department of Oregon circular, 18 March 1916, box 4, folder 20, Grand Army of the Republic Collection, OHS; Speech of Rev. Dr. Clark to Lincoln-Garfield Post No. 3, quoted in minute book entry, 11 April 1919, box 3, folder 4, Grand Army of the Republic Collection, OHS.

44. Minute book entry, Lincoln-Garfield Post No. 3, 18 May 1917, box 3, folder 6, Grand Army of the Republic Collection, OHS; Letter of Robert C. Markee to Gideon Stolz, 18 February 1918, box 5, folder 15, Grand Army of the Republic Collection, OHS; "Would Oust Alien Employes [sic]," *Oregon Daily Journal* [Portland, OR], 5 March 1918, 4; "Soldiers Loyal to Chinese," *Oregon Statesman* [Salem, OR], 5 March 1918, 6; *Journal of the Forty-Ninth National Encampment, Grand Army of the Republic, Washington, D.C., Sept. 27 to Oct. 2, 1915* (Washington, D.C.: Government Printing Office, 1916), 211. For more on late nineteenth- and early twentieth-century Asian immigration, see Ronald

Takaki, *Strangers from a Different Shore: A History of Asian Americans* (New York: Penguin Books, 1989), esp. chapter 1.

45. Minute book entry, Lincoln-Garfield Post No. 3, 23 April 1920, box 3, folder 8, Grand Army of the Republic Collection, OHS; GAR Department of Oregon circular, 21 July 1894, box 4, folder 16, Grand Army of the Republic Collection, OHS; Preamble of the Constitution of the Industrial Workers of the World, quoted in *Thirteenth Annual Report on Strikes and Lockouts for the Year 1912* (Boston: Wright and Potter, 1913), 29. Despite taking a rather dim view overall of the GAR's prolabor credentials in the late nineteenth century, Matthew E. Stanley nevertheless identifies a cohort of Grand Army veterans who participated amicably alongside members of the Knights of Labor and American Federation of Labor in parades, rallies, and other events. See Stanley, *Grand Army of Labor: Workers, Veterans, and the Meaning of the Civil War* (Urbana: University of Illinois Press, 2021), 91, 170.

46. "G.A.R. Post Condemns Outlaws," *Pullman Herald* [Pullman, WA], 12 November 1909, 1; "Plan to Bar Anarchists," *San Francisco Call*, 10 April 1912, 1; "I.W.W. Flayed by Heroes of the Civil War," *San Francisco Call*, 26 July 1912, 5; Minute book entry, Lincoln-Garfield Post No. 3, 19 February 1915, box 3, folder 5, Grand Army of the Republic Collection, OHS. For more on the Spokane free speech protests, see Gregory R. Woirol, ed., "Two Letters on the Spokane Free Speech Fight," *Pacific Northwest Quarterly* 77, no. 2 (April 1986): 68–71. For contested labor-related appeals to Lincoln's memory, see Stanley, *Grand Army of Labor*, 210–14.

47. Minute book entry, Lincoln-Garfield Post No. 3, 20 August 1915, box 3, folder 5, Grand Army of the Republic Collection, OHS; Minute book entry, Lincoln-Garfield Post No. 3, 19 November 1915, box 3, folder 5, Grand Army of the Republic Collection, OHS; "Portland Citizens Pay High Tribute to Colored Leader," *Oregon Daily Journal* [Portland, OR], 22 November 1915, 2; Minute book entry, Lincoln-Grant Post No. 3, 5 March 1920, box 3, folder 8, Grand Army of the Republic Collection, OHS; Johnston, *The Radical Middle Class*, 235, 238; GAR Department of Oregon circular, 1921, box 4, folder 20, Grand Army of the Republic Collection, OHS. For more on the GAR's resistance to the popularity of *The Birth of a Nation*, see "Trying to Get G.A.R. Up Over 'Birth of a Nation,'" *Moving Picture World* 25, no. 9 (28 August 1915): 1510; and Richard Maltby, "Blackface, Disguise and Invisibility in the Reception of *The Birth of a Nation*," in *In the Shadow of* The Birth of a Nation: *Racism, Reception and Resistance*, ed. Melvyn Stokes and Paul McEwan (Cham, Switzerland: Palgrave Macmillan, 2013), 58 fn. 45.

48. Steven Hahn, *A Nation Without Borders: The United States and Its World in an Age of Civil Wars, 1830–1910* (New York: Viking, 2016), 517.

4. Clasping Hands Across the Sea

1. "Headquarters," *Daily Pacific Commercial Advertiser* [Honolulu, HI], 24 May 1884, 2; *Memorial Services in Honor of America's Patriot Dead at Honolulu, H.I., on Sunday Eve., May 25th, and Friday, May 30th, 1884* (Honolulu: Thomas G. Thrum, 1884), 6, 8, 16–17, in Sedgwick Post [Salem, OR] scrapbook, box 1, book 2, Grand Army of the Republic Collection, Oregon Historical Society, Portland, OR; "Memorial Servise [sic] at the Fort Street Church," *Daily Bulletin* [Honolulu, HI], 26 May 1884, 2; "Decoration Day," *Daily*

Bulletin [Honolulu, HI], 31 May 1884, 2. For more on Nuuanu Cemetery's GAR plot, see Ralph Thomas Kam, "Commemorating the Grand Army of the Republic in Hawai'i: 1882–1930," *Hawaiian Journal of History* 43 (2009): 127–32.

2. Daniel T. Rodgers, "In Search of Progressivism," *Reviews in American History* 10, no. 4 (December 1982): 113–32; William E. Leuchtenburg, "Progressivism and Imperialism: The Progressive Movement and American Foreign Policy, 1898–1916," *Mississippi Valley Historical Review* 39, no. 3 (December 1952): 500, 501; Gerald E. Markowitz, "Progressivism and Imperialism: A Return to First Principles," *The Historian* 37, no. 2 (February 1975): 264. For other wide-ranging works that discuss the compatibility of progressivism and imperialism, see Richard Hofstadter, *The Age of Reform: From Bryan to F.D.R.* (New York: Alfred A. Knopf, 1955), 272; Joseph M. Siracusa, "Progressivism, Imperialism, and the Leuchtenburg Thesis, 1952–1974: An Historiographical Appraisal," *Australian Journal of Politics and History* 20, no. 3 (December 1974): 312–25; Steven J. Diner, *A Very Different Age: Americans of the Progressive Era* (New York: Hill and Wang, 1998), 261–62; Kristin Hoganson, "'As Badly off as the Filipinos': U.S. Women's Suffragists and the Imperial Issue at the Turn of the Twentieth Century," *Journal of Women's History* 13, no. 2 (Summer 2001): 9–33; Michael McGerr, *A Fierce Discontent: The Rise and Fall of the Progressive Movement in America* (New York: Oxford University Press, 2003), 281–82; Allison L. Sneider, *Suffragists in an Imperial Age: U.S. Expansion and the Woman Question, 1870–1929* (New York: Oxford University Press, 2008); Steven Hahn, *A Nation Without Borders: The United States and Its World in an Age of Civil Wars, 1830–1910* (New York: Viking, 2016), 400, 500; and Mark Elliott, "'Our God-Given Mission': Reconstruction and the Humanitarian Internationalism of the 1890s," in *Reconstruction and Empire: The Legacies of Abolition and Union Victory for an Imperial Age*, ed. David Prior (New York: Fordham University Press, 2022), 161–90.

3. *Journal of the Eighteenth Annual Session of the National Encampment, Grand Army of the Republic, Minneapolis, Minn., July 23, 24 and 25, 1884* (Philadelphia: Town Book and Job Printing House, 1884), 258; *Proceedings of the Twenty-First Annual Encampment of the Department of California, Grand Army of the Republic, Held at Santa Rosa, March 14th, 15th and 16th, 1888* (San Francisco: George Spaulding and Co., 1888), 177.

4. For a still-influential economic perspective on late nineteenth-century US expansionism and how its currents went back decades, see Walter LaFeber, *The New Empire: An Interpretation of American Expansion, 1860–1898* (Ithaca, NY: Cornell University Press, 1963; repr. 1998). For studies that use the lenses of gender and race to interpret US imperialism, see Gail Bederman, *Manliness and Civilization: A Cultural History of Gender and Race in the United States, 1880–1917* (Chicago: University of Chicago Press, 1995); Kristin L. Hoganson, *Fighting for American Manhood: How Gender Politics Provoked the Spanish-American and Philippine-American Wars* (New Haven, CT: Yale University Press, 1998); and Eric T. Love, *Race Over Empire: Racism and U.S. Imperialism, 1865–1900* (Chapel Hill: University of North Carolina Press, 2004). For broader historiographical discussion of late nineteenth-century US imperialism, see Edward P. Crapol, "Coming to Terms with Empire: The Historiography of Late Nineteenth-Century American Foreign Relations," *Diplomatic History* 16 (Fall 1994): 52–70; and Joseph A. Fry, "Phases of Empire: Late Nineteenth-Century U.S. Foreign Relations," in *The Gilded Age: Perspectives on*

the Origins of Modern America, second edition, ed. Charles W. Calhoun (Lanham, MD: Rowman & Littlefield, 2007), 307–32. For a more recent interpretation that links the Reconstruction era with late nineteenth-century American imperialism, see the excellent contributions in David Prior, ed., *Reconstruction and Empire: The Legacies of Abolition and Union Victory for an Imperial Age* (New York: Fordham University Press, 2022).

    5. "A G.A.R. Post in Alaska," *National Tribune* [Washington, D.C.], 16 January 1890, 4; Alexander Badlam, *The Wonders of Alaska* (San Francisco: n.p., 1891), 29; *Journal of the Thirty-Sixth National Encampment of the Grand Army of the Republic, Washington, D.C., October 9th to 10th, 1902* (Minneapolis: Kimball and Storer Co., 1903), 267; "Washington and Alaska," *National Tribune*, 21 June 1894, 6; "Decoration Day in Juneau," *Douglas Island News* [Douglas City, AK], 31 May 1899, 2; "A Headquarters Bulletin," *National Tribune* [Washington, D.C.], 20 May 1897, 6; "Juneau Ladies Aid in Red Cross Work," *San Francisco Call*, 25 July 1898, 2. On national-level officers' assumption that the Alaska posts had died out, see Allan C. Bakewell, *Report of Allan C. Bakewell, Chief Aide on Military Instruction and Patriotic Education in Schools, to John R. King, Commander-in-Chief, Grand Army of the Republic* (n.p., 1905), 78. For evidence of Grand Army veterans in Alaska continuing to organize for Memorial Day ceremonies several years later, see "Memorial Day Near at Hand," *Alaska Daily Empire* [Juneau, AK], 28 May 1913, 1; and "Juneau Bows Head in Honor of War Veterans," *Alaska Daily Empire* [Juneau, AK], 30 May 1916, 1. Historian Stephen Haycox argues that Alaska's early settlers "sought to replicate the culture they came from," reproducing the amenities and institutions they were familiar with in their former homes. In this sense, it is logical that Union veterans desired to quickly organize in Alaska the fraternal bonds they likely were used to in the continental United States. See Haycox, *Alaska: An American Colony* (Seattle: University of Washington Press, 2002), 162.

    6. "From Far Hawaii," *Pittsburgh Press*, 23 July 1894, 7; "James D. Arnold," *Pittsburgh Press*, 16 March 1907, 3; John William Siddall, ed., *Men of Hawaii: Being a Biographical Reference Library, Complete and Authentic, of the Men of Note and Substantial Achievement in the Hawaiian Islands*, vol. 1 (Honolulu: Honolulu Star-Bulletin, 1917), 87; "C. H. Dickey, Veteran Law Member, Dies," *Honolulu Advertiser*, 22 January 1932, 1, 4; "Solons Extend Sympathy to Dickey Family," *Honolulu Advertiser*, 23 January 1932, 4.

    7. *National Tribune* [Washington, D.C.], 9 September 1882, 4; "G.A.R.," *Daily Herald* [Honolulu, HI], 27 September 1886, 3; Kam, "Commemorating the Grand Army of the Republic," 130; "The Drummer Boy," *Pacific Commercial Advertiser* [Honolulu, HI], 11 April 1887, 2. Newspaper reports place the De Long Post's initial membership estimate between forty and fifty veterans. Historian Ralph Thomas Kam places total membership throughout the post's nearly half century of existence at around 110. See "A Post in the Sandwich Islands," *National Tribune* [Washington, D.C.], 9 September 1882, 3; "Cheering News from the Coast Concerning the Growth of the Order," *National Tribune* [Washington, D.C.], 26 October 1882, 3; and Kam, "Commemorating the Grand Army of the Republic in Hawai'i," 126. Cecelia Elizabeth O'Leary suggests that "the formalization of Memorial Day molded personal statements of grief into a movement to build the nation." It seems reasonable to extend this argument to the lands and peoples associated

with expansionist America's growing empire. For quote, see O'Leary, *To Die For: The Paradox of American Patriotism* (Princeton, NJ: Princeton University Press, 1999), 108.

8. "The Flag of a New Republic," *Akron Beacon and Republican* [Akron, OH], 31 July 1894, 1; *An Address by the Hawaiian Branches of the Sons of the American Revolution, Sons of Veterans, and Grand Army of the Republic to Their Compatriots in America Concerning the Annexation of Hawaii* (Washington, D.C.: Gibson Brothers, 1897), 7. On the Bayonet Constitution, see Kam, "Commemorating the Grand Army of the Republic," 134–37; and Tom Coffman, *Nation Within: The History of the American Occupation of Hawai'i*, rev. ed. (Durham, NC: Duke University Press, 2016), chapter 7. For a fuller history of Lili'uokalani's overthrow, see Coffman, *Nation Within*, chapter 9.

9. Andrew Smith, "Confederation as a Hemispheric Anomaly: Why Canada Chose a Unique Model of Sovereignty in the 1860s," in *Remaking North American Sovereignty: State Transformation in the 1860s*, ed. Jewel L. Spangler and Frank Towers (New York: Fordham University Press, 2020), 44–47; Ryan Hall, "Negotiating Sovereignty: U.S. and Canadian Colonialisms on the Northwest Plains, 1855–1877," in *Remaking North American Sovereignty: State Transformation in the 1860s*, ed. Jewel L. Spangler and Frank Towers (New York: Fordham University Press, 2020), 143; *Journal of the Eighteenth Annual Session, of the National Encampment, Grand Army of the Republic, Minneapolis, Minn., July 23, 24, and 25, 1884* (Philadelphia: Town Book and Job, 1884), 126. For more on, for instance, the turbulent *Trent* and *Chesapeake* affairs and the raid on St. Albans, Vermont, launched by Confederate agents in Montreal, see John Boyko, *Blood and Daring: How Canada Fought the American Civil War and Forged a Nation* (Toronto: Alfred A. Knopf Canada, 2013), 90–105, 153–55, 179–85. Boyko estimates that for every one Canadian fighting for the Confederacy, fifty fought for the North. See *Blood and Daring*, 9.

10. Hancock Post circular, ca. 1895, folder: appeals for donations, Grand Army of the Republic Subject Files, State Historical Society of Iowa, Des Moines, IA (hereafter SHSI); "Hancock Post, G.A.R., in Montreal," *Burlington Daily Free Press* [Burlington, VT], 31 May 1894, 1; "Day Observed in Canada," *National Tribune* [Washington, D.C.], 18 June 1896, 6; "City and Vicinity," *Burlington Free Press and Times* [Burlington, VT], 3 July 1900, 8; *Rochester Democrat and Chronicle* [Rochester, NY], 22 September 1901, 6. Citing the many Canadians who served in the Union army, the newspaper concluded that it was "[n]o wonder Canada is Americanized, and feels almost as deeply the loss of President McKinley as citizens of the United States."

11. *National Tribune* [Washington, D.C.], 21 June 1894, 6; "Manitoba Post, G.A.R.," *Winnipeg Tribune*, 19 December 1893, 5; "Manitoba Post G.A.R.," *Manitoba Morning Free Press* [Winnipeg, MB], 24 January 1894, 8; "Our Comrades in Canada," *National Tribune* [Washington, D.C.], 4 April 1895, 6; "Our Comrades in Canada," *National Tribune* [Washington, D.C.], 6 November 1902, 5. The *Manitoba Morning Free Press* further reported that "too much could not be said of the good offices done by" Wilson, who "[w]ithout any hope of reward…has looked up needy cases, reported them to Washington and got the pension granted. This he has done for many years and only wishes to know of other cases, that the good work may go on." See "Veteran Discipline," *Manitoba Morning Free Press* [Winnipeg, MB], 20 August 1906, 3. For Wilson obituary, see "Captain Wilson Funeral Sunday," *Winnipeg Tribune*, 29 August 1914, 2. For the obstacles that

Canadian veterans faced in applying for US pensions, see Richard M. Reid, *African Canadians in Union Blue: Enlisting for the Cause in the Civil War* (Vancouver: UBC Press, 2014), 185–201.

12. "New York," *National Tribune* [Washington, D.C.], 10 January 1895, 6. For enlistment estimates, biography of Abbott's life, and Abbott speech, see Reid, *African Canadians in Union Blue*, 4–5, 163–69, 174–76, and 206–12. As Reid explains, those Black Canadians and Canadian Americans who enlisted in the Union military during the Civil War "conceived of their world as being broader than just their province." Further, the Lincoln administration's Emancipation Proclamation and utilization of Blacks in the military "gave the war a new international dimension." See Reid, *African Canadians in Union Blue*, 4, 209.

13. "Manitoba Post G.A.R.," *Manitoba Morning Free Press* [Winnipeg, MB], 6 May 1896, 8; *The Vermonter*, vol. 4, no. 12 (St. Albans, VT: Charles Spooner Forbes, 1899): 230; "Montreal," *Burlington Weekly Free Press* [Burlington, VT], 22 June 1899, 1; "Vermont Encampment," *National Tribune* [Washington, D.C.], 13 July 1899, 6; "Sam and John," *Buffalo Commercial*, 24 May 1899, 9; "Two Splendid Flags Waving Together," *Buffalo Evening News*, 24 May 1899, 1.

14. "G.A.R. Post in Mexico," *Chicago Tribune*, 21 August 1891, 9. For southerners' migration abroad after the Civil War and Confederate veterans' alliance with Maximilian I during the French intervention in Mexico, see Gaines M. Foster, *Ghosts of the Confederacy: Defeat, the Lost Cause, and the Emergence of the New South, 1865–1913* (New York: Oxford University Press, 1987), 15–17; and Evan C. Rothera, "'The Men Are Understood to Have Been Generally Americans, in the Employ of the Liberal Government': Civil War Veterans and Mexico, 1865–1867," in *The War Went On: Reconsidering the Lives of Civil War Veterans*, ed. Brian Matthew Jordan and Evan C. Rothera (Baton Rouge: Louisiana State University Press, 2020), 41–42. For the Díaz regime (or "Porfiriato") and the mutual accommodation between the United States and Mexico's liberal leadership, see John Mason Hart, *Empire and Revolution: The Americans in Mexico Since the Civil War* (Berkeley: University of California Press, 2002), 45.

15. "Col. W. J. DeGress," *The Station Agent* 5, no. 5 (July 1891): 200–201; "Record Deal on Main," *Los Angeles Daily Times*, 24 September 1909, 15; *Weekly Herald-Despatch* [sic] [Decatur, IL], 15 April 1893, 3; "Mustered Out," *National Tribune* [Washington, D.C.], 11 May 1893, 6; "A Lost Daughter," *Parsons Daily Sun* [Parsons, KS], 2 June 1884, 4; "Captain Howe Dead," *Scioto Gazette* [Chillicothe, OH], 13 March 1909, 1; *27th Annual Encampment of the Department of Tennessee, Grand Army of the Republic, Held at Newport, May 20–21, 1910, Journal of 1909–10* (Chattanooga, TN: Thompson Printing Co., 1910). William Schell Jr. draws a distinction in Mexico City's American colony between the wealthy (or the "*popolo grosso*") and the middling (or "*popolo minuto*") classes. The latter, according to Schell, usually comprised the community's "professionals, managers, shopkeepers, clerks, and the better-paid railway workers" and were attracted to the colony's burgeoning civic organizations to enhance their social standing. For Union veterans, the Ord Post was just one of these groups. Others included the colony's American Club, American Cemetery Association, Society of the American Colony, YMCA, and the Mexico City Country Club. Schell further argues that the Ord Post's members "were

overwhelmingly concerned with the betterment of Mexican-American relations, that is to say, the promotion of American investment in Mexico." See William Schell Jr., *Integral Outsiders: The American Colony in Mexico City, 1876–1911* (Wilmington, DE: Scholarly Resources, 2001), xix, 10–11, 18, 72, 79, 97.

16. "U.S. Cemetery in Mexico City," *Brownsville Herald* [Brownsville, TX], 16 January 1907, 2; "Unknown but Honored," *Indianapolis Star*, 26 May 1907, 54; *National Tribune* [Washington, D.C.], 22 June 1893, 6; "Memorial Day in Mexico," *National Tribune* [Washington, D.C.], 18 June 1896, 6; *National Tribune* [Washington, D.C.], 17 June 1897, 6; "Mexican War Veterans," *National Tribune* [Washington, D.C.], 1 November 1906, 2; "Mexican Troubles," *National Tribune* [Washington, D.C.], 29 December 1910, 6. William Schell, Jr., argues that the GAR's Memorial Day observance "re-created an American ritual observance in a Mexican context to demonstrate loyalty to the regime, not to transplant *yanqui* custom." This seems correct as the American colony required good relations with the Mexican government's leadership to achieve social stability and financial success in a foreign land where they were vastly outnumbered. Conversely, Memorial Day observances by Hawaii's De Long Post more noticeably served the purpose of acculturating Native Hawaiians to American custom and paving the way for US annexation of the islands. See Schell Jr., *Integral Outsiders*, 73. For more on the American colony during the Mexican Revolution, see Schell Jr., *Integral Outsiders*, 190–92; and Hart, *Empire and Revolution*, chapter 9. For Mexicans' longstanding suspicions about foreign incursions on their territory, see Marcela Terrazas y Basante, "Indian Raids in Northern Mexico and the Construction of Mexican Sovereignty," in *Remaking North American Sovereignty: State Transformation in the 1860s*, ed. Jewel L. Spangler and Frank Towers (New York: Fordham University Press, 2020), 153–54.

17. "American Dead in Peru," *Philadelphia Times*, 10 July 1899, 5; Lester W. Strauss, "The Casapalca Smelter, Peru," *The Mining Magazine* 5, no. 1 (July 1911): 59–66; Florencia E. Mallon, *The Defense of Community in Peru's Central Highlands: Peasant Struggle and Capitalist Transition, 1860–1940* (Princeton, NJ: Princeton University Press, 1983), 126; Lawrence A. Clayton, *Peru and the United States: The Condor and the Eagle* (Athens: University of Georgia Press, 1999), 87; Joseph Gaston, *Portland, Oregon: Its History and Builders in Connection with the Antecedent Explorations, Discoveries and Movements of the Pioneers that Selected the Site for the Great City of the Pacific*, volume 3 (Chicago: S. J. Clarke Publishing Company, 1911), 16, 19–22. For more on the War of the Pacific and escalating interactions between the United States and Peru, see Clayton, *Peru and the United States*, esp. chapters 2 and 3.

18. "With the Veterans," *Philadelphia Inquirer*, 23 October 1898, 24; *Proceedings of the 41st Annual Encampment, Department of Pennsylvania, Grand Army of the Republic, Easton, June 5 and 6, 1907* (Harrisburg, PA: Harrisburg Publishing Company, 1907), 262; "A G.A.R. Outpost," *Philadelphia Times*, 12 February 1898, 6; "State Encampment Commences," *Wilkes-Barre Daily News* [Wilkes-Barre, PA], 8 June 1899, 3; "G.A.R. Post in Peru," *Record Times* [Wilkes-Barre, PA], 7 July 1899, 2; "Convention Notes," *National Tribune* [Washington, D.C.], 10 October 1901, 6. The Lincoln Post also planned to establish a small hospital in Lima for the care of ailing US veterans. There is no evidence, however, to confirm whether this hospital was ever formally opened. See "State Encampment Commences," *Wilkes-Barre Daily News* [Wilkes-Barre, PA], 8 June 1899, 3.

19. "Turn Her This Way," *Saint Paul Daily Globe*, 15 March 1896, 7; *National Tribune* [Washington, D.C.], 31 October 1895, 4. Advocating strong US foreign policy, the *National Tribune* also published as part of its *"National Tribune* Library" series a five-cent pamphlet, which included a biography of James Monroe, text of the Monroe Doctrine, map of South America, and other pertinent information for its readers. See "The Monroe Doctrine," *National Tribune* [Washington, D.C.], 26 December 1895, 4.

20. "Demanding Full Emancipation," *New York Daily Tribune*, 23 February 1887, 2. Rally attendees were particularly incensed about a recent decision by the city's Young Men's Christian Association (YMCA) Institute to deny the application of Wiltshire Payne, a young Black man seeking to attend classes in mechanical drawing. Interestingly, New York's African American community leveraged the 1886 abolition of slavery in Cuba to protest a "second inflicted slavery" in the United States. For the Payne case, see "A Case of Color Line," *The Christian Union* 35, no. 8 (24 February 1887): 5. For African American Union veterans imagining their own emancipation struggle as merely a chapter in a larger international movement, see Donald R. Shaffer, *After the Glory: The Struggles of Black Civil War Veterans* (Lawrence: University Press of Kansas, 2004), 172–73; and Barbara A. Gannon, *The Won Cause: Black and White Comradeship in the Grand Army of the Republic* (Chapel Hill: University of North Carolina Press, 2011), 175–76. For veterans broadly perceiving the international dimensions of the Civil War, see Rothera, "Civil War Veterans and Mexico," 53.

21. *Journal of the Twelfth Annual Encampment of the Grand Army of the Republic, Department of Michigan, Held at Adrian, Mich., April 1, 2, 3, 1890* (Big Rapids, MI: Daily Pioneer Printing House, 1890), 13, at Bentley Historical Library, Ann Arbor, MI (hereafter BHL); "News of Interest to the Veterans," *Philadelphia Inquirer*, 8 May 1898, 35. Barbara A. Gannon rightly cautions that while northern veterans' engagement with the emancipationist legacy of the war often involved celebration of the expansion of liberty abroad, it often did not extend to an interest in improving the status of African Americans at home. See Gannon, *The Won Cause*, 174–75.

22. Alfred S. Johnson, ed., *The Cyclopedic Review of Current History*, vol. 5 (Buffalo, NY: Garretson, Cox, and Co., 1896), 793; "G.A.R. Post Commends Cleveland," *Omaha Daily Bee*, 22 December 1895, 3; "Santa Cruz Veterans," *San Francisco Call*, 21 December 1895, 2; "Ready to Enlist," *Evening Star* [Washington, D.C.], 24 December 1895, 1; "Congress," *National Tribune* [Washington, D.C.], 9 January 1896, 8. Despite the GAR's self-imposed mandate to remain apolitical, its hostility to Cleveland was frequently palpable. Besides his affiliation with the Democratic Party, Cleveland garnered acrimony for hiring a substitute to take his place in the Union army after Congress passed the Conscription Act in 1863. While president, Cleveland incurred further wrath for his unsympathetic stance on veterans' pensions (deeming the policy to be expensive and teeming with corruption) and for suggesting in 1887 the return of captured Confederate battle flags to southern states. On Cleveland and pensions, see Theda Skocpol, *Protecting Soldiers and Mothers: The Political Origins of Social Policy in the United States* (Cambridge, MA: Harvard University Press, 1992), 124–27. On Cleveland and the proposed return of Confederate battle flags, see David W. Blight, *Race and Reunion: The Civil War in American Memory* (Cambridge, MA: Harvard University Press, 2001), 203; and Caroline E. Janney, *Remembering the Civil War: Reunion and the Limits of Reconciliation*

(Chapel Hill: University of North Carolina Press, 2013), 174–75. For more on the Venezuelan crisis and the role the US played in settling the dispute, see LaFeber, *The New Empire*, 242–83. For more on the so-called "Olney Corollary" to the Monroe Doctrine, see George B. Young, "Intervention Under the Monroe Doctrine: The Olney Corollary," *Political Science Quarterly* 57, no. 2 (June 1942): 247–80.

23. "The Davis Resolution and the Monroe Doctrine," *Public Opinion: A Weekly Journal* 20, no. 5 (30 January 1896): 134; Minute book entry, 11 February 1896, box 1, folder 1, Grand Army of the Republic records, Northeast Minnesota Historical Center, University of Minnesota Duluth, Duluth, MN (hereafter NMHC); "Comrade Davis' Speech," *St. Paul Daily Globe*, 23 February 1896, 5; *Journal of the Twenty-Second Annual Encampment, Department of Iowa, Grand Army of the Republic, Under the New Organization, and the Thirtieth under the Old Organization, Held at Cedar Rapids, April 28-29-30, 1896* (Des Moines, IA: Register Printing House, 1896), 65; *Journal of the Thirtieth Annual Encampment, Department of Massachusetts, Grand Army of the Republic...Held in Lowell, Feb. 12 and 13, 1896* (Boston: E. B. Stillings and Co., 1896), 225; Rothera, "Civil War Veterans and Mexico," 38–39. For more on Cushman, see Marion D. Shutter, ed., *Progressive Men of Minnesota: Biographical Sketches and Portraits of the Leaders in Business, Politics and the Professions; Together with an Historical and Descriptive Sketch of the State* (Minneapolis: Minneapolis Journal, 1897), 33–34; and Kent Kreuter and Gretchen Kreuter, "The Presidency or Nothing: Cushman K. Davis and the Campaign of 1896," *Minnesota History* 41 (Fall 1969): 301–16.

24. "Cuban Debate Continues," *Austin Weekly Statesman* [Austin, TX], 19 March 1896, 1; "Martial Scenes," *Minneapolis Times*, 13 March 1896, 1, newspaper clipping in box 2, folder 18, Henry A. Castle Papers, Minnesota Historical Society, St. Paul, MN (hereafter MinnHS); Letter of Rafael Navarro to unidentified Iowa GAR post, 27 May 1896, folder: politics, Grand Army of the Republic Subject Files, SHSI. Weyler reputedly learned his total war techniques during the Civil War while serving as a Spanish military attaché accompanying Union General William T. Sherman on his 1864 march through Georgia. For more on Weyler's *reconcentrado* and total war policies, as well as Sherman's influence on Weyler, see Stuart Creighton Miller, *"Benevolent Assimilation": The American Conquest of the Philippines, 1899–1903* (New Haven, CT: Yale University Press, 1982), 9–10; G. J. A. O'Toole, *The Spanish War: An American Epic—1898* (New York: W. W. Norton, 1984), 55–58; Susan A. Brewer, *Why America Fights: Patriotism and War Propaganda from the Philippines to Iraq* (New York: Oxford University Press, 2009), 18; and Elliott, "Humanitarian Internationalism," 172–73. For more on Navarro and his work to provide relief funds to the sick and wounded of the Cuban army, see "For Suffering Cuba," *Passaic Daily News* [Passaic, NJ], 19 May 1896, 4.

25. "Grand Army Men Aroused," *New York Times*, 14 December 1896, 1; "They're for Cuba Libre," *San Francisco Call*, 5 February 1897, 14; "Sympathy for Cuba," *Salt Lake Herald* [Salt Lake City, UT], 12 February 1897, 2; "Would Recognize Cuba," *Copper Country Evening News* [Calumet, MI], 17 June 1897, 1. Mark Elliott identifies a "humanitarian internationalism" among some figures who lived through the Civil War and Reconstruction and believed the federal government should intervene on behalf of just causes in the late nineteenth century (as it had in striking down slavery in the 1860s). Many Grand

Army veterans embraced this ideal that Elliott has described. See Elliott, "Humanitarian Internationalism," 161–90.

26. "General Gobin's Views," *Lawrence Daily Journal* [Lawrence, KS], 18 February 1898, 1; Minute book entry, Allegheny County Grand Army Association, 26 February 1898, box 30, folder 27, Grand Army of the Republic Collection, Soldiers and Sailors Memorial Hall, Pittsburgh, PA (hereafter SSMH); Samuel W. Thornton diary entry, 25 April 1898, box 1, folder 12, Thornton Family Collection, U.S. Army Heritage and Education Center, Carlisle, PA (hereafter USAHEC); "Destruction of the Maine," *Evening Star* [Washington, D.C.], 21 February 1898, 13.

27. *Journal of the Thirty-First Annual Encampment of the Department of New Hampshire, Grand Army of the Republic, Held at Concord, April 13 and 14, 1898, Together with General Orders and Circulars of 1897 and Unofficial Proceedings* (Concord: Ira C. Evans, 1898), 96, at New Hampshire Historical Society, Concord, NH (hereafter NHHS); "The Old Soldiers on Deck," *Sacramento Daily Record-Union*, 26 February 1898, 3; "Artillery Regiment in Maine," *New York Times*, 21 March 1898, 2; "Ex-Soldiers Want to Fight," *San Francisco Call*, 2 March 1898, 2.

28. "For a Volunteer Reserve," *New York Times*, 28 March 1898, 3. In truth, schemes like the National Volunteer Reserve played havoc with the McKinley administration's desire to forego armies of volunteer "citizen-soldiers" and instead reorganize and enlarge the regular army. At the same time GAR veterans promoted the National Volunteer Reserve and other volunteer proposals in March and April 1898, the War Department was backing a congressional effort by Iowa Republican John A. T. Hull to reform the US Army. The so-called Hull Bill, however, incurred the ire of the many supporters of the National Guard (and the Guard's association with local- and state-level voluntary recruitment) and the opponents of a large standing army. The bill was defeated handily in early April, as state and federal officials were even then inundated with local-level offers of voluntary military service. For more on Hull Bill advocates, detractors, and the bill's ultimate defeat, see Graham A. Cosmas, *An Army for Empire: The United States Army in the Spanish-American War* (Columbia: University of Missouri Press, 1971), 87–97.

29. Department of Michigan circular, 9 April 1898, box 7, folder 11, L. B. Quackenbush Post No. 205, Grand Army of the Republic Collection, Archives of Michigan, Lansing, MI; "Call to Arms at Asbury Park," *Philadelphia Inquirer*, 29 April 1898, 6; "National Veterans' Reserve," *Los Angeles Herald*, 6 April 1898, 7; *Proceedings of the Seventeenth Annual Encampment of the Department of Missouri, Grand Army of the Republic, Held at Carthage, Missouri, May 19 and 20, 1898* (St. Louis, MO: Commercial Printing Company, 1898), 122; "National Volunteer Reserves," *St. Johnsbury Caledonian* [St. Johnsbury, VT], 27 April 1898, 4. Although anecdotal newspaper evidence suggests healthy interest in the National Volunteer Reserves, its quantitative success is difficult to assess. Graham A. Cosmas estimates that at least 15,000 enrolled in just a few weeks before the declaration of war against Spain. See Cosmas, *An Army for Empire*, 93.

30. "Colored Veterans Ready," *Morning News* [Wilmington, DE], 14 April 1898, 1; "Shaw Post's Campfire," *Kansas City Journal* [Kansas City, MO], 19 April 1898, 5; "Host of Volunteers," *Detroit Free Press*, 23 April 1898, 5; "They Want to Fight," *Indianapolis Journal*, 27 April 1898, 2; "At Harmony Cemetery," *Evening Star* [Washington, D.C.], 31

May 1898, 11. On the promises and limitations of Black military service in the Spanish-American War, see Joseph T. Glatthaar, *Forged in Battle: The Civil War Alliance of Black Soldiers and White Officers* (Baton Rouge: Louisiana State University Press, 1990), 263; and Gannon, *The Won Cause*, 174–77.

31. *Journal of the Thirty-Second Annual Encampment of the Department of New Hampshire, Grand Army of the Republic, Held at Concord, April 12 and 13, 1899, Together with General Orders and Circulars of 1898 and Unofficial Proceedings* (Concord, NH: n.p., 1899), 33, at NHHS; Ezra J. Warner, *Generals in Blue: Lives of the Union Commanders* (Baton Rouge: Louisiana State University Press, 1964), 46–47, 321–24; Ronald H. Spector, *Admiral of the New Empire: The Life and Career of George Dewey* (Baton Rouge: Louisiana State University Press, 1974); David Traxel, *1898: The Birth of the American Century* (New York: Alfred A. Knopf, 1999), 144. As a Civil War officer himself, William McKinley exercised close supervision over the appointment of officers for the war with Spain. As stipulated under an April 22 law, the individual states commissioned lower-level officers for volunteer units, while the administration selected commanders for upper-echelon positions along the volunteer and regular army chain of command. McKinley clearly favored professional soldiers over civilians, and of the latter, many had served in the Civil War. On the establishment of the Spanish-American War chain of command and statistics on commissioned officers' military experience, see Cosmas, *An Army for Empire*, 148–50.

32. *Minutes of the Eighth Annual Meeting and Reunion of the United Confederate Veterans, Held in the City of Atlanta, Ga., on Wednesday, Thursday, Friday and Saturday, July 20, 21, 22 and 23, 1898* (New Orleans: Hopkins Printing Office, 1899), 27; *Journal of the Thirty-Second National Encampment of the Grand Army of the Republic, Cincinnati, Ohio, September 8th and 9th, 1898* (Philadelphia: Town Printing Company, 1898), 68, 193.

33. "Full Honors of War for Col. A. L. Hawkins," *Pittsburgh Press*, 2 August 1899, 1; "Hero of Two Wars," *Pittsburgh Commercial Gazette*, 2 August 1899, 4; "Troops Ready for Big Pageant," *Pittsburgh Gazette*, 11 June 1904, 1; "Great Line of Marching Men," *Pittsburgh Gazette*, 12 June 1904, 2; "Taps Sound for Veteran Warrior, Gen. O. Summers," *Oregon Daily Journal* [Portland, OR], 22 January 1911, 1, 4; "Simple Services Mark Funeral of Oregon Fighter," *Oregon Daily Journal* [Portland, OR], 23 January 1911, 6. Many historians have identified the Spanish-American War as a moment when North and South—fighting a common foe—permanently cemented the long post–Civil War healing process, firmly abandoned the emancipationist memory of the war, and supplanted it with a reconciliationist bond between white northerners and white southerners. More recently, however, some scholars have questioned the extent to which the Spanish-American War could heal the deep wounds of fratricidal sectionalism and the disturbing legacy of southern chattel slavery. Indeed, the disinterest and even outright aversion that many GAR veterans exhibited in sharing glory with the South suggests a rethinking of the completeness of reconciliationism during and after the 1898 conflict. For the former school of thought, see Foster, *Ghosts of the Confederacy*, 149; Nina Silber, *The Romance of Reunion: Northerners and the South, 1865–1900* (Chapel Hill: University of North Carolina Press, 1993), 178, 181; and Blight, *Race and Reunion*, 347. For the latter, see Gannon, *The Won Cause*, 174–77; and Janney, *Remembering the Civil War*, 199.

34. See *Annual Report of the Quartermaster-General of the Army to the Secretary of War for the Fiscal Year Ended June 30, 1900* (Washington, D.C.: Government Printing Office, 1900), 30; "Death of Past Commander Goodale," *National Tribune* [Washington, D.C.], 16 February 1911, 4; National Headquarters circular, 20 March 1911, folder SC 361, Grand Army of the Republic, Department of New York Collection, Syracuse University Special Collections Research Center, Syracuse, NY; Letter of Senator William E. Chandler to Joab N. Patterson, 8 January 1900, box 2, folder 9, Joab N. Patterson Papers, NHHS; *The Granite Monthly: New Hampshire State Magazine*, vol. 54 (Concord, NH: Harlan C. Pearson, 1922), 173–74; "Gen. Joab N. Patterson Dies at Concord, N.H.," *Fitchburg Sentinel* [Fitchburg, MA], 18 July 1923, 3; Newspaper clipping pasted in minute book, Tower Post No. 17, 9 May 1898, box 7, subgroup 5, Rhode Island Department, Grand Army of the Republic, Rhode Island Historical Society, Providence, RI (hereafter RIHS); "Ready to Muster Out," *Wilkes-Barre Record* [Wilkes-Barre, PA], 30 August 1898, 1; "War of Rebellion Chaplain," *Harrisburg Daily Independent* [Harrisburg, PA], 5 September 1898, 1. Returning from the war, the Rev. Joseph J. Woolley resumed his pastorship of Park Place Congregational Church and active involvement in the GAR, becoming Rhode Island department chaplain from 1900 to 1901 and department commander in 1904. Woolley died in 1906. For more on Woolley's life, see *Newport Mercury* [Newport, RI], 7 July 1906, 1; and *Journal of the Fortieth Annual Encampment of the Department of Rhode Island, G.A.R., Thursday, February 21, 1907* (Providence: Rhode Island Printing Company, 1907), 71.

35. "Waiting for the Word to Move," *Cincinnati Enquirer*, 27 April 1898, 3; "Iowa Militia Is in Camp," *Omaha Daily Bee* [Omaha, NE], 27 April 1898, 6; "Name of Dewey on Every Lip," *San Francisco Call*, 8 May 1898, 4. McKinley's call for 125,000 volunteers surprised military administrators who expected a volunteer force of fewer than half that number. McKinley and some of his close advisers, however, remembered the Lincoln administration's mistake in requesting too few volunteers at the onset of the Civil War. Further, the larger number ensured that all National Guard units across the country could be readily subsumed into the volunteer service intact (thereby preventing the politically powerful guardsmen from feeling slighted or overlooked during the mobilization process). See Cosmas, *An Army for Empire*, 107–10. For more on the mobilization of the National Guard and tensions between the regular and volunteer service, see Cosmas, *An Army for Empire*, 111–38; and Jerry Cooper, *The Rise of the National Guard: The Evolution of the American Militia, 1865–1920* (Lincoln: University of Nebraska Press, 1997), 97–107. On patriotism and military service as a locally inspired phenomenon in the nineteenth century, see Gerald F. Linderman, *The Mirror of War: American Society and the Spanish-American War* (Ann Arbor: University of Michigan Press, 1974), 62–85.

36. "At Camp Tunnell," *Evening Journal* [Wilmington, DE], 16 May 1898, 1; "Can't Take Part in the Parade," *Morning News* [Wilmington, DE], 30 May 1898, 3; Josiah B. Chaney diary entry, 11 and 15 May 1898, box 6, volume 44, Josiah B. Chaney and Family Papers, MinnHS.

37. Transcribed letter dated 30 May 1898 in minute book entry, Roberts Post No. 14, 27 September 1898, GAR Roberts Post No. 14 Record Books Collection, Vermont Historical Society, Barre, VT; Donald H. Wickman, "Henry Ripley Dorr in the Splendid

Little War of 1898," *Rutland Historical Society Quarterly* 28, no. 3 (1998): 42–63; Minute book entries, Sedgwick Post No. 17, 8 May 1898, 12 August 1898, and 26 August 1898, box 4, Grand Army of the Republic, Sedgwick Post No. 17, USAHEC.

38. Speech of Josiah B. Chaney entitled "Care of Sick Soldiers in 1862 and 1898," 24 September 1898, box 4, folder 4, Josiah B. Chaney and Family Papers, MinnHS; "Funeral of Corporal Gilmartin," *Scranton Tribune*, 7 July 1898, 3; "Private Angiers's Funeral," *New York Times*, 5 September 1898, 5. Some 5,200 Spanish-American War soldiers died of disease, compared with just 460 combat deaths. See Nell Irvin Painter, *Standing at Armageddon: The United States, 1877–1919* (New York: W. W. Norton, 1987), 157.

39. "The Fighting Thirteenth Has Reached Home Again," *Buffalo Enquirer*, 15 September 1898, 1; Speech of Isaac N. Carr, ca. 1898, box 6, folder 3, Isaac N. Carr Collection, SHSI, Iowa City, IA. As David V. Holtby has concluded, sentiments like these indicate that many GAR veterans consciously linked imperial expansion with the safeguarding of the republic they had saved. See Holtby, "Connected Lives: Albert Beveridge, Benjamin Tillman, and the Grand Army of the Republic," in *Reconstruction and Empire: The Legacies of Abolition and Union Victory for an Imperial Age* (New York: Fordham University Press, 2022), 131.

40. "Soldiers Reach Madison," *Inter Ocean* [Chicago, IL], 11 September 1898, 7; "At Hollidaysburg," *Altoona Tribune* [Altoona, PA], 19 September 1898, 1, 4; "History Repeats Itself," *Democrat and Chronicle* [Rochester, NY], 13 September 1898, 9. On the Chickamauga battlefield and Camp George H. Thomas during the Spanish-American War, see "Volunteers Acted Badly," *Buffalo Review*, 10 September 1898, 1; and Bradley S. Keefer, *Conflicting Memories on the 'River of Death': The Chickamauga Battlefield and the Spanish-American War, 1863–1933* (Kent, OH: Kent State University Press, 2013), esp. chapters 11 and 12.

41. Minute book entry, Tower Post No. 17, 6 June 1898, box 7, subgroup 5, Rhode Island Department, Grand Army of the Republic, RIHS; Minute book entry, Col. James C. Hull Post No. 157, 16 June 1898, box 12, folder 16, Grand Army of the Republic Collection, SSMH; "Shall New Veterans Enter the Grand Army?," *Brooklyn Daily Eagle*, 7 July 1899, 14. Barbara A. Gannon has rightly argued that some GAR veterans balked at offering membership to Spanish-American War veterans. Such leniency would have hypothetically opened membership to former Confederates and to young men who came of age during a time of sectional reconciliation—thereby minimizing Union veterans' sacrifices and the emancipationist memory of the Civil War. However, there are many examples of GAR veterans advocating inclusion of Spanish-American War veterans that are difficult to explain away. Examining local GAR post records, as opposed to state- and national-level GAR materials, may provide a clue. Posts that had comrades serving in the military in 1898 (like the Tower Post) or that likely would not have been directly affected by the specter of Confederate veterans entering their post rooms may have been more amenable to the idea of intergenerational veteran membership. See Gannon, "'They Call Themselves Veterans': Civil War and Spanish War Veterans and the Complexities of Veteranhood," *Journal of the Civil War Era* 5, no. 4 (December 2015): 528–50.

42. *Journal of the Thirty-Second National Encampment of the Grand Army of the Republic, Cincinnati, Ohio, September 8th and 9th, 1898* (Philadelphia: Town Printing Company, 1898), 49; *Proceedings of the 33rd Annual Encampment of the Department of*

Pennsylvania, Grand Army of the Republic, at Wilkes-Barre, June 7–8, 1899 (Harrisburg, PA: William Stanley Ray, 1899), 128; Thomas J. McCrory, *Grand Army of the Republic, Department of Wisconsin* (Black Earth, WI: Trails Books, 2005), 46.

43. *Constitution and Rules and Regulations of the United Spanish War Veterans* (Chicago: H. L. Ruggles and Co., 1929), viii, x. For more on Spanish-American War veteran fraternalism and the establishment of the USWV, see Rodney G. Minott, *Peerless Patriots: Organized Veterans and the Spirit of Americanism* (Washington, D.C.: Public Affairs Press, 1962), chapter 2.

44. Newspaper clipping (unidentified publication), "Sherman Is Against One-Man Memorial," 31 October 1916, box 1, folder 13, Grand Army of the Republic Records, NMHC; Minute book entry, Allegheny County Grand Army Association, 24 May 1902, box 30, folder 27, Grand Army of the Republic Collection, SSMH; *Constitution and Rules and Regulations*, ix–x; *Proceedings of the Seventeenth Department Encampment, United Spanish War Veterans, June 30th, and July 1st 1916, Racine, Wisconsin* (n.p., 1916), 11.

45. Minute book entry, Lyon Post No. 266, 30 May 1902, box 1, folder: Menominee, Grand Army of the Republic, Jean Worth Papers, BHL; *Journal of the Thirty-Ninth National Encampment of the Grand Army of the Republic, Denver, Colorado, September 7th and 8th, 1905* (Boston: Griffith-Stillings Press, 1905), 235; Department of New York circular, 26 June 1909, box 94, folder 5, New York State Historian Grand Army of the Republic Records, New York State Archives, Albany, NY.

46. In 1919, for example, USWV national headquarters estimated a membership of around 50,000. At the same time, the GAR fielded more than double the members (despite Union veterans' advanced age). See Thomas F. Gannon, ed., *Proceedings of the United Spanish War Veterans, Department of New York, For the Year 1919, New Rochelle, N.Y., July 13, 14, 15 and 16, 1919* (Albany, NY: J. B. Lyon Company, 1920), 152–53.

5. Rally Once Again

1. "Home Folks to Open Hearts to Soldiers Today," *Minneapolis Morning Tribune*, 1 September 1917, 1; "City Turns Out to Pay Tribute to Its Soldiers," *Minneapolis Sunday Tribune*, 2 September 1917, 1; Ell Torrance, "Address Delivered to Departing Soldiers," 1 September 1917, box 34, folder 2, Ell Torrance Papers, Minnesota Historical Society, St. Paul, MN (hereafter MinnHS).

2. *Journal of Proceedings of the Fifty-Second Annual Encampment of the Department of Minnesota, Grand Army of the Republic, Held in Assembly Hall, Minneapolis, Minnesota, June 13th–14th, 1918* (Minneapolis: Syndicate Printing Company, 1918), 40–41; Minute book entry, Lincoln-Grant Post No. 3, 25 April 1919, box 3, folder 4, Grand Army of the Republic Collection, Oregon Historical Society, Portland, OR; "Veterans Draw Tears and Cheers," *Indianapolis Star*, 11 May 1917, 10; "Patriotic Scenes at Flag Raisings," *Philadelphia Inquirer*, 23 April 1917, 2; "G.A.R. Aids Recruiting," *Harrisburg Telegraph*, 30 May 1917, 7; "G.A.R.'s [sic] Secure 19 Recruits," *Daily Times* [Davenport, IA], 8 May 1917, 18.

3. For statistics, see *Journal of the Forty-Ninth National Encampment, Grand Army of the Republic, Washington, D.C., Sept. 27 to Oct. 2, 1915* (Washington, D.C.: Government Printing Office, 1916), 167; and *Journal of the Fifty-Fourth National Encampment, Grand Army of the Republic, Indianapolis, Ind., September 19 to 25, 1920* (Washington,

D.C.: Government Printing Office, 1921), 137; For the terms "gerontophobia" and "cult of youth," see David Hackett Fischer, *Growing Old in America* (New York: Oxford University Press, 1977), 101, 132. See also Howard P. Chudacoff, *How Old Are You? Age Consciousness in American Culture* (Princeton, NJ: Princeton University Press, 1989). Most studies of the Grand Army rarely carry the organization's story into the twentieth century, merely mentioning the fraternity's steady decline in membership after 1890. Others magnify the twentieth-century Union veteran's preoccupation with nostalgia and increasing disengagement with the bustling modern world. See for instance, Stuart McConnell, *Glorious Contentment: The Grand Army of the Republic, 1865–1900* (Chapel Hill: University of North Carolina Press, 1992); and Brian Matthew Jordan, *Marching Home: Union Veterans and Their Unending Civil War* (New York: W. W. Norton, 2014), 192–203.

4. "Few Veterans Remain Here," *Gettysburg Times*, 5 July 1913, 1; "Students' Camp Next in Order," *Gettysburg Times*, 5 July 1913, 1; "Students to Attend Camp," *Pittsburgh Post-Gazette*, 1 July 1913, 6; "Military Camps Teach Young Americans Art of Modern Warfare," *Asbury Park Press* [Asbury Park, NJ], 23 July 1913, 2. Recently, historians have provided important nuance to the typical interpretation of the 1913 Gettysburg semicentennial as a symbolic moment in the reconciliation between North and South. They have uncovered ample instances of Union veterans refusing to equate the righteousness of their cause with the Confederate Cause in the lead-up to the reunion and highlighted previously overlooked African American veteran participation at the event. See for instance, Barbara A. Gannon, *The Won Cause: Black and White Comradeship in the Grand Army of the Republic* (Chapel Hill: University of North Carolina Press, 2011), 182–91; Caroline E. Janney, *Remembering the Civil War: Reunion and the Limits of Reconciliation* (Chapel Hill: University of North Carolina Press, 2013), 266–69; and Jordan, *Marching Home*, 195–97.

5. For a brief and cogent summary of the development and policy objectives of preparedness advocates, see Nancy Gentile Ford, *The Great War and America: Civil-Military Relations During World War I* (Westport, CT: Praeger Security International, 2008), 1–25. On the difficulty of pinning down commonalities among preparedness advocates, see John Garry Clifford, *The Citizen Soldiers: The Plattsburg Training Camp Movement, 1913–1920* (Lexington: University Press of Kentucky, 1972), 31.

6. David M. Kennedy, *Over Here: The First World War and American Society* (New York: Oxford University Press, 1980), 44. For the Progressive Party's platform at its 1916 national convention in Chicago, see Harrold E. Klise, ed., *Official Register, Twenty-Seventh Number* (Des Moines: State of Iowa, 1917), 362–64. For more on the National Defense Act of 1916 and the related Naval Act of 1916, see Ford, *The Great War and America*, 20–23. For Wilson's evolution in supporting "reasonable preparedness," see Kennedy, *Over Here*, 31–34; and David Traxel, *Crusader Nation: The United States in Peace and the Great War, 1898–1920* (New York: Alfred A. Knopf, 2006), 212–13. Nancy Gentile Ford suggests that universal military training advocates adopted much of the same social justice rhetoric of other progressive reformers. Both groups "sought to 'uplift' the lower classes, build character, instill moral values (defined by the upper class), and provide wholesome outdoor activities." See Ford, *The Great War and America*, 8.

7. John A. Logan, *The Volunteer Soldier of America with Memoir of the Author and Military Reminiscences from General Logan's Private Journal* (Chicago: R. S. Peale and Company, 1887), 605, 606; *Journal of the Thirty-Fourth National Encampment of the Grand Army of the Republic, Chicago, Illinois, August 29th and 30th, 1900* (Philadelphia: Town Printing Co., 1900), 63; *Journal of the Thirtieth National Encampment of the Grand Army of the Republic, St. Paul, Minn., September 2^{d}, 3^{d} and 4th, 1896* (Indianapolis, IN: William B. Burford, 1896), 159–69. John A. Logan also suggested that West Point and Annapolis be decentered in their importance to the nation's military training, insinuating that these institutions were undemocratic and promoted an aristocratic martial class. He charged that West Point, in particular, bred incompetent and—in the case of southern graduates who defected to the Confederacy—disloyal officers before the Civil War. Ultimately, Logan endeavored to disseminate military education broadly and cultivate a democratic—even progressive—military system, shared by all men and which preserved the icon of the volunteer citizen-soldier. For more, see McConnell, *Glorious Contentment*, 198–99.

8. "Banks and Trust Companies Encourage Employees to Attend Military Training Camps," *Trust Companies* 22, no. 1 (January 1916): 370. For a lengthier history of Leonard Wood's training camps and the expansion of the program from its roots at the 1913 Gettysburg camp, see Clifford, *Citizen Soldiers*; and Ford, *The Great War and America*, 6–25.

9. *Journal of the Forty-Ninth National Encampment, Grand Army of the Republic, Washington, D.C., Sept. 27 to Oct. 2, 1915* (Washington, D.C.: Government Printing Office, 1916), 120; *Journal of the Fortieth Annual Encampment of the Department of Nebraska, Grand Army of the Republic, Held at Lexington, Nebraska, May 16, 17, 18, 1916* (Lincoln, NE: A. M. Trimble, 1916), 82; *Journal of Proceedings of the Fiftieth Annual Encampment of the Department of New Hampshire, Grand Army of the Republic Held at Concord, April 12 and 13, 1917, Together with General Orders and Circulars of 1916 and Unofficial Proceedings* (Concord, NH: Evans Printing Company, 1917), 41. For the Nebraska Telephone Company's policy notice, see "Favors Military Training," *Lincoln Daily News* [Lincoln, NE], 17 June 1916, 1. Nancy Gentile Ford notes that many companies, particularly in the East, enacted similarly generous policies for employees to attend the camps. Newspapers that summer made a habit of printing the names of these businesses to recognize their patriotism. See Ford, *Great War and America*, 24.

10. "What Is the Sons of Veterans Reserve?" *Minneapolis Morning Tribune*, 5 April 1915, 4; "Sons of Veterans Reserves," *The Scranton Truth* [Scranton, PA], 20 June 1907, 6. For the amendments to the SV constitution that created the order's Military Division and the SVR, see "The Sons of Veterans in National Encampment," *National Tribune* [Washington, D.C.], 1 October 1903, 6.

11. Souvenir program, 30th Annual Encampment, Pennsylvania Division, Sons of Veterans, U.S.A., June 20–25, 1910, Wilkes-Barre, PA, Pennsylvania Division, Sons of Veterans Collection, Pennsylvania State Archives, Harrisburg, PA (hereafter PSA); *Journal of Proceedings of the 33rd Annual Encampment of the Division of Ohio, Sons of Veterans, Held June 21, 22, 23, and 24th, in the Year of Nineteen Hundred Fifteen* (Dayton, OH: William A. Selz Printing Company, 1915), 35, U.S. Army Heritage and Education Center, Carlisle, PA (hereafter USAHEC); *Journal of Proceedings of the Thirty-Second Annual Encampment of*

the Division of Ohio, Sons of Veterans, Held June Twenty-Second, Twenty-Third, Twenty-Fourth and Twenty-Fifth, in the Year of Nineteen Hundred Fourteen, Held at East Liverpool, Ohio (Findlay, OH: L. E. Kennedy, 1914), 23; *Journal of Proceedings of the Thirty-Fourth Annual Encampment of the Division of Ohio, Sons of Veterans, Held June 12, 13, 14 and 15, in the Year of Nineteen Hundred Sixteen, Held at Marion, Ohio* (Findlay, OII: L. E. Kennedy, 1916), 31–32, USAHEC; "Sons of Veterans Reserves Make Plans for Encampment," *The Mansfield News* [Mansfield, OH], 22 May 1915, 4; "Fill Company of S. of V. Reserves," *The Mansfield News* [Mansfield, OH], 28 February 1916, 4; *Acts and Resolves Passed by the General Assembly of the State of Rhode Island and Providence Plantations, at the January Session, 1912* (Providence, RI: E. L. Freeman Company, 1912), 544; *Journal of Proceedings of the Fiftieth Annual Encampment of the Department of Minnesota, Grand Army of the Republic, Held in State Capitol, St. Paul, Minnesota, June 5th–6th, 1917* (Minneapolis: Syndicate Printing Company, 1917), 66.

12. Newspaper clipping pasted in minute book entry, April 1915, box 16, folder 4, Grand Army of the Republic, Department of Wisconsin Records, Wisconsin Veterans Museum, Madison, WI (hereafter WVM); Speech of Ell Torrance, 20 May 1916, box 34, folder 5, Ell Torrance Papers, MinnHS; *Proceedings of the 49th Annual Encampment, Department of New Jersey, G. A. R., Atlantic City, New Jersey, June 15, 16, 1916* (Trenton, NJ: MacCrellish and Quigley Co., 1916), 28. John Garry Clifford notes that "preparedness" was a vague term in the years before American involvement in World War I. For some, preparedness implied a first step toward military intervention in the European war. For others, preparedness might only imply a self-defense measure to ensure American neutrality. Although Grand Army veterans, like Americans at large, had different definitions of just what "preparedness" meant, most seemed to genuinely believe that it was the best hope to keep the nation safe and at peace. For more on differing definitions of preparedness, see Clifford, *Citizen Soldiers*, 30–38.

13. Minute book entry, 28 November 1914, box 1, folder 3, Grand Army of the Republic records, Northeast Minnesota Historical Center, University of Minnesota Duluth, Duluth, MN (hereafter NMHC); *Journal of Proceedings of the Forty-Ninth Annual Encampment of the Department of New Hampshire, Grand Army of the Republic, Held at Concord, April 6 and 7, 1916, Together with General Orders and Circulars of 1915 and Unofficial Proceedings* (Concord, NH: Ira C. Evans Co., 1916), 41; "Preach Message of Preparedness," *Essex County Herald* [Guildhall, VT], 9 July 1915, 6; *Journal of the Forty-Second Annual Encampment, Department of Iowa, Grand Army of the Republic, under the New Organization and the Forty-Fourth under the Old Organization, Held at Marshalltown, Iowa, June 20-21-22, 1916 with General Orders and Circulars for 1915 and 1916, and the Official Rosters for 1916 and 1917* (Des Moines, IA: n.p., 1916), 68.

14. Minute book entries, Lt. James M. Lysle Post No. 128, 11 September 1914; 5 November 1915; and 23 March 1917, box 7, folder 8, Grand Army of the Republic Collection, Soldiers and Sailors Memorial Hall, Pittsburgh, PA (hereafter SSMH); "G. A. R. Men Hold Annual Banquet," *Wilkes-Barre Record* [Wilkes-Barre, PA], 3 February 1916, 5; "'Prepare' Urges Judge L. F. Burpee," *Hartford Courant* [Hartford, CT], 19 April 1916, 13.

15. "Better Than a Banquet," *Emporia Weekly Gazette* [Emporia, KS], 3 December 1914, 3; "Old Soldiers Help," *The Hutchinson News* [Hutchinson, KS], 21 November 1914, 6; "W.R.C. Donation," *The Frankfort Daily Index* [Frankfort, KS], 2 December 1914, 1;

Journal of the Thirty-First Annual Convention, Department of Kansas, Woman's Relief Corps, Auxiliary to the Grand Army of the Republic, May 11, 12, and 13, 1915, Hutchinson, Kansas (Olathe, KS: Mirror Publishing Co., 1915), 34; Minute book entry, 7 December 1914, box 16, folder 3, Grand Army of the Republic, Department of Wisconsin Records, WVM.

    16. "History of League," *Evening Star* [Washington, D.C.], 21 July 1916, 11; "Support President, Col. Palmer Urges," *Evening Star* [Washington, D.C.], 4 October 1915, 1; "Security League on the Army," *Army and Navy Register* 57, no. 1819 (29 May 1915): 680; National Security League, *Report of Director of Branches Read at the Annual Meeting, May 3, 1916* (New York: NSL Headquarters, 1916); "National Security League," *Hearings Before a Special Committee of the House of Representatives*, 65th Congress, 3rd session (19 December 1918), 4. The May 1865 Grand Review was a huge parade in Washington, D.C., of some 200,000 soldiers of the Union armies who marched in one last, great show of strength of the forces that had put down the rebellion. Just as notably, in a matter of weeks after the review, the Union soldiers became civilians again—putting down their weapons, disbanding their units, and returning home, fulfilling the final obligation of the republican citizen-soldier. For more on the Grand Review and its links to the GAR, see McConnell, *Glorious Contentment*, 1–17; Jordan, *Marching Home*, 9–19; and Robert Bonner, "1860s Capitalscapes, Governing Interiors, and the Illustration of North American Sovereignty," in *Remaking North American Sovereignty: State Transformation in the 1860s*, ed. Jewel L. Spangler and Frank Towers (New York: Fordham University Press, 2020), 83–85.

    17. "More Action for Security League," *Brooklyn Daily Eagle* [Brooklyn, NY], 28 July 1915, 18; "Preparedness Need Urgent, Speakers Say," *Pittsburgh Post*, 10 April 1916, 7; "It Is Time to Think of Preparedness," *Brooklyn Daily Eagle* [Brooklyn, NY], 1 April 2016, 3.

    18. "Veterans in Big Parade," *Plainfield Courier-News* [Plainfield, NJ], 31 May 1916, sect. 2, p. 4; "Veterans Speak in Schools," *Philadelphia Inquirer*, 30 May 1916, 5.

    19. "52,000 in Providence," *The Hartford Courant* [Hartford, CT], 4 June 1916, sect. three, p. 12; *Journal of the Fiftieth Annual Encampment of the Department of Rhode Island, G.A.R., Monday, April 9, 1917* (Providence: Rhode Island Printing Company, 1917), 15–16; "Million Viewed Parade," *Wichita Eagle* [Wichita, KS], 4 June 1916, 28; "Bomb Explosion Kills 6 and Maims 40 Preparedness Parade Spectators," *San Francisco Chronicle*, 23 July 1916, 1. For more on preparedness parades and their supporters and detractors, see David Montgomery, *The Fall of the House of Labor: The Workplace, the State, and American Labor Activism, 1865–1925* (New York: Cambridge University Press, 1987), 363–64; Marc Leepson, *Flag: An American Biography* (New York: St. Martin's Griffin, 2005), 179–80; and Ross J. Wilson, *New York and the First World War: Shaping an American City* (New York: Routledge, 2014), 117. For more on the San Francisco preparedness parade bombing and the ensuing investigation, see Michael L. Radelet, Hugo Adam Bedau, and Constance E. Putnam, *In Spite of Innocence: Erroneous Convictions in Capital Cases* (Boston: Northeastern University Press, 1992), 79–97.

    20. "Vitagraph's Patriotic Picture," *Moving Picture World* 25, no. 5 (31 July 1915): 795; "A Growing Sentiment," *The Daily Argus-Leader* [Sioux Falls, SD], 9 February 1916, 4; *Moving Picture World* 25, no. 8 (21 August 1915): advertisement between pp. 1350 and 1351; "An Old Friend Is at the Strand This Week," *Washington Times* [Washington, D.C.],

8 April 1917, 8. For a complete biography of Crawford, see Darlis A. Miller, *Captain Jack Crawford: Buckskin Poet, Scout, and Showman* (Albuquerque: University of New Mexico Press, 1993).

21. "Poet-Scout Writes Preparedness Song," *Washington Times*, 22 January 1916, 4; "General Miles Will Command at Grand Army Encampment," *Des Moines Register*, 1 September 1915, 6; "Three Generations of Fighters at War Film as Guests of Post," *Houston Daily Post*, 25 January 1916, 2; "New Experience for War Veteran," *Fitchburg Daily Sentinel* [Fitchburg, MA], 29 September 1916, 2. Crawford's lyrics became the preparedness movement's response to the popular pacifist song of the time, "I Didn't Raise My Boy to Be a Soldier," whose chorus featured the lines, "I didn't raise my boy to be a soldier, / I brought him up to be my pride and joy. / Who dares to place a musket on his shoulder, / To shoot some other mother's darling boy?" On the song, its reception, and its roots in feminist pacifism, see Susan Zeiger, "She Didn't Raise Her Boy to Be a Slacker: Motherhood, Conscription, and the Culture of the First World War," *Feminist Studies* 22, no. 1 (Spring 1996): 6–39; and Mark W. Van Wienen, *Partisans and Poets: The Political Work of American Poetry in the Great War* (New York: Cambridge University Press, 1997), 56–60.

22. Allegheny County Grand Army Association minute book entry, 25 July 1903, Allegheny County Grand Army Association Records, 1898–1940, microfilm reel 1, Archives of Industrial Society, University of Pittsburgh, Pittsburgh, PA; Theodore Roosevelt, *The New Nationalism* (New York: The Outlook Company, 1910), 6–7. Tracking presidential candidate support in local GAR post records is nearly impossible, as comrades mostly made good on their organization's pledge to remain nonpartisan (a directive since the 1870s when the GAR feared that their overt Republican sympathies hampered their membership growth). Still, it is clear there was a close relationship between the GAR and the Republican Party, whose elected officials proved most amenable to using treasury surpluses on Union veterans' pensions. The post–Civil War string of Republican presidents with war service (Grant, Hayes, Garfield, Arthur, Harrison, and McKinley in the Civil War; Roosevelt in the Spanish-American War) further cemented a tacit bond between most GAR members and the Republican Party. For GAR directives against overt partisanship, see McConnell, *Glorious Contentment*, 33. For the links between the GAR, pension rights, and the Republican Party, see Theda Skocpol, *Protecting Soldiers and Mothers: The Political Origins of Social Policy in the United States* (Cambridge, MA: Harvard University Press, 1992), 102–51.

23. "Wilson Here for One Hour," *Adams County News* [Gettysburg, PA], 5 July 1913, 1; "Gettysburg Cold to Wilson's Speech," *New York Times*, 5 July 1913, 1; "G. A. R. Men Protest," *Topeka State Journal*, 26 November 1913, 6; "Members of G. A. R. to Voice Protest," *Evening Star* [Washington, D.C.], 25 May 1914, 1; "Wilson Snubs G. A. R.," *Scranton Tribune-Republican*, 26 May 1914, 8. For Wilson's speech, see Albert Bushnell Hart, ed., *Selected Addresses and Public Papers of Woodrow Wilson* (New York: Modern Library, 1918), 32. For more on veteran reaction to Wilson's Gettysburg speech, see Gannon, *The Won Cause*, 182–83, 248 fn. 11. For the United Daughters of the Confederacy's unveiling of the Arlington Confederate Memorial, see Janney, *Remembering the Civil War*, 261–64.

24. "President to Take Part in Exercises of G. A. R.," *Washington Times*, 2 April 1915, 8; "Heroes Live Again in the Memory of American People," *Evening Star* [Washington, D.C.], 31 May 1915, 1; "President Wilson to the G. A. R.," *Evening Star* [Washington, D.C.], 29 September 1915, 5; "Wilson in Tears as Old Soldiers Pass in Review," *Evening Public Ledger* [Philadelphia, PA], 29 September 1915, 3; "Wilson's Peace Policy Lauded at Camp Emery," *Washington Herald*, 30 September 1915, 1; "Many Union Veteran[s] Will Vote for President Wilson," *Watauga Democrat* [Boone, NC], 21 October 1915, 1. Wilson's encampment address went on to further cement his typical reconciliationist sympathies, stating that the Civil War was "one of the very few wars in which in one sense everybody engaged may take pride."

25. "Wilson's Peace Policy Lauded at Camp Emery," *Washington Herald*, 30 September 1915, 1; *Journal of Proceedings of the Forty-Ninth Annual Encampment, Department of Vermont, Grand Army of the Republic, City Hall, Burlington, VT., April 18 and 19, 1916* (n.p., 1916), at Vermont Historical Society, Barre, VT (hereafter VHS); *Journal of Proceedings of the Forty-Eighth Annual Encampment of the Department of the Potomac, Grand Army of the Republic, Held at Washington, D. C., February 9th, 14th and 19th, 1916* (Washington, D.C.: R. Beresford, 1916), 51, 52.

26. "Grand Army Behind Wilson," *Baltimore Sun*, 9 February 1917, 2; "Nation Speeds Course to Real Preparedness," *Washington Herald*, 9 February 1917, 2; "G. A. R. Chief Pledges Aid," *Evening Public Ledger* [Philadelphia, PA], 10 February 1917, 3; "President Praised by State G. A. R.," *Daily Arkansas Gazette* [Little Rock, AR], 16 March 1917, 4; Newspaper clipping pasted in minute book, 5 February 1917, box 17, folder 1, Grand Army of the Republic, Department of Wisconsin Records, WVM; "Grand Army Men Are Firm in Allegiance," *Honolulu Star-Bulletin*, 12 February 1917, 3.

27. Minute book entry, 10 March 1917, box 1, folder 3, Grand Army of the Republic records, NMHC; "Northern Veterans Are with President," *Wilmington Dispatch* [Wilmington, NC], 7 March 1917, 8; "Wants War Now," *Vancouver Daily World* [Vancouver, BC], 19 March 1917, 1; Newspaper clipping pasted in minute book entry, 29 April 1917, box 2, folder 5, Grand Army of the Republic Memorial Hall Records; Series: Hall Custodians; Subseries: Hosea W. Rood, WVM.

28. Patriotic instructor's address, 3 May 1917, manuscript book 5, box 10, GAR Records, Department of Delaware, General Orders Scrapbook, 1916–1917, 14, Delaware Historical Society, Wilmington, DE; Newspaper clipping pasted in minute book entry, 8 April 1917, Grand Army of the Republic Memorial Hall Records, Series: Hall Custodians; Subseries: Hosea W. Rood, WVM; Minute book entry, 10 March 1917, box 1, folder 3, Grand Army of the Republic records, NMHC; Minute book entries, O. H. Rippey Post No. 41, 2 April 1918 and 4 June 1918, box 4, folder 4, Grand Army of the Republic Collection, SSMH; Letter from C. E. Harrington to Joab N. Patterson, 15 September 1917, box 2, folder 15, Joab N. Patterson Papers, New Hampshire Historical Society, Concord, NH.

29. *Proceedings of the 49th Annual Encampment, Department of New Jersey, G.A.R., Atlantic City, New Jersey, June 15, 16, 1916* (Trenton, NJ: MacCrellish and Quigley Co., 1916), 34–35; *Journal of Proceedings of the Fifty-Second Annual Encampment of the Department of Minnesota, Grand Army of the Republic, Held in Assembly Hall, Minneapolis, Minnesota, June 13th–14th, 1918* (Minneapolis: Syndicate Printing Company, 1918), 40; "Peissner

Post, G. A. R., Will Buy Liberty Bond," *Democrat and Chronicle* [Rochester, NY], 16 October 1917, 17. Both Theodore Roosevelt and Woodrow Wilson referred contemptuously to "hyphenated Americans"—individuals with supposed divided loyalties between the country of their birth and the country of their naturalization. The concept was used to perhaps its most infamous effect in a 1919 speech by Wilson in which he warned that "any man who carries a hyphen about him carries a dagger that he is ready to plunge into the vitals of this Republic whenever he gets ready." For quote, see Wilson's "Address at Pueblo, Colo., September 25, 1919," in Woodrow Wilson, *Addresses of President Wilson: Addresses Delivered by President Wilson on His Western Tour, September 4 to September 25, 1919, on the League of Nations, Treaty of Peace with Germany, Industrial Conditions, High Cost of Living, Race Riots, etc.* (Washington, D.C.: Government Printing Office, 1919), 359. For more on German American contributions in the Civil War, see Ella Lonn, *Foreigners in the Union Army and Navy* (Baton Rouge: Louisiana State University Press, 1951), 663–64; and David L. Valuska and Christian B. Keller, *Damn Dutch: Pennsylvania Germans at Gettysburg* (Mechanicsburg, PA: Stackpole Books, 2004).

30. "G.A.R. and Elks Offer Services," *Mount Carmel Item* [Mt. Carmel, PA], 9 April 1917, 1; "Veterans Offer Services," *Boston Post*, 13 April 1917, 6; "Board Credits Patriotic Acts," *The Daily Gate City* [Keokuk, IA], 4 May 1917, 7.

31. Minute book entry, James C. Hull Post No. 157, 15 March 1918, box 13, folder 19, Grand Army of the Republic Collection, SSMH; "Grand Army Man, 77, Ready to Fight Again," *Brooklyn Daily Eagle* [Brooklyn, NY], 26 March 1917, 8; "Veteran Offers Services," *Pittsburgh Gazette Times*, 17 August 1917, 2; "Judge Moulton Eager to Organize Regiment," *Washington Herald*, 12 April 1917, 3. For more on Moulton's biography and professional accolades, see Henry W. Moulton, *Moulton Annals* (Chicago: Edward A. Claypool, 1906), 343–44. Incidentally, nothing seems to have come from Moulton's offer to President Wilson (who subsequently forwarded Moulton's proposal on to Secretary of War Newton Baker). Besides Moulton's advanced age, one reason for the inaction is likely that the Wilson administration was strongly opposed to individuals offering to raise volunteer units (in the style of Theodore Roosevelt's "Rough Riders").

32. "Menominee Tribe Offers to Fight Nation's Enemies," *Green Bay Press-Gazette*, 18 April 1917, 4; "Indorse Gov. Capper," *Topeka Daily Capital*, 23 March 1918, 5. Over one hundred Menominee Indians enlisted in the Union army during the Civil War, many serving in the 17th and 37th Wisconsin Volunteer Infantry regiments. The Joseph A. Ledergerber Post was organized in 1889 and named after the beloved commander under whom many Menominee volunteers served. Ledergerber, a white man, was killed in November 1863 outside Atlanta at the Battle of Ringgold Gap during the Chattanooga campaign. The twenty-two charter members named their post after Ledergerber, the first comprised exclusively of Native Americans. The post peaked at fifty members in 1892, but dwindled to just seventeen by the time of the United States' entry into World War I. For more on the history of the Ledergerber Post, see Thomas J. McCrory, *Grand Army of the Republic, Department of Wisconsin* (Black Earth, WI: Trails Books, 2005), 276–77. For young Native American men enlisting in World War I to flee poor conditions on their reservations, see Thomas A. Britten, *American Indians in World War I: At Home and at War* (Albuquerque: University of New Mexico Press, 1997), 62.

33. GAR department circular, 12 April 1917, box 1, folder 6, Grand Army of the Republic, Department of Nebraska records, Nebraska State Historical Society, Lincoln, NE (hereafter NSHS); "Support Pledged to the Nation," *The Daily Gate City* [Keokuk, IA], 23 April 1917, 8; "Veterans to Offer Services to Govt.," *Akron Evening Times* [Akron, OH], 14 April 1917, 1; *Burlington Weekly Free Press* [Burlington, VT], 12 July 1917, 8.

34. Letter of Governor Emanuel L. Philipp to Hosea W. Rood, 18 April 1917, box 17, folder 1, Grand Army of the Republic, Department of Wisconsin records, WVM; *Journal of the House of Representatives of the United States, Sixty-First Congress, First Session, Begun and Held at the City of Washington, April 2, 1917, in the One Hundred and Forty-First Year of the Independence of the United States* (Washington, D.C.: Government Printing Office, 1917), 464; "Work for the Veterans," *Indianapolis News*, 7 May 1917, 5; *Abstract of General Orders and Proceedings of the Fifty-Third Annual Encampment, Department of New York, G. A. R., Held at Elmira, June 24, 25, 26, 1919* (Albany, NY: J. B. Lyon Company, 1919), 163; William E. Connelley, *A Standard History of Kansas and Kansans*, vol. 4 (Chicago: Lewis Publishing Company, 1919), 1824.

35. GAR department circular, 12 April 1917, box 1, folder 6, Grand Army of the Republic, Department of Nebraska records, NSHS; "The Iowa Drive for 4,000 Recruits," *Webster City Freeman* [Webster City, IA], 10 April 1917, 1; "Country Needs You, Is Appeal," *Lansing State Journal* [Lansing, MI], 7 April 1917, 1.

36. "Were Civil War Volunteers Failures?," *New York Tribune*, 23 April 1917, 6; Speech of Jerome A. Watrous, ca. 1917, box 2, folder 21, Jerome A. Watrous Papers, Wisconsin Historical Society, Madison, WI; *Proceedings of the 50th Annual Encampment, Department of New Jersey, G.A.R., Held in the Arcade, Asbury Park, N.J., June 13, 14, 1917* (Trenton, NJ: MacCrellish and Quigley Co., 1917), 21; GAR department circular, 12 April 1917, box 1, folder 6, Grand Army of the Republic, Department of Nebraska records, NSHS. Many Union veterans were averse to those who were either conscripted into Civil War service or were incentivized by way of lucrative state and federal bounties. A competing Union veterans' organization to the GAR—the Union Veteran Legion (UVL)—was established in 1884 with the express purpose of barring veterans who were drafted or those who accepted recruitment bounties. For Civil War–era conscription, see J. Matthew Gallman, *Defining Duty in the Civil War: Personal Choice, Popular Culture, and the Union Home Front* (Chapel Hill: University of North Carolina Press, 2015), 252.

37. "G.A.R. Ready for Call," *The Advertiser* [Lawrence, KS], 26 April 1917, 1; "Thousands Plan to Enter Parade," *Wausau Daily Herald* [Wausau, WI], 18 April 1917, 1; "Whole City to Turn Out for Civic Parade," *Harrisburg Telegraph* [Harrisburg, PA], 16 October 1917, 12; "Grand Army Big Recruiting Aid," *Evening News* [Harrisburg, PA], 19 November 1917, 4.

38. "Salem Turns Out to Give First Quota Rousing Send Off," *Daily Capital Journal* [Salem, OR], 1 April 1918, 1; "Draft Boards Prepare Lists of Men Ordered to Camp November 3," *Carlisle Evening Herald* [Carlisle, PA], 29 October 1917, 1; "Soldiers of Two Wars in Parade," *Evening Times-Republican* [Marshalltown, Iowa], 13 June 1918, 2.

39. "A Suggestion," *The Fort Wayne News and Sentinel* [Fort Wayne, IN], 29 November 1919, 11; "Sons of Veterans Reserves Join Home Defense Guard," *Allentown Morning Call* [Allentown, PA], 13 September 1917, 5; "Sons of Veterans to Join the Home Guard,"

Allentown Morning Call, 12 September 1917, 5; "Company A to Be Mustered into State Service," *Allentown Morning Call*, 2 October 1917, 5. Another eleven states reported at least some of their SV members in the service. For report, see *Journal of Proceedings of the Thirty-Ninth Annual Encampment of the Division of Pennsylvania, Sons of Veterans*, 145–46, at PSA.

40. Minute book entry, 2 May 1917, box 1, folder 3, Grand Army of the Republic records, NMHC; Newspaper clipping pasted in minute book, 19 August 1917, box 2, folder 5, Grand Army of the Republic Memorial Hall records, WVM; "Berkeley Women Arrange July Fourth Celebration," *Oakland Tribune*, 4 July 1917, 4. The distribution of the cards at so-called Hoover pledge drives was an illustrative way for women associational members to prove their patriotism. An estimated fourteen million households adhered to the pledge. For more on Hoover pledge drives, see Elaine F. Weiss, *Fruits of Victory: The Woman's Land Army of America in the Great War* (Washington, D.C.: Potomac Books, 2008), 61; and Christopher Capozzola, *Uncle Sam Wants You: World War I and the Making of the Modern American Citizen* (New York: Oxford University Press, 2008), 96–97. For text of the pledge, see United States Food Administration, *Bulletin No. 2* (Washington, D.C.: Government Printing Office, 1917), 5. For more on Hoover, food conservation, and the establishment of the US Food Administration, see Kennedy, *Over Here*, 117–23; and Traxel, *Crusader Nation*, 300–302.

41. Minute book entry, ca. September 1918, box 1, Grand Army of the Republic, General James B. McPherson Post No. 117 Records, Detre Library and Archives, Heinz History Center, Pittsburgh, PA; "Civil War Veterans Buy Liberty Bonds," *Butler Eagle* [Butler, PA], 2 June 1917, in Grand Army of the Republic Vertical File, Butler Area Public Library, Genealogy and Special Collections Room, Butler, PA; Minute book entry, 28 February 1920, series nine, box 4, folder 16, Grand Army of the Republic, Department of Nebraska Records, NSHS; Minute book entry, 26 October 1917, box 4, Grand Army of the Republic, Sedgwick Post No. 17, USAHEC; Minute book entry, 20 November 1917, Duquesne Post No. 259, box 22, folder 20, Grand Army of the Republic Collection, SSMH; Edward A. Weed letter to A. B. Hay, 23 August 1918, letterbook 1, Union Veteran Legion Collection, SSMH; "Veteran Cyclist Makes Long Trip," *San Francisco Call*, 29 August 1910, 3. Interestingly, McAdoo considered the nation's financial state for the coming war through the context of the Civil War. Secretary McAdoo chastised his 1860s counterpart Salmon P. Chase for "not attempt[ing] to capitalize the emotion of the people" to sustain the country's finances during the Civil War. Instead, McAdoo pledged to go "direct to the people, and that means everybody—to business men, workmen, farmers, bankers, millionaires, school-teachers, laborers. We capitalized the profound impulse called patriotism." McAdoo's system clearly relied on veterans who served as both participants and boosters of the Liberty Bond drives. For quotes, see Kennedy, *Over Here*, 105. For the logistics of the Liberty Bonds as economic policy, see Kennedy, *Over Here*, 98–105.

42. *Congressional Record: Containing the Proceedings and Debates of the First Session of the Sixty-Fifth Congress of the United States of America*, vol. 55 (Washington, D.C.: Government Printing Office, 1917), 5 May 1917, 1845; "Building a Solid Foundation," *The Social Hygiene Bulletin* 5, no. 12 (December 1918): 1; Katharine Bement Davis, "Women's Education in Social Hygiene," *The Annals of the American Academy of Political and Social*

Science 79 (Sept. 1918): 175; *Journal of the Thirty-Fifth Annual Convention of the Department of Wisconsin, Woman's Relief Corps, Auxiliary to the Grand Army of the Republic, Held at Ashland, June 17, 18, 19, 1918* (Evansville, WI: The Antes Press, 1918), 128; *Journal of the Fifty-Third Annual Encampment, Department of Maine, Grand Army of the Republic, June 16th and 17th, 1920* (Auburn, ME: Merrill & Webber Company, 1920), 47. For a complete history of the founding, objectives, and results of the CTCA, see Nancy K. Bristow, *Making Men Moral: Social Engineering During the Great War* (New York: New York University Press, 1996).

43. Newspaper clipping pasted in record book, 20 October 1918, box 2, folder 5, book 2, Grand Army of the Republic Memorial Hall Records; Series: Hall Custodians; Subseries: Hosea W. Rood, WVM; 1919 program for Rhode Island Grand Army Flag Day, 8–9, at Rhode Island Historical Society, Providence, RI; *Journal of Proceedings, Fifty-Second Annual Encampment, Department of Vermont, Grand Army of the Republic, G. A. R. Hall, Rutland, Vermont, May 21, 1919* (Rutland, VT: n.p., 1919), 32, at VHS. In her important work, historian Chandra Manning convincingly "rescues slavery from the periphery of soldiers' mental worlds, where subsequent generations have tried to relegate it, and returns slavery to its rightful place at the center of soldiers' views of the struggle." Statements from Union veterans linking their role in emancipating slaves in the 1860s to modern efforts to liberate Europe from autocracy suggest that slavery remained at the heart of their memory of the Civil War's cause, even a half century later. For quote, see Manning, *What This Cruel War Was Over: Soldiers, Slavery, and the Civil War* (New York: Knopf, 2007), 11.

44. Massachusetts department circular, 24 December 1918, carton 4, folder: Orders/Circulars, 1912–1922, Grand Army of the Republic, E. W. Kinsley Post No. 113 Records, Massachusetts Historical Society, Boston, MA; "Croton Drum Corps to Play at G.A.R. Reception Monday," *New Castle Herald* [New Castle, PA], 22 February 1919, 2; "Welcome Home Celebration to the Boys Who Served," *Burlington Free Press and Times* [Burlington, VT], 12 November 1919, 12; "Civil War Heroes to Fete Soldiers," *Port Huron Times-Herald* [Port Huron, MI], 21 April 1919, 2; "Vets, Old and Young Gather," *Port Huron Times-Herald* [Port Huron, MI], 24 April 1919, 2; "Colored Fighters of 92nd Division Honored by City," *Topeka Daily Capital* [Topeka, KS], 30 July 1919, 1.

45. *Proceedings of the 50th Annual Encampment, Department of Pennsylvania, Grand Army of the Republic, Held at Harrisburg, PA, June 8th and 9th, 1916* (Harrisburg, PA: William Stanley Ray, 1916), 214; *Journal of the 53rd Annual Encampment of the Department of Ohio, Grand Army of the Republic, Held at Lima, Ohio, June 16, 17, 18, 19, 1919* (Columbus, OH: F. J. Heer Printing Co., 1919), 83; Minute book entry, 5 July 1919, box 1, folder 5, Grand Army of the Republic records, NMHC. For the LEP and other organizations that laid the groundwork for the idea of the League of Nations, see Kennedy, *Over Here*, 30–31; and Traxel, *Crusader Nation*, 244–45.

46. *Journal of the Forty-First Annual Encampment of the Department of Colorado and Wyoming, Grand Army of the Republic, Held at Canon City, Colorado, June 2, 3, and 4, 1920* (Denver, CO: Work Printing Works, 1920), 35; *Proceedings of the 55th Annual Encampment, Department of Pennsylvania, Grand Army of the Republic, Allentown, June 8th and 9th, 1921* (Harrisburg, PA: J. L. L. Kuhn, 1922), 40.

47. *Journal of Proceedings of the Fifty-Third Annual Encampment of the Department of Minnesota, Grand Army of the Republic, Held in Old Capitol Building, St. Paul, Minnesota, June 5th–6th, 1919* (Minneapolis: Syndicate Printing, 1919), 25; "Stop Taft's Talk," *Topeka Daily State Journal*, 23 May 1919, 10.

48. *Journal of Proceedings of the Fifty-Second Annual Encampment of the Department of New Hampshire, Grand Army of the Republic, Held at Concord, April 17 and 18, 1919, Together with General Orders and Circulars of 1918 and Unofficial Proceedings* (Concord, NH: Evans Printing Co., 1919), 39; *Abstract of General Orders and Proceedings of the Fifty-Third Annual Encampment, Department of New York, G. A. R., Held at Elmira, June 24, 25, 26, 1919* (Albany, NY: J. B. Lyon Co., 1919), 269.

49. *Journal of Proceedings of the Fifty-First Annual Encampment of the Department of the Potomac, Grand Army of the Republic, Held at Washington, D. C., February 18th, 20th and 22^{d}, 1919* (Washington, D.C.: R. Beresford, 1919), 37–38; *Topeka Daily State Journal*, 16 December 1918, 4; *Journal of the Forty-First Annual Encampment of the Department of Colorado and Wyoming, Grand Army of the Republic, Held at Canon City, Colorado, June 2, 3, and 4, 1920* (Denver, CO: Work Printing Works, 1920), 65.

50. On the spirit and methods of progressivism that guided the Wilson administration's war needs and the subsequent postwar retreat from government activism, see Michael McGerr, *A Fierce Discontent: The Rise and Fall of the Progressive Movement in America* (New York: Oxford University Press, 2003), 280–313.

51. *Journal of Proceedings, Fifty-Second Annual Encampment, Department of Vermont, Grand Army of the Republic, G. A. R. Hall, Rutland, Vermont, May 21, 1919* (n.p., 1919), 31, at VHS.

Conclusion: From Their Battlements in Heaven

1. Loren C. Grieves, *The New Grand Army of the Republic and Its Publication* (Kansas City, MO: Post Printing and Publishing Co., 1919), 3, 17, 18. For newspaper reaction to Grieves's publication, see "The New Grand Army," *Arizona Republican* [Phoenix, AZ], 11 May 1919, sect. 3, p. 14; and "The New Grand Army," *Nashville Tennessean*, 8 June 1919, sect. B, p. 4. For biography of Loren C. Grieves, see "Ionia Farmer Has Two Sons Wearing the Blue and Serving Their Country," *Detroit Free Press*, 3 November 1907, 8; and "Body of Retired Officer to Rest in National Cemetery," *Lansing State Journal* [Lansing, MI], 7 August 1951, 37.

2. Frederick E. Schortemeier, ed., *Rededicating America: Life and Recent Speeches of Warren G. Harding* (Indianapolis, IN: Bobbs-Merrill Company, 1920), 223.

3. *Journal of the Fortieth Annual Encampment, Department of Iowa, Grand Army of the Republic…Held at Burlington, Iowa, June 17-18-19, 1914* (Des Moines, IA: J. H. Welch Printing Company, 1914), 183; Minute book entry, James C. Hull Post No. 157, 21 February 1919, box 13, folder 19, Grand Army of the Republic Collection, Soldiers and Sailors Memorial Hall, Pittsburgh, PA. Union veterans' debate about including World War I veterans in the GAR was in many ways a replay of similar debates that occurred two decades earlier when Spanish-American War veterans returned home. See Barbara A. Gannon, "'They Call Themselves Veterans': Civil War and Spanish War Veterans and the

Complexities of Veteranhood," *Journal of the Civil War Era* 5, no. 4 (December 2015): 528–50.

    4. Minute book entry, 9 July 1918, box 1, Grand Army of the Republic, General James B. McPherson Post No. 117 Records, Detre Library and Archives, Heinz History Center, Pittsburgh, PA; "Federation of Loyalty Bodies Meet," *Long Beach Press* [Long Beach, CA], 16 January 1920, 12; *Proceedings of the 53rd Annual Encampment, Department of Pennsylvania, Grand Army of the Republic, Lancaster, June 11th and 12th, 1919* (Harrisburg, PA: J. L. L. Kuhn, 1919), 191.

    5. Christopher Nehls, "The American Legion and Striking Workers During the Interwar Period," in *The Right and Labor in America: Politics, Ideology, and Imagination*, ed. Nelson Lichtenstein and Elizabeth Tandy Shermer (Philadelphia: University of Pennsylvania Press, 2012), 32; "He Would Permit Private Soldiers to Incorporate," *Fort Wayne News and Sentinel* [Fort Wayne, IN], 2 August 1919, 4.

    6. "The American Legion," *New York Sun*, 19 March 1919, 8; "A. E. F. Boys Still Fighting," *Iola Daily Register* [Iola, KS], 12 February 1921, 8; *Journal of Proceedings of the Fifty-Fifth and Fifty-Sixth Annual Encampments of the Department of Minnesota, Grand Army of the Republic* (Minneapolis: Syndicate Printing Co., 1922), 136; Pamphlet, "First Annual Picnic, American Legion, Berrien County Posts," 17 July 1920, 8, Gertrude Conrad Collection, Western Michigan University Archives and Regional History Collection, Kalamazoo, MI. For the early organizational history of the American Legion, see William Pencak, *For God and Country: The American Legion, 1919–1941* (Boston: Northeastern University Press, 1989), 48–77.

    7. "Young Vets Honor G. A. R.," *Indianapolis Star*, 23 September 1920, 10; "Take No Action of Federation" and "Legion Will Not Act on Resolution," *The Sun* [Pittsburg, KS], 25 September 1920, 1; *Journal of Proceedings of the Fifty-Fourth Annual Encampment of the Department of Minnesota, Grand Army of the Republic, Held in Memorial Hall, Minneapolis, Minnesota, June 3d and 4th, 1920* (Minneapolis: Syndicate Printing Co., 1920), 51; Sons of Veterans membership book, "The Organization, Sons of Veterans, U.S.A., the Reasons for Existence, Its Duties and Privileges and Methods for Increasing Its Membership," 1924, 4, in carton 9, Pennsylvania Division, Sons of Veterans Collection, Pennsylvania State Archives, Harrisburg, PA.

    8. Newspaper clipping pasted in minute book entry, 23 April 1920, box 1, folder: Menominee, Grand Army of the Republic, Jean Worth Papers, Bentley Historical Library, Ann Arbor, MI (hereafter BHL); Annual Report of Post Patriotic Instructor, Kenosha, WI, 31 May 1920 and Annual Report of Post Patriotic Instructor, Manitowoc, WI, 9 June 1920, box 7, folder 5, Grand Army of the Republic, Department of Wisconsin records, Wisconsin Veterans Museum, Madison, WI (hereafter WVM); *Journal of Proceedings of the Fifty-Fourth Annual Encampment of the Department of Minnesota, Grand Army of the Republic, Held in Memorial Hall, Minneapolis, Minnesota, June 3^{d} and 4th, 1920* (Minneapolis: Syndicate Printing Co., 1920), 32. The divided sentiments between comrades representing the state and national encampments on the one hand and the local posts on the other is perhaps not altogether surprising. Officials at the state and national encampments were typically healthier, more active, and a bit younger than the average GAR comrade. The significant work and travel associated with being

a high-level GAR official may have masked the reality that many veterans, by this time, did indeed see that their lives were nearing the end. Members of the local posts were always cognizant of the steady decline of their units. At nearly every post meeting, reports and resolutions of respect were issued in honor of the latest comrade who had passed away. This phenomenon, although acknowledged at state and national encampments, was more often glossed over by GAR officials whose duty it was to advertise a still-robust and active organization.

 9. Marc Leepson, *Flag: An American Biography* (New York: St. Martin's Griffin, 2005), 194; Larry Ceplair, *Anti-Communism in Twentieth-Century America: A Critical History* (Santa Barbara, CA: Praeger, 2011), 38. For more on the American Legion's conflict with the WWV, see Regin Schmidt, *Red Scare: FBI and the Origins of Anticommunism in the United States, 1919–1943* (Copenhagen, Denmark: Museum Tusculanum Press, 2000), 109–15.

 10. Pencak, *For God and Country*, 69; Anthony F. Gero, *Black Soldiers of New York State: A Proud Legacy* (Albany: State University of New York Press, 2009), 67; "The Grand Army of Americans Being Formed at Capital," *Monitor* [Omaha, NE], 24 May 1919, 4; Chad L. Williams, *Torchbearers of Democracy: African American Soldiers in the World War I Era* (Chapel Hill: University of North Carolina Press, 2010), 279; 1923 American Legion national convention resolution quoted in Jonathan H. Ebel, *Faith in the Fight: Religion and the American Soldier in the Great War* (Princeton, NJ: Princeton University Press, 2010), 185. For comparison's sake, a concurrent resolution from a Wisconsin Sons of Veterans camp (which, by this point, contained a number of Great War veterans) took a much stronger stand against the Klan. Taking their cue from their GAR fathers and grandfathers, the Sons resolved "that membership in [the] Klan is incompatible with membership in any Patriotic Order, and a proper cause for expulsion from the same." See resolutions of Henry Harnden Camp No. 2, Division of Wisconsin, Sons of Veterans, ca. 1920s, box 1, folder 5, Sons of Union Veterans Henry Harden Camp No. 2 Records, WVM.

 11. National encampment circular, 1926, folder: miscellaneous papers, Grand Army of the Republic, C. J. Dickerson Post No. 6, BHL; Old Guard Post No. 7 resolutions, GAR Department of Nebraska, box 3, folder 1, Grand Army of the Republic, Department of Nebraska Records, Nebraska State Historical Society, Lincoln, NE; GAR Department of Illinois resolutions, 26 June 1924, box 62, folder 8, William K. Buchanan Papers, U.S. Army Heritage and Education Center, Carlisle, PA; Minute book entry, 27 December 1928, George Washington Post No. 103 minute book, box 91, folder 1, New York State Historian Grand Army of the Republic Records, New York State Archives, Albany, NY; "G.A.R. Protests in Vain On 'Gone With the Wind,'" *Pittsburgh Post-Gazette*, 1 September 1939, 6; "Union Veterans Name Leaders, Evacuate City," *Pittsburgh Press*, 1 September 1939, 38.

 12. Letter of George H. Pounder to comrade, 26 January 1934, box 1, folder 2, Grand Army of the Republic, Department of Wisconsin Records, WVM; "Last Few Survivors Sound Taps Over GAR," *Indianapolis News*, 1 September 1949, 21; Photocopy of "Taps Sound for Grand Army of the Republic," *The Banner* 60, no. 5 (August 1956) in vertical file, Albert Woolson Papers, Northeast Minnesota Historical Center, University of

Minnesota Duluth, Duluth, MN; Brian Matthew Jordan, "Grand Old Men: The Last Veterans and Civil War Memory in the Mid-Twentieth Century," in *Civil War Monuments and Memory: Favorite Stories and Fresh Perspectives from the Historians at Emerging Civil War*, ed. Jonathan Tracey and Chris Mackowski (El Dorado Hills, CA: Savas Beatie, 2022), 255–63.

13. Speech of J. C. Plank before the encampment of the Department of Colorado and Wyoming at Grand Junction, Colorado, June 1924, box 5, folder 15, Grand Army of the Republic Collection, Oregon Historical Society, Portland, OR. As this book has emphasized, Grand Army veterans had long identified their organization as one of accomplishment. For a Union veteran's much earlier use of the phrase "a monument of achievement" to describe the GAR's activism, see Robert B. Beath, *History of the Grand Army of the Republic* (New York: Bryan, Taylor and Co., 1889), 358.

Bibliography

Primary Sources

Manuscripts

Andrew Carnegie Free Library and Music Hall, Carnegie, Pennsylvania
    Thomas Espy Post Collection
Archives of Industrial Society, University of Pittsburgh, Pittsburgh, Pennsylvania
    Allegheny County Grand Army Association Records
Archives of Michigan, Lansing, Michigan
    Grand Army of the Republic Collection
Bentley Historical Library, University of Michigan, Ann Arbor, Michigan
    Grand Army of the Republic, C. J. Dickerson Post No. 6 Records
    Jean Worth Papers
    William Herbert Withington Papers
Butler Area Public Library, Genealogy and Special Collections Room, Butler, Pennsylvania
    Grand Army of the Republic Vertical File
Delaware Historical Society, Wilmington, Delaware
    Ada Anderson Collection
    GAR Records, Department of Delaware
Detre Library and Archives, Heinz History Center, Pittsburgh, Pennsylvania
    Grand Army of the Republic, General James B. McPherson Post No. 117 Records
    Grand Army of the Republic, Major William G. Lowry Post No. 548 Records
Filson Historical Society, Louisville, Kentucky
    Grand Army of the Republic, 1895 Encampment Records
Lyon County History Center, Emporia, Kansas
    Lyon County Photograph Collection
Mason City Public Library, Lee P. Loomis Archive, Mason City, Iowa
    Memorial University Collection
Massachusetts Historical Society, Boston, Massachusetts
    Grand Army of the Republic, E. W. Kinsley Post No. 113 Records
Minnesota Historical Society, St. Paul, Minnesota
    Ell Torrance Papers
    Grand Army of the Republic, Department of Minnesota Records
    Henry A. Castle Papers
    Josiah B. Chaney and Family Papers
Nebraska State Historical Society, Lincoln, Nebraska
    Grand Army of the Republic, Department of Nebraska Records

New England Civil War Museum and Research Center, Rockville, Connecticut
    Thomas F. Burpee Post No. 71 Collection
New Hampshire Historical Society, Concord, New Hampshire
    Concord Public Library Historical Materials
    GAR Sheridan Post No. 14 Records
    Joab N. Patterson Papers
    Journal of the Encampments, Department of New Hampshire Records
New York State Archives, Albany, New York
    New York State Historian, Grand Army of the Republic Records
Northeast Minnesota Historical Center, University of Minnesota Duluth, Duluth, Minnesota
    Albert Woolson Papers
    Grand Army of the Republic Records
Office of the Livingston County Historian, Mount Morris, New York
    Livingston County Military; Monuments, Memorials, and Organizations Collection
Oregon Historical Society, Portland, Oregon
    Grand Army of the Republic Collection
Pennsylvania State Archives, Harrisburg, Pennsylvania
    Pennsylvania Division, Sons of Veterans Collection
Rhode Island Historical Society, Providence, Rhode Island
    Elisha Hunt Rhodes Papers
    Rhode Island Department, Grand Army of the Republic Collection
Soldiers and Sailors Memorial Hall and Museum, Pittsburgh, Pennsylvania
    Allegheny County Grand Army Association Collection
    Grand Army of the Republic Collection
    Soldiers' Memorial Hall Committee Collection
    Union Veteran Legion Collection
State Historical Society of Iowa, Des Moines, Iowa
    Grand Army of the Republic Correspondence Records
    Grand Army of the Republic Post Records
    Grand Army of the Republic Subject Files
    Woman's Relief Corps Records
State Historical Society of Iowa, Iowa City, Iowa
    Isaac N. Carr Papers
Syracuse University Special Collections Research Center, Syracuse, New York
    Grand Army of the Republic, Department of New York Collection
Toledo-Lucas County Public Library, Toledo, Ohio
    Toledo Soldiers Memorial Association Collection
Tulane University, Howard-Tilton Memorial Library, New Orleans, Louisiana
    Grand Army of the Republic, Joseph A. Mower Post No. 1 Records
US Army Heritage and Education Center, Carlisle, Pennsylvania
    Civil War Pamphlets: Massachusetts Monuments and Memorials
    Grand Army of the Republic, Sedgwick Post No. 17 Records
    Thornton Family Collection

William K. Buchanan Papers
Vermont Historical Society, Barre, Vermont
 GAR Roberts Post No. 14 Record Books Collection
Western Michigan University Archives and Regional History Collection, Kalamazoo, Michigan
 Gertrude Conrad Collection
Wisconsin Historical Society, Madison, Wisconsin
 James Whitehead Papers
 Jerome A. Watrous Papers
Wisconsin Veterans Museum, Madison, Wisconsin
 Augustus Weissert Collection
 Grand Army of the Republic, Department of Wisconsin Records
 Grand Army of the Republic, Memorial Hall Records
 Panoramic Photographs of Veterans Organizations Collection
 Sons of Veterans Henry Harnden Camp No. 2 Records

Manuscript Collection (Internet)

Uriah W. Oblinger Collection, Library of Congress / Nebraska State Historical Society, http://memory.loc.gov/ammem/award98/nbhihtml/aboutoblinger.html.

Periodicals

Adams County News (Gettysburg, PA)
Advertiser (Lawrence, KS)
Age (York, PA)
Akron Beacon and Republican (Akron, OH)
Akron Evening Times (Akron, OH)
Alaska Daily Empire (Juneau, AK)
Albuquerque Daily Citizen (Albuquerque, NM)
Allentown Morning Call (Allentown, PA)
Altoona Tribune (Altoona, PA)
Argus-Leader (Sioux Falls, SD)
Arizona Daily Star (Tucson, AZ)
Arizona Republican (Phoenix, AZ)
Army and Navy Register (Washington, D.C.)
Asbury Park Press (Asbury Park, NJ)
Aurora Beacon News (Aurora, IL)
Austin Weekly Statesman (Austin, TX)
Baltimore Sun (Baltimore, MD)
Bangor Daily Whig and Courier (Bangor, ME)
Belleville Telescope (Belleville, KS)
Boston Globe (Boston, MA)
Boston Post (Boston, MA)
Brooklyn Daily Eagle (Brooklyn, NY)

Brownsville Herald (Brownsville, TX)
Buffalo Commercial (Buffalo, NY)
Buffalo Enquirer (Buffalo, NY)
Buffalo Evening News (Buffalo, NY)
Buffalo Evening Times (Buffalo, NY)
Buffalo Review (Buffalo, NY)
Burlington Daily Free Press (Burlington, VT)
Burlington Weekly Free Press (Burlington, VT)
Bystander (Des Moines, IA)
Carlisle Evening Herald (Carlisle, PA)
Charleston Daily Mail (Charleston, WV)
Chicago Tribune (Chicago, IL)
Christian Union (New York, NY)
Cincinnati Enquirer (Cincinnati, OH)
Clare Democrat and Press (Clare, MI)
Commercial Herald (Vicksburg, MS)
Copper Country Evening News (Calumet, MI)
County Record (Kingstree, SC)
Daily American (Nashville, TN)
Daily Argus-Leader (Sioux Falls, SD)
Daily Arkansas Gazette (Little Rock, AR)
Daily Bulletin (Honolulu, HI)
Daily Capital Journal (Salem, OR)
Daily Gate City (Keokuk, IA)
Daily Herald (Honolulu, HI)
Daily Leader (Lexington, KY)
Daily Nebraska State Journal (Lincoln, NE)
Daily New Era (Lancaster, PA)
Daily Northwestern (Oshkosh, WI)
Daily Pacific Commercial Advertiser (Honolulu, HI)
Daily Picayune (New Orleans, LA)
Daily Telegram (Eau Claire, WI)
Daily Times (Davenport, IA)
Dalton Enterprise (Dalton, NY)
Democrat and Chronicle (Rochester, NY)
Des Moines Register (Des Moines, IA)
Deseret Weekly (Salt Lake City, UT)
Detroit Free Press (Detroit, MI)
Douglas Island News (Douglas City, AK)
Eau Claire Leader (Eau Claire, WI)
Emporia Gazette (Emporia, KS)
Emporia Weekly Gazette (Emporia, KS)
Essex County Herald (Guildhall, VT)
Evening Dispatch (York, PA)

BIBLIOGRAPHY 249

Evening Journal (Wilmington, DE)
Evening News (Harrisburg, PA)
Evening Public Ledger (Philadelphia, PA)
Evening Star (Washington, D.C.)
Evening State Journal (Lincoln, NE)
Evening Times-Republican (Marshalltown, IA)
Fitchburg Daily Sentinel (Fitchburg, MA)
Fort Wayne News and Sentinel (Fort Wayne, IN)
Frankfort Daily Index (Frankfort, KS)
Freeport Journal-Standard (Freeport, IL)
Genesee County Express (Dansville, NY)
Gettysburg Times (Gettysburg, PA)
Grand Army Advocate (Des Moines, IA)
Grand Rapids Press (Grand Rapids, MI)
Granite Monthly (Concord, NH)
Green Bay Press-Gazette (Green Bay, WI)
Harrisburg Daily Independent (Harrisburg, PA)
Harrisburg Telegraph (Harrisburg, PA)
Hartford Courant (Hartford, CT)
Hinton Daily News (Hinton, WV)
Honolulu Advertiser (Honolulu, HI)
Honolulu Star-Bulletin (Honolulu, HI)
Houston Daily Post (Houston, TX)
Huntington Democrat (Huntington, IN)
Hutchinson News (Hutchinson, KS)
Indiana Gazette (Indiana, PA)
Indianapolis Journal (Indianapolis, IN)
Indianapolis News (Indianapolis, IN)
Indianapolis Recorder (Indianapolis, IN)
Indianapolis Star (Indianapolis, IN)
Inter Ocean (Chicago, IL)
Iola Daily Register (Iola, KS)
Kalamazoo Gazette (Kalamazoo, MI)
Kansas City Advocate (Kansas City, KS)
Kansas City Gazette (Kansas City, KS)
Kansas City Journal (Kansas City, MO)
Lancaster Examiner (Lancaster, PA)
Lansing State Journal (Lansing, MI)
Lawrence Daily Journal (Lawrence, KS)
Leavenworth Times (Leavenworth, KS)
Lincoln Daily News (Lincoln, NE)
Lincoln Star (Lincoln, NE)
Livingston Republican (Geneseo, NY)
Long Beach Press (Long Beach, CA)

Los Angeles Times (Los Angeles, CA)
Los Angeles Herald (Los Angeles, CA)
Manitoba Morning Free Press (Winnipeg, MB)
Mansfield News (Mansfield, OH)
Mason City Globe-Gazette (Mason City, IA)
Mining Magazine (London, UK)
Minneapolis Journal (Minneapolis, MN)
Minneapolis Morning Tribune (Minneapolis, MN)
Minneapolis Sunday Tribune (Minneapolis, MN)
Minneapolis Times (Minneapolis, MN)
Monitor (Omaha, NE)
Morning News (Lancaster, PA)
Morning News (Wilmington, DE)
Morning Oregonian (Portland, OR)
Mount Carmel Item (Mt. Carmel, PA)
Moving Picture World (New York, NY)
Muncie Morning Star (Muncie, IN)
Nashville American (Nashville, TN)
Nashville Tennessean (Nashville, TN)
Natchez Democrat (Natchez, MS)
National Republican (Washington, D.C.)
National Tribune (Washington, D.C.)
Nebraska State Journal (Lincoln, NE)
New Bern Weekly Journal (New Bern, NC)
New Berne Daily Journal (New Bern, NC)
New Castle Herald (New Castle, PA)
New Era (Lancaster, PA)
New Haven Evening Register (New Haven, CT)
New York Daily Tribune (New York, NY)
New York Sun (New York, NY)
New York Times (New York, NY)
New York Tribune (New York, NY)
Newport Mercury (Newport, RI)
Newton Daily Republican (Newton, KS)
North Adams Transcript (North Adams, MA)
North American Review (Boston, MA)
North Carolinian (Elizabeth City, NC)
Nunda News (Nunda, NY)
Oakland Tribune (Oakland, CA)
Omaha Daily Bee (Omaha, NE)
Oregon Daily Journal (Portland, OR)
Oregon Statesman (Salem, OR)
Oshkosh Daily Northwestern (Oshkosh, WI)
Parsons Daily Sun (Parsons, KS)

BIBLIOGRAPHY   251

Passaic Daily News (Passaic, NJ)
Philadelphia Inquirer (Philadelphia, PA)
Philadelphia Times (Philadelphia, PA)
Pittsburgh Commercial Gazette (Pittsburgh, PA)
Pittsburgh Gazette (Pittsburgh, PA)
Pittsburgh Gazette Times (Pittsburgh, PA)
Pittsburgh Post (Pittsburgh, PA)
Pittsburgh Post-Gazette (Pittsburgh, PA)
Pittsburgh Press (Pittsburgh, PA)
Plainfield Courier-News (Plainfield, NJ)
Port Huron Times-Herald (Port Huron, MI)
Postville Graphic (Postville, IA)
Providence News (Providence, RI)
Public Opinion (New York, NY)
Pullman Herald (Pullman, WA)
Reading Times (Reading, PA)
Record Times (Wilkes-Barre, PA)
Rochester Times-Union (Rochester, NY)
Rockford Daily Register-Gazette (Rockford, IL)
Rockford Republic (Rockford, IL)
Sacramento Daily Record-Union (Sacramento, CA)
Salt Lake Herald (Salt Lake City, UT)
Salt Lake Tribune (Salt Lake City, UT)
San Francisco Call (San Francisco, CA)
San Francisco Chronicle (San Francisco, CA)
Scioto Gazette (Chillicothe, OH)
Scranton Republican (Scranton, PA)
Scranton Tribune (Scranton, PA)
Scranton Tribune-Republican (Scranton, PA)
Scranton Truth (Scranton, PA)
Social Hygiene Bulletin (New York, NY)
Springfield Republican (Springfield, MA)
St. Johnsbury Caledonian (St. Johnsbury, VT)
St. Paul Daily Globe (St. Paul, MN)
Standard Union (Brooklyn, NY)
State (Columbia, SC)
Station Agent (Chicago, IL)
Successful American (New York, NY)
Sun (New Bern, NC)
Sun (Pittsburg, KS)
Times-Democrat (New Orleans, LA)
Topeka Capital-Commonwealth (Topeka, KS)
Topeka Daily Capital (Topeka, KS)
Topeka Plaindealer (Topeka, KS)

Topeka State Journal (Topeka, KS)
Topeka State Press (Topeka, KS)
True Northerner (Paw Paw, MI)
Trust Companies (New York, NY)
Vancouver Daily World (Vancouver, BC)
Vermont Phoenix (Brattleboro, VT)
Vermonter (St. Albans, VT)
Washington Herald (Washington, D.C.)
Washington Standard (Olympia, WA)
Washington Times (Washington, D.C.)
Watauga Democrat (Boone, NC)
Wausau Daily Herald (Wausau, WI)
Webster City Freeman (Webster City, IA)
Weekly Democrat (Natchez, MS)
Weekly Herald-Despatch [sic] (Decatur, IL)
Weekly Press (Kansas City, KS)
Weekly Star (Wilmington, NC)
West Bay City Times-Press (West Bay City, MI)
Wichita Daily Eagle (Wichita, KS)
Wilkes-Barre Daily News (Wilkes-Barre, PA)
Wilkes-Barre Record (Wilkes-Barre, PA)
Wilmington Dispatch (Wilmington, NC)
Wilmington Messenger (Wilmington, NC)
Winnipeg Tribune (Winnipeg, MB)
Wyandotte Gazette (Kansas City, KS)
York Democratic Press (York, PA)

Published Primary Sources

Acts and Resolves Passed by the General Assembly of the State of Rhode Island and Providence Plantations, at the January Session, 1912. Providence, RI: E. L. Freeman Company, 1912.

Address of Department Commander Samuel S. Burdett, at the 16th Annual Encampment of the Department of the Potomac, G.A.R., Washington, D.C., Jan. 30, 1884. Washington, D.C.: n.p., 1884.

Aikens, Andrew Jackson, and Lewis A. Proctor, eds. *Wisconsin Men of Progress in 1897: A Selected List of Biographical Sketches and Portraits of the Leaders in Business, Professional and Official Life, Together with Short Notes on the History and Character of Wisconsin*. Milwaukee: The Evening Wisconsin Company, 1897.

An Address by the Hawaiian Branches of the Sons of the American Revolution, Sons of Veterans, and Grand Army of the Republic to Their Compatriots in America Concerning the Annexation of Hawaii. Washington, D.C.: Gibson Brothers, 1897.

"Annual Catalogue of Grant University, Chattanooga and Athens, Tenn., 1902, with Announcements for 1902–1903." Athens, TN: Grant Memorial University, 1902.

BIBLIOGRAPHY

Annual Report of the President to the Corporation of Brown University, October 13, 1909. Providence, RI: Brown University, 1909.

Annual Report of the Quartermaster-General of the Army to the Secretary of War for the Fiscal Year Ended June 30, 1900. Washington, D.C.: Government Printing Office, 1900.

Armstrong, Samuel Chapman. *Ideas on Education Expressed by Samuel Chapman Armstrong.* Hampton, VA: Hampton Institute Press, 1908.

Badlam, Alexander. *The Wonders of Alaska.* San Francisco, CA: n.p., 1891.

Bakewell, Allan C. *Report of Allan C. Bakewell, Chief Aide on Military Instruction and Patriotic Education in Schools, to John R. King, Commander-in-Chief, Grand Army of the Republic.* n.p., 1905.

Barton, Clara. *The Story of My Childhood.* New York: The Baker & Taylor Co., 1907.

Bateman, Newton, and Paul Selby, eds. *Historical Encyclopedia of Illinois and History of Kendall County.* Vol. 2. Chicago: Munsell Publishing Company, 1914.

Beath, Robert B. *History of the Grand Army of the Republic.* New York: Bryan, Taylor and Co., 1889.

"Bulletin of Memorial University, Mason City, Iowa." Mason City, IA: n.p., dates vary.

Carnahan, J. Worth. *Manual of the Civil War and Key to the Grand Army of the Republic and Kindred Societies.* Chicago: Easel Monument Association, 1897.

"Catalogue, Grant Memorial University, 1887–1888." Athens, TN: Grant Memorial University, 1887.

Ceremony of Flag Presentation to Columbia University of the City of New York, May Second, 1896, and May Seventh, 1898 by Lafayette Post, No. 140, Department of New York, Grand Army of the Republic. New York: n.p., 1899.

Champlin, John Denison, ed. *Orations, Addresses and Speeches of Chauncey M. Depew.* Vol. 1. New York: n.p., 1910.

Chipman, N. P. *The Tragedy of Andersonville: Trial of Captain Henry Wirz, the Prison Keeper.* San Francisco, CA: Blair Murdock Company, 1911.

Compendium of History, Reminiscence, and Biography of Nebraska Containing a History of the State of Nebraska. Chicago: Alden Publishing Company, 1912.

Congressional Record: Containing the Proceedings and Debates of the First Session of the Sixty-Fifth Congress of the United States of America. Vol. 55. Washington, D.C.: Government Printing Office, 1917.

Connelley, William E., ed. *A Standard History of Kansas and Kansans.* Various volumes. Chicago: Lewis Publishing Company, 1919.

Constitution and Rules and Regulations of the United Spanish War Veterans. Chicago: H. L. Ruggles and Co., 1929.

Custer, Elizabeth B. *"Boots and Saddles"; or, Life in Dakota with General Custer.* New York: Harper & Brothers, 1885.

———. *Tenting on the Plains; or, General Custer in Kansas and Texas.* New York: Charles L. Webster & Company, 1887.

Cutter, William Richard, ed. *New England Families, Genealogical and Memorial: A Record of the Achievements of Her People in the Making of Commonwealths and the Founding of a Nation.* Vol. 2. New York: Lewis Historical Publishing Co., 1914.

Davis, Katharine Bement. "Women's Education in Social Hygiene." *The Annals of the American Academy of Political and Social Science* 79 (September 1918): 167–77.

Davis, Washington. *Camp-Fire Chats of the Civil War; Being the Incident, Adventure and Wayside Exploit of the Bivouac and Battle Field, as Related by Veteran Soldiers Themselves.* Chicago: Lewis Publishing Company, 1888.

Dedication Services of the Memorial Library and Grand Army Hall at Manchester-by-the-Sea, Massachusetts, October 13, 1887. Boston: Franklin Press, 1888.

Donaldson, Thomas. *The Public Domain: Its History, with Statistics.* Washington, D.C.: Government Printing Office, 1884.

Early History of the Department of Massachusetts, G.A.R., from 1866 to 1880 Inclusive. Boston: E. B. Stillings and Co., 1895.

Eliot, Charles W. *A National University. Report Made by Charles W. Eliot, President of Harvard University, to the National Educational Association, (Department of Higher Instruction) August 5, 1873.* Cambridge, MA: Charles W. Sever, 1874.

Erastus Milo Cravath. New York: Devinne Press, 1900.

Fletcher, Thomas C., et al. *Life and Reminiscences of General William T. Sherman by Distinguished Men of His Time.* Baltimore, MD: R. H. Woodward Co., 1891.

Gannon, Thomas F., ed. *Proceedings of the United Spanish War Veterans, Department of New York, for the Year 1919, New Rochelle, N.Y., July 13, 14, 15 and 16, 1919.* Albany, NY: J. B. Lyon Company, 1920.

Gaston, Joseph. *Portland, Oregon: Its History and Builders in Connection with the Antecedent Explorations, Discoveries and Movements of the Pioneers that Selected the Site for the Great City of the Pacific.* Vol. 3. Chicago: S. J. Clarke Publishing Company, 1911.

Gaston, W. L., and A. R. Humphrey. *History of Custer County, Nebraska.* Lincoln, NE: Western Publishing and Engraving Company, 1919.

Grand Army of the Republic. *Journal of the National Encampment.* Publishers, dates, and places of publication vary.

Grand Army of the Republic, Department of California. *Proceedings of the Annual Encampment of the Department of California.* Publishers, dates, and places of publication vary.

Grand Army of the Republic, Department of Colorado and Wyoming. *Journal of the Annual Encampment of the Department of Colorado and Wyoming.* Publishers, dates, and places of publication vary.

Grand Army of the Republic, Department of Delaware. *Journal of the Annual Encampment of the Department of Delaware.* Publishers, dates, and places of publication vary.

Grand Army of the Republic, Department of Iowa. *Journal of the Annual Encampment of the Department of Iowa.* Publishers, dates, and places of publication vary.

Grand Army of the Republic, Department of Kansas. *Journal of the Annual Encampment of the Department of Kansas.* Publishers, dates, and places of publication vary.

Grand Army of the Republic, Department of Maine, *Journal of the Annual Encampment of the Department of Maine.* Publishers, dates, and places of publication vary.

Grand Army of the Republic, Department of Massachusetts. *Journal of the Annual Encampment of the Department of Massachusetts.* Publishers, dates, and places of publication vary.

Grand Army of the Republic, Department of Michigan. *Journal of the Annual Encampment of the Department of Michigan.* Publishers, dates, and places of publication vary.

Grand Army of the Republic, Department of Minnesota. *Journal of Proceedings of the Annual Encampment of the Department of Minnesota.* Publishers, dates, and places of publication vary.

Grand Army of the Republic, Department of Missouri. *Proceedings of the Annual Encampment of the Department of Missouri.* Publishers, dates, and places of publication vary.

Grand Army of the Republic, Department of Nebraska. *Journal of the Annual Encampment of the Department of Nebraska.* Publishers, dates, and places of publication vary.

Grand Army of the Republic, Department of New Hampshire, *Journal of Proceedings of the Annual Encampment of the Department of New Hampshire.* Publishers, dates, and places of publication vary.

Grand Army of the Republic, Department of New Jersey. *Proceedings of the Annual Encampment of the Department of New Jersey.* Publishers, dates, and places of publication vary.

Grand Army of the Republic, Department of New York. *Abstract of General Orders and Proceedings of the Annual Encampment of the Department of New York.* Publishers, dates, and places of publication vary.

Grand Army of the Republic, Department of Ohio. *Journal of the Annual Encampment of the Department of Ohio.* Publishers, dates, and places of publication vary.

Grand Army of the Republic, Department of Pennsylvania. *Proceedings of the Annual Encampment of the Department of Pennsylvania.* Publishers, dates, and places of publication vary.

Grand Army of the Republic, Department of Rhode Island. *Journal of the Annual Encampment of the Department of Rhode Island.* Publishers, dates, and places of publication vary.

Grand Army of the Republic, Department of Tennessee. *Journal of Proceedings of the Annual Encampment of the Department of Tennessee.* Publishers, dates, and places of publication vary.

Grand Army of the Republic, Department of the Potomac. *Journal of Proceedings of the Annual Encampment of the Department of the Potomac.* Publishers, dates, and places of publication vary.

Grand Army of the Republic, Department of Vermont. *Journal of Proceedings of the Annual Encampment of the Department of Vermont.* Publishers, dates, and places of publication vary.

Grieves, Loren C. *The New Grand Army of the Republic and Its Publication.* Kansas City, MO: Post Printing and Publishing Co., 1919.

Haddad, George. *Mt. Lebanon to Vermont: Autobiography of George Haddad, Taken Down by His Daughter Emily Marie Haddad with the Assistance of Berenice Rachel Tuttle.* Rutland, VT: Tuttle Company, 1916.

Hand, H. Wells, ed. *Centennial History of the Town of Nunda, 1808–1908.* Rochester, NY: Rochester Herald Press, 1908.

Hart, Albert Bushnell, ed. *Selected Addresses and Public Papers of Woodrow Wilson*. New York: Modern Library, 1918.
Hartshorn, W. N., ed. *An Era of Progress and Promise, 1863–1910: The Religious, Moral, and Educational Development of the American Negro Since His Emancipation*. Boston: Priscilla Publishing Company, 1910.
Harwood, W. S. "Secret Societies in America." *North American Review* 164, no. 486 (May 1897): 617–24.
Hay, John. *Pike County Ballads and Other Pieces*. Boston: James R. Osgood and Co., 1871.
History of Mason County, Michigan, with Illustrations and Biographical Sketches of Some of Its Prominent Men and Pioneers. Chicago: H. R. Page and Co., 1882.
History of Porter County, Indiana: A Narrative Account of Its Historical Progress, Its People and Its Principal Interests. Vol. 1. Chicago: Lewis Publishing Company, 1912.
House Journal. Proceedings of the House of Representatives of the State of Kansas. Sixth Biennial Session, Begun at Topeka, January 8, 1889. Topeka: Kansas Publishing House, 1889.
Howard, Oliver O. "Lincoln's Monument in the Mountains." *The National Magazine: An Illustrated American Monthly* 22 (April–September 1905): 299–304.
Hoyt, John W. *Memorial in Regard to a National University*. Washington, D.C.: Government Printing Office, 1892.
Hunter, Paul F., ed. *Wisconsin Blue Book, 1919*. Madison, WI: Democrat Printing Company, 1919.
Jennings, Janet. *The Blue and the Gray*. Madison, WI: Cantwell Printing Co., 1910.
Johnson, Alfred S., ed. *The Cyclopedic Review of Current History*. Vol 5. Buffalo, NY: Garretson, Cox, and Co., 1896.
Journal of the House of Representatives of the Twenty-Fourth General Assembly of the State of Iowa, Which Convened at the Capitol in Des Moines, Iowa, January 11, 1892. Des Moines, IA: G. H. Ragsdale, 1892.
Kellogg, Paul Underwood, ed. *The Pittsburgh Survey: Wage-Earning Pittsburgh*. New York: Survey Associates, 1914.
Kennedy, Joseph C. G. *Population of the United States in 1860; Compiled from the Original Returns of the Eighth Census, Under the Direction of the Secretary of the Interior*. Washington, D.C.: Government Printing Office, 1864.
Klise, Harrold E., ed. *Official Register, Twenty-Seventh Number*. Des Moines: State of Iowa, 1917.
Leonard, A. C. *Grand Army of the Republic Hand Book*. n.p., 1884.
———. *The Boys in Blue of 1861–1865: A Condensed History Worth Preserving*. Lancaster, PA: New Era Printing Company, 1904.
Lester, John C., and D. L. Wilson. *Ku Klux Klan: Its Origin, Growth and Disbandment*. New York: Neale Publishing Company, 1905.
Letters and Messages of Rutherford B. Hayes, President of the United States, Together with Letters of Acceptance and Inaugural Address. Washington, D.C.: n.p., 1881.
Logan, John A. *The Volunteer Soldier of America with Memoir of the Author and Military Reminiscences from General Logan's Private Journal*. Chicago: R. S. Peale and Company, 1887.

Lovering, Joseph F. *Services for the Use of the Grand Army of the Republic.* Boston: E. B. Stillings and Co., 1881.
Martin, George W., ed. *Collections of the Kansas State Historical Society, 1909–1910.* Vol. 11. Topeka, KS: State Printing Office, 1910.
Martin, John A. *Addresses: By John A. Martin, Delivered in Kansas.* Topeka: Kansas Publishing House, 1888.
———. "The Progress of Kansas." *North American Review* 142, no. 353 (April 1886): 348–55.
McGillicuddy, T. D., ed. *Proceedings of the Annual and Semi-Annual Encampments of the Department of Ohio, Grand Army of the Republic, for the First Fourteen Years of Its Existence.* Columbus, OH: F. J. Heer Printing Co., 1912.
McKinney, William M. *Federal Statutes Annotated: Second Edition, Containing All the Laws of the United States of a General, Permanent and Public Nature in Force on the First Day of January, 1916.* Vol. 3. Northport, NY: Edward Thompson Co., 1917.
Myers, Frank Elliott. "Defenders of the Union." *Overland Monthly* 28 (July 1896): 53–81.
———. "Defenders of the Union: Grand Army of the Republic on the Pacific Coast." *Overland Monthly* 27 (March 1896): 434–62.
Moulton, Henry W. *Moulton Annals.* Chicago: Edward A. Claypool, 1906.
National Security League. *Report of Director of Branches Read at the Annual Meeting, May 3, 1916.* New York: NSL Headquarters, 1916.
Nichols, Charles Sumner. "A Patriotic Ideal." *The National Magazine: An Illustrated American Monthly* 14 (April–September 1901): 443–45.
Ninth Report of the Free Public Library Commission of Massachusetts. Boston: Wright and Potter, 1899.
Ordinances of the City of Philadelphia, from January 1 to December 31, 1906 and Opinions of the City Solicitor. Philadelphia: Dunlap Printing Company, 1907.
Orton, Edward, Jr. *The Status of the Military Department in the Land-Grant Colleges.* Washington, D.C.: Government Printing Office, 1914.
Osborn, John R. *An Historical Sketch of the Rise and Progress of the Toledo Soldiers Memorial Association.* Toledo, OH: Barkdull Printing, 1883.
Parker, George F., ed. *The Writings and Speeches of Grover Cleveland.* New York: Cassell Publishing Co., 1892.
Past and Present of Adams County, Nebraska. Vol. 2. Chicago: S. J. Clarke Publishing Co., 1916.
Portrait and Biographical Album of Lancaster County, Nebraska, Containing Full Page Portraits and Biographical Sketches of Prominent and Representative Citizens of the County. Chicago: Chapman Brothers, 1888.
Presentation of a National Flag to the College of the City of New York on Friday Evening, June 8, 1888 in the Academy of Music by Lafayette Post, No. 140, Department of New York, Grand Army of the Republic. New York: J. J. Little, 1888.
Proceedings of the Seventeenth Department Encampment, United Spanish War Veterans, June 30th, and July 1st 1916, Racine, Wisconsin. n.p., 1916.
Report of the Proceedings of the Society of the Army of the Tennessee at the Fourteenth Annual Meeting, Held at Cincinnati, Ohio, April 6th and 7th, 1881. Cincinnati, OH: Society of the Army of the Tennessee, 1885.

Roosevelt, Theodore. *The New Nationalism*. New York: The Outlook Company, 1910.

———. *The Rough Riders*. New York: Charles Scribner's Sons, 1899.

Schortemeier, Frederick E., ed. *Rededicating America: Life and Recent Speeches of Warren G. Harding*. Indianapolis, IN: Bobbs-Merrill Company, 1920.

Schuyler, Montgomery. "The Building of Pittsburgh." *Architectural Record* 30, no. 3 (September 1911): 204–82.

Shutter, Marion D., ed. *Progressive Men of Minnesota: Biographical Sketches and Portraits of the Leaders in Business, Politics and the Professions; Together with an Historical and Descriptive Sketch of the State*. Minneapolis: Minneapolis Journal, 1897.

Siddall, John William, ed. *Men of Hawaii: Being a Biographical Reference Library, Complete and Authentic, of the Men of Note and Substantial Achievement in the Hawaiian Islands*. Vol. 1. Honolulu, HI: Honolulu Star-Bulletin, 1917.

Smith, Harry Conklin, ed. *A Century of Vernon, Connecticut, 1808–1908*. Rockville, CT: T. F. Rady and Co., 1911.

Smith, James H. *History of Livingston County, New York with Illustrations and Biographical Sketches of Some of Its Prominent Men and Pioneers, 1687–1881*. Syracuse, NY: D. Mason and Co., 1881.

Soldiers' Memorial Building, Toledo, Ohio, in Honor and in Memory of Those Who Fought and Those Who Fell in Defense of Our Country During the War of the Rebellion. Toledo, OH: B. F. Wade Co., 1886.

Sons of Veterans. *Journal of Proceedings of the Annual Encampment of the Sons of Veterans*. Publishers, dates, and places of publication vary.

Sons of Veterans, Division of Ohio. *Journal of Proceedings of the Annual Encampment of the Division of Ohio, Sons of Veterans*. Publishers, dates, and places of publication vary.

Sons of Veterans, Division of Pennsylvania. *Journal of Proceedings of the Annual Encampment of the Division of Pennsylvania, Sons of Veterans*. Publishers, dates, and places of publication vary.

Sparks, Jared. *The Writings of George Washington*. Vol. 11. Boston: Russell, Shattuck, and Williams, 1838.

Stiles, Henry R. *The History and Genealogies of Ancient Windsor, Connecticut; Including East Windsor, South Windsor, Bloomfield, Windsor Locks, and Ellington, 1635–1891*. Vol. 1. Hartford, CT: Case, Lockwood, and Brainard, 1891.

Stocker, Corinne. "Northern Veterans Making Southern Homes." *The Illustrated American* 19, no. 318 (21 March 1896): 368–70.

Stolz, Gideon. *Memoirs of Sedgwick Post No. 10 G.A.R.* Salem, OR: n.p., 1931.

Stuart, I. L., ed. *History of Franklin County, Iowa: A Record of Settlement, Organization, Progress and Achievement*. Vol. 1. Chicago: S. J. Clarke, 1914.

Thayer, Christopher T. *Address Delivered at the Dedication of Memorial Hall, Lancaster, June 17, 1868*. Boston: Nichols and Noyes, 1868.

"The Catalogue of Brown University, One Hundred and Fifty-Sixth Year, 1919–1920." Providence, RI: Brown University, 1919.

Thirteenth Annual Report on Strikes and Lockouts for the Year 1912. Boston: Wright and Potter, 1913.

United Confederate Veterans. *Minutes of the Annual Meeting and Reunion of the United Confederate Veterans*. Publishers, dates, and places of publication vary.

United States Census Office. *Report on Population of the United States at the Eleventh Census: 1890*. Vol. 2. Washington, D.C.: Government Printing Office, 1897.

United States Congress. *Congressional Record: Containing the Proceedings and Debates of the Fifty-Ninth Congress, Second Session.* Vol. 41. Washington, D.C.: Government Printing Office, 1907.

———. *Journal of the House of Representatives of the United States, Being the Second Session of the Forty-Ninth Congress Begun and Held at the City of Washington, December 6, 1886, in the One Hundred and Eleventh Year of the Independence of the United States.* Washington, D.C.: Government Printing Office, 1886.

———. *Journal of the House of Representatives of the United States, Sixty-First Congress, First Session, Begun and Held at the City of Washington, April 2, 1917, in the One Hundred and Forty-First Year of the Independence of the United States.* Washington, D.C.: Government Printing Office, 1917.

United States Congress, Special Committee to Investigate the National Security League. *Hearings Before a Special Committee of the House of Representatives, Sixty-fifth Congress, Third Session on H. Res. 469 and H. Res. 276, to Investigate and Make Report as to the Officers, Activities and Purposes of the National Security League, a Corporation of New York, and of Any Associated Organizations, Parts 1–13.* Washington, D.C.: Government Printing Office, 1918.

United States Department of the Interior. *Report of the Commissioner of Education for the Year Ended June 30, 1909.* Vol. 2. Washington, D.C.: Government Printing Office, 1910.

United States Food Administration. *Bulletin No. 2.* Washington, D.C.: Government Printing Office, 1917.

"University of Pittsburgh Bulletin: General Catalog." Pittsburgh, PA: University of Pittsburgh, 1923.

Ward, Joseph Ripley Chandler. *History of George G. Meade Post No. One, Department of Pennsylvania Grand Army of the Republic.* Philadelphia: n.p., 1889.

Ward, William H., ed. *Records of Members of the Grand Army of the Republic with a Complete Account of the Twentieth National Encampment.* San Francisco, CA: H. S. Crocker and Co., 1886.

Washington, Booker T. "Industrial Education for the Negro." In *The Negro Problem: A Series of Articles by Representative American Negroes of Today.* New York: James Pott, 1903.

Watkins, Albert, ed. *History of Nebraska: From the Earliest Explorations to the Present Time with Portraits, Maps, and Tables.* Vol. 3. Lincoln, NE: Western Publishing and Engraving Company, 1913.

Weed, Cora Chaplin. *Hand Book for Iowa Soldiers' and Sailors' Monument.* n.p., 1897.

Whittemore, Edwin Carey. *The Centennial History of Waterville, Kennebec County, Maine.* Waterville, ME: Executive Committee of the Centennial Celebration, 1902.

Wilson, Henry. *History of the Rise and Fall of the Slave Power in America.* 3 vols. Boston: Houghton, Mifflin and Co., 1872.

Wilson, Oliver M. *The Grand Army of the Republic Under Its First Constitution and Ritual. Its Birth and Organization.* Kansas City, MO: Franklin Hudson Publishing Co., 1905.

Wilson, Woodrow. *Addresses of President Wilson: Addresses Delivered by President Wilson on His Western Tour, September 4 to September 25, 1919, on the League of Nations, Treaty of Peace with Germany, Industrial Conditions, High Cost of Living, Race Riots, etc.* Washington, D.C.: Government Printing Office, 1919.

Woman's Relief Corps. *Journal of the National Convention of the Woman's Relief Corps.* Publishers, dates, and places of publication vary.

Woman's Relief Corps, Department of Kansas. *Journal of the Annual Convention of the Department of Kansas, Woman's Relief Corps.* Publishers, dates, and places of publication vary.

Woman's Relief Corps, Department of Massachusetts. *Journal of the Annual Convention of the Department of Massachusetts, Woman's Relief Corps.* Publishers, dates, and places of publication vary.

Woman's Relief Corps, Department of South Dakota. *Journal of the Annual Convention of the Department of South Dakota, Woman's Relief Corps.* Publishers, dates, and places of publication vary.

Woman's Relief Corps, Department of Wisconsin. *Journal of the Annual Convention of the Department of Wisconsin, Woman's Relief Corps.* Publishers, dates, and places of publication vary.

"Yearbook, U.S. Grant University, Athens and Chattanooga, Tenn., 1891–1892." Athens, TN: Grant Memorial University, 1891.

Secondary Sources

Books

Anderson, James D. *The Education of Blacks in the South, 1860–1935.* Chapel Hill: University of North Carolina Press, 1988.

Attie, Jeanie. *Patriotic Toil: Northern Women and the American Civil War.* Ithaca, NY: Cornell University Press, 1998.

Ayers, Edward L. *The Promise of the New South: Life After Reconstruction.* New York: Oxford University Press, 1992.

Bederman, Gail. *Manliness and Civilization: A Cultural History of Gender and Race in the United States, 1880–1917.* Chicago: University of Chicago Press, 1995.

Bensel, Richard Franklin. *Yankee Leviathan: The Origins of Central State Authority in America, 1859–1877.* New York: Cambridge University Press, 1990.

Bigler, David L., and Will Bagley. *The Mormon Rebellion: America's First Civil War, 1857–1858.* Norman: University of Oklahoma Press, 2011.

Blair, William A. *Cities of the Dead: Contesting the Memory of the Civil War in the South, 1865–1914.* Chapel Hill: University of North Carolina Press, 2004.

Blight, David W. *Race and Reunion: The Civil War in American Memory.* Cambridge, MA: Harvard University Press, 2001.

Blumin, Stuart M. *The Emergence of the Middle Class: Social Experience in the American City, 1760–1900.* New York: Cambridge University Press, 1989.

Boyer, M. Christine. *Dreaming the Rational City: The Myth of American City Planning.* Cambridge, MA: MIT Press, 1983.

Boyko, John. *Blood and Daring: How Canada Fought the American Civil War and Forged a Nation*. Toronto: Alfred A. Knopf Canada, 2013.
Breisch, Kenneth A. *Henry Hobson Richardson and the Small Public Library in America: A Study in Typology*. Cambridge, MA: MIT Press, 1997.
Brewer, Susan A. *Why America Fights: Patriotism and War Propaganda from the Philippines to Iraq*. New York: Oxford University Press, 2009.
Bristow, Nancy K. *Making Men Moral: Social Engineering During the Great War*. New York: New York University Press, 1996.
Britten, Thomas A. *American Indians in World War I: At Home and at War*. Albuquerque: University of New Mexico Press, 1997.
Brubacher, John S., and Willis Rudy. *Higher Education in Transition: A History of American Colleges and Universities*. 4th edition. New Brunswick, NJ: Transaction Publishers, 1997.
Capozzola, Christopher. *Uncle Sam Wants You: World War I and the Making of the Modern American Citizen*. New York: Oxford University Press, 2008.
Carnes, Mark C. *Secret Ritual and Manhood in Victorian America*. New Haven, CT: Yale University Press, 1989.
Catton, Bruce. *Waiting for the Morning Train: An American Boyhood*. New York: Doubleday, 1972.
Ceplair, Larry. *Anti-Communism in Twentieth-Century America: A Critical History*. Santa Barbara, CA: Praeger, 2011.
Cherny, Robert W. *Populism, Progressivism, and the Transformation of Nebraska Politics, 1885–1915*. Lincoln: University of Nebraska Press, 1981.
Chudacoff, Howard P. *How Old Are You? Age Consciousness in American Culture*. Princeton, NJ: Princeton University Press, 1989.
Cimbala, Paul A. *Veterans North and South: The Transition from Soldier to Civilian After the American Civil War*. Santa Barbara, CA: Praeger, 2015.
Clawson, Mary Ann. *Constructing Brotherhood: Class, Gender, and Fraternalism*. Princeton, NJ: Princeton University Press, 1989.
Clayton, Lawrence A. *Peru and the United States: The Condor and the Eagle*. Athens: University of Georgia Press, 1999.
Clifford, John Garry. *The Citizen Soldiers: The Plattsburg Training Camp Movement, 1913–1920*. Lexington: University Press of Kentucky, 1972.
Coffman, Tom. *Nation Within: The History of the American Occupation of Hawai'i*. Rev. Ed. Durham, NC: Duke University Press, 2016.
Cohen, Michael David. *Reconstructing the Campus: Higher Education and the American Civil War*. Charlottesville: University of Virginia Press, 2012.
Cooper, Jerry. *The Rise of the National Guard: The Evolution of the American Militia, 1865–1920*. Lincoln: University of Nebraska Press, 1997.
Cosmas, Graham A. *An Army for Empire: The United States Army in the Spanish-American War*. Columbia: University of Missouri Press, 1971.
Cox, Karen L. *Dixie's Daughters: The United Daughters of the Confederacy and the Preservation of Confederate Culture*. Gainesville: University Press of Florida, 2003.
Crockett, Norman L. *The Black Towns*. Lawrence: Regents Press of Kansas, 1979.

Curti, Merle, and Roderick Nash. *Philanthropy in the Shaping of American Higher Education*. New Brunswick, NJ: Rutgers University Press, 1965.
Davies, Wallace Evan. *Patriotism on Parade: The Story of Veterans and Hereditary Organizations in America, 1783–1900*. Cambridge, MA: Harvard University Press, 1955.
Dean, Eric T., Jr. *Shook Over Hell: Post-Traumatic Stress, Vietnam, and the Civil War*. Cambridge, MA: Harvard University Press, 1997.
Dearing, Mary R. *Veterans in Politics: The Story of the G.A.R.* Baton Rouge: Louisiana State University Press, 1952.
Diner, Steven J. *A Very Different Age: Americans of the Progressive Era*. New York: Hill and Wang, 1998.
———. *Universities and Their Cities: Urban Higher Education in America*. Baltimore, MD: Johns Hopkins University Press, 2017.
Dittmer, John. *Black Georgia in the Progressive Era, 1900–1920*. Urbana: University of Illinois Press, 1980.
Ditzion, Sidney. *Arsenals of a Democratic Culture: A Social History of the American Public Library in New England and the Middle States from 1850 to 1900*. Chicago: American Library Association, 1947.
Doyle, Don Harrison. *The Social Order of a Frontier Community: Jacksonville, Illinois, 1825–1870*. Urbana: University of Illinois Press, 1978.
DuBois, Ellen Carol. *Feminism and Suffrage: The Emergence of an Independent Women's Movement in America, 1848–1869*. Ithaca, NY: Cornell University Press, 1998.
Dumenil, Lynn. *Freemasonry and American Culture, 1880–1930*. Princeton, NJ: Princeton University Press, 1984.
Du Mont, Rosemary Ruhig. *Reform and Reaction: The Big City Public Library in American Life*. Westport, CT: Greenwood Press, 1977.
Ebel, Jonathan H. *Faith in the Fight: Religion and the American Soldier in the Great War*. Princeton, NJ: Princeton University Press, 2010.
Edwards, Rebecca. *New Spirits: Americans in the "Gilded Age," 1865–1905*. New York: Oxford University Press, 2006.
Etcheson, Nicole. *Bleeding Kansas: Contested Liberty in the Civil War Era*. Lawrence: University Press of Kansas, 2004.
Fahs, Alice. *The Imagined Civil War: Popular Literature of the North and South, 1861–1865*. Chapel Hill: University of North Carolina Press, 2001.
Faust, Drew Gilpin. *This Republic of Suffering: Death and the American Civil War*. New York: Vintage Books, 2008.
Fischbeck, Arthur M., R. Duane Umberger, and James Chimbidis, eds. *Mason City: A Historical Album*. Lake Mills, IA: Graphic Printing Company, 1985.
Fischer, David Hackett. *Growing Old in America*. New York: Oxford University Press, 1977.
Foglesong, Richard E. *Planning the Capitalist City: The Colonial Era to the 1920s*. Princeton, NJ: Princeton University Press, 1986.
Foner, Eric. *Reconstruction: America's Unfinished Revolution, 1863–1877*. New York: Harper & Row, 1988.

Ford, Nancy Gentile. *The Great War and America: Civil-Military Relations During World War I*. Westport, CT: Praeger Security International, 2008.
Foster, Gaines M. *Ghosts of the Confederacy: Defeat, the Lost Cause, and the Emergence of the New South*. New York: Oxford University Press, 1987.
Gallman, J. Matthew. *Defining Duty in the Civil War: Personal Choice, Popular Culture, and the Union Home Front*. Chapel Hill: University of North Carolina Press, 2015.
Gannon, Barbara A. *Americans Remember Their Civil War*. Santa Barbara, CA: Praeger, 2017.
———. *The Won Cause: Black and White Comradeship in the Grand Army of the Republic*. Chapel Hill: University of North Carolina Press, 2011.
Garrison, Dee. *Apostles of Culture: The Public Librarian and American Society, 1876–1920*. New York: The Free Press, 1979.
Geiger, Roger L. *The History of American Higher Education: Learning and Culture from the Founding to World War II*. Princeton, NJ: Princeton University Press, 2015.
Gero, Anthony F. *Black Soldiers of New York State: A Proud Legacy*. Albany: State University of New York Press, 2009.
Gilmore, Glenda Elizabeth. *Gender and Jim Crow: Women and the Politics of White Supremacy in North Carolina, 1896–1920*. Chapel Hill: University of North Carolina Press, 1996.
Glatthaar, Joseph T. *Forged in Battle: The Civil War Alliance of Black Soldiers and White Officers*. Baton Rouge: Louisiana State University Press, 1990.
Goodwyn, Lawrence. *The Populist Moment: A Short History of the Agrarian Revolt in America*. New York: Oxford University Press, 1978.
Grantham, Dewey W. *Southern Progressivism: The Reconciliation of Progress and Tradition*. Knoxville: University of Tennessee Press, 1983.
Guenter, Scot M. *The American Flag, 1777–1924: Cultural Shifts from Creation to Codification*. Rutherford, NJ: Farleigh Dickinson University Press, 1990.
Gutman, Yifat, and Jenny Wüstenberg, eds. *The Routledge Handbook of Memory Activism*. New York: Routledge, 2023.
Hahn, Steven. *A Nation Without Borders: The United States and Its World in an Age of Civil Wars, 1830–1910*. New York: Viking, 2016.
Handley-Cousins, Sarah. *Bodies in Blue: Disability in the Civil War North*. Athens: University of Georgia Press, 2019.
Harp, Gillis J. *Positivist Republic: Auguste Comte and the Reconstruction of American Liberalism*. University Park: Pennsylvania State University Press, 1995.
Harris, M. Keith. *Across the Bloody Chasm: The Culture of Commemoration Among Civil War Veterans*. Baton Rouge: Louisiana State University Press, 2014.
Hart, John Mason. *Empire and Revolution: The Americans in Mexico Since the Civil War*. Berkeley: University of California Press, 2002.
Haycox, Stephen. *Alaska: An American Colony*. Seattle: University of Washington Press, 2002.
Herbst, Jurgen. *And Sadly Teach: Teacher Education and Professionalization in American Culture*. Madison: University of Wisconsin Press, 1989.
Hess, Earl J. *Lincoln Memorial University and the Shaping of Appalachia*. Knoxville: University of Tennessee Press, 2011.

Hofstadter, Richard. *The Age of Reform: From Bryan to F.D.R.* New York: Alfred A. Knopf, 1955.

Hoganson, Kristin L. *Fighting for American Manhood: How Gender Politics Provoked the Spanish-American and Philippine-American Wars.* New Haven, CT: Yale University Press, 1998.

Horwitz, Tony. *Confederates in the Attic: Dispatches from the Unfinished Civil War.* New York: Vintage, 1998.

Hunter, Tera W. *To 'Joy My Freedom: Southern Black Women's Lives and Labors After the Civil War.* Cambridge, MA: Harvard University Press, 1997.

Isenberg, Andrew C. *The Destruction of the Bison: An Environmental History, 1750–1920.* New York: Cambridge University Press, 2000.

Jackson, Brenda K. *Domesticating the West: The Re-creation of the Nineteenth-Century American Middle Class.* Lincoln: University of Nebraska Press, 2005.

Janney, Caroline E. *Remembering the Civil War: Reunion and the Limits of Reconciliation.* Chapel Hill: University of North Carolina Press, 2013.

Johnston, Robert D. *The Radical Middle Class: Populist Democracy and the Question of Capitalism in Progressive Era Portland, Oregon.* Princeton, NJ: Princeton University Press, 2003.

Jordan, Brian Matthew. *A Thousand May Fall: Life, Death, and Survival in the Union Army.* New York: W. W. Norton, 2021.

———. *Marching Home: Union Veterans and Their Unending Civil War.* New York: W. W. Norton, 2014.

Kauffman, Christopher J. *Faith and Fraternalism: The History of the Knights of Columbus, 1882–1982.* New York: Harper & Row, 1982.

Kaufman, Jason. *For the Common Good? American Civic Life and the Golden Age of Fraternity.* New York: Oxford University Press, 2002.

Keefer, Bradley S. *Conflicting Memories on the 'River of Death': The Chickamauga Battlefield and the Spanish-American War, 1863–1933.* Kent, OH: Kent State University Press, 2013.

Kelly, Patrick J. *Creating a National Home: Building the Veterans' Welfare State, 1860–1900.* Cambridge, MA: Harvard University Press, 1997.

Kennedy, David M. *Over Here: The First World War and American Society.* New York: Oxford University Press, 1980.

Kennedy, Thomas. *A History of Southland College: The Society of Friends and Black Education in Arkansas.* Fayetteville: University of Arkansas Press, 2009.

LaFeber, Walter. *The New Empire: An Interpretation of American Expansion, 1860–1898.* Ithaca, NY: Cornell University Press, 1963. Reprint 1998.

Lagemann, Ellen Condliffe. *The Politics of Knowledge: The Carnegie Corporation, Philanthropy, and Public Policy.* Chicago: University of Chicago Press, 1989.

Leepson, Marc. *Flag: An American Biography.* New York: St. Martin's Griffin, 2005.

Leslie, W. Bruce. *Gentlemen and Scholars: College and Community in the "Age of the University," 1865–1917.* University Park: Pennsylvania State University Press, 1992.

Linderman, Gerald F. *The Mirror of War: American Society and the Spanish-American War.* Ann Arbor: University of Michigan Press, 1974.

Link, William A. *The Paradox of Southern Progressivism, 1880–1930*. Chapel Hill: University of North Carolina Press, 1992.
Logan, Rayford W. *The Betrayal of the Negro: From Rutherford B. Hayes to Woodrow Wilson*. 1954. Reprint, New York: Da Capo Press, 1997.
Logue, Larry M. *To Appomattox and Beyond: The Civil War Soldier in War and Peace*. Chicago: Ivan R. Dee, 1996.
Lonn, Ella. *Foreigners in the Union Army and Navy*. Baton Rouge: Louisiana State University Press, 1951.
Love, Eric T. *Race Over Empire: Racism and U.S. Imperialism, 1865–1900*. Chapel Hill: University of North Carolina Press, 2004.
Lucas, Marion B. *A History of Blacks in Kentucky: From Slavery to Segregation, 1760–1891*. Frankfort: Kentucky Historical Society, 2003.
Luebke, Frederick C. *Bonds of Loyalty: German-Americans and World War I*. De Kalb: Northern Illinois University Press, 1974.
Mallon, Florencia E. *The Defense of Community in Peru's Central Highlands: Peasant Struggle and Capitalist Transition, 1860–1940*. Princeton, NJ: Princeton University Press, 1983.
Manning, Chandra. *What This Cruel War Was Over: Soldiers, Slavery, and the Civil War*. New York: Alfred A. Knopf, 2007.
Marten, James. *Sing Not War: The Lives of Union and Confederate Veterans in Gilded Age America*. Chapel Hill: University of North Carolina Press, 2011.
Masich, Andrew E. *The Civil War in Arizona: The Story of the California Volunteers, 1861–1865*. Norman: University of Oklahoma Press, 2006.
McConnell, Stuart. *Glorious Contentment: The Grand Army of the Republic, 1865–1900*. Chapel Hill: University of North Carolina Press, 1992.
McCrory, Thomas J. *Grand Army of the Republic, Department of Wisconsin*. Black Earth, WI: Trails Books: 2005.
McGerr, Michael. *A Fierce Discontent: The Rise and Fall of the Progressive Movement in America*. New York: Oxford University Press, 2003.
McPherson, James M. *For Cause and Comrades: Why Men Fought in the Civil War*. New York: Oxford University Press, 1997.
Miller, Darlis A. *Captain Jack Crawford: Buckskin Poet, Scout, and Showman*. Albuquerque: University of New Mexico Press, 1993.
Miller, Stuart Creighton. *"Benevolent Assimilation": The American Conquest of the Philippines, 1899–1903*. New Haven, CT: Yale University Press, 1982.
Minott, Rodney G. *Peerless Patriots: Organized Veterans and the Spirit of Americanism*. Washington, D.C.: Public Affairs Press, 1962.
Montgomery, David. *The Fall of the House of Labor: The Workplace, the State, and American Labor Activism, 1865–1925*. New York: Cambridge University Press, 1987.
Moorman, Donald R. *Camp Floyd and the Mormons: The Utah War*. Salt Lake City: University of Utah Press, 1992.
Neff, John R. *Honoring the Civil War Dead: Commemoration and the Problem of Reconciliation*. Lawrence: University Press of Kansas, 2005.
Neiberg, Michael S. *Making Citizen-Soldiers: ROTC and the Ideology of American Military Service*. Cambridge, MA: Harvard University Press, 2000.

Nelson, Megan Kate. *Ruin Nation: Destruction and the American Civil War*. Athens: University of Georgia Press, 2012.

———. *The Three-Cornered War: The Union, the Confederacy, and Native Peoples in the Fight for the West*. New York: Scribner, 2020.

O'Leary, Cecelia Elizabeth. *To Die For: The Paradox of American Patriotism*. Princeton, NJ: Princeton University Press, 1999.

O'Toole, G. J. A. *The Spanish War: An American Epic—1898*. New York: W. W. Norton, 1984.

Oakes, James. *Freedom National: The Destruction of Slavery in the United States, 1861–1865*. New York: W. W. Norton, 2013.

Ogren, Christine A. *The American State Normal School: "An Instrument of Great Good."* New York: Palgrave Macmillan, 2005.

Orvell, Miles. *The Death and Life of Main Street: Small Towns in American Memory, Space, and Community*. Chapel Hill: University of North Carolina Press, 2012.

Painter, Nell Irvin. *Exodusters: Black Migration to Kansas After Reconstruction*. New York: Alfred A. Knopf, 1977.

———. *Standing at Armageddon: The United States, 1877–1919*. New York: W. W. Norton, 1987.

Pencak, William. *For God and Country: The American Legion, 1919–1941*. Boston: Northeastern University Press, 1989.

Peterson, Merrill D. *Lincoln in American Memory*. New York: Oxford University Press, 1994.

Putnam, John C. *Class and Gender Politics in Progressive-Era Seattle*. Reno: University of Nevada Press, 2008.

Putnam, Robert D. *Bowling Alone: The Collapse and Revival of American Community*. New York: Simon & Schuster, 2000.

Radelet, Michael L., Hugo Adam Bedau, and Constance E. Putnam. *In Spite of Innocence: Erroneous Convictions in Capital Cases*. Boston: Northeastern University Press, 1992.

Ragan, Diane. *Grand Army of the Republic, Department of Pennsylvania, Personal War Sketches of the African American Members of Col. Robert G. Shaw Post No. 206, Pittsburgh*. Pittsburgh: Western Pennsylvania Genealogical Society, 2003.

Reid, Richard M. *African Canadians in Union Blue: Enlisting for the Cause in the Civil War*. Vancouver: UBC Press, 2014.

Rinella, Steven. *American Buffalo: In Search of a Lost Icon*. New York: Spiegel and Grau, 2008.

Rockefeller, Steven C. *John Dewey: Religious Faith and Democratic Humanism*. New York: Columbia University Press, 1991.

Rohrbough, Malcolm J. *The Land Office Business: The Settlement and Administration of American Public Lands, 1789–1837*. New York: Oxford University Press, 1968.

Rosenburg, R.B. *Living Monuments: Confederate Soldiers' Homes in the New South*. Chapel Hill: University of North Carolina Press, 1993.

Rudolph, Frederick. *The American College and University: A History*. Athens: University of Georgia Press, 1962.

Sandage, Scott A. *Born Losers: A History of Failure in America*. Cambridge, MA: Harvard University Press, 2005.
Savage, Kirk. *Standing Soldiers, Kneeling Slaves: Race, War, and Monument in Nineteenth-Century America*. Princeton, NJ: Princeton University Press, 1997.
Schell, William, Jr. *Integral Outsiders: The American Colony in Mexico City, 1876–1911*. Wilmington, DE: Scholarly Resources, 2001.
Schmidt, Regin. *Red Scare: FBI and the Origins of Anticommunism in the United States, 1919–1943*. Copenhagen, Denmark: Museum Tusculanum Press, 2000.
Shaffer, Donald R. *After the Glory: The Struggles of Black Civil War Veterans*. Lawrence: University Press of Kansas, 2004.
Silber, Nina. *Gender and the Sectional Conflict*. Chapel Hill: University of North Carolina Press, 2009.
———. *The Romance of Reunion: Northerners and the South, 1865–1900*. Chapel Hill: University of North Carolina Press, 1993.
Skocpol, Theda. *Diminished Democracy: From Membership to Management in American Civic Life*. Norman: University of Oklahoma Press, 2003.
———. *Protecting Soldiers and Mothers: The Political Origins of Social Policy in the United States*. Cambridge, MA: Harvard University Press, 1992.
Sloane, David Charles. *The Last Great Necessity: Cemeteries in American History*. Baltimore, MD: Johns Hopkins University Press, 1991.
Smith, Stacey L. *Freedom's Frontier: California and the Struggle over Unfree Labor, Emancipation, and Reconstruction*. Chapel Hill: University of North Carolina Press, 2013.
Smith, Timothy B. *Altogether Fitting and Proper: Civil War Battlefield Preservation in History, Memory, and Policy, 1861–2015*. Knoxville: University of Tennessee Press, 2017.
Sneider, Allison L. *Suffragists in an Imperial Age: U.S. Expansion and the Woman Question, 1870–1929*. New York: Oxford University Press, 2008.
Snyder, Thomas D., ed. *120 Years of American Education: A Statistical Portrait*. Washington, D.C.: US Department of Education, 1993.
Sommerville, Diane Miller. *Aberration of Mind: Suicide and Suffering in the Civil War-Era South*. Chapel Hill: University of North Carolina Press, 2018.
Spector, Ronald H. *Admiral of the New Empire: The Life and Career of George Dewey*. Baton Rouge: Louisiana State University Press, 1974.
Stanley, Matthew E. *Grand Army of Labor: Workers, Veterans, and the Meaning of the Civil War*. Urbana: University of Illinois Press, 2021.
Takaki, Ronald. *Strangers from a Different Shore: A History of Asian Americans*. New York: Penguin Books, 1989.
Taliaferro, John. *All the Great Prizes: The Life of John Hay, from Lincoln to Roosevelt*. New York: Simon & Schuster, 2013.
Tetrault, Lisa. *The Myth of Seneca Falls: Memory and the Women's Suffrage Movement, 1848–1898*. Chapel Hill: University of North Carolina Press, 2014.
Thelin, John R. *A History of American Higher Education*. 2nd edition. Baltimore, MD: Johns Hopkins University Press, 2011.

Thomas, George. *The Founders and the Idea of a National University: Constituting the American Mind*. New York: Cambridge University Press, 2015.
Traxel, David. *1898: The Birth of the American Century*. New York: Alfred A. Knopf, 1999.
———. *Crusader Nation: The United States in Peace and the Great War, 1898–1920*. New York: Alfred A. Knopf, 2006.
Valuska, David L., and Christian B. Keller. *Damn Dutch: Pennsylvania Germans at Gettysburg*. Mechanicsburg, PA: Stackpole Books, 2004.
Van Slyck, Abigail A. *Free to All: Carnegie Libraries and American Culture, 1890–1920*. Chicago: University of Chicago Press, 1995.
Van Wienen, Mark W. *Partisans and Poets: The Political Work of American Poetry in the Great War*. New York: Cambridge University Press, 1997.
Veysey, Laurence R. *The Emergence of the American University*. Chicago: University of Chicago Press, 1965.
Warner, Ezra J. *Generals in Blue: Lives of the Union Commanders*. Baton Rouge: Louisiana State University Press, 1964.
Weiss, Elaine F. *Fruits of Victory: The Woman's Land Army of America in the Great War*. Washington, D.C.: Potomac Books, 2008.
Wiebe, Robert H. *The Search for Order, 1877–1920*. New York: Hill and Wang, 1967.
Wiegand, Wayne A. *Part of Our Lives: A People's History of the American Public Library*. New York: Oxford University Press, 2015.
Williams, Chad L. *Torchbearers of Democracy: African American Soldiers in the World War I Era*. Chapel Hill: University of North Carolina Press, 2010.
Wilson, Ivy G., ed. *At the Dusk of Dawn: Selected Poetry and Prose of Albery Allson Whitman*. Boston: Northeastern University Press, 2009.
Wilson, Ross J. *New York and the First World War: Shaping an American City*. New York: Routledge, 2014.
Wilson, William H. *The City Beautiful Movement*. Baltimore, MD: Johns Hopkins University Press, 1989.
Woodward, C. Vann. *Origins of the New South, 1877–1913*. Baton Rouge: Louisiana State University Press, 1951.
Young, James E. *The Texture of Memory: Holocaust Memorials and Meaning*. New Haven, CT: Yale University Press, 1993.

Articles, Essays, and Reports

Blanck, Peter, and Chen Song. "'Never Forget What They Did Here': Civil War Pensions for Gettysburg Union Army Veterans and Disability in Nineteenth-Century America." *William and Mary Law Review* 44, no. 3 (February 2003): 1109–71.
Bonner, Robert. "1860s Capitalscapes, Governing Interiors, and the Illustration of North American Sovereignty." In *Remaking North American Sovereignty: State Transformation in the 1860s*, edited by Jewel L. Spangler and Frank Towers, 80–103. New York: Fordham University Press, 2020.
Bright, Thomas R. "Yankees in Arms: The Civil War as a Personal Experience." *Civil War History* 19, no. 3 (September 1973): 197–218.

Butler, Anne S. "Black Fraternal and Benevolent Societies in Nineteenth-Century America." In *African American Fraternities and Sororities: The Legacy and the Vision*, 2nd ed., edited by Tamara L. Brown, Gregory S. Parks, and Clarenda M. Phillips, 75–100. Lexington: University Press of Kentucky, 2012.

Cadbury, Henry J. "Negro Membership in the Society of Friends." *Journal of Negro History* 21, no. 2 (April 1936): 151–213.

Camp, Bayliss J., and Orit Kent. "'What a Mighty Power We Can Be': Individual and Collective Identity in African American and White Fraternal Initiation Rituals." *Social Science History* 28, no. 3 (Fall 2004): 439–83.

Casey, Marion. "Efficiency, Taylorism, and Libraries in Progressive America." *Journal of Library History* 16, no. 2 (Spring 1981): 265–79.

Chalker, Fussell M. "Fitzgerald: Place of Reconciliation." *Georgia Historical Quarterly* 55, no. 3 (Fall 1971): 397–405.

Clark, Christopher. "State, Market, and Popular Sovereignty in Agrarian North America: The United States, 1850–1920." In *Remaking North American Sovereignty: State Transformation in the 1860s*, edited by Jewel L. Spangler and Frank Towers, 177–99. New York: Fordham University Press, 2020.

Costa, Dora L. "Displacing the Family: Union Army Pensions and Elderly Living Arrangements." *Journal of Political Economy* 105, no. 6 (December 1997): 1269–92.

———. "Pensions and Retirement Among Black Union Army Veterans." *Journal of Economic History* 70, no. 3 (September 2010): 567–92.

Crapol, Edward P. "Coming to Terms with Empire: The Historiography of Late Nineteenth-Century American Foreign Relations." *Diplomatic History* 16 (Fall 1994): 52–70.

Elliott, Mark. "'Our God-Given Mission': Reconstruction and the Humanitarian Internationalism of the 1890s." In *Reconstruction and Empire: The Legacies of Abolition and Union Victory for an Imperial Age*, edited by David Prior, 161–90. New York: Fordham University Press, 2022.

Fahs, Alice. "The Feminized Civil War: Gender, Northern Popular Literature, and the Memory of the War, 1861–1900." *Journal of American History* 85, no. 4 (March 1999): 1461–94.

Filene, Peter G. "An Obituary for 'The Progressive Movement.'" *American Quarterly* 22, no. 1 (Spring 1970): 20–34.

Fry, Joseph A. "Phases of Empire: Late Nineteenth Century U.S. Foreign Relations." In *The Gilded Age: Perspectives on the Origins of Modern America*, second edition, edited by Charles W. Calhoun, 307–32. Lanham, MD: Rowman & Littlefield, 2007.

Gallagher, Gary W., and Kathryn Shively Meier. "Coming to Terms with Civil War Military History." *Journal of the Civil War Era* 4, no. 4 (December 2014): 487–508.

Gannon, Barbara A. "Sites of Memory, Sites of Glory: African-American Grand Army of the Republic Posts in Pennsylvania." In *Making and Remaking Pennsylvania's Civil War*, edited by William Blair and William Pencak, 165–87. University Park: Pennsylvania State University Press, 2001.

———. "'They Call Themselves Veterans': Civil War and Spanish War Veterans and the Complexities of Veteranhood." *Journal of the Civil War Era* 5, no. 4 (December 2015): 528–50.

Glasco, Laurence A. "Optimism, Dilemmas, and Progress: The Pittsburgh Survey and Black Americans." In *Pittsburgh Surveyed: Social Science and Social Reform in the Early Twentieth Century*, edited by Maurine W. Greenwald and Margo Anderson, 205–20. Pittsburgh, PA: University of Pittsburgh Press, 1996.

Hackemer, Kurt. "Civil War Veteran Colonies on the Western Frontier." In *The War Went On: Reconsidering the Lives of Civil War Veterans*, edited by Brian Matthew Jordan and Evan C. Rother, 61–80. Baton Rouge: Louisiana State University Press, 2020.

Hahn, Steven. "The United States from the Inside Out and the Southside North." In *Remaking North American Sovereignty: State Transformation in the 1860s*, edited by Jewel L. Spangler and Frank Towers, 25–35. New York: Fordham University Press, 2020.

Hall, Ryan. "Negotiating Sovereignty: U.S. and Canadian Colonialisms on the Northwest Plains, 1855–1877." In *Remaking North American Sovereignty: State Transformation in the 1860s*, edited by Jewel L. Spangler and Frank Towers, 132–52. New York: Fordham University Press, 2020.

Hoganson, Kristin. "'As Badly off as the Filipinos': U.S. Women's Suffragists and the Imperial Issue at the Turn of the Twentieth Century." *Journal of Women's History* 13, no. 2 (Summer 2001): 9–33.

Holtby, David V. "Connected Lives: Albert Beveridge, Benjamin Tillman, and the Grand Army of the Republic." In *Reconstruction and Empire: The Legacies of Abolition and Union Victory for an Imperial Age*, edited by David Prior, 191–213. New York: Fordham University Press, 2022.

Hopkins, Leroy T. "No Balm in Gilead: Lancaster's African American Population and the Civil War Era." In *African Americans in Pennsylvania: Shifting Historical Perspectives*, edited by Joe William Trotter Jr. and Eric Ledell Smith, 177–97. University Park: Pennsylvania State University Press, 1997.

Howard, Rebecca. "Lost to the Lost Cause: Arkansas's Union Veterans." In *The War Went On: Reconsidering the Lives of Civil War Veterans*, edited by Brian Matthew Jordan and Evan C. Rothera, 262–82. Baton Rouge: Louisiana State University Press, 2020.

Johnston, Robert D. "The Possibilities of Politics: Democracy in America, 1877 to 1917." In *American History Now*, edited by Eric Foner and Lisa McGirr, 96–124. Philadelphia: Temple University Press, 2011.

Jordan, Brian Matthew. "Grand Old Men: The Last Veterans and Civil War Memory in the Mid-Twentieth Century." In *Civil War Monuments and Memory: Favorite Stories and Fresh Perspectives from the Historians at Emerging Civil War*, edited by Jonathan Tracey and Chris Mackowski, 255–63. El Dorado Hills, CA: Savas Beatie, 2022.

Kahler, Bruce R. "John A. Martin, Soldier State Visionary." *Kansas History: A Journal of the Central Plains* 34 (Spring 2011): 50–59.

Kam, Ralph Thomas. "Commemorating the Grand Army of the Republic in Hawai'i: 1882–1930." *Hawaiian Journal of History* 43 (2009): 125–51.

Klotter, James C. "The Black South and White Appalachia." *Journal of American History* 66, no. 4 (March 1980): 832–49.

Kreuter, Kent, and Gretchen Kreuter. "The Presidency or Nothing: Cushman K. Davis and the Campaign of 1896." *Minnesota History* 41 (Fall 1969): 301–16.
Lee, Chulhee. "Health, Information, and Migration: Geographic Mobility of Union Army Veterans, 1860–1880." *Journal of Economic History* 68, no. 3 (September 2008): 862–99.
Leuchtenburg, William E. "Progressivism and Imperialism: The Progressive Movement and American Foreign Policy, 1898–1916." *Mississippi Valley Historical Review* 39, no. 3 (December 1952): 483–504.
Link, Arthur S. "The Progressive Movement in the South, 1870–1914." *North Carolina Historical Review* 23, no. 2 (April 1946): 172–95.
Logue, Larry M. "Union Veterans and Their Government: The Effects of Public Policies on Private Lives." *Journal of Interdisciplinary History* 22, no. 3 (Winter 1992): 411–34.
Logue, Larry M., and Peter Blanck. "'There Is Nothing That Promotes Longevity Like a Pension': Disability Policy and Mortality of Civil War Union Army Veterans." *Wake Forest Law Review* 39, no. 1 (2004): 49–67.
Makker, Kirin J. "Mary G. Hopkins and the Origins of Village Improvement in Antebellum Stockbridge, Massachusetts." *Landscape Journal* 34, no. 1 (2015): 1–14.
———. "Village Improvement and the Development of Small Town America, 1853–1893." *Journal of Planning History* 13 (February 2014): 68–87.
Maltby, Richard. "Blackface, Disguise and Invisibility in the Reception of *The Birth of a Nation*." In *In the Shadow of* The Birth of a Nation: *Racism, Reception and Resistance*, edited by Melvyn Stokes and Paul McEwan, 35–62. Cham, Switzerland: Palgrave Macmillan, 2013.
Markowitz, Gerald E. "Progressivism and Imperialism: A Return to First Principles." *The Historian* 37, no. 2 (February 1975): 257–75.
McAfee, Ward M. "California's House Divided." *Civil War History* 33, no. 2 (June 1987): 115–30.
McClintock, Megan J. "Civil War Pensions and the Reconstruction of Union Families." *Journal of American History* 83, no. 2 (September 1996): 456–80.
McConnell, Stuart. "Who Joined the Grand Army?: Three Case Studies in the Construction of Union Veteranhood, 1866–1900." In *Toward a Social History of the American Civil War: Exploratory Essays*, edited by Maris A. Vinovskis, 139–70. New York: Cambridge University Press, 1990.
McCormick, Richard L. "Public Life in Industrial America, 1877–1917." In *The New American History*, edited by Eric Foner, 107–32. Philadelphia: Temple University Press, 1997.
Morgan, Stephen T. "Fellow Comrades: The Grand Army of the Republic in South Dakota." *South Dakota History* 36, no. 3 (Fall 2006): 229–59.
Myers, John L. "The Writing of *History of the Rise and Fall of the Slave Power in America*." *Civil War History* 31, no. 2 (June 1985): 144–62.
Nehls, Christopher. "The American Legion and Striking Workers During the Interwar Period." In *The Right and Labor in America: Politics, Ideology, and Imagination*, edited by Nelson Lichtenstein and Elizabeth Tandy Shermer, 27–41. Philadelphia: University of Pennsylvania Press, 2012.

Neu, Jonathan D. "A Building Very Useful: The Grand Army Memorial Hall in U.S. Civic Life, 1880–1920." In *The War Went On: Reconsidering the Lives of Civil War Veterans*, edited by Brian Matthew Jordan and Evan C. Rothera, 173–90. Baton Rouge: Louisiana State University Press, 2020.

———. "'Produce Patriots As Well As Scholars': GAR Educational Reform and the Establishment of Mason City's Memorial University." *The Annals of Iowa* 79, no. 3 (Summer 2020): 211–46.

Nord, David Paul. "Minneapolis and the Pragmatic Socialism of Thomas Van Lear." *Minnesota History* 45 (Spring 1976): 2–10.

Ogle, Maureen. "Beyond the Great City: Finding and Defining the Small City in Nineteenth Century America." In *American Cities and Towns: Historical Perspectives*, edited by Joseph F. Rishel, 48–66. Pittsburgh, PA: Duquesne University Press, 1992.

Peterson, Jon A. "The City Beautiful Movement: Forgotten Origins and Lost Meanings." *Journal of Urban History* 2, no. 4 (August 1976): 415–34.

Pettegrew, John. "'The Soldier's Faith': Turn-of-the-Century Memory of the Civil War and the Emergence of Modern American Nationalism." *Journal of Contemporary History* 31, no. 1 (January 1996): 49–73.

Ranftle, Robert. "Rutland in the Civil War (Part I)." *Rutland Historical Society Quarterly* 41, no. 2 (2011): 3–18.

Riotto, Angela M. "Remembering 'That Dark Episode': Union and Confederate Ex-Prisoners of War and Their Captivity Narratives." In *The War Went On: Reconsidering the Lives of Civil War Veterans*, edited by Brian Matthew Jordan and Evan C. Rothera, 121–36. Baton Rouge: Louisiana State University Press, 2020.

Rippley, La Vern J. "Conflict in the Classroom: Anti-Germanism in Minnesota Schools, 1917–19." *Minnesota History* 47 (Spring 1981): 170–83.

Rodgers, Daniel T. "In Search of Progressivism." *Reviews in American History* 10, no. 4 (December 1982): 113–32.

Rothera, Evan C. "'The Men Are Understood to Have Been Generally Americans, in the Employ of the Liberal Government': Civil War Veterans and Mexico, 1865–1867." In *The War Went On: Reconsidering the Lives of Civil War Veterans*, edited by Brian Matthew Jordan and Evan C. Rothera, 37–60. Baton Rouge: Louisiana State University Press, 2020.

Sherman, Jacob. "Lost Buildings of Old Rutland: A Calendar." *Rutland Historical Society Quarterly* 33, no. 4 (2003): 3–7.

Smith, Andrew. "Confederation as a Hemispheric Anomaly: Why Canada Chose a Unique Model of Sovereignty in the 1860s." In *Remaking North American Sovereignty: State Transformation in the 1860s*, edited by Jewel L. Spangler and Frank Towers, 36–60. New York: Fordham University Press, 2020.

Smith, John David. "'A Credit to the Author and an Honor to the Dead Heroes': George Washington Williams's *A History of the Negro Troops in the War of the Rebellion, 1861–1865*." In George Washington Williams, *A History of the Negro Troops in the War of the Rebellion, 1861–1865*, ix–xxxvi. New York: Fordham University Press, 2012.

Sinisi, Kyle S. "Veterans as Political Activists: The Kansas Grand Army of the Republic, 1880–1893." *Kansas History: A Journal of the Central Plains* 14, no. 2 (Summer 1991): 89–99.

Siracusa, Joseph M. "Progressivism, Imperialism, and the Leuchtenburg Thesis, 1952–1974: An Historiographical Appraisal." *Australian Journal of Politics and History* 20, no. 3 (December 1974): 312–25.

Sklar, Kathryn Kish. "American Female Historians in Context, 1770–1930." *Feminist Studies* 3, no. 1/2 (Summer–Autumn 1975): 171–84.

Sodergren, Steven E. "'Exposing False History': The Voice of the Union Veteran in the Pages of the *National Tribune*." In *The War Went On: Reconsidering the Lives of Civil War Veterans*, edited by Brian Matthew Jordan and Evan C. Rothera, 137–56. Baton Rouge: Louisiana State University Press, 2020.

Terrazas y Basante, Marcela. "Indian Raids in Northern Mexico and the Construction of Mexican Sovereignty." In *Remaking North American Sovereignty: State Transformation in the 1860s*, edited by Jewel L. Spangler and Frank Towers, 153–74. New York: Fordham University Press, 2020.

Vinovskis, Maris A. "Have Social Historians Lost the Civil War? Some Preliminary Demographic Speculations." *Journal of American History* 76, no. 1 (June 1989): 34–58.

Walsh, John Evangelist. "Forgotten Angel: The Story of Janet Jennings and the Seneca." *Wisconsin Magazine of History* 81, no. 4 (Summer 1998): 267–93.

Wickman, Donald H. "Henry Ripley Dorr in the Splendid Little War of 1898." *Rutland Historical Society Quarterly* 28, no. 3 (1998): 42–63.

Wilson, Sven. "Prejudice and Policy: Racial Discrimination in the Union Army Disability Pension System, 1865–1906." *American Journal of Public Health* 100, S1 (April 2010): S56–S65.

Wilson, William H. "The Ideology, Aesthetics and Politics of the City Beautiful Movement." In *The Rise of Modern Urban Planning*, edited by Anthony Sutcliffe, 165–98. New York: St. Martin's Press, 1980.

Woirol, Gregory R., ed. "Two Letters on the Spokane Free Speech Fight." *Pacific Northwest Quarterly* 77, no. 2 (April 1986): 68–71.

Wongsrichanalai, Kanisorn. "Lessons of War: Three Civil War Veterans and the Goals of Postwar Education." In *So Conceived and So Dedicated: Intellectual Life in the Civil War-Era North*, edited by Lorien Foote and Kanisorn Wongsrichanalai, 129–52. New York: Fordham University Press, 2015.

Woods, Randall B. "Integration, Exclusion, or Segregation? The 'Color Line' in Kansas, 1878–1900." *Western Historical Quarterly* 14, no. 2 (April 1983): 181–98.

Woodson, C. G. "Early Negro Education in West Virginia." *Journal of Negro History* 7, no. 1 (January 1922): 23–63.

Young, George B. "Intervention Under the Monroe Doctrine: The Olney Corollary." *Political Science Quarterly* 57, no. 2 (June 1942): 247–80.

Zeiger, Susan. "She Didn't Raise Her Boy to Be a Slacker: Motherhood, Conscription, and the Culture of the First World War." *Feminist Studies* 22, no. 1 (Spring 1996): 6–39.

Dissertations

Breisch, Kenneth Alan. "Small Public Libraries in America, 1850–1890: The Invention and Evolution of a Building Type." PhD diss. University of Michigan, 1982.

Mujic, Julie A. "Between Campus and War: Students, Patriotism, and Education at Midwestern Universities During the American Civil War." PhD diss. Kent State University, 2012.

Walters, Glenda Jane. "Union Colony in the Confederate South: Lynn Haven, Florida, 1910–1920." PhD diss. Florida State University, 1995.

Index

Abbott, Anderson, 114–15
abolitionism, 10, 26, 40, 61, 92, 120, 126
accommodation (race), 61
Acker Post (St. Paul, Minnesota), 119, 129
activism. *See* civic engagement; reform activism
Adams, Clarendon F., 168, 169
Adams, John G. B., 78
Adams, Massachusetts, 48
African American GAR posts: and battle for Civil War memory, 6, 10, 22, 25–26, 40–41, 83–85, 92, 120, 125–26; and Blacks' political rights, 120, 125–26, 157; and education, 29, 62–64; and interactions with community members, 22, 25–26, 28–29, 40–41, 120, 137, 161, 166; and interactions with white veterans, 5, 22, 25, 40–41, 82–85, 93, 190n16, 210n14; and Memorial Day ceremonies, 40, 84–85, 126; providing entertainments, 22, 25–26, 84–85, 166; providing opportunities for leadership, 5, 62–64, 83, 114, 177; and war mobilization, 125–26, 137, 157, 161
African American newspapers, 11, 62
African American veterans: and discrimination, 79, 82–85, 102, 120, 125–26, 157, 177–78; and education, 29, 62–64; GAR attitude toward, 5, 17, 79, 82–85, 92–93, 102, 114, 166, 177–78; in Canada, 114; in integrated posts, 5, 25, 40, 62, 93, 177, 190n16; in the South, 76, 79, 82–85; in the West, 92–93, 102
African Americans: discrimination against, 4–5, 56, 82, 92–93, 102, 120, 125–26, 157, 177–78, 223n20; military experience of during the Civil War, 6, 25–26, 40–41, 76, 92, 114, 125–26; self-improvement and education of, 25, 54, 56, 60–64, 69–70, 87, 114; using military service to advance freedom struggle, 26, 92, 114, 125–26, 157, 161, 166, 177. *See also* Historically Black Colleges and Universities; United States Colored Troops (USCT)
age consciousness. *See* Grand Army of the Republic: elder activism of
Alaska, GAR in, 96, 109, 219n5
Alger, Russell A., 126
Allegheny County Grand Army Association, 7, 37–38
amendments, constitutional, 82, 99, 120, 126
American Civil Liberties Union (ACLU), 177
American Expeditionary Force (AEF), 175
American history, 66, 68
American Legion, 10, 34, 172–73, 175–78; and race, 177–78; and rivalry with Sons of Veterans, 176, 242n10
American Missionary Association (AMA), 61, 62
anarchy, GAR attitude toward, 66, 67, 101–2, 148, 204n37
Andersonville prison, 15, 78; and memory of, 52
Andrews, Egbert T., 164
Appalachia, 58–59
Apsley, Lewis D., 51, 198n13
Arlington House, 178

Arlington National Cemetery, 152
Armstrong, Samuel C., 61
Asian Americans, 100–1, 216n42
Athens, Tennessee, 59
Atlanta, Georgia, 60, 79–80, 127
Atlanta University, 60
Aurora, Illinois, 49
auxiliaries. *See* Ladies of the Grand Army of the Republic; Sons of Veterans; Woman's Relief Corps

Backus, Jacob, 118
Baker, Newton, D., 156, 236n31
Ball, Isabel Worrell, 70
Bangor, Maine, 50
Barton, Clara, 51, 68
Battle Cry of Peace (film), 148–50
Baugh, William G., 60
"Bayonet Constitution," 111
Beaver, James A., 62
Beecher, Henry Ward, 168
Belgium, during World War I, 146
Bengough, Herbert H., 158, 174
Benn Post (Lancaster, Pennsylvania), 28
Bill, Arminius W., 52–53
Birth of a Nation, The (film), 102, 178
Black freedom struggle. *See* African Americans: using military service to advance freedom struggle; civil rights
Blackton, J. Stuart, 148–50
Blight, David W., 9–10
Blue and the Gray, The (book), 51
Blue-Gray reunions, 140, 152
Blundon Post (Charleston, West Virginia), 63
Bolshevism. *See* socialism
Boy Scouts, 41, 147, 150
Brazil, 120
Brooke, John R., 126
Brown, John, 26, 94, 213n30
Brown, Robert B., 78
Brown Post (Detroit, Michigan), 125
Brown Post (Valparaiso, Indiana), 32
Brown University, 57–58
Bryson, James, 93

Buffalo, New York, 63, 116, 131
Burdsall, Edmund, 167
Bureau of Indian Affairs, 157
Burpee Post (Rockville, Connecticut), 27–28

California, GAR in, 7, 20, 24, 79, 95–100, 102, 108, 117–18, 122–23, 124, 129, 163, 215n36
Campaigns of the Civil War (book), 50–51
Canada, GAR in, 112–16; relationship with the United States, 109, 112–16, 220n9, 220n10
Canton, Massachusetts, 48
Carnegie, Andrew, 46, 52
Carnegie, Pennsylvania, 52
"carpetbaggers," 76, 207n3
Carr, Isaac N., 131
Carter, John J., 34
Carty, Henry, 118
Catton, Bruce, 172
cemeteries: antebellum, 47; veteran maintenance and visitation of, 26, 40, 77–79, 84–85, 105–6, 110, 113, 116, 117, 135, 147, 152
Chaney, Josiah P., 129, 130
charity, 6, 18–21, 60, 61, 77–78, 80–82, 113, 134
Chickamauga, training camp, 129, 130, 132
children, GAR relation to, 13, 23–24, 26, 40, 41, 44, 46, 51, 59, 71, 87, 98, 109, 137, 141–42, 147–48, 155, 161. *See also* Sons of Veterans
Chinese Exclusion Act (1882), 100
Chipman, Norton P., 52
Cimbala, Paul A., 9
citizen-soldiers, 48, 51, 140, 141, 143, 158–60, 225n28, 231n7, 233n16
City Beautiful Movement, 38
City College of New York, 54
civic engagement, 3, 5, 13–14, 30–41, 43–44, 74, 77, 90–91, 97, 106, 109, 110, 135, 137–39, 156–64, 170, 177, 185–86n4. *See also* Grand Army of the Republic: and

community involvement and localism; reform activism
civil rights, 5, 41, 56, 85, 125–26, 157
Civil War: and amnesia about slavery as a cause, 9–10; and comradeship, 5–6; death and suffering during, 9, 32, 37–38, 47, 130, 138, 145, 196n6; lectures on, 24–26; northern veterans' understanding about its causes, 9–10, 21–22, 105–6, 114, 125–26; teaching, 13, 30, 50–52, 68, 71, 148, 205n41
Clark Atlanta University. *See* Atlanta University
Clarkson, Floyd, 54
Clement, Percival W., 166
Cleveland, Grover, 67, 121; GAR attitude toward, 121, 223n22
colleges and universities, 1–2, 44–45, 53–71, 98, 101, 140, 141–42, 196n2, 200n19, 205n40, 205n41. *See also* education; Historically Black Colleges and Universities (HBCUs)
colonization. *See* soldiers' colonies
Columbia University (and College), 55
Commission on Training Camp Activities (CTCA), 164
Committee on Public Information, 163
Compson Post (Portland, Oregon), 63
comradeship: bonds of, from Civil War, 6–7, 14, 19, 76, 85–87, 93, 96, 209n12; intergenerational, 128–30, 131–35, 137–38, 151, 160–62, 165–66, 172–78; international, 169; interracial, 5, 25, 40–41, 83, 85, 177, 190n16, 191n20
Confederate veterans, 44, 79, 124, 140, 150; GAR attitude toward, 10, 21, 73, 87, 133; homes for, 80–82; during the Spanish-American War, 124–27. *See also* United Confederate Veterans
conscription. *See* citizen-soldier; mobilization, war; voluntarism
consumerism, 170
Converse Post (Windsor Locks, Connecticut), 35
Cravath, Erastus M., 61–62

Crawford, John Wallace, 149–50
Cuba, 105, 107, 120, 122–25, 128, 130
Cuban Army Sanitary Corps, 122
Culver Post (Duluth, Minnesota), 50, 121, 134, 145, 154, 155, 162, 167
Curry, Henry M., 57
Custer, George Armstrong and Elizabeth Bacon, 51, 198n14

"dark turn" (historiography), 9, 186–87n10
Davis, Cushman K., 121
Davis, Jefferson, 79
Davis, William H., 63
Dean, Eric T., 9
Dearing, Mary, 8
deaths, of veterans, 7, 52–53, 178–79
Decoration Day. *See* Memorial Day
DeGress, William J., 116–17
Delany Post (Indianapolis, Indiana), 22, 125, 137
De Long Post (Honolulu, Hawaii), 105–6, 110–12, 154, 219n7, 222n16
demobilization, 6, 9, 74, 88, 134, 172–73; and veteran migration, 73–75, 76–77, 85–87, 88–90, 92, 94–98
Democratic Party, 121, 151–53, 223n22
Dependent Pension Act (1890), 3, 8
DePew, Chauncey M., 67–68
Detroit, Michigan, 36–37, 83, 125
Devens, Charles, Jr., 19
Dewey, George, 126
Díaz, Porfirio, 116–18
Dillard University. *See* Straight University
disabled veterans, 8–9, 80–82, 175
disease, 1, 127, 130, 132, 164
Dole, Sanford B., 111
Douglass, Frederick, 40
draft, military, 124, 137, 158–60, 170, 237n36
Draper, William B., 156
Drew, Daniel, 25, 63
drill, military, 36, 124, 129, 140, 143, 144, 162; Logan argues for, 141–42; in schools and universities, 54, 68, 69, 141–42
Duluth, Minnesota, 24, 50, 121, 134, 145, 154, 155, 162, 167, 179

East Tennessee Wesleyan University. *See* Grant Memorial University
Edmunds-Tucker Act, 99, 216n40
education: and GAR, 2, 14, 43–72, 87, 98. *See also* African American GAR posts: and education; African American veterans: and education; African Americans: self-improvement and education of; colleges and universities; Historically Black Colleges and Universities (HBCUs); graduate education; public schools; South: education in; White Civil War veterans: attitudes toward Black education
elections: local, 32, 34, 39; national, 117, 151
emancipation, GAR memory of, 5, 6, 10, 22, 25–26, 40–41, 62, 75, 83–85, 92, 93–94, 102, 105–6, 114, 120, 125–26, 166, 179
Emancipation Day, 26, 85
Emancipation Proclamation, 26, 221n12
employment, veteran preference in, 15, 37, 92, 134, 135, 152, 174
Emporia, Kansas, 1–2, 146
encampments. *See* Grand Army of the Republic encampments
enlistment. *See* mobilization, war
entertainment, 2, 18, 20–26, 29, 32, 34, 38, 85, 128, 131, 145, 146, 166
Espy Post (Carnegie, Pennsylvania), 52, 199n16
ethnicity: in GAR posts, 17, 154–56; in Union Army, 17
Everest, Wesley, 177
Exodusters, 92–93

Fairchild, Lucius, 41–42
Fairchild Post (Madison, Wisconsin), 55–56, 87, 146, 154, 165, 200n21
Farragut Post (Lincoln, Nebraska), 90, 163
Federal Bureau of Investigation (FBI), 177
Fiebig, Paul Herman, 89–90
Fisk, Clinton B., 61
Fisk University, 60–62
Fitzgerald, Georgia, 85–86

Fitzgerald, Philander, 85–86
flags: Confederate, 80; donations, 54–55; living, 148; GAR promotion of, 44, 77–78, 87, 111, 137, 138, 155, 158, 199–200n19
Florida, GAR in, 86–87, 208n4
Florida A&M University (formerly State Normal and Industrial College for Colored Students), 70
Foner, Eric, 61, 207n3
Ford, Elliot W., 51
Forsyth Post (Toledo, Ohio), 154
Fort Pillow Post (Topeka, Kansas), 26, 157, 166, 214n30
Foster Post (Lansing, Michigan), 159
Fountain, Oliver, 114
Fourteen Points, 168
Fourth of July, 1, 113, 118, 140, 163
Foxboro, Massachusetts, 47–48
fraternalism: influenced by GAR, 131–35; 173–78; influences on GAR, 14, 16–18, 96, 186n6, 188n5
fraud, 86, 90, 92, 117
Freedmen's Bureau, 59, 61, 76
Freemasonry. *See* Masonry
funerals, 79, 90, 110, 130, 143

Galveston, Texas, 77
Gannon, Barbara A., 5, 9, 10, 22, 60, 70, 210n14, 211n17, 213–14n30, 223n21, 228n41
Garfield, James A., 65, 109
Garrison, Lindley M., 140, 142
Garrison Post (New York, New York), 22
Geraldine, Texas, 86
Germans: as GAR members, 89–90, 155–56; nativist hostility toward, 154–55
Germany, during World War I, 145, 146, 153–57, 162, 166, 169
"gerontophobia." *See* Grand Army of the Republic (GAR): decline and death of last members
Gerwig, Charles W., 145
Gettysburg: battle of, 140, 148; reunions at, 140, 152, 230n4; training camp at, 140, 142

Gettysburg, South Dakota, 93
Gobin, John P. S., 123, 133
Gone with the Wind (film), 178
Goodale, George L., 128
Gordon, John B., 127
grade system, 18
graduate education, 57–58
Grady, Henry W., 80
Grand Army of Americans, 177
Grand Army of the Republic (GAR): auxiliary groups of, 3, 6, 11, 21, 23, 34, 36, 59, 66, 91, 161, 163, 166 (*see also* Ladies of the Grand Army of the Republic; Sons of Veterans; Woman's Relief Corps); cardinal principles of, 6, 16–17, 134, 174; and community involvement and localism, 2–3, 5, 7, 8, 9, 12, 14–15, 16, 20, 30–41, 47–50, 53–54, 74–75, 137–38, 146, 156–59, 162–64, 166; controversies in, regarding race, 82–85, 210n14, 211n17; decline and death of last members, 7, 52–53, 138–39, 173–80, 230n3, 241–42n8; elder activism of, 138–39, 147, 156–64, 170, 173, 178; eligibility for, 6, 17, 132–35, 173–74; and ethnicity, 17, 154–56; founding and origins of, 6, 16–20; initial decline of (1870s), 6, 16, 18, 77, 96; installations and elections in, 7, 20–22, 189n13; international and extracontinental posts of, 6, 105–6, 109–19; as interracial organization, 5, 22, 25, 40–41, 82–85, 93, 114, 125; middle-class values in, 4, 16, 98, 215n38; and open meetings, 20–21, 23–26, 137, 145, 166, 190n19; organizational structure of, 7, 17; as a pension lobby, 3, 5, 6, 8, 15, 37, 113–14; and politics, 3, 5, 8, 18, 90–92, 151–54, 234n22; and race, 5, 9–10, 25–26, 28–29, 40–41, 60–64, 82–85, 92–93, 102, 114, 120, 125–26, 177–78, 190n16, 191n20; and resistance to reconciliation, 9–10, 79–82, 106, 133, 152, 178, 191n20; southern posts of, 74–75, 76–88, 177, 208n4; western posts of, 73–75, 88–103; white members of, remembering Blacks' service, 25, 102. *See also* African American GAR posts; integrated GAR posts
Grand Army of the Republic encampments: national, 7, 19, 20, 53, 56–57, 63, 73, 83, 93–94, 96, 99, 108, 109, 112, 114, 127, 132, 133, 142–43, 146, 150, 152–53, 175, 176, 178, 179, 201n22; state, 7, 18, 19, 20, 45–46, 60, 65, 85, 87, 96, 102, 114–16, 123, 133, 142, 143, 145, 153, 161, 166, 168, 169, 174, 175, 179
Grand Army of the Republic memorial halls, 3, 13–14, 26–41, 43, 47, 48–49, 86, 87, 98, 133, 166; and relationship between veterans and nonveterans, 27–28, 31–34, 38–39; in rural areas, 32–34; in towns and cities, 34–41; veterans' advocacy for, 26–27, 31–41. *See also* Soldiers and Sailors Memorial Hall, Pittsburgh, Pennsylvania
Grand Review (1865), 146, 152, 233n16
Grange, 34, 35
Grant, Ulysses S., 58–59, 65, 85, 109, 148
Grant Memorial University, 58–59
Grant Post (Brooklyn, New York), 149–50
Gray, Jacob, 79
Great Britain. *See* United Kingdom
Grieves, Loren C., 172

Hall, Daniel M., 96
Hampton University (formerly Hampton Normal and Agricultural Institute), 60, 61
Hancock Post (Montreal, Quebec), 113, 115
Harding, Warren G., 144, 173
Hawaii: annexation of, 110–12; GAR in, 105–6, 109–12, 117, 154
Hawkins, Alexander L., 127
Hayes, Rutherford B., 65, 109
Head, Albert, 145
Hendershot, Robert Henry, 110
higher education. *See* colleges and universities
Hill, Martha Basella, 63

Historically Black Colleges and Universities (HBCUs), 60–64, 70
Hoagland, Henry V., 90, 91
Holland, William J., 56–57
Homestead Act of 1862, 88, 90
Homestead steel strike, 101
homesteading, 1, 88–90, 91, 92, 93, 94, 108
Hoover, Herbert, 162–63
Hoover Pledge Cards, 163, 238n40
Housatonic, SS (ship), 154
House, Edward M., 168
Howard, Oliver Otis, 59, 61, 124, 202n27
Howard Post (Clear Lake, Iowa), 67
Howard University, 60, 63
Hunter College, 58
Huntley Post (Mason City, Iowa), 67
Hurlbut, Stephen A., 118
Hurley, R. French, 40–41
hygiene, 140, 142, 164

immigrants, 3, 14, 16, 17, 46, 67, 89, 90, 99, 108, 177, 236n29; GAR attitude toward, 17, 67, 99–101, 154–55
imperialism, 4, 106–31, 135, 159, 228n39
Indianapolis, Indiana, 22, 26, 32, 125, 175, 179
Illinois State University, 69
Industrial Workers of the World (IWW), 101–2, 177
industrialization, 3, 14, 67, 108–9
integrated GAR posts: Blacks holding elected offices in, 63, 114; intentional creation of, 5, 25, 40, 63, 70, 83, 84, 93, 114, 177–78, 190n16, 214n30
integration of the military, 2, 126, 166
Iowa Soldiers' and Sailors' Monument, 31
isolationism, 167–70
Ives Post (Providence, Rhode Island), 22, 26

Jennings, Janet, 51
Jim Crow, era of, 4, 102
jingoism. *See* imperialism; Spanish-American War; United States: emerging as world power

Johnson, Andrew, 152, 153
Johnston, Albert Sidney, 79
Jordan, Brian Matthew, 9

Kalākaua, David, 105, 110–11
Kalamazoo, Michigan, 31
Kansas: African American posts in, 26, 28, 125, 157, 166, 213–14n30; GAR in, 1, 2, 21, 24, 25, 43, 82, 89, 91–93, 94, 146, 151, 158, 161, 163, 213n28
Kansas Historical Society, 43, 195n1
Kapiʻolani, 110
Kearney Post (Richmond, Virginia), 80–81
Kennedy, David M., 141
Knights of Columbus, 16, 17
Knights of Pythias, 16, 35
Ku Klux Klan, 4, 76, 102, 177–78, 242n10

labor, GAR attitude toward, 60, 100, 101–2, 106, 217n45; unions, 101–2; unrest, 101–2, 108, 173, 177
Ladies of the Grand Army of the Republic, 17, 163–64
Lafayette Post (New York, New York), 43, 54–55
Lancaster, Massachusetts, 47, 197n7
Lancaster, Pennsylvania, 15, 26, 28
Latin America, 106–7, 109, 116–19, 120–31
League for Democracy, 177
League of Nations, 167–70
League to Enforce Peace (LEP), 167
Ledergerber Post (Keshena, Wisconsin), 157, 236n32
Lee, Fitzhugh, 126, 127
Lee, Robert E., 24, 178
Lee Camp (Richmond, Virginia), 80–81
Leggett, James, 69–70
Leonard, Albert C., 15–16
Leuchtenburg, William E., 106
Lexington, Kentucky, 22, 29
Libby Post (Rockland, Maine), 48–49
Liberty Bonds, 137, 156, 163, 167
libraries, 10, 13, 27, 29, 35, 36, 38, 44–53, 87, 197n7, 197n9
Liliʻuokalani, 111–12

Index

Lincoln, Abraham, 13, 24, 26, 40, 41, 55, 58, 59, 68, 69, 85, 100, 102, 112, 153, 154, 165, 202n27
Lincoln, Nebraska, 24, 90, 94, 163, 164
Lincoln-Garfield Post (Portland, Oregon), 98, 102
Lincoln Legion, 177
Lincoln Memorial Cemetery (Pittsburgh, Pennsylvania), 40
Lincoln Memorial University, 58–59, 202n27
Lincoln Post (Lima, Peru), 118–19, 222n18
Lincoln University, 62, 63
Livingston County, New York, 32–34
Logan, John A., 19, 141–42, 231n7
Longfellow, Levi, 176
Longstreet, James, 124
Loomis, Dwight, 27
Lost Cause, 52, 66, 75, 78, 79, 84, 178
Louisville, Kentucky, 83
Low, Seth, 55
Lowry Post (Wilkinsburg, Pennsylvania), 37–38
Lusitania, RMS (ship), 142
Lynn Haven, Florida, 87
Lyon Post (Menominee, Michigan), 21–22, 135
Lyon Post (Oakland, California), 100
Lysle Post (Pittsburgh, Pennsylvania), 145

MacArthur, Douglas, 172
Maceo Grajales, Antonio, 122
Madison, Wisconsin, 13, 55–56, 132, 146, 154, 165, 187n1
Maine, USS (battleship), 123
Manassas Industrial School for Colored Youth, 60
Manchester-by-the-Sea, Massachusetts, 48
manliness and masculinity, 16–17, 53, 55, 92, 143, 144, 163–64
Marietta National Cemetery (Georgia), 78
Marten, James, 9
Martin, John A., 91, 92, 93
Mason City, Iowa, 66–71
Masonry, 16–18, 28, 188n6
Massachusetts: Fifty-fourth Infantry (Colored), 26; public library laws, 47–48
McAdoo, William G., 163, 238n41
McCall Post (West Chester, Pennsylvania), 167
McConnell, Stuart, 8
McKinley, William, 41, 48, 112, 113, 123, 126, 128, 130, 226n31, 227n35
McPherson, James, 44
McPherson Post (Pittsburgh, Pennsylvania), 163
Meade Post (Philadelphia, Pennsylvania), 49–50
Memorial Day: African Americans commemorating, 40, 84–85, 126; commemoration of, 1, 8, 27, 34, 49, 52, 105–6, 90, 92, 109, 135, 143, 147–48, 152, 168, 169, 175–76; commemorations abroad, 105–6, 110, 113, 117, 169, 219–20n7, 222n16; decorating cemeteries during, 77–79, 84–85, 135, 147, 176; in the South, 77–79, 84–85, 208n7
memorial halls. *See* Grand Army of the Republic memorial halls
Memorial University (Mason City, Iowa), 64–71, 205n41, 205n42, 206n44
memory, 9, 23–26, 30, 31, 34, 37–38, 41, 43, 44, 47, 48, 52, 57, 59, 66, 67, 68, 70, 78, 102, 112, 123, 125–26, 130, 132, 135, 154, 159, 165–66, 169, 175, 178, 211n16; GAR collective, 3–6, 9–10, 14, 27, 46, 60, 71, 83–85, 93–94, 102, 106, 118, 132, 138, 178, 228n41, 239n43
Menken, S. Stanwood, 147
Menominee, Michigan, 21–22, 52–53, 135, 176
Merrill, George Sargent, 77
Merritt, Wesley, 126
Mexican Revolution, 117–18, 142
Mexico, former Confederates in, 116; GAR in, 116–18, 221–22n15
Miles, Nelson A., 126
militarism, 129, 141, 145, 156–62
military drill. *See* drill, military
Minneapolis, Minnesota, 50, 81, 108, 137

Mitchel Post (Atlanta, Georgia), 79–80
mobilization, war, 124–30, 137–38, 156–64, 170, 227n35
Monfort, Elias R., 153
Monroe Doctrine, 119–20, 121, 223n19
monuments, 27, 30–31, 32, 33, 35, 36, 37–38, 40, 43, 47, 48, 49, 52, 59, 87, 116, 117, 134, 191n24, 194n45; Confederate, 79–80
Mordough, John C., 117
Morgan, John Hunt, 24
Mormons, GAR attitude toward, 73, 98–99
Morrill Land Grant Act (1862), 54
motion pictures, 34, 102, 148–50, 178
Moulton, Hosea B., 156–57, 236n31
Mulholland, St. Clair A., 120

Nashville, Tennessee, 61–62
National Cemetery System, 62, 77–78, 85, 152
National Defense Act (1916), 141
National Defense League, 146
national encampments. *See* Grand Army of the Republic encampments
National Guard, 36, 40, 124, 127, 128, 129, 141, 142, 143, 146–47, 156, 158–59, 225n28, 227n35
National Origins Act (1924), 100
National Reform Press Association, 91
National Security League (NSL), 146–47
National Tribune (newspaper), 49–51, 61, 65, 66, 76, 81, 87, 98, 110, 119, 172, 197–98n11, 223n19
national university, 64–67, 204n36
National Volunteer Reserve, 124–25, 225n28, 225n29
Native Americans, 51, 89, 93, 95, 157, 236n32
nativism, 99–101, 154–55, 177
Navarro, Rafael, 122
Nebraska, GAR in, 1, 24, 28, 45–46, 89–91, 93, 94, 121, 123, 143, 157, 159, 160, 178
New Hampshire College of Agriculture and the Mechanic Arts, 63
New Nationalism, 151
New Orleans, Louisiana, 62, 79, 83, 84, 126

New South, 75, 76
Normal College of the City of New York. *See* Hunter College
normal (teachers') schools, 58, 60, 61, 63, 201n24, 202n25
Nunda, New York, 33–34

Oberlin College, 61
Odd Fellows, Independent Order of, 16, 17, 28, 120
Official Records of the War of the Rebellion, The (book), 51
Oklahoma, settlement in, 93
Olney, Richard, 121
Ord Post (Mexico City, Mexico), 116–18, 221–22n15
Order of Elks, 16
Order of Red Men, 16
Oregon, GAR in, 7, 25, 63, 95, 96, 97, 98, 99, 100, 101, 102, 127–28, 137, 161
Oregon Trail, 95

pacifism, 123, 144–45, 148–150, 234n21
Palmer, David J., 101, 145, 146
Palmer, John, 83, 210n14
Panic of 1893, 86
parades, 26, 40, 73, 80, 83, 128, 129, 131, 137, 143, 147–48, 150, 160–61, 163, 177, 178–79; preparedness, 147–48
Paris Peace Conference, 168
patriotic instruction, 20, 23, 53, 58, 59, 66–71, 90–91, 98, 100–1, 109, 137–38, 145, 147–48, 162, 168, 176
Patterson, Joab N., 128
Patterson, William J., 133, 153, 159, 173
Patterson Post (Pittsburgh, Pennsylvania), 29
Peissner Post (Rochester, New York), 155–56
Penland, Theodore A., 179
pensions, military, 3, 5, 6, 8, 9, 15, 37, 79, 87, 90, 113–14, 223n22, 234n22. *See also* Dependent Pension Act (1890)
Pershing, John J., 175
Peru, GAR in, 118–19

INDEX

Philadelphia, Pennsylvania, 29, 49–50, 120, 137, 147–48, 150
Philipp, Emanuel L., 158
Philippines, The, 105, 126, 127, 128, 131, 134, 172, 175
Pillsbury, George A., 108
Pittsburgh, Pennsylvania, 7, 21, 25, 29, 37–41, 56–57, 60, 63, 110, 112, 122, 123, 133, 134, 145, 147, 155, 156, 163, 173, 178, 194n43
Plank, Josephus C., 180
Plattsburg training camp movement, 142–43
Plumb Post (Emporia, Kansas), 1–2, 146
polygamy, 73, 99, 216n40
Populists, 91
Portland, Oregon, 25, 63, 96, 97, 98, 100, 101, 102, 137
postgraduate education. *See* graduate education
post room, 3, 14, 20–21, 23, 28–30, 36, 41, 74, 109, 130, 133, 145, 166, 189n13; libraries in, 49–51; physical arrangement of, 17
post-traumatic stress disorder (PTSD). *See* trauma
preparedness, 123–24, 130, 138, 140–51, 153–54, 167, 232n12
Preparedness Day bombing (San Francisco), 148
Proctor, David E., 145, 168
Progressive Party, 141, 151
Progressivism and Progressive Era, 3–5, 9, 14, 28, 44, 71, 74–75, 91, 106–7, 138, 141, 151, 170, 173, 174, 176–77, 178, 179–80, 185n3, 194n43, 196n4; definition of, 4, 185–86n4; limitations of, 4; middle-class influence of, 4, 44, 46
Providence, Rhode Island, 22, 26, 57–58, 148
public schools, 44, 53, 54, 70, 87, 90–91, 98, 141–42, 147–48, 155
Puerto Rico, 105, 126
Putnam, Robert D., 14

Race and Reunion (book), 9
racism, 4–5, 82–85, 92–93, 107, 173, 177–78
Ransom Post (Natchez, Mississippi), 84
Rawlins Post (Minneapolis, Minnesota), 50
reconciliation, 9, 71, 74, 126–27, 134–35, 140, 152, 235n24; in the South, 79–82; Union veterans' opposition to, 10, 79–82, 106, 134–35, 152, 168, 178, 191n20, 226n33, 230n4
Reconstruction, 61, 75, 76–77, 126, 207n3
recruitment. *See* mobilization, war
Red Cross, 34, 51, 109, 137, 163, 167
Red Scare, 173, 174
reform activism, 3–6, 8–9, 12, 14, 28, 34–35, 38, 44, 46, 53, 71, 76, 91, 98–99, 106–7, 135, 138, 140–42, 147, 151, 157, 170, 173, 174, 179–80, 185n3, 196n4, 243n13
Republican Party, 3, 6, 8, 18, 19, 76–77, 88, 92, 140–41, 151, 167, 207n3, 234n22
Reserve Officers' Training Corps (ROTC), 141
reunions, 29, 41, 85, 140, 152, 169
Richmond, Virginia, 1, 60, 78, 80–81, 130, 148
Rippey Post (Pittsburgh, Pennsylvania), 155
rituals, GAR, 3, 6, 16–20
Roberts Post (Rutland, Vermont), 129–30
Rochester, New York, 13, 132, 155–56
Rockford, Illinois, 35–36
Rockland, Maine, 48–49
Rockville, Connecticut, 26–28
Rood, Hosea W., 13–14, 155, 165–66
Roosevelt, Theodore, 55, 142, 151, 173
Roosevelt, Theodore, Jr., 175
Rough Riders, 55, 130
Rutland, Vermont, 48, 129–30

Salem, Oregon, 95, 97, 100, 161
Salt Lake City, Utah, 73, 96
Sayles Post (Adams, Massachusetts), 48
Schofield, John M., 124
scholarships, 56–58, 59, 63, 200–1n22
Scott, Alice M., 63–64

secessionism, 66, 71, 105, 204n37
Sedgwick Post (Orange, Massachusetts), 130, 163
Sedgwick Post (Salem, Oregon), 97
segregation, 4, 41, 60–61, 82–85, 92–93, 102, 120, 125–26
sentimentalism, 3, 14, 126–27, 152, 179
"separate but equal," 83
Seward, William, 109
Seward Post (Juneau, Alaska), 109
Shaw, Albert, 80, 142
Shaw Post (Pittsburgh, Pennsylvania), 40–41, 63
Sherman, William T., 14, 145, 224n24
Sherwood, Isaac R., 154, 174
Shute, Charles H., 62, 83–84, 210n15
Skocpol, Theda, 8, 14
slavery: amnesia about, 9, 205n41; GAR attitude toward, 73, 120, 165–66; northern culpability over, 62; remembering as key reason for the Civil War, 10, 25–26, 40–41, 66, 68, 92, 105–6, 126, 150, 165–66, 178, 239n43; romanticization of, 120
Small, David E., 63
Smyth Post (Wilmington, Delaware), 129
social security, 139
socialism, 67, 101, 173, 177
Society of California Volunteers, 96
Soldiers and Sailors Memorial Hall (Pittsburgh, Pennsylvania), 37–41
soldiers' colonies, 85–87, 93, 116
soldiers' homes, 9, 14–15, 31, 80, 90, 92, 101, 146; Confederate, 80–82
Sons of the American Revolution, 112
Sons of Veterans (Sons of Union Veterans of the Civil War), 6, 10, 40, 41, 66–67, 70, 124, 130, 143–44, 145, 162, 172, 176, 179
Sons of Veterans Reserves, 143–44, 162, 238n39
Sortor, Alexander Louis, Jr., 66–67
South: education in, 58–64, 87, 201–2n25; GAR in, 7, 59, 61–62, 74–75, 76–88, 177, 208n4; "redeemer" governments in, 76–77, 92
Southern Memorial Fund, 78–79
Spanish-American War, 51, 55, 100, 106, 109, 118, 122–35, 140, 173, 226n33, 227n35; death in, 130, 228n38; veterans of, 40, 131–35, 161, 174, 175, 228n41
Spence, John F., 59
St. Cloud, Florida, 87
state encampments. *See* Grand Army of the Republic encampments
Stevens, Thaddeus, 26
Stolz, Gideon, 97
Stone Mountain Memorial, 178
Straight University, 62
Stuart, Edward S., 40
Summers, Owen, 127–28
Sumner, Charles, 26
Sumner Post (Kansas City, Kansas), 28–29, 93, 213–14n30

Taft, William Howard, 13, 151, 167, 168
Tanner, James, 152–53, 168–69
temperance, 17, 34, 91
Templeton, Charlotte, 45–46
textbooks, GAR campaigns to influence, 44
Thayer, Christopher T., 47
Toledo, Ohio, 36, 154
Toledo Soldiers Memorial Association, 36
Topeka, Kansas, 24, 26, 43, 94, 157, 163–64, 166
Torrance, Eliakim, 58, 67, 68, 80–82, 137, 144
Tower Post (Pawtucket, Rhode Island), 128, 132
transcontinentalism, United States, 74–75, 94–103, 108
trauma, 6, 9
treason, GAR charging Confederates with, 10, 73, 79, 82, 178
Treaty of Versailles, 167–70
Tuskegee Institute (University), 60

INDEX

Uncle Tom's Cabin (book), 150
Union, preservation of, 10, 179
Unionists, southern, 58–59
United Confederate Veterans, 87, 127, 150
United Daughters of the Confederacy, 52, 152
United Kingdom, 112, 115–16, 121–22
United Spanish War Veterans, 41, 134–35, 175, 229n46
United States: emerging as world power, 3, 105–31, 140–41, 144–47, 152, 167–70
United States Colored Troops (USCT), 25, 61, 63, 82, 85, 92, 114, 127, 213–14n30
United States Food Administration, 162
United States military, 2, 61, 124–30, 131–32, 137–38, 140–41, 146–47, 150, 155, 156–62, 172, 175, 179
United States Military Academy. *See* West Point
universal military training, 141, 158, 230n6
universities. *See* colleges and universities
University of Michigan, 67
University of Pittsburgh, 56–57, 63
University of Wisconsin, 55–56
urbanization, 3, 8, 14, 16, 36, 38, 44, 46, 67
Utah, GAR in 73, 96, 98–99

Van Sant, Samuel R., 122
Vandervoort, Paul, 73, 91, 94
Venezuela, boundary crisis in (1890s), 121–22
veterans, Confederate. *See* Confederate veterans
veterans, Union. *See* Grand Army of the Republic
Veterans of Foreign Wars (VFW), 10, 175
Victory gardens, 162–63
voluntarism, 129, 140, 141–42, 143, 158–60, 162
Volunteer Soldier of America, The (book), 141–42

Wadsworth Post (Nunda, New York), 33–34
Wait, Addison, 89

Walker, Ivan N., 122
Walsh, Frank A., 51
War of the Pacific, 118
war reminiscence, 2, 24–26
Washington, Booker T., 60–61, 63, 102
Washington, George, 24, 41, 64, 65, 166, 167
Watrous, Jerome, 133–34, 144, 159
Webb, Alexander S., 54–55
Weed, Edward A., 163
West: Civil War in, 95; GAR in, 6, 73–75, 88–103
West Point, 172, 231n7
West Virginia Colored Institute (West Virginia State University), 63
Western College and Industrial Institute (Missouri), 63
Western University. *See* University of Pittsburgh
Weyler y Nicolau, Valeriano, 122, 129, 224n24
Wheeler, Joseph, 124, 126, 127
white Civil War veterans: attitudes toward Asian Americans, 99–101, 216n42; attitudes toward Black civil and political rights, 2, 40–41, 76, 102, 177–78, 190n16; attitudes toward Black education, 60–62, 87; in relation to integration of GAR posts, 25, 40, 82–85, 93, 114, 177–78
Whitehead, James, 1–3
Whitman, Albery A., 25
widows of soldiers, 19, 51, 100
Wilhelm II, Kaiser, 155, 166, 169
Williams, Alonzo, 57
Williams, George Washington, 63
Wilson, Harper, 114, 220n11
Wilson, Woodrow, 140, 141, 145, 151–57, 162, 163, 164, 166, 167–70, 173, 236n29
Windsor Locks, Connecticut, 35
Wirz, Henry, 52
"Wobblies." *See* Industrial Workers of the World (IWW)
Wolff, James H., 62–63

Womanhood, the Glory of the Nation
  (film), 148–50
Woman's Relief Corps (WRC), 21, 22, 29,
  32, 41, 52, 63–64, 67, 70, 71, 91, 93, 98,
  99, 118, 130, 132, 163, 164, 172, 204n36;
  and charity, 77, 78, 109, 146; origins of,
  6, 17
women, GAR attitude toward, 16–18, 51,
  63–64, 157, 205n42. *See also* Woman's
  Relief Corps
Women's Christian Temperance Union, 34
women's suffrage, 157
Wood, Leonard, 140, 142, 147
Woodruff, Wilford, 99
Woolley, Joseph J., 128, 132, 227n34
Woolson, Albert, 179

Worker, Georgia B., 67
World War I, 7, 98, 100, 135, 137–71, 172–78;
  death in, 168–69; food conservation,
  158, 162–63; GAR advocacies during,
  2, 156–64; home front, 137–38, 160–64,
  167; veterans of, 98, 166, 169, 170,
  172–78, 240n3
World War II, 178
World War Veterans (WWV),
  174, 177
Wyandotte Constitution, 92

xenophobia. *See* nativism

Young, Brigham, 73
Young, James E., 10

Jonathan D. Neu holds a PhD in history from Carnegie Mellon University and works in publishing. His writings have appeared in the *Pittsburgh Post-Gazette, Gettysburg Magazine, Annals of Iowa,* and in the volume *The War Went On*. He lives in Pittsburgh, Pennsylvania.

RECONSTRUCTING AMERICA
Andrew L. Slap, series editor

Hans L. Trefousse, *Impeachment of a President: Andrew Johnson, the Blacks, and Reconstruction.*

Richard Paul Fuke, *Imperfect Equality: African Americans and the Confines of White Ideology in Post-Emancipation Maryland.*

Ruth Currie-McDaniel, *Carpetbagger of Conscience: A Biography of John Emory Bryant.*

Paul A. Cimbala and Randall M. Miller, eds., *The Freedmen's Bureau and Reconstruction: Reconsiderations.*

Herman Belz, *A New Birth of Freedom: The Republican Party and Freedmen's Rights, 1861 to 1866.*

Robert Michael Goldman, *"A Free Ballot and a Fair Count": The Department of Justice and the Enforcement of Voting Rights in the South, 1877–1893.*

Ruth Douglas Currie, ed., *Emma Spaulding Bryant: Civil War Bride, Carpetbagger's Wife, Ardent Feminist—Letters, 1860–1900.*

Robert Francis Engs, *Freedom's First Generation: Black Hampton, Virginia, 1861–1890.*

Robert F. Kaczorowski, *The Politics of Judicial Interpretation: The Federal Courts, Department of Justice, and Civil Rights, 1866–1876.*

John Syrett, *The Civil War Confiscation Acts: Failing to Reconstruct the South.*

Michael Les Benedict, *Preserving the Constitution: Essays on Politics and the Constitution in the Reconstruction Era.*

Andrew L. Slap, *The Doom of Reconstruction: The Liberal Republicans in the Civil War Era.*

Edmund L. Drago, *Confederate Phoenix: Rebel Children and Their Families in South Carolina.*

Mary Farmer-Kaiser, *Freedwomen and the Freedmen's Bureau: Race, Gender, and Public Policy in the Age of Emancipation.*

Paul A. Cimbala and Randall Miller, eds., *The Great Task Remaining Before Us: Reconstruction as America's Continuing Civil War.*

John A. Casey Jr., *New Men: Reconstructing the Image of the Veteran in Late-Nineteenth-Century American Literature and Culture.*

Hilary N. Green, *Educational Reconstruction: African American Schools in the Urban South, 1865–1890.*

Christopher B. Bean, *Too Great a Burden to Bear: The Struggle and Failure of the Freedmen's Bureau in Texas.*

David E. Goldberg, *The Retreats of Reconstruction: Race, Leisure, and the Politics of Segregation at the New Jersey Shore, 1865–1920.*

David Prior, ed., *Reconstruction in a Globalizing World.*

Jewel L. Spangler and Frank Towers, eds., *Remaking North American Sovereignty: State Transformation in the 1860s.*

Adam H. Domby and Simon Lewis, eds., *Freedoms Gained and Lost: Reconstruction and Its Meanings 150 Years Later.*

David Prior, ed., *Reconstruction and Empire: The Legacies of Abolition and Union Victory for an Imperial Age.*

Sandra M. Gustafson and Robert S. Levine, eds., *Reimagining the Republic: Race, Citizenship, and Nation in the Literary Work of Albion W. Tourgée.* Foreword by Carolyn L. Karcher.

Brian Schoen, Jewel L. Spangler, and Frank Towers, eds., *Continent in Crisis: The U.S. Civil War in North America.*

Raymond James Krohn, *Abolitionist Twilights: History, Meaning, and the Fate of Racial Egalitarianism, 1865–1909.*

Hilary N. Green and Andrew L. Slap, eds., *The Civil War and the Summer of 2020*.

Ian Delahanty, *Embracing Emancipation: A Transatlantic History of Irish Americans, Slavery, and the American Union, 1840–1865*.

AnneMarie Brosnan, *A Contested Terrain: Freedpeople's Education in North Carolina During the Civil War and Reconstruction*.

Hilary N. Green, *Unforgettable Sacrifice: How Black Communities Remembered the Civil War*. Foreword by Edda L. Fields-Black.

Jonathan D. Neu, *Our Onward March: The Grand Army of the Republic in the Progressive Era*

www.ingramcontent.com/pod-product-compliance
Lightning Source LLC
Jackson TN
JSHW021112310125
78134JS00004B/14